T0368764

GERMAN
CANADIANS

Community Formation,
Transformation
and Contribution
to Canadian Life

Arthur **Grenke**

Order this book online at www.trafford.com
or email orders@trafford.com

Most Trafford titles are also available at major online book retailers.

Print information available on the last page.

ISBN: 978-1-4120-2076-3 (sc)
ISBN: 978-1-4907-7203-5 (hc)
ISBN: 978-1-4907-7202-8 (e)

Trafford rev.   12/04/2020

 www.trafford.com

North America & international
toll-free: 844-688-6899 (USA & Canada)
fax: 812 355 4082

CONTENTS

INTRODUCTION

German Canadians, or Canadians who report their ethnic origin as solely or partly from Germany or German ancestry, have been intrinsic to Canada's earliest beginnings. They arrived as explorers, adventurers, scientists, bona fide immigrants and refugees. Once here, German-Canadians sought to create an institutional life that would help them maintain their ethnic community and preserve their identity. They established churches, clubs, schools and other institutions. Essential to preserving this identity was preserving their linguistic heritage, which included transmitting a knowledge of the German language to their children.

This survey history of Germans in Canada will explore different aspects of German Canadian life, beginning with the arrival of Germans in Canada and concluding with an examination of German contributions to this country. It will examine German settlement patterns, secular formal voluntary associations and churches, and the function these served to meet everyday community needs, as well as their role in preserving the community's identity. The German Canadian war experiences will be looked at, as well as their effect on community life. The role of Germans in opening up the country and their contribution to Canada's agricultural and industrial development will be examined, as well as their contributions in the arts and sciences.

The focus will not be on the community at any specific point in time, but on a community in flux. In particular, the work will explore the dynamics that encouraged Germans to create an institutional life that would help them preserve their identity in this country, especially their linguistic identity. Despite their efforts, the language, in most instances, tended to be lost after several generations. With it came an additional loss of other aspects of the German identity, as children, grandchildren or great-grandchildren of immigrants merged into and became part of the larger English or French-speaking host societies.

There are few survey histories of Germans in Canada. The major work in this area is Heinz Lehmann's *Das Deutschtum in Ostkanada* and *Das Deutschtum in Westkanada*.[1] Written in the 1930s, the studies concentrate on German immigration and settlement. Rudolf A. Helling's *A Socio-Economic History of German-Canadians: They, Too, Founded Canada* was written as part of the history series sponsored by the Department of the Secretary of State in the 1970s.[2] While paying some attention to early German Canadian history, the work concentrates on the more recent experiences of Germans in Canada. Hartmut Fröschle's *Die Deutschen in Kanada*, provides an overview of the German experience in Canada, with a focus on German contributions in different areas of Canadian life.[3] Gerhard Bassler's *The German Canadian Mosaic Today and Yesterday: Identities, Roots, and Heritage*[4] is a succinct account of the German Canadian experience, written essentially for students at the grade school level.

While presenting an overview of the German Canadian experience, this study will concentrate on the relationship between language and community. Focusing on German churches, the study will look at the influences that caused congregations to give up the German language

[1] Heinz Lehmann, *Das Deutschtum in Ostkanada*. Schriften des deutschen Auslandsinstituts Stuttgart, Kulturhistorische Reihe, No. 31. Stuttgart: Ausland und Heimat, Verlags-Aktiengesellschaft, 1931, and *Das Deutschtum in Westkanada*. Veröffentlichung der Hochschule für Politik, Forschungsabteilung, Sachgebiet Volkskunde, No. 1. (Berlin: Junker & Dünnhaupt Verlag, 1939). The two volumes were translated and published under the title *The German Canadians: Immigration, Settlement and Culture*, ed. and transl. by Gerhard Bassler (St. John's, NL: Breakwater Books, 1986).

[2] Rudolf A. Helling's *A Socio-Economic History of German-Canadians: They, Too, Founded Canada. A Research Report.* Ed. Bernd Hamm. Vierteljahrschrift f. Sozial-und Wirtschaftsgeschichte, Beiheft, No. 75. (Wiesbaden: Franz Steiner Verlag, 1984).

[3] Hartmut Fröschle, *Die Deutschen in Kanada: Eine Volksgruppe im Wandel*. Eckartschriften, No. 101. Wien: Österr. Landsmannschaft, 1987. The volume was translated by Georg K. Weissenborn under the title *The German Canadians: A Concise History* (Toronto: Historical Society of Mecklenburg Upper Canada, 1992).

[4] Gerhard P. Bassler, *The German Canadian Mosaic Today and Yesterday: Identities, Roots, and Heritage* (Ottawa: German-Canadian Congress, 1991).

in favor of the dominant languages in the host society. This study concentrates on the churches because congregations were the most important community organizations. They tended to have a much longer lifespan than other organizations. Although many clubs or other secular organizations disappeared after a few years, churches continued generation after generation. They did so because churches survived the language transition of their members, simply changing services from German to the dominant language spoken in a particular locality. In most cases, the language transition was from German to English. Churches not only survived the language transition but also retained a record of the transition, allowing one to observe not only the language change but also the reasons for it.

While German churches tended to survive the challenges of linguistic assimilation, German clubs primarily served the immigrant generation. Although they often outlived the first generation, they nevertheless served primarily the immigrants, with people leaving as they became increasingly integrated into the host society. At the same time, clubs tended to arise mostly in urban centers. Also, they essentially met secular social needs of the community, with groups that sought to make the church the centre of their community life frequently avoiding them.

In a sense, the examination of the German community involves the study of several communities. Not only were Germans divided by origin, time of arrival and areas of settlement, they were also divided by religion. At times, communities formed by earlier arrivals were disintegrating as their members were being assimilated, while new communities were being established by new arrivals. Mennonites, Catholics, Lutherans and other religious communities, while German-speaking, tended to have little interaction with each other. They often followed different patterns of accommodation and assimilation. The study will look at patterns of change, in particular language change, in these different groups.

In addition to looking at German immigration, settlement and community formation and transformation, the work will explore the German contributions to Canadian life, be this in agriculture, business, the arts or the sciences. This becomes problematic particularly where names were changed or where women married outside their ethnic community. In these instances, names provide little information on ethnic identity and/or background. Despite these problems, the study will nevertheless make an effort to explore the contributions of Germans in different areas of endeavor as they lost their identity and were integrated into the larger society.

This work seeks to provide readers with insight into: the different German communities that emerged in Canada over time and the forces that caused them to gradually disintegrate; and the structure of the German ethnic identity and how it altered in time and with changing circumstances. The objective is to fill an important gap in the historical literature. To date, German Canadian historical literature has concentrated on immigration and, to an extent, community formation. Little attention has been given to the language transition in the German Canadian community and to what brings it about. Also, it is generally assumed that the immigrants are the hewers of wood and the drawers of water, and that it's the succeeding generations that make the most important contributions to Canadian society as they move up the social ladder and are assimilated into the larger society. This study examines the accuracy of that premise. At the same time, it looks at what remains of the German Canadian identity after the language, the main feature differentiating and separating Germans from the host societies, is lost.

GERMAN IMMIGRATION AND SETTLEMENT

Immigration and Settlement in Eastern Canada

First contacts

The first mention of a German having set foot on what today is Canada dates back to the Icelandic sagas which speak of a German by the name of Tykir being a member of Leif Erikson's expedition that discovered Vinland around 1001 AD. Tykir is credited with giving the name to the newly discovered land because of the abundance of grapes he discovered there. The Norwegian explorer Helge Ingstad, who discovered a Norse landing site at L'Anse au Meadows, in northern Newfoundland, argues that this was the elusive Vinland and that the wild grapes of which Tykir spoke were actually wild berries.

Germans in New France

There is some dispute as to whether Vinland was in fact located in Newfoundland. Tykir's account was part of the oral tradition that forms the basis of the Norse saga. More reliable information on the German experience in Canada dates back to New France. Although France settled Germans in Louisiana, in particular during the first part of the 18th century, there is little evidence that it made an effort to recruit

Germans for settlement in New France.[5] Yet, there is some evidence of
Germans taking up land in New France, forming, for example, the small
settlement of Allemande, not far from Lévis, on the south shore of the St.
Lawrence River, opposite Quebec City.[6] Sometimes, France also recruited
German specialists. It used German miners to exploit copper discoveries
in New France in the 1730s. It used mercenaries from German-speaking
countries to extend its territorial holdings in North America. For
example, Swiss soldiers were included in the small expeditionary force
under Monsieur de Monts who established a colony on Sainte Croix (now
Dorchester) Island in Acadia, in 1604. Ravaged by disease, in 1605 the
settlement was relocated to Port Royal. Again, between 1721 and 1745
two detachments of the Swiss Karrer regiment served France to reinforce
the defences of the fortress of Louisbourg. Swiss contingents tended to
be made up not only of Swiss but also of soldiers from other areas of
German-speaking Europe.

---

[5] However, there is evidence of the occasional German going to France and
then to New France. An example is Anne Marie Faneséque. Born in 1657, in
Hamburg, Germany, she ended up in France after the death of her father, with
little evidence of how and why she went there. She was included among the
"Filles de Roi", sent by King Louis XIVth to provide brides for bachelors of
the colony. Soon after landing in Québec (September 3, 1673), she married the
fur trader Hubert Le Roux, with whom she had three children. After his death
in 1681, she married the 21-year-old wage earner Gabriel Cardinal, who was
both bad tempered and a drunk, a situation worsened by the couple's financial
difficulties. To support the family, he worked as a "coureur de bois", while she
operated a bar which also served as a brothel. The couple separated in 1692.
Burdened by debt, Anne Marie was first forced to rent out and then sell her
house. In 1703, she was accepted as as a patient in the hospital for the poor and
sick in the Hôpital de Québec. She died on December 4, 1722. From Rémi
Tougas, *L'Allemande: La Scandaleuse Histoire D'Une Fille du Roi,1657-1722*
(Québec: Québec, 2003).

[6] It appears that the seigniorial system discouraged Germans from settling in
New France. There is some evidence of Germans having settled in Acadia,
which did not have the seigniorial system. However, here they had difficulty
receiving title to their land and found themselves facing unfriendly neighbours,
which discouraged further settlement in Acadia. (See France. Archives des
Colonies. MG1, G1, vol. 466, no.82, bobine F-769).

By the 1660s German names such as Steiner (or Steimer) were included among inhabitants of the fortress of Quebec and the Île d'Orléans facing it. W.H. Debor found evidence of habitants of German origin living in and around the fortress of Quebec as early as 1664, when the city had a population of 2000. Searching property and church records, he found mention of Hans Bernhardt from the Mosel valley, Jean Daigre from Speyer, Hans Daigle from Vienna, and Joseph Brissac from Breisach. In the case of Daigle, evidence of his origin was reinforced in that he was given the nickname "Jean dit L'Allemand" and his grandchildren were still singled out as L'Allemand.

Although there is little information on French recruitment of Germans for New France, one may speculate what brought Germans to the colony. Germans in New France would have included mercenary soldiers who, when leaving the service, chose to remain in New France. The annexation of Alsace-Lorraine by France in 1648 may have brought some settlers as well as German draftees from these areas as early as 1665 to fight the Indians. Other Germans may have arrived through the activities of German and Dutch Protestant merchants who in the early 17th century worked out of Rouen, France. Others may have been brought out by the Company of Adventurers. Its agreement with the government stipulated that it was to bring out a certain number of settlers in return for its monopoly in the fur trade.

Germans in the French and British Service

As Germans were minimally aware of their common national identity prior to the French revolution and the Napoleonic invasions that followed, they were readily recruited by both the British and the French in their struggle for control of North America. In 1745 Samuel Waldo's Palatinates laid siege to and captured the Fortress of Louisbourg which was garrisoned and defended by the Swiss-German Karrer regiment. In the 1755 Battle of Lake George, the French troops were under the supreme command of the Saxon Baron von Dieskau, who that year had come from Europe with 3,000 soldiers to strengthen the French position against the Anglo-Americans. General Wolfe's attack on Quebec in 1759 included the Royal American Regiment, among which were a considerable number of Germans and German Americans. One of these was the Swiss-born Sir Frederick Haldimand, who served as the second in command of the British forces in 1760, as military governor of Montreal and Trois Rivières from 1760-64, and, from 1776 to 1786, as Governor-General of Quebec.

The British conquest brought an expansion of German settlement in Quebec and Lower Canada, which had previously been discouraged, not only by France but also by Germans, who preferred the more open British society to the hierarchical seigniorial system of New France. Many of the first Germans who came to Quebec during the first years of British rule after 1759 came as hired soldiers or as members of British militias that had been raised in New England to help in the conquest of New France. They included Johann Peter Arnoldi, a silversmith by trade, who in 1760 served in the British expeditionary force that laid siege to and took Montreal for the British crown. Among them, also, was Joseph Wexler, who later became active in the fur trade. Immigrants to the colony shortly after the British conquest included the Swiss German Lawrence Ermatinger, who became involved in the fur trade. The Wurtele family emigrated directly from Württemberg to Lower Canada, in about 1780. Here they became active as general merchants, becoming wealthy enough to acquire the seigneuries of Bourg Marie de l'Est and De Grir, commonly known as River David.

The "Foreign Protestants" and German settlement in the Maritimes

The first major recruitment of Germans for what was to become British North America happened when Britain recruited so-called foreign Protestants to serve as a bulwark against French influence in Acadia. They came to be seen as potential settlers after impressing the British with their industriousness while building the fortress of Halifax, in 1749. Conditions in Germany were favourable for their recruitment. South-western Germany suffered from overpopulation. Economic development in the area was hampered by the guild system in the towns, by antiquated agricultural practices and by the dues and tolls at the borders of the patchwork of states in the region. In addition, the states in the area had suffered severely from war, the wars of Louis XIV of France having wreaked havoc on lands that had hardly recovered from the Thirty Years War.

They were recruited in Europe by John Dick, a merchant at Rotterdam, with the help of local agents in the various duchies and local municipalities in the south-western part of the German Empire. Dick's first assignment from the Lords of Trade in 1750 was to recruit a number "not exceeding 1500." He was to receive one guinea for every immigrant delivered. Immigrants in Nova Scotia in turn were each to receive a grant of fifty acres of land, free of quit-rents and taxes for ten years, as well as additional land for every dependent woman or child. They were further to be given twelve months' free subsistence and to be furnished with a proper quantity of materials and utensils for husbandry, clearing and cultivating their lands, erecting their homes and carrying on the fishery.

The first ship sent out by Dick, the *Anne,* docked in Halifax on the 13th of September, with some 322 passengers, including 190 adults, 77 children ranging from four to 14, and approximately 55 infants. In 1751, Dick sent four more ships, with a total of 1000 immigrants. In 1752, he sent out an about equal number on five ships. Johann Michael Schmidt, who crossed over on the "Gale" in 1752, relates his experiences in his family Bible:

> 1752. The 9th of May we left Leimen (a village in the Palatinate four or five miles south of Heidelberg) for America, and arrived at Halifax on the 6th of September in the same year...The ship with which we travelled across the great sea bore the name Goehl, and in Rotterdam 262 souls embarked in her. On the voyage to America 12 children were born, of which all but one died. Of the above 262 souls, 53 died on the ocean and the remaining 210 landed safely at Halifax. There were 183 freights and 53 sleeping places. From the 8th of July 1752 to the 28th of February 1753, 83 persons from the above-mentioned ship died in Halifax. We were 14 days travelling down the Rhine and 14 weeks on the ocean, not counting the time we were on the ship in Rotterdam and again in Halifax before we were put ashore, all of which together amounted to 22 weeks.[7]

Between 1750 and 1752 a total of 2,700 Foreign Protestants arrived. Of the 2,450 whose ethnic origin can be determined, approximately 65.5%

---

[7]   Quoted in Herbert W.Debor, "Early German Immigration in Nova Scotia," *Deutschkanadisches Jahrbuch/German Canadian Yearbook,* volume I, ed. H. Fröschle (Toronto: Historical Society of Mecklenburg Upper Canada Inc., 1973) 68-69.

came from Germany; 18% from Montbelliard; 13-14% from Switzerland and 3% from the Netherlands. The influx ceased when towards the end of 1752 the government in London decided to end the migrations to Nova Scotia, largely because of the antagonism of the French and the active hostility of the Indians. This was seen as a "temporary departure." However, no further recruitment efforts were made.

Because of the hostility of the natives, incited by the French in the hope of using them to regain Acadian territory ceded to Britain by the Treaty of Utrecht, in 1713, Germans were obligated to remain in Halifax after their arrival. Settled in an enclave in the north of the city, they were used by the governor to construct fortifications and roads, work used to repay expenditures incurred by the government for bringing them over. When Indian hostility decreased, 1,453 Germans left Halifax for Merliguesh Bay, in May 1753, where they founded the settlement of Lunenburg. Except for Germans brought in by Joseph Pernette in 1765, and settled on his land on the La Have River, Lunenburg received few new immigrants after the initial settlement. Still, natural increase led to the gradual expansion of the original settlement both along the coast in either direction and up the La Have River into the interior. The expansion was largely the result of the initiative of individual families who moved into yet undeveloped areas to find land for their offspring. Gradually almost the entire Lunenburg County was occupied by settlers of German descent.

During this time, also, German Americans were attracted to the Maritimes. In the 1760s, close to 1000 Germans from New England and Europe were recruited to settle on land held by Pennsylvania businessmen in the Annapolis Valley. In 1765 New Brunswick politicians and businessmen settled Pennsylvania Germans in Hillsborough Township and also in 1765, a conglomerate of four Philadelphia land companies began settling Pennsylvania Germans in Moncton Township. Germantown was founded in 1765 on the northern shore of the Bay of Fundy by a group of land speculators headed by a Pennsylvania German businessman. That year, also, several German families went up the Petitcodiac and founded what became the city of Moncton. Shortly thereafter other Germans established the settlement of Coverdale on the opposite bank. In time, the Germans from the original Moncton and Hopewell Townships spread through the Petitcodiac River district.

German Loyalists and Auxiliary Troops

The natural flow of Germans into the Maritimes was interrupted by the outbreak of the American Revolution. The victory of the rebels resulted in an influx of new settlers, made up of Loyalists and German auxiliary troops. Of the some 45,000 Loyalists who settled in British North America after the American War of Independence, some 10 to 30per cent were of German origin. For example, The King's Royal Regiment of New York, the 60th or Royal American Regiment, and Butler's Rangers all included a considerable number of Germans. In addition, of the some 30,000 German auxiliary troops raised by Britain to help in its struggle against the rebellious colonists, about 2,400 chose to remain in British North America. Of German troops, some 1,400 remained in Quebec, where they settled in the larger centres or local villages where they had frequently been stationed during the war. The majority of these intermarried with the local population and pursued whatever trade or profession they had on arrival in the New World.

An estimated 950 to 1,000 of the soldiers went either to Nova Scotia or Upper Canada. A good number of them settled in Halifax where they may have spent some time after prison exchanges or when first arriving in Canada as new recruits. The inflow of Loyalists and disbanded Hessians following the American War of Independence expanded the German community in Halifax to over 1000, which had shrunk from 900 in 1753 to 264 in 1766. Others settled on land allotted to them in the Annapolis Valley and in other parts of the Maritimes, German auxiliary troops and Loyalists being given 300 acres of land, freedom from taxation for 12 years, as well as other privileges. In 1783, two large parallel settlements of Waldeck and Hessian troops were established in Clement Township. German American Loyalists were settled in Shelbourne County, Hants County, Halifax County, and German American Loyalists and disbanded German auxiliaries were placed in the village of Saint John and along the Saint John River. Unlike Lunenburg, where Germans formed a large block settlement, Germans who settled in other areas of the Maritimes seldom formed cohesive communities but rather were generally dispersed among the more numerous population of British background.

In Upper Canada, Loyalists, in addition to provisions in food and clothing, received 100 acres on the riverfront and two hundred acres in the hinterland. If a Loyalist was married and had a family, or if at any future time he should marry, he was entitled to fifty acres more for his wife, and fifty for every child. Besides this, each son or daughter, on coming of age or at the time of their marriage, was entitled to a further grant of 200 acres. Of the Loyalist settlements established by the British in Upper Canada, a number were inhabited predominantly by people of German origin. This did not come about by intent but rather because soldiers in a number of the regiments recruited in the United States were predominantly of German origin. This was true in particular of the 1st Battalion of the King's Royal Regiment of New York, which was settled in Williamsburg and Matilda, Dundas County, and in Cornwall and Osnabruck, Stormont County.

Williamsburg and Mathilda were made up entirely of German Americans, while the majority of settlers in Cornwall and Osnabruck were German Americans. Troops of Johnson's Second Battalion (comprising some 470 men), under the leadership of Sir John Johnson or under Colonel Rogers, were settled in Ernesttown or Fredericksburg, along the Bay of Quinte. More than half of these consisted of Palatines from New York State. Marysburg, the fifth and last of the Loyalist settlements along the Bay of Quinte, included not only German Americans but also a good number of German auxiliary troops. Unlike in Nova Scotia, auxiliary troops in Upper Canada were not granted the same privileges as Loyalists. This, combined with the unsuitability of many of the soldiers for a farming life, made it difficult for them to adjust. Only their poverty prevented most of them from leaving their farms and making their livelihood elsewhere.

Butler's Rangers, which included a sizable proportion of Germans from New York State, had its fixed headquarters in Fort Niagara during the war. At that time, Butler had some of the disabled soldiers open farms in the area so as to supply the garrison with grain. As the soil was good, many of Butler's soldiers took up land here after they were demobilized in June, 1784. A good number of the 620 persons who settled in Queenston, which was established by these settlers, were of German American origin.

A number of features characterize these soldier settlements. For the most part they were small, consisting of villages and surrounding land. Except for places like Williamsburg or Matilda, Germans were intermingled throughout the settlements with English-speaking peoples. Furthermore, what identified these people was not their national origin but rather the fact that they had fought on Britain's side in its attempt to suppress the American rebels. As a result, many of them were not welcome in the rebel states that had won the war against the "motherland."

The Late Loyalists

Somewhat different motives caused the so-called "late" Loyalists to take up land in British North America. The most significant of these among German Americans were the Mennonites, who, although they hadn't supported the British cause openly, also hadn't participated in the open rebellion against the "motherland" because of their pacifism. They were therefore frequently suspect among their neighbours. Also, land scarcity was becoming a problem in the Mennonite settlements in Pennsylvania. It was therefore natural that they should look north for a potential area of settlement. The first group of Mennonites that came to Upper Canada settled at Twenty Mile Creek in 1786, in present-day Lincoln County. They appear to have been the forerunners for a larger Mennonite settlement planned for the area. This did not materialize, however, because Lieutenant-Governor Simcoe, who served as Lieutenant-Governor of Upper Canada from 1791-1796, refused to support the establishment of a large-scale settlement of pacifists of foreign descent.

Despite this, Mennonites continued to arrive in Upper Canada. A small settlement, the Rainham settlement, was established north of Lake Erie, in 1791. Another settlement was established between Grimsby and Queenston in the Niagara Peninsula in 1799. Still other Pennsylvania Mennonites began settling in Vaughan Township, near Markham, where they bought land sold by Loyalists of the gentry class who wanted to give up farming. The major settlement of Mennonites, however, was established along the Grand River. Mennonite settlement there began in 1800, when Mennonite families from Franklin County, Pennsylvania, bought land from a speculator by the name of Richard Beasley. By 1803, some 20 Mennonite families had already settled in Waterloo, and more were on their way from different parts of Pennsylvania, when it was discovered that the land they had purchased was still mortgaged. In order to claim ownership, Mennonites were told that they had to purchase the entire mortgaged 60,000 acres. In order to raise the £10,000.00 demanded for the property, they turned to their wealthier brethren in Pennsylvania. Convinced that the land in question was fertile, and to help their friends, Mennonites in Lancaster County set up the German Land Company which raised the £10, 000.00 and bought the entire tract of land.

The problems raised by the Beasley purchase made the Grand River settlement known among Mennonites in Pennsylvania in general, encouraging them to move steadily into the area, so that within a few years the 60,000 acres were distributed. In 1807, the German Land Company bought an additional 45,195 acres in the adjacent Woolwich Township, and settlers also began to stream into this township. This enabled Mennonites to establish a large block settlement, which originally they had been prevented from doing by Lieutenant-Governor Simcoe.

Non-Mennonite arrivals from the United States

Of German Americans, only the Mennonites succeeded in establishing a larger block settlement. Except in cases where they were settled in groups by the British government, as was the case with some of the Loyalist settlements, German Americans not of the Mennonite faith tended to be dispersed among the British population, and they left little record of themselves. One exception was the Berczy settlement in Markham Township. Cheated out of his partnership in the Pulteney settlement project in the Genesee Valley of New York, for which he was to recruit 30,000 to 50,000 immigrants from Germany, Berczy took up Lieutenant-Governor Simcoe's offer of land grants for developers. Together with New York investor-speculators, who banded together to form the German Company, Berczy petitioned Lieutenant-Governor Simcoe for one million acres on which they initially planned to settle 200 people, to be supported by the company until they were self-sufficient. These were to be followed by many more Germans from Germany, Pennsylvania and New York State.

To facilitate this undertaking, Berczy and his associates were granted 64, 000 acres in 1794, with the promise of additional grants as more settlers were brought in. In 1794, Berczy settled 190 German immigrants he had recruited for his New York settlement on his land grant. Settlers received a 200-acre freehold lot in return for agreeing to work for Berczy for six years. In order to reach their settlement, the immigrants were obligated to construct a road through virgin forest from Lake Ontario to Lake Simcoe, a road that eventually became Toronto's

Yonge Street. Following this, they began clearing their own land. Within three years the settlers had cleared one-quarter of their land, and erected a church and school. Despite this, in 1803 the Executive Council of Upper Canada, distrusting an alien land developer who had backers they considered to have republican tendencies, declared the reserved lands forfeited and the enterprise ended in bankruptcy.

At the time the Berczy settlement was founded, not only Mennonites but also German American Lutherans established themselves in the Markham area. The first of these to arrive appear to have been Jacob Fischer and Jacob Keffer, who took up land in Vaughan Township in 1798 and 1799 respectively. It seems they were part of a group of community leaders from Somerset, Pennsylvania, who came to Canada several years in advance of their relatives and friends, established homesteads and then returned to guide back a larger group of their people. As such, they followed a pattern of migration very similar to that of the Mennonites who moved to Upper Canada.

Immigrants from Germany

The flow of Germans from the United States had not yet ceased when Germans from Europe started to arrive and settle in Upper Canada in larger numbers, in particular during the 1820s and 1830s. A number of forces motivated Germans to leave their homeland. One was overpopulation, with the population of Europe doubling in the century after 1750. Then with the Industrial Revolution spreading from England to the continent, countless artisans were thrown out of work. Furthermore, the rise of large-scale scientific farming led to the old communal system of agriculture being replaced by large-scale production. All these factors, combined with political uncertainty and repression, brought an exodus of Germans from Europe in the half century before Confederation, with some 50 to 60 thousand of these emigrants settling in Canada.

A number of factors caused these people to remain here, rather than make their way through Canada on their way to the western United States. One was the immigration route itself. The two main overland routes to the American West from Quebec along the St. Lawrence River and from New York along the Hudson River to Lake Ontario intersected in south-western Ontario in the early 19th century. Some of the immigrants coming by way of New York decided to remain in Upper Canada because they found employment with German-speaking farmers. German immigrants coming via Quebec were encouraged to remain in Canada by the German interpreter working there. Moreover, many of the immigrants landing at Quebec did not have the means to continue to the United States and therefore were forced to remain in Canada.

On board an Emigrant Ship in the 1830s. Sketch by C. W. Jefferys. *Library and Archives Canada,* C-73435.

The first of the new arrivals settled in the Niagara Peninsula, Haldimand, Lincoln, or Welland counties, with the majority going to Waterloo County. These included the Amish Mennonites. In 1822, Christian Nafziger, a tenant farmer from Bavaria, had arrived in Lancaster County, Pennsylvania, in search of land for himself and a number of his Amish brethren in Europe. Referred to the Mennonite settlement of the German Company, Nafziger came to Waterloo. The Mennonite leaders in Waterloo directed him westward to the township later called Wilmot, an untouched Crown Reserve, except for three road lines running into it. Nafziger conferred with Governor Maitland, who reserved the land for Nafziger's people, naming it the German Block. On his way back to Germany, Nafziger spread the good news in the Palatinate, from where it quickly spread to Amish settlements in Alsace and America. Nafziger did not emigrate until 1826, three years after Amish settlers had actually begun to arrive, first from Pennsylvania and then from Europe. With the help of a Mennonite settlement committee from Waterloo County, they settled on 200-acre plots along the township roads in the German Block.

The next major group of Germans from Europe drawn to Waterloo were German Catholics. The first Catholic in St. Agatha parish and perhaps also in Waterloo Township, Theobald Spetz, arrived in America in about 1826. Landing in New York, he moved on to Buffalo, where he attached himself to a caravan of Mennonites going to Canada. He settled in Waterloo Township, and his letters home to friends and relatives drew other Catholics to the area, many of whom eventually settled in St. Agatha. Reports home by new arrivals drew an increasing number of friends, relatives and acquaintances, and by 1850 the German Catholic population in the Waterloo area, coming primarily from south-western Germany and Alsace, had risen to about eight to ten thousand. By that time, the Catholic inflow to the Waterloo area was being supplanted by an influx of Lutherans, coming largely from central and northern Germany. In some areas, such as Berlin and Waterloo, Lutherans and Catholics settled in the same neighbourhood. In other cases, the different religious groups settled separately, with Catholic settlements concentrated in the north-eastern part of Waterloo Township, where St. Agatha and New Germany became major Catholic settlements; Lutherans, again, were concentrated in centres such as Preston, New Hamburg and Heidelberg.

Like the German Catholic immigrants, the Lutherans at first worked for the more wealthy Mennonites to familiarize themselves with the country and earn sufficient money to establish themselves. Following this, many of them took up farming, on land usually purchased from the Mennonites or the German Land Company. Others, in particular those with a trade, bought small plots of land in centres such as Waterloo, Preston, or Ebytown (Berlin after 1833), and in addition to working for the Mennonites, worked in their trades, be this as butchers, blacksmiths, or cabinetmakers.

As by the end of the 1820s the price of land was already relatively high in Waterloo County, Germans were also beginning to move into areas being opened for settlement to the north-west of the county by the Canada Land Company. Incorporated in 1826, the Canada Land Company had received all Crown Reserves in addition to the immense area of land known as the Huron Tract. In order to open this area for settlement, the company cut a road to Lake Huron, a project which was completed between 1828 and 1832. The company had no sooner been founded, when it made a special effort to attract Germans to its lands. It had its brochures printed in German and distributed in German-speaking areas of Europe. For a period of one and a half years, the Company also hired a man named Rischmuller as a full-time agent to recruit settlers from German-speaking areas of Europe.

By the end of the 1840s, little German villages had sprung up on both sides of the road to Goderich, west of Sebastopol: Freiburg (1848), Inkerman (1857), and Tavistock (1857). If in the 1820s, 30s and 40s the majority of Germans who picked up land in Upper Canada had come directly from Europe, those in the 1850s had in many cases lived for some time in the Waterloo settlement, where they had worked to earn sufficient money to help them make a start on the land. It was especially these people who were caught up in what came to be known as the "Saugeen-fever," which saw German settlement spilling over into Bruce and Grey counties. New settlements were founded, such as Hannover, Neustadt, Alsfeld and others.

Several examples may be given showing the movement of peoples to the new areas of settlement. Thus, when by the middle of the 1850's much of the good land in St. Agatha was taken up, many of the Alsatian Catholics of this settlement moved on to Bruce County, to found the essentially German Catholic village of Formosa. Many of the German settlers who went on to settle in the Crediton area of the Huron Tract were immigrants from Europe who had first stayed among the Mennonites in Lincoln County after their arrival from New York. Many of them moved on to Morriston, in Puslinch Township. Feeling at home here, many of them stayed for a couple of years before moving on to Stephen, eighty miles away. A good number of the families then moved on to Crediton. Most of these had originally come from Baiersbronn, Württemberg, in southern Germany.

Once the good land had been taken up in southern Ontario, Germans turned to north-western parts of the province, first to the Ottawa Valley and then to what is traditionally known as Northern Ontario. The majority of German settlers for the Ottawa Valley were recruited through the work of Canadian immigration agents in Germany, in particular in West Prussia and Mecklenburg. Here modernized farming techniques had given rise to a surplus farm population. If the American Civil War had not started, these people would likely have emigrated to the United States. With civil war raging in the United States, many people wishing to leave Germany looked to other areas where they might settle. To recruit them, Wilhelm Wagner, in the employ of the federal government, prepared the immigration pamphlet *Anleitung für Diejenigen welche sich am Ottawa-Flusse niederlassen wollen*, which described the settlement possibilities in the Ottawa Valley in highly laudatory terms. In addition, he placed newspaper advertisements in German papers and made use of sub-agents. As a result, some 5,000 German immigrants were drawn to the Ottawa Valley between 1861 and 1870. As many arrived in the Ottawa Valley between 1870 and the early 1890s. They settled in virtually all the townships of Renfrew County and were concentrated in particular in Alice Township, to the north, in the area surrounding the present town of Eganville, and west of the present town of Arnprior. In Pontiac County, on the Quebec side of the Ottawa River, they settled some 75 km north of the present town of Shawville, in Ladysmith (before 1902 Bretzlaff Corners), and in Schwarz. Their third area of concentration was Labelle County, between the present town of Buckingham and Poltimore.

About this time, German Swiss were attracted to Northern Ontario, largely through the recruitment efforts of Baroness Elise de Koerber, who worked on behalf of Canada in Switzerland during the 1870s. On her instigation, Swiss agriculturists toured Northern Ontario to look for suitable land to found a Swiss settlement. She herself undertook speaking tours, particularly in the Berne, Liestal and Saanen areas of Switzerland. By the end of 1875, de Koerber had sent some 400 immigrants to Canada. Some of these settled in the Magnetawan area, where they formed a small Swiss settlement. Later immigrants recruited by her settled at Hungry Lake and Doe Lake. She planned to create two concentrations of Swiss: one at Doe Lake for French-speaking Swiss and the other at Magnetawan for German-speaking Swiss, with the two settlements merging north of Magnetawan. She was never able to complete this project because her contract with the government as Special Immigration Agent was not renewed in 1879. She was replaced by Dr. Otto Hahn, who continued de Koerber's work, settling German immigrants in particular in the Lake Nipissing region. At the same time, also, Germans from Renfrew County took up land in Northern Ontario, where some of them settled in Temperance Valley, south of Massey.

By the 1870s and 1880s, opportunities to obtain fairly good and inexpensive land were coming to an end in Eastern Canada and new arrivals turned increasingly to Western Canada. Those who took up land in Ontario had to settle on increasingly marginal land, indicating that in the province the period of land settlement was drawing to a close, as it had drawn to a close in the Maritimes nearly 100 years earlier.

Settlement Patterns of German Immigrants

A number of generalisations can be made about the settlement of German immigrants in Eastern Canada. Other than during the French regime, German settlement moved from east to west, following the opening up of the frontier by the British colonizers. Like other settlers, Germans spread out along the major settlement routes. At first, this was the ocean shoreline, then the lake and the river shorelines which stretched into the interior. In this way, the Lunenburg settlement in Nova Scotia expanded along the La Have River and other river systems. In New Brunswick, Germans were drawn in particular to land along the St. John River system.

In Upper Canada, German settlements spread out along various colonization roads that had been constructed to direct settlers into the interior. Thus, German settlements grew up along the Huron Road, constructed by the Canada Company to direct settlers into areas that were being opened for settlement. German immigrants arriving in the Ottawa Valley were directed to their land by roads such as the Ottawa and Opeongo Road. Both roads and rivers were the main communication routes settlers used to bring their produce to market and obtain products they needed from the outside world.

Generally, Germans tended to settle in areas that were opening to settlement. Sometimes they preceded the establishment of settlement routes by a few years, but for the most part they followed them. This meant that they generally moved into areas where other people were also taking up land.

A number of influences contributed to the formation of German settlements. To an extent, these were encouraged by British immigration and settlement policy. German American Loyalists and German auxiliary troops were settled according to the company to which they belonged. This had an influence on the number of Germans in a particular settlement, with the proportion of Germans increasing according to the proportion of German American Loyalists or German auxiliary troops found in a particular company.

In the case of Lunenburg, the British government made a conscious effort to recruit German Protestants to counterbalance the preponderance of French Catholics in the Maritimes. With this end in mind, it financed the recruitment of German Protestants, providing them with employment to facilitate the repayment of debts immigrants had acquired to pay for their trip over. Following this, the government selected an area where the immigrants might be settled and then helped them establish themselves.

Religion and family relationships had a major influence on the formation of block settlements. So the first Mennonite settlements in Upper Canada were formed when small groups of Mennonites in Pennsylvania decided to find new homes for themselves in Upper Canada. Waterloo County emerged as a major German settlement, in part because of the dishonesty of Richard Beasley. Mennonites could take advantage of this situation only because they possessed the unity to raise the money needed to acquire the entire tract of land that was for sale. Once the land was purchased, they coordinated their efforts to settle the area.

Later German immigrants were drawn to the area. Amish Mennonites, enticed by their co-religionists. German Catholic and Lutheran immigrants settled there because Mennonite farmers sought to hire farm hands that spoke their language. At the same time, new arrivals were sent to the area by the German interpreter who worked in Quebec. Once settled in the area, Lutherans and Catholics sought to establish settlements consisting only of their co-religionists. In the more urban centres, such as in the emerging Berlin, the different German religious groups coordinated their efforts to expand the economic opportunities of the centre's citizens.

In other instances, as in the Berczy settlement, German settlements were established through the efforts of land speculators. Others, in particular German American Lutherans, sent out delegates to seek out a suitable area for settlement. Following this, their friends and co-religionists followed.

Settlements, once established, served to direct Germans to surrounding areas once most of the good land in the original settlement had been taken up. This occurred, for example, in Lunenburg, where the children of the original settlers gradually spread through the entire county. Especially in Waterloo County, once most of the good land was taken, the children of the original settlers took up land in surrounding counties where the land was cheaper. As in the case of the formation of original settlements, new settlements that were founded were structured largely by religion and family ties.

In most instances, religious and family affiliations contributed to the establishment of small German settlements, with many of the German settlements established consisting in particular of people with a common religious background. It was only in the Waterloo County area where the continuous influx of new German arrivals led to the establishment of a large German block settlement.

Canadian Immigration Policy and German immigration to the Canadian Prairies

As the Canadian government made a great effort to demonize Germans after World War I broke out in 1914, this chapter will focus on the government's pre-war efforts to recruit German settlers for this country. The division of powers between the different levels of government made immigration essentially a federal responsibility after 1872. Following a series of agreements between the federal government and the provinces in 1868 and 1871, the national government became increasingly involved in the work of recruiting immigrants, especially for the Canadian West. Prior to that, primarily provincial agents and agents working for private organizations had been active in recruiting immigrants from German-speaking areas of Europe. To carry out its new responsibility, in 1872 the federal government appointed Jacob E. Klotz and William Hespeler as its agents to recruit immigrants from Germany.

What appeared as the "wandering spirit" evident among Germans suggested these agents might have some success. Germans were attracted by the promises of higher wages and, especially, by freedom from military service that emigration offered them. Stationed in Bremen, Klotz worked to recruit immigrants from northern Germany; Hespeler worked in southern Germany. In addition to carrying out the regular work of an immigration agent, such as distributing pamphlets or holding public meetings, Hespeler was also authorized to organize a system of immigration in Germany.

German emigration laws made it extremely difficult for Canadian agents working in that country. Anyone who made a business of enticing Germans to emigrate by laying before them false facts or circumstances was subject to a fine. The Prussian law of 7 May 1853, which after unification applied to all of Germany, allowed only native Germans to become involved in forwarding emigrants from that country, and then only when in the possession of a concession from the government of their district. An agent of a foreign country could work only under the concession obtained by steamship lines that had given a security to the government as a guarantee of good behaviour. The Canadian work was further hampered by the unwillingness of the German government to respond favourably to Hespeler's attempt to introduce into Germany, with the aid of the British government, a system of Dominion immigration. Nor could either Hespeler or Klotz, both naturalized Canadians, hope to obtain the aid of the British government, should they be arrested in Germany in pursuit of their work, as Canadian naturalization laws provided the naturalized person the rights of a British citizen only within Canada. Under these conditions, Canadian government agents such as Hespeler could work for the cause of emigration to Canada only through the concession of Allan Line agents and under the name of one of them. In this capacity, he could publish statements about Canada, call upon intending emigrants and distribute pamphlets.

It was while working under these restrictive conditions that Hespeler was advised by the Ottawa government to explore the possibility of inducing Mennonites, who wanted to leave Russia, to emigrate to Canada. Rapid population growth had created in the Mennonite colonies of southern Russia a class of day labourers and conditions of social unrest, both of which found expression in the desire for new land. Mennonites were also dissatisfied with government measures to curtail their local self-government and make Russian the main language of instruction in Mennonite schools. More important, however, and the immediate cause of the desire to emigrate was the Government Ukaz of 1871, which threatened to deprive German colonists of their exemption from military service. The Ukaz caused disquietude and a desire to emigrate among all German colonists in Russia, no matter whether these were Lutheran, Catholic, or Mennonite. Groups such as the Mennonites were more closely affected as the belief in non-resistance was fundamental to their Christian faith. In search of a home where their religious values would be respected, as were those of the Quakers, a Mennonite delegation requested information from the British Consul at Berdiansk, Zohrab, regarding the possibility of emigrating to America, more specifically to Canada. When informed that the Mennonites were considering emigrating from Russia, the Canadian government spelled out for them the status of conscientious objectors in Canada. Mennonites were further promised a reserve of free land. Mennonite delegates were invited to come to Canada to inspect the land and social conditions at government expense. Also, Hespeler was directed to proceed to Berdiansk to explain the government's terms to the Mennonites and persuade them to emigrate to Canada.

As a further inducement, the government guaranteed to Mennonites that they would face no restrictions in the practice of their religion in Canada. Similar privileges were extended to them for the education of their children in schools. Although the Canadian government had hoped to make arrangements to ship the Mennonites via a port in southern Russia directly to Canada, this objective was not realized because the Russian government refused to allow any aid that would facilitate the departure of the Mennonites. Through arrangements made with the Dominion Line, the government sought to obtain for Mennonites relatively cheap ocean fares via German ports. The government also made arrangements to provide for them a relatively inexpensive travel route between Quebec and Winnipeg. To help emigrants who could not pay their way, a government loan of $96,400 was made available, which was guaranteed by Mennonites in Ontario.

Meanwhile, immigration work was cumbersomely proceeding in Germany, where Klotz remained to work under the direction of the Agent-General in London. Unlike Hespeler, who in his work in Germany sought to recruit German immigrants through the clergy, Klotz worked primarily in co-operation with shipping agents, especially those of the Allan Line. He recruited in particular local shipping agents. In return for distributing

Canadian immigration literature, contributing financially towards having it printed, and for directing emigrants to Canada, an agent was paid $2.00 for each adult German he sent to Canada. In support of the cause of Canadian immigration, Klotz also spoke at fairs and markets, as well as answered letters requesting information about Canada.

In addition to its special agents, the Canadian government also employed commissioned agents for its work in Germany, Austria-Hungary and Switzerland. For the most part, these wrote articles about Canada, which they would then seek to have printed in the German language press. Also, Swiss and German delegates were invited to Canada and their reports printed and distributed. At the same time, propaganda literature was printed in Canada for distribution in Europe.

On the advice of Klotz, a passenger warranty was offered for a brief period to continental emigrants to make steamship rates to Canada more competitive with rates paid by European emigrants who went to other countries. As it was considered important that nuclei of foreign settlements be established to attract continental European emigrants to the Canadian West, land was reserved for the purpose of establishing foreign colonies. With this as its objective, the Government entered into an agreement with the German Society of Montreal, whereby land was reserved for German and German-Russian immigrants, who were to be brought out by the Society.

Except for the Mennonites, the immigration work sponsored by the Canadian government in German-speaking areas of Europe failed to recruit the desired influx of settlers. Even Mennonite immigration, while significant immediately after 1873, dwindled to a trickle by 1881. This lack of success may be attributed, in part, to the experimental and inconsistent nature of Canadian policy. For example, the £1 warranty, introduced in 1873, was abolished in 1874, when it was found that steamship companies were appropriating the money rather than reducing the ocean fare of their customers sailing for Canada. While the $2.00 bonus was retained, it was an insufficient inducement to motivate agents to work in the cause of emigration to Canada, as other countries often paid more. The German Society had neither sufficient staff nor expertise to carry out immigration work successfully. Propaganda work sponsored by the Canadian government to advertise the country, which was almost unknown in Germany, was considerably less than that undertaken by American railway companies. Furthermore, steamship agents working in the interest of emigration to the Canadian West were also paid by American companies to recruit immigrants for the United States. This did little to attract German-speaking immigrants to Canada, or to alter the unfavourable bias against Canada, which, when known, was considered the "bad corner" of the United States, with grasshoppers, a wintry climate and late frosts.

Even when the short-lived warranty was offered, inducements offered to immigrants by South American countries surpassed those offered by Canada. Argentina and Brazil offered free transportation from German ports to South America. The indirect Canadian Lines, which shipped via Liverpool, also were at a disadvantage when rates were compared to German Lines sailing directly between Hamburg or Bremen and New York. Also, the comparative cost of railway transportation from New York to the American and Canadian West favoured settling in the United States. Finally, the Canadian West had no nuclei of emigrants from Germany to attract settlers. Germans were attracted in large numbers to the United States where they had friends or relatives who forwarded favourable reports or paid the passage for them.

The failure of the immigration policy pursued by the Liberal Mackenzie administration to attract continental immigrants induced the Conservative government, when returning to power in 1878, to introduce changes in the continental work. Special Canadian immigration agents who had been active in the cause of emigration to Canada were dismissed. Whereas formerly both special agents and a bonus policy were used to recruit immigrants, the basis of the immigration work in continental Europe, as introduced by J. H. Pope, was the existing structure of steamship agents. To prepare for this change, Alexander T. Galt and John Dyke made several journeys to Sweden, Norway, Denmark, Germany, Austria, Switzerland, Belgium and France to secure the co-operation of most of the representatives of steamship lines sailing from British and continental ports to North America so as to promote a comprehensive system of emigration from those countries to Canada. By the arrangement that emerged, the Canadian government paid to a shipping agent a "bonus of $5.00 for every adult (over the age of 18) whom he sent to Manitoba." As the government had no agency by which it could reach immigrants either in Germany or Scandinavia, the Department of Agriculture in 1880 entered into negotiations with the New York and Erie Railway Company to recruit its extensive connections with emigration agencies in the German Empire and the Scandinavian kingdoms in the interest of emigration to Canada. It also made arrangements with the company to provide for continuous transportation from New York to Winnipeg and the Canadian West. Similar arrangements with Canadian companies provided immigrants with reduced railway rates between Quebec and Winnipeg.

Under the new government, propaganda work on the continent, through the distribution of literature, was also greatly expanded. While officially under the direction of the High Commissioner's office, such work was carried out largely under the supervision of John Dyke of the Liverpool Agency. This Agency replied to correspondence arriving from continental Europe, collected addresses, often from immigrants passing through Liverpool, and forwarded literature to them. While prepared in consultation with the steamship agents, immigration literature was printed and distributed to agents in continental Europe under Dyke's direction. The $5.00 bonus was looked upon as compensation to the agent for efforts and expenses incurred in distributing the material. Dyke reported that in 1885 the Agency distributed 154,000 pamphlets and other German language advertising material to steamship agents in Germany, Austria, Belgium, Holland and France, as well as to emigrants and boarding-house keepers on the continent.[8]

In addition to this work, the government also invited German-speaking delegates, such as Prince Hohenlohe-Langenburg of the *Kolonialverein* to visit the Canadian West. Attempts to interest the *Kolonialverein* to start colonies in the Canadian West failed, however, because of the disinclination of the Canadian government to reserve land for the settlers that the colonizers intended to bring out. Similar attempts at persuasion with Swiss delegates, who represented German-speaking Cantons, also failed. Nevertheless, the reports of delegates were printed and distributed. On occasion, the government also had pamphlets and other suitable literature printed in Canada; these were then distributed in North America and Europe. Special agents like Dr. O. Hahn, who recruited delegates or published material on Canada, also continued to be employed.

---

[8]   See Arthur Grenke, "The Formation and Early development of an Urban Ethnic Community: A case Study of the Germans in Winnipeg, 1872-1919" (PhD thesis, University of Manitoba, Winnipeg, 1975) 24, 57-58.

Meanwhile, the base was laid for the first German settlements in the Territories. In 1884, Neu Elsass was established, followed by Hohenlohe and Langenburg in 1885. While the work of recruiting immigrants and settling them was supported by the federal government, colonization in these projects was carried out largely by Germans who for some time had been residing in Winnipeg. Through an agreement between the Farmers North-West Land and Colonization Company and D. W. Riedle and Aaron J. Schantz of Winnipeg, the company would pay them $50.00 for each settler they placed on its land. To support his work, D.W. Riedle sometimes also received $2.00 from Zwilchenbart, a Swiss steamship agent working in the interest of Canada, for each adult immigrant sent out by him from southern Germany. In addition, the colonizers received free railway passes from the federal government when accompanying immigrants from Winnipeg to their respective homesteads. The government agency in Liverpool also printed pamphlets advertising the colonies that were being established, and distributed these in Europe.

The government also supported immigration work to recruit German American settlers for the Canadian West. During the slack season at the Brandon Agency, the German interpreter, H.J. Maass, undertook several trips through the western United States, carrying with him immigration literature which he distributed at various points along the railway lines as he visited German and Scandinavian settlers whose addresses he had previously obtained. He also recruited immigrants at farmers' meetings or fairs. As a result of his work several smaller German settlements were started in 1884 at Broken Head, Fishing Lake and Prichard Creek.

A few small settlements were also established by Germans whose coming to Canada appears to have been the result largely of conditions in their homelands. In 1885 a small cluster of Germans from Romania formed the settlement of Neu Toulcha. In 1887 German Baptists from Volhynia, Russia, established themselves in Ebenezer. Also, during the 1880s and early 1890s German Americans arrived in smaller numbers to settle near Yorkton and Shehla. Germans from Galicia were beginning to arrive and German Lutherans and Catholics from Southern Russia or Volhynia began to settle in increasing numbers among the Mennonites in Southern Manitoba.

German Americans often came to the Canadian West to escape drought conditions and high interest rates in the U.S. Others came to obtain sufficient land for themselves and their children. Social and economic conditions caused Germans to leave Galicia, Bukowina, Romania and Volhynia. Rapid population increase had produced a landless proletariat in all German settlements in these areas. In Galicia and Bukowina, this problem was at first overcome by the founding of daughter colonies in the southern parts of the Habsburg Empire. Later, the surplus population emigrated to Russia and then to America. Although in the Banat, in Austria-Hungary, there was room for expansion, this was extremely difficult because of the high cost of land, which was largely in the hands of the gentry. In Russia, laws were passed in 1887 that prevented non-naturalized persons from buying land. Further laws in 1889 and 1892 prevented German-Russians of Volhynia from buying land. In Volhynia and southern Russia, where many German colonies had been established on virgin land leased from nobles, German farmers, once they had deforested their plots, found themselves landless when the nobles refused to renew the leases, or chose to renew them at exorbitant rates. In Romania, to where many German-Russians emigrated to escape these conditions, the introduction of military service in 1883 and the difficulties which non-naturalized persons had in obtaining land presented other problems. Emigration offered an escape from these conditions.

Emigration from Russia was encouraged further by the continued attack upon German language instruction. In 1891, schools in the German villages were taken from under the control of the community and, on various occasions, Russian was made the main language of instruction. German religious leaders were persecuted and Germans were hindered from building churches. In many ways, this was an expression of a broader antagonism towards the German colonists in the country, who were accused of acquiring all the good land. Under these conditions, German settlers in southern Russia, as well as in Volhynia, looked to America as a possible area for settlement.

Germans who left Romania in 1884 were Baptists who found themselves harassed by Lutherans, whose churches they had left to embrace the new faith. There is some indication that Germans left Austria-Hungary to escape the Polonization policies in Galicia and the Magyarization policies in Hungary. The *Ausgleich* of 1867 had placed Germans of Bukowina and the Banat under the control of the Hungarians, a situation used by the Hungarians to assimilate non-Magyar minorities. When the 1869 Austrian Public School Law removed education from the control of the clergy and placed it under the direction of secular authorities, the Poles used their dominant position in Galicia to assimilate their minorities.

Recurring drought in Southern Russia and Austria-Hungary also motivated the colonists to seek new areas of settlement. In the 1890s an immigration agency was established in Odessa which was active in the cause of emigration to America. Furthermore, German colonists of Eastern Europe, often having left their original homelands to improve their economic condition by settling among a larger alien population, did not have the traditional roots tying a peasant to the soil. Relatively favourable opportunities to improve their economic situation could induce them to wander on.

Only a few of these German emigrants chose Canada as their destination. Rather, in numerous instances, they left for South America where the governments offered favourable shipping rates. When going to North America, emigrants usually went to the United States, whose shipping and railway companies carried out considerable immigration propaganda. German-Russian colonists also often sent their delegates to the United States to explore conditions for the purpose of eventual settlement. Also, Germans continued to be drawn to their friends and relatives in the United States, who often prepaid for their passage.

Settlers in the Canadian West, still in the beginning stages of settlement, were not yet in the position to bring their friends over. Dyke estimated that about 75% of the emigrants from Germany and Scandinavia had their passages paid by friends in the United States.[9] Also, despite Canadian propaganda work, Canada remained little known in continental Europe. That which was known was unappealing: Canada continued to be seen as the cold and uninhabitable part of America. Furthermore, the unfavourable economic conditions generally prevalent in the Canadian West at the time were not conducive to attracting immigrants.

Transportation rates, which continued to work against Canada, made it difficult to recruit immigrants. Canada also had difficulty persuading the major German Lines to work on its behalf, as these were wary of sending emigrants to an area where they might fail. German emigration laws continued to hamper the distribution of immigration pamphlets

---

[9]   *Ibid.* 31.

and newspaper articles favourable to Canada. Also, people who were carrying out emigration work successfully in Europe, such as Riedle, were not supported by the Canadian government. Prior to the cessation of the agreement between the German colonizers and the land company in 1890, Riedle and his co-workers sought to persuade the government to give direct support to their venture. The government ignored their appeals, apparently because it feared that employing agents who worked from Canada would offend the steamship agents working on Canada's behalf and thereby disrupt its bonus policy.

As the bonus policy failed to bring the inrush of immigrants that had been expected, the Minister of Agriculture sought to abolish it in 1889. The instruction directing the High Commissioner's Office to abolish the $5.00 bonus was, however, unfavourably received in London. The reply acknowledging Minister Carling's instructions maintained that the $5.00 bonus was the only means Canada had of inducing continental European booking agents to work in Canada's interests and that emigration laws, especially in Germany, made it impossible for Canada to resort to the alternative of establishing her own emigration offices in these countries. These arguments were supported by Sir Charles Tupper, who added that although the $5.00 bonus did not bring the expected inrush, the beginnings of foreign settlement had been made since its introduction. It was necessary to be patient and persevering.[10] Abolishing the bonus system at a moment's notice would antagonize the agents, thereby harming the chances of recruiting immigrants, should Canada at some time in the future again wish to pursue an active policy in continental Europe.

Rather than abolish the bonus system, immigration work in continental Europe was expanded in 1890 through the introduction of a settler's bonus. In cooperation with Canadian steamship lines and the C.P.R., the Canadian government agreed to pay $15.00 to an immigrant who picked up land, $7.50 to his wife, and an additional $7.50 for each child over the age of twelve. In 1890, the policy of return men or farmer delegates was also introduced. In payment for their carrying out immigration work in their old homeland, the government offered successful farmers in the West a free trip home, and a free return trip to anyone who brought back at least ten potential settlers. The government

---

[10]   *Ibid.* 32.

also paid a commission for each person who came as a result of the work of the return men, if such a person picked up land. Under these conditions, several German Canadian settlers, such as Klaas Peters, were sent to Europe to work among their old-country friends.

To encourage immigration work among Germans in the United States, the government continued to support the activity of agents south of the border. For example, Aaron J. Schantz was paid $2.50 per day in 1892 while working to recruit Pennsylvania Germans for Western Canada. Government salary and expense accounts for 1893 show four German names among the people recruiting immigrants from the United States. These agents were generally paid travel and/or living expenses while recruiting Americans.[11]

The policy of return men and the settler's bonus policy were, however, to be in effect only for a short period. In 1894, the settlement bonus was abolished because Canadian steamship companies refused to share in the cost. Also, emigration laws in countries such as Germany prevented these benefits from being widely advertised. The policy of return men was also phased out because it was opposed by the continental shipping agents, who looked upon the agents from Canada as competitors. While dissatisfaction with the bonus policy continued to be expressed in government circles, there were few suggested alternatives. When in 1896 the Liberal administration came to power, Canada's continental European work was seen to be badly in need of a new approach. The Boer War had increased wages in Britain, so few arrivals were expected from there, and Canada was not considered to be securing the desired class of immigrant from Germany and the continent. To improve the work on the continent, W. T. R. Preston, Canada's first Commissioner of Immigration, suggested that the $5.00 bonus that had been granted to continental shipping agents cease to be paid and that efforts should be made in Germany, Austria-Hungary, Belgium, Holland and Denmark to secure the cooperation of a colonization society, a company, or individual shipping agent with extended connections throughout continental Europe.

Preston attributed the failure of the old bonus policy to the lack of a directing hand on the continent with responsibility for emigration to Canada. Under the old system, it was also difficult to determine whether

---

[11]   Ibid. 33, 65.

agents were distributing the immigration literature sent to them.[12] Another weakness, as seen by Lord Strathcona, was the uncertainty of the old bonus policy. As the policy could be abolished at any moment, an agent could never be sure of reaping the rewards, and therefore was not motivated to work wholeheartedly in the interest of Canada.[13]

Organizing the continental work through a central Agency was seen to give the government greater control over emigration personnel than had previously existed. It would also secure departmental control over any bonus paid. With these ends in mind, The North Atlantic Trading Company, a syndicate of continental shipping agencies, was established. To escape interference with its activities by the emigration laws of various continental countries, the company was to operate from Amsterdam, and its agreement with the Canadian government was kept secret. To enable the government to monitor its work, the company was required to submit periodical reports, which were checked by the Commissioner of Immigration, as well as by departmental officials in Ottawa. To give to the company some assurance that it could expect a return on its investment, the government entered into agreements with the company which generally lasted five or ten years. However, the government retained the right to cancel the arrangement, should it be dissatisfied with the company's work.

Arrangements were also made to certify that the company would recruit "desirable" immigrants. By the first arrangement with the North Atlantic Trading Company, the bonus was paid only on agriculturists (farm labourers and domestic servants included) who settled on the land. Each family head was to possess at least $100.00, or, where there was a community of families working together, they were to average an amount sufficient not to become a public burden. These financial restrictions were increasingly focused on immigrants from Galicia and Bukowina, and the agreement in 1900 placed financial restrictions only on immigrants from those parts of Europe. In the 1902 agreement, special financial restrictions applied "in respect to settlers from Galicia, Roumania, Serbia, and Russia, excepting Germans."[14]

---

[12]   *Ibid.* 35.

[13]   *Ibid.* 35.

[14]   *Ibid.* 36.

To forward the cause of emigration from German-speaking areas of Europe to Canada, the North Atlantic Trading Company printed and distributed literature such as pamphlets and maps. To circumvent the surveillance officers enforcing emigration laws, the Company also printed and distributed its own small newspaper in German-speaking areas of Europe. Addresses were collected and the relevant literature was forwarded to them. Literature was also distributed through the steamship agencies, or forwarded to public reading rooms, libraries and other places frequented by the general public. Where it was difficult to use printed material, as in Germany, Austria-Hungary or Russia, sub-agents were employed, usually travelling merchants, or other equally mobile persons. The company was supported by the immigration agency in Winnipeg, as well as by immigration workers in Ottawa, who replied to letters and distributed immigration literature.

The Liberal government also reorganized the immigration work in the United States. The number of state agencies was increased and more commissioned agents or sub-agents were appointed, their numbers rising from 64 in 1894 to 129 in 1898, and then to 270 in 1900 and 291 in 1903. The sub-agent worked under the state agent and served to put the state agent into direct contact with the populace in his territory. Of agents appointed, most tended to be railway ticket agents or local farmers, who were selected because of their knowledge of local conditions and their ability to recruit potential immigrants. Agents were also selected because of their ability to circulate among a specific ethnic or minority group. Of agents working among German Americans, three might be mentioned. The first was Jacob C. Koehn of Mountain Lake, Minnesota, who was appointed to his position in 1898, primarily on the strength of his ability to work among the large German Mennonite community of Minnesota. He was himself a Mennonite, who as a child had come from Russia to the United States. Another sub-agent was F.J. Lange, president of the Catholic Settlement Society, who worked in the interest of German Catholic emigration to Canada. A Mr. Stoner worked among the German Dunkards or Baptists.

In carrying out his work, the sub-agent distributed literature among German Americans who were likely to emigrate. He also might insert his name with that of a state agent in advertisements in newspapers subscribed to by the group among which he was working. The sub-agents also held meetings to recruit settlers. They answered letters from

German-speaking settlers requesting information on the Canadian West. At times, they assisted state agents by setting up and manning displays at fairs and by keeping in contact with local German communities and reporting to state agents on the possibility of Germans emigrating from a certain locality. On various occasions, they accompanied farm delegates or settlers, who went to the Canadian West to pick up land or explore the possibility of settlement.

In addition to employing sub-agents in the United States, the federal government appointed persons from the Canadian West to encourage the emigration of German Americans. In 1897 and 1899 Mr. Gerhardt Ens, a Mennonite businessman from Rosthern was paid $75.00 per month plus expenses to recruit Mennonite settlers from Kansas. In 1901, Mr. T. Unruh was employed under the same financial conditions to recruit Mennonites from the Dakotas for the Rosthern district. Mr. D. Friesen of southern Manitoba worked to recruit settlers among the Mennonites of Kansas. The work of the agents sent from Canada tended to be seasonal, generally carried out during the winter. The agents distributed German language pamphlets or held meetings in the interest of emigration to Western Canada. In the spring, they worked to help the emigrants who had been recruited locate their homesteads.

To encourage German American emigration, advertisements were placed in German American newspapers. Of the 211 advertisements placed in 1902 by Lord and Thomas Newspapers and Magazine Advertising, an advertising agency through which the Canadian government worked, two advertisements were placed in German language newspapers. In addition, Lord and Thomas were authorized in 1902 to insert a 53 line advertisement of the Department of the Interior six times in leading German agricultural papers of Wisconsin - the *Ackerbau* and the *Gartenbau*. The Department of Interior also subscribed that year to some 10,000 issues weekly of *Der Nordwesten* and other German language newspapers, which were forwarded to a rotating series of addresses that had been collected in the United States by the Department. On occasion, special immigration issues of *Der Nordwesten* were subscribed to and distributed by the Department, especially among Germans in the United States.

In addition to its direct sponsorship of immigration work, the federal government also provided indirect support to the recruitment of German Americans, for example through the Catholic Settlement Society.

Believing that the price of land in the United States made it imperative for the younger elements to emigrate, German American Catholic leaders sought to direct this flow of emigrants into larger German Catholic settlements in the Canadian West. Group settlement, it was hoped, would help German Catholics perpetuate their faith and their German culture, as well as aid German Catholic priests to serve their parishioners. To establish larger settlements in Canada, the Catholic Settlement Society, which had formerly been occupied in this work in the United States, turned its attention to recruiting German Catholics for Western Canada.

To pay its expenses, estimated at $5.00 to $7.00 in advertisements for each family recruited, the Settlement Society charged the settlers $15.00 for its services in addition to the $10.00 homestead entry fee charged by the government. While the government disapproved of the extra fee, it was unwilling to prevent it being charged as long as settlers were willing to pay, primarily because it saw the Society as doing useful work. To meet its expenses, the Society also applied to the government to have its president appointed government sub-agent. As a sub-agent from September 1902 to June 1903, F.J. Lange received $1.50 for each male and $.75 for each female over eighteen years, and $.50 for all recruits under eighteen years of age. It has been estimated that during this period some 1,500 homesteaders were recruited by the Society. While it is not certain whether Lange received a bonus on all the settlers, even if he had received payment for some of them, this would have aided the Society substantially in carrying out its work. At the request of the Society, one of its agents, H. Bens, was appointed Land Guide at a salary of $2.00 a day to help it meet the expenses it incurred in advertising. In addition, the government aided Catholic settlement by ordering 3,000 subscriptions of the *St. Peter's Bote* at $1.00 each per year and by advertising in German American Catholic newspapers.

Government immigration work, as well as push-pull influences in the country of origin, encouraged Germans to emigrate. For example, between 1903 and 1911 some 23,733 German Americans emigrated to Canada. A major reason for their leaving was the closing of the American frontier. This brought an increase in the price of good, readily available land, which caused in particular new arrivals to the United States to leave. While it is difficult to determine the effect which German language newspapers, or the propaganda aimed at the American population at large, had upon the movement of Germans, government sponsored work no doubt helped to direct the attention of German Americans to Canada as a potential area of settlement.

Reports from settlement agents give some indication of the success of government-sponsored work. A report by Ens shows that during his work in Kansas, in 1898, he recruited 23 Mennonite farmers for Rosthern.[15] Koehn's reports show that he had on different occasions received a bonus on 30 or 40 people who emigrated to Western Canada.[16] While there is no indication of the number of German American settlers recruited by Stoner and Lange, the reason given for reducing the bonus paid to them was to save bonus money paid out by the government because of the large number of settlers each was recruiting.

Reports from settlers themselves give an indication why Germans migrated. German Americans, for example, ascribe their coming to Canada to the high cost of land, repeated crop failures, poor land, dishonest agents, or the opportunity to obtain good land cheaply.[17] Of German American Catholic settlers who had been recruited for the St. Peter's Colony, many left the United States because of their desire to live in a larger Catholic settlement. Once established, or having located suitable homesteads, new arrivals sought to induce their friends or relatives to follow. More frequently, a group of farmers in a district or community elected delegates to locate an area suitable for settlement. There is little mention in reports from settlers of immigration literature or government-sponsored agents having induced them to emigrate. However, settlers frequently mentioned that they had been aided by agents or other services offered by the Canadian government when coming to Canada.[18]

This does not mean that government-sponsored work was not an important influence in inducing German Americans to emigrate to the Canadian West. Judging by their letters, the emigrants tended not to be aware of this work. The same may be observed in the movement of Germans from Europe. The North Atlantic Trading Company, which for the year 1903-1904 printed 335 copies of the pamphlet *Canada* in seventeen languages, 115 copies of the *Canadakarten* in eight languages,

---

[15] Ibid. 42.

[16] Ibid. 42.

[17] *Ibid.* 42.

[18] *Ibid.* 43.

180,000 copies of the German pamphlet *Canada*, 5,000 pamphlets in Dutch, and 100,000 copies of the Swedish paper *Meddalande*, claimed that the increase of continental European emigration after the turn of the century was due largely to its work.[19] Walter Kuhn, when discussing the motives for the emigration of Germans from Galicia (a prime area of recruitment for Canada) attributed it to the adverse conditions in Galicia.[20]

The influence of the North Atlantic Trading Company upon the migratory patterns of Germans may also be observed by examining German emigration after the company ceased its work. In 1906, the Canadian government broke its agreement with the North Atlantic Trading Company, maintaining that the company neglected work among desirable continental Europeans, such as Scandinavians and Germans, and concentrated on recruiting the less desirable, but more easily obtainable Ruthenians.[21] After 1906, the Canadian government almost ceased emigration work among Germans in Europe.

This may in part be attributed to the unfavourable attitude towards Eastern Europeans held by the new Minister of Immigration, Frank Oliver. Once the agreement with the North Atlantic Trading Company was broken and the company was further discredited by parliamentary inquiries into its work, the government was at a loss as to how to pursue its immigrant recruitment activities in Germany. It refused to return to the old policy of supporting German booking agents directly because they were not allowed to direct emigrants to a specific country. This was further motivated by the refusal of German shipping companies to establish a direct line between Germany and Canada. The absence of such a line from German ports was seen as being in part responsible for directing the more desirable continental Europeans away from Canada. It was further argued that, as German shipping companies would keep the bonus rather than pay it to their booking agents, the bonus would do little to encourage immigration, but rather would help to subsidize German Lines, thereby aiding them to undercut British Lines in the competition for shipping emigrants from the continent.[22]

---

[19]   *Ibid.* 43.

[20]   *Ibid.*, 44.

[21]   *Ibid.* 44.

[22]   *Ibid.* 45.

However, the immigration work that had already been carried out, as well as world conditions and conditions in the homelands from which Germans originated, served to bring 40,000 German immigrants to Canada between 1896 and 1914. A number of influences encouraged these migrants to make Canada their destination. The depression of the late 1880s and early 1890s which had hampered the immigration efforts of the Conservatives had ended. Immediately following 1896, conditions essential to the successful settlement of Western Canada improved. The first of these was a favourable ratio between the price of wheat and the cost of transportation. Although the Canadian Pacific was completed in 1885, it was not until the late nineties that the advance in the price of wheat and the decline in the cost of transportation produced the favourable ratio. The second requirement was a variety of wheat adapted to the short growing season in Western Canada, thereby eliminating the recurring damage from frost. By 1896, Red Fife, wheat suitable for Western Canadian prairie conditions, was generally planted. The third essential was the introduction of farming methods suitable to the prairie environment. By the close of the century the dry farming technique, developed on the great plains of the United States, had crossed the border into Canada.

These developments within Canada were contemporaneous with a world-wide economic expansion. Late in 1896, the depression which for several years had gripped the world began to lift, encouraged by the rise in the world gold supply as a result of the development of the cyanide process for extracting gold from low-grade ores, combined with major new discoveries of gold in South Africa, the Yukon and the Klondike. Further impetus to the economic expansion in the world was given by the huge increase in investment, primarily at home in the case of Germany and the United States, and abroad in the case of Britain. International prosperity contributed to the improved fortunes of the wheat economy. Rising living standards throughout the Western World brought a pronounced shift in demand from inferior meal products to wheat based foods, while reduced world crops during the later nineties and the earlier years of the twentieth century enhanced the upward pressure on world wheat prices. Important reductions in transportation charges, resulting from the expansion of Western Canadian railways, the Crow's Nest Pass Agreement and the price wars between the steamship lines, brought increased revenues for wheat sales. The competition between steamship lines also lowered emigration costs for Europeans. These conditions created in Canada a favourable economic climate which brought prosperity to the German Canadian farmers and wage earners and induced them to report favourably on local conditions and also provided them with the means to help their friends join them in this country.

German Settlement Patterns on the Canadian Prairies prior to World War I

Between 1817 and 1914, 80,000 German-speaking immigrants settled on the Canadian prairies – the area north of the 49th parallel between the Canadian Shield and the Rockies that now comprises the provinces of Manitoba, Saskatchewan and Alberta. Except where the immigration movement was organized, Germans tended to arrive in small groups, coming largely from Russia, the United States and the predominantly non-German speaking areas of Austria-Hungary. Various influences determined where these immigrants settled on the Canadian prairies, including land type, railway construction, religious affiliation and friendship and family ties among the immigrants. The following explores some of these influences.

The first German-speaking immigrants to arrive in Western Canada were the De Meuron mercenaries, brought to Red River by Lord Selkirk in 1817. They were followed by Swiss immigrants in 1821. Both groups left Red River in 1826, and St. Boniface (named after the patron saint of the Germans by Bishop Provencher in honour of these settlers) became a French Canadian settlement. The next important influx of German-speaking immigrants to Western Canada came with the arrival of the Russian Mennonites. Believing that the Government Ukase of 1871 threatened the right to non-resistance granted to them by Catherine II in the 1760s, some 7,800 Mennonites left Russia between 1874 and 1881 and settled in southern Manitoba. Here they formed two block settlements - the East Reserve and the West Reserve.

Between 1881 and 1896 a further 14,500 German-speaking immigrants arrived in Western Canada, mostly from Russia and Austria-Hungary. Some 50 small German settlements were founded by them, including Langenburg, Neu Elsass and Neu Tulcea. In the 1890s German Moravians from Volhynia, Russia, founded the settlements of Bruderfeld and Bruderheim in the Edmonton area. German-speaking Catholics from southern Russia settled in the Regina area, where they established a number of settlements, including St. Joseph's Colony, started in 1886, and Rastatt and Katharinenthal, where settlement began in 1890.

The boom in the prairie economy between 1896 and World War I brought 40,000 German-speaking immigrants from Europe and the United States. During this period, the Catholic Colonization Society settled about 5,000 German American Catholic farmers in St. Peter's Colony, east of Saskatoon. When most of the good land there was taken up, the colonizers turned their attention to St. Joseph's Colony, west of Saskatoon. During this period, the Didsbury area, where Mennonite settlement had begun in about 1892, received additional settlers from the United States. After 1896, the Mennonite block settlement in the Rosthern District, begun in 1891, started to receive a large number of settlers from both Europe and the United States. A large number of smaller primarily Lutheran and Catholic settlements were also formed at this time, including Thalberg and Oldenburg in the Whitemouth area of Manitoba, where settlement began in 1896; Odessa, Saskatchewan, where settlement began in 1901; Marienthal, Saskatchewan, established in 1902; Gartenland, Saskatchewan, established in 1905; Kramer, Saskatchewan, established in 1910; and Blumenau, Alberta, established in 1903.

As German-speaking immigrants were predominantly agriculturists, they were interested in taking up land and, insofar as possible, homestead land. It was the availability of free land that directed them, first to Manitoba and later to the still sparsely populated areas of Saskatchewan and Alberta. Reports from German settlers in the West, as well as inquiries from persons seeking a suitable area of settlement, show that land type, rainfall and crops raised were important considerations in drawing Germans to different areas of the West. They tended to be attracted to areas that still had free homesteads, were suitable for grain growing and allowed for mixed farming.

Frequently, German-speaking immigrants were attracted to terrain that was similar to that of their homeland. The experiences which Mennonites had with dry farming techniques on the Russian steppes encouraged them to begin farming on the open plain of the West Reserve where, in 1876, they were to form the first large agricultural settlement on the Canadian prairies. The Reverend R. A. Mueller settled German Baptists from Volhynia in the Leduc area of Alberta, where he found the land type similar to that of their homeland. Similar motives attracted

German Lutherans from Volhynia to the parkland of Manitoba, where they formed a number of small settlements near Beausejour, Moosehorn and along the Grass River. The first German Russian Catholic immigrants tended to settle in the Regina area, where they found the treeless plain similar to the steppes in southern Russia. Many of the German American farmers attracted to the St. Joseph's Colony, west of Saskatoon, originated from southern Russia and preferred grassland to the parkland of the St. Peter's Colony.

As with settlement in general, once steel rails began dissecting the prairie landscape, railways and railway development channeled German-speaking immigrants to different areas of the West. Frequently, settlers or settlement agents anticipated the construction of a railway, as in the case of Neu Elsass, which was established by D.W. Riedle and Aaron J. Schantz at a point near where they expected the Manitoba and Northwest Railway to pass. When it was shown that they had miscalculated, many of the settlers left. As the Manitoba and Northwest Railway pushed into Saskatchewan, small German settlements arose in its proximity, including Langenburg, established in 1885, and Wilhelmshoehe, established in 1896. A.S. Morton observed that between 1891 and 1894 no fewer than 14 small German settlements were founded subsidiary to a railway. These included Rosenthal, established in 1891, Josephsburg, established in 1892, and Bruderfeld and Bruderheim, the Moravian settlements in the Edmonton area.[23]

The influence of the railway is also evident in the development of block settlements formed by German-speaking groups. By 1900 the large Mennonite settlement in the Rosthern District stretched along both sides of the railway between the stations Rosthern, Hague and Osler. By 1906, the Mennonite settlement in the Didsbury area stretched some 30 miles on either side of the Calgary and Edmonton Railway. Advertisements of the Catholic Colonization Society, which recruited German American farmers for the Canadian West, pointed out that one attractive feature of St. Joseph's Colony, west of Saskatoon, was that a settler there would be within 20 miles of a railway that had been built or was about to be built.

---

[23] Arthur Grenke. "Settlement Patterns of German-Speaking Immigrants on the Prairies," *German-Canadian Yearbook* XIV Ed. H. Fröschle (Toronto: Historical Society of Mecklenburg Upper Canada Inc., 1995) 4.

As railways were the primary means whereby a farmer could transport his grain to market, farmers sought to take up land as close to them as possible. For European immigrants, who, unlike the German Americans, tended to come with insufficient money to take up land immediately, the railway and railway centers offered the opportunity to earn the money required to begin farming. For settlers on the land, work on the nearby railway provided a supplement to their often meager farm income. Settlers in the Langenburg area, for example, used money earned from working on the Manitoba and Northwest Railway to build their houses and purchase household goods. Railway companies also advanced loans to settlers to help them purchase machinery or aided them following a crop failure. Railway centers with a large German-speaking population in their hinterland, such as Langenburg and Gretna, attracted a considerable number of German-speaking businessmen to serve the settlers in their own language.

The major railway centers, such as Winnipeg, Regina or Calgary, which were pivotal links in the western railway system, attracted a considerable number of Germans. Sizeable German enclaves arose in Elmwood and North Winnipeg, in the so-called "Germantown" in Regina, and in Bowville, near Calgary. While some of the German-speaking elements of these cities were business or tradespeople, most were agriculturists from Europe, who tended to remain in these centers for about three or four years, working as labourers to pay off any debt incurred by their trip to Canada and to earn sufficient money to make a start on the land. When moving to the land, these people frequently settled near the city, as was the case with Winnipeggers who moved to Whitemouth, Thalberg and other areas of rural Manitoba.

Community ties that Germans formed at urban churches helped to channel them to different areas of the west. Members of First German Baptist Church, Winnipeg, for example, chose to move to Baptist congregations in Whitemouth and Oak Bank, where local Baptist churches had close ties with the urban church. Many of the first settlers of Josephsburg, Saskatchewan, were at one time members of Trinity Reformed Church, Winnipeg. The first German settlers of Wolfsheim, Saskatchewan, were predominantly former members of St. Joseph's (Catholic) Church, Winnipeg. Pastors such as the Reverend G. Gehrke of the Ohio Synod used his position as synod president to channel people from German-speaking congregations of his synod in Winnipeg to rural congregations of the Ohio Synod that were in need of additional membership if they were to become independent.

German centers, once established, attracted German immigrants and served to distribute them in the hinterland. German Lutherans and Catholics who followed the Mennonites to Manitoba worked for the Mennonite farmers until they had sufficient money to acquire their own land. Lutherans settled in the Mennonite reserves. An example is Friedensthal, near Steinbach, Manitoba. The Catholics moved on to the Regina area. By the 1890s Edenwald became a distributing centre for German Lutherans who remained there long enough to gain farming experience and to earn the money required to make a start on the land. Many of them later settled in Kimmel, Southey and Grey. The German Catholic settlements in the Regina area served similar purposes for German Catholics arriving from southern Russia.

In a few instances, business organizations with weak ties to the German immigrant community sought to forward their financial interests through settlement work among Germans. Examples are the London and Ontario Investment Company, whose representative, William Harvey, as part of his work among Germans organized small German settlements near Emerson and Dominion City. The German American Land Company, organized in 1905 by a number of German businessmen, envisaged establishing a number of German settlements. Incorporated with capital of $500,000.00, the company purchased 10,000 acres of land near Dominion City. A further 16,000 acres near Lipton, Saskatchewan, were acquired, as well as 10,000 acres north of the Pheasant Hill Railway. The company was successful in settling some Germans on its land but does not appear to have established a German settlement. Germans preferred the free homestead land offered by the government. Nor did the plan, whereby the company offered to help immigrants buy their farm machinery and market their products, prove attractive.

German language newspapers appear to have played some part in channeling Germans into different areas of the West. From the time that the first German language newspaper in the West was founded, the federal government subscribed to German language papers and distributed them to addresses in Europe and the United States to help recruit settlers. Special immigration issues of *Der Nordwesten, Saskatchewan Courier* or the *Alberta Herold* were purchased to provide German-speaking elements in the United States and Europe with reports on German settlements in Western Canada. Government reports do not indicate what effect these newspapers had on influencing the people who received them. But the use of these papers by settlers to attract new immigrants to their area does indicate that they had some influence in directing German-speaking immigrants to specific parts of Western Canada. In the columns of the papers, settlers reported on their progress and invited other Germans to settle in their area. Also, Germans wishing to emigrate to Western Canada used German language newspapers to find a settlement where they might locate. In other instances, individuals such as Karl Stetter, who established a German Swiss settlement in Blumenau, Alberta, used the German language press to attract Germans of a variety of backgrounds to his settlement.

Religious affiliation had a profound effect on the settlement patterns of Germans in Western Canada, as demonstrated by the settlement patterns of the different German religious groups. More than any other religious group of German Canadians, except possibly the Hutterites, Mennonites sought to establish settlements large enough to afford a fair degree of local independence, sufficient to give them control of the most important community organizations such as churches and schools. These objectives were pursued from the beginning of Mennonite settlement in the Canadian West. In 1873 and 1876 this was done through an agreement between Mennonites and the federal government whereby land was reserved for Mennonite settlement. This resulted in the formation of the Mennonite East Reserve and West Reserve in Manitoba. In 1895 and again in 1904 *Ältester* Wiebe, serving as a representative of Old Colony Mennonites, entered into agreements with the Canadian government to reserve land for younger members of his Church, first in the Herbert area and later near Swift Current. In 1903, Senator Peter Jansen of Nebraska, in pursuit of his own settlement schemes for Mennonites, reserved land both of the Saskatchewan Valley Land Company and homestead land.

On other occasions, Mennonites succeeded in forming block settlements without reserving land. An example is the Mennonite settlement in the Rosthern District. When towards the end of the 1880s good land on the Mennonite reserves in Manitoba was becoming scarce and expensive, Mennonite delegates examined land for the purpose of founding a settlement further west and, as a result, a few Mennonites settled near Gleichen. Finding the area too arid, they were advised by Klaas Peters, an employee of the Calgary and Edmonton Railway, to select land in the

Rosthern District. When reports reached southern Manitoba that good homestead land was available near Rosthern, local villages sent out delegates to examine land there. Settlement excursions were organized to enable those who were interested to locate suitable homesteads. Mennonite delegates also arrived from Russia, Germany and the United States to examine the district and settlers from these countries began to take up land. Immigration agents such as J.C. Koehn, G. Ens and especially Klaas Peters directed their attention towards recruiting Mennonites from the United States, southern Manitoba and Russia for settlement in the Rosthern District.

Although church elders were generally involved in negotiations with the government for reserving land for Mennonite settlement, the practical settlement work was carried out largely by Mennonite businessmen such as Ens, Schanz or Peters. They recruited the settlers. Schanz, for example, when establishing a settlement near Didsbury, Alberta, recruited settlers from among Mennonite farmers in Pennsylvania and especially sought to recruit Mennonites in Waterloo County, Ontario, who were living on rented land. Senator Peter Jansen, when seeking to establish a Mennonite settlement in the Quill Lake area sought to recruit settlers from southern Manitoba, Waterloo County and Nebraska.

Like the Mennonites, German American Catholic leaders sought to organize settlements that would serve the religious needs of the community. As viewed by German American Catholic priests, preservation of the German language among their parishioners was an integral part of preserving the faith. Systematically organized settlements were also seen as a means whereby a limited number of priests would be able to serve their parishioners. To forward these goals, German American Benedictines of Cluny, Illinois, took a leading role in establishing St. Peter's Colony, in Saskatchewan. They worked together with Catholic laymen, such as F.J. Lange, president of the Catholic Settlement Society, and German American capitalists, such as Henry Haskamp, president of the German American Land Company.

Prior to establishing St. Peter's Colony, delegates representing German Catholic interests in the United States, including Father Bruno Doerfler, a Benedictine from Cluny, explored several locations in Western Canada to locate land suitable for establishing a German Catholic block settlement. They decided upon land in the Hoodoo District, east of Saskatoon, which was soon to be opened for settlement. The Catholic Settlement Society thereupon requested and received permission from the federal government to register the claims of the settlers it represented prior to the area's being thrown open to general settlement. The Catholic claim was further strengthened through the purchase of 108,000 acres of non-homestead land by the German American Land Company from the North Saskatchewan Land Company. Meanwhile, the Catholic Settlement Society conducted an extensive campaign to advertise this land in German American Catholic newspapers and through circulars, thereby recruiting a large enough number of German American Catholics to settle most of the good land of St. Peter's in about two years.

Having too many applications to accommodate all of them on suitable land in the St. Peter's Colony, and having many potential settlers who preferred grassland to the parkland of the St. Peter's Colony, German Catholic colonizers decided to establish a new settlement, St. Joseph's Colony, west of Saskatoon. Again, delegates served to locate suitable land. To carry out the settlement work the Catholic Settlement Society was reorganized, this time under the spiritual leadership of the Oblates. The colonizers again concentrated on recruiting German Catholics from the United States. No land company was organized, however, to purchase non-government land. The Society's request that the government allow it to reserve the odd-numbered sections for sale to the settlers it recruited was refused. Unlike St. Peter's, St. Joseph's Colony was, therefore, not settled almost exclusively by German-speaking Catholics.

German-speaking members of other denominations also undertook major settlement projects. In 1907, German Lutherans of the Nebraska Synod purchased 100,000 acres of land from the Luseland Company to establish a German Lutheran settlement in Saskatchewan. Attempts to have homestead land in the area also reserved for Lutherans failed when the government refused a request to that effect by the land company. In 1908, German Seventh-Day Adventists from North Dakota formed a colony by settling 35 sections of land that they had purchased from the German American Land Company. In 1893 the Reverend R.A. Mueller served as a delegate for persecuted German Baptists in Volhynia who wished to settle together in the Canadian west, and in the mid-1890s the Reverend A. Lilge of the Moravian Brethren entered into agreements with the Canadian government to reserve land in the Edmonton area, where he established the settlements of Bruderheim and Bruderfeld. In 1899 Hutterite Brethren from South Dakota bought land and established a "Hof" near Dominion City, south of Winnipeg. The settlement broke up again when repeated flooding of the Roseau River and the inability to attract members of the sect from South Dakota induced inhabitants to return to the United States.

Among German Protestant denominations, other than the Mennonites and Hutterites, the attempt to organize settlements systematically was more the exception than the rule. Even when Protestant groups such as the Baptists or Lutherans pursued a strategy to organize settlements, they seldom did so to preserve the religious or linguistic characteristics of the immigrants. Pastor Mueller, for example, was more interested in settling his approximately 100 families of German Baptists closely together than in establishing a nucleus for a German Baptist block settlement. The Lutheran Luseland settlement was formed following a quarrel over dogma that had erupted among German Lutherans in Nebraska.

Protestant groups such as the Baptists and Lutherans placed little emphasis on organizing block settlements because they did not feel that their religious identity was threatened by the forces of assimilation in the American environment. As the Reverend G.A. Heimann, a Lutheran pastor who had worked among the pioneers asserted: "Unlike in Russia, in Canada the Germans had nothing to fear. They felt a kinship for their Anglo-Saxon countrymen. Also, the Lutherans are Protestant and Canada and the United States are Protestant countries." [24] Similar attitudes are evident among groups such as the Baptists, who often felt a greater kinship with their English-speaking brethren than with Germans of other denominational backgrounds.

North American conditions motivated German American Catholics to organize block settlements. German Catholics from Europe did not establish block settlements because they originated largely from a Catholic environment in east-central Europe where assimilation did not threaten their religious identity. In fact, a good number of German Catholics living in smaller German enclaves in Eastern Europe were assimilated into the Polish national group. It was in the United States, where assimilation to the larger Anglo-Saxon Protestant majority also meant loss of the Catholic faith, that German Catholic priests took a leading role in organizing Catholic settlements. At the turn of the century, their eyes turned to Canada because it still had sufficient free land to enable them to establish block settlements.

---

[24] *Ibid.* 13.

As important as religious influences on structuring the settlement patterns of German-speaking immigrants were the forces of family, friendship and neighborhood ties. These had a profound effect on the settlement patterns of all German immigrants, no matter what their denominational background. All of the approximately 65 German-speaking pre-1914 immigrants interviewed by me in the course of preparing this analysis had chosen to come to Western Canada and had chosen their area of settlement because of the influence of friends, relatives or former neighbors already settled there. The people interviewed included members of the Catholic, Baptist, Lutheran and Reformed denominations.

For groups that consciously pursued a settlement strategy, these influences contributed to the establishment of block settlements. This is evident in the case of St. Peter's Colony, for example, where friendship, family and neighborhood ties contributed to the growth of the different local communities. Similar influences are evident in the formation of the Mennonite block settlements. The establishment of the East and West Reserve in Manitoba involved the recreation on the Canadian prairies of Russian Mennonite communities from which the settlers originated. In Saskatchewan, family and friendship relations channeled Mennonites from Rosenort, West Prussia, to Tiefengrund in the Rosthern District. Similar forces are evident in the Mennonite settlement in the Didsbury area, where Mennonites from Waterloo County were concentrated closest to the town; then came Mennonites from Minnesota, and furthest from the town were Mennonites from Manitoba.

Among groups that placed little emphasis on organizing block settlements, friendship and neighbourhood ties contributed to the formation of a great number of small settlements, which, like the block settlements, tended to consist of members with a common denominational background. In Eastern Europe and the United States whence most German immigrants to Western Canada originated, Germans were settled largely according to denominational affiliation. Family, friendship and neighbourhood ties, therefore, worked towards organizing new denominational settlements. This was the case, for example, with Friedensthal and Brunkild in Manitoba, with Friedensthal being settled by German Lutherans from Volhynia and Brunkild by German Lutherans from East Prussia. Edenwald, although originally founded by German Baptists from Romania, became populated largely by German Lutherans from Bukowina who attracted their friends and relatives from the homeland. Josephsburg, Saskatchewan, became largely a German Reformed settlement because of the ability of the original settlers to encourage their friends and relatives to follow them. Settlers of the original German-Russian Catholic settlements in the Regina area also drew their families and friends after them, which resulted in their establishing about a dozen small settlements near Regina. The same forces resulted in Mariahilf, south of Regina, being populated largely by German Catholics from Bukowina.

Influences affecting the settlement patterns of German-speaking immigrants in Western Canada can be divided into two broad categories. Under one category might be placed all the impersonal forces affecting settlement, be this land type, railways or the availability of free land, influences which in themselves would have had little effect on the formation of German settlements. In fact, one might say that, independent of community influences, Germans would have been generally dispersed through the Canadian west among peoples of other national backgrounds. But influences such as denominational membership and family and friendship relations brought about the formation of German settlements, with German settlements forming in those areas of the West where they found the land type, transportation facilities and other conditions suitable to meet their needs. In the formation of these settlements religious influences, family, friendship and neighborhood ties were especially important, with block settlements being established by groups that saw in such settlements a means of retaining their religious identity. Family, friendship and neighborhood ties brought about the formation of small German settlements whose members tended to belong to a common denomination.

German Immigration and Settlement during the Inter-War years

Prior to World War I the desirability of European immigrants was determined by the benefits they were seen to bring to the country; after World War I their admissibility was very much influenced by whether they originated from an allied or an enemy country. The Canadian government all but forgot that it had laid out considerable sums to recruit Germans for this country, essentially because they were considered to be good settlers. The war had made these people be seen as a potential fifth column.

In February 1919, the Canadian government decreed that any person's complaint "evidencing a feeling of public apprehension entertained by the community" was sufficient cause to detain an enemy alien, or those individuals originating from enemy countries who had not been naturalized. The suspect was entitled neither to legal counsel nor the right to be informed of the proceedings against him. The Canadian government also gave consideration to petitions demanding the internment and mass expulsion of all registered enemy aliens. This was not acted upon. However, the government repatriated over 1,800 of the Germans and 302 of the Austrians it had interned during the war. At the same time, the Canadian government frequently didn't return property it had confiscated from enemy aliens for administrative purposes. The Canadian government had no proof that these people had betrayed the country in any way. Rather, people lost their belongings and were shipped back essentially because of their assumed beliefs and attitudes. There was room for only one old world loyalty at the time: loyalty to Britain and its war time allies.

Attitudes such as these also resulted in hostility toward conscientious objectors. Toward the end of the war approximately 1,000 German-speaking Hutterites and 600 Mennonites came to Canada from the United States. They fled to Canada despite the anti-German sentiment sweeping the country, because of the far greater American intolerance toward pacifists in the United States after its entry into the war. In some instances, Mennonite churches had been burned and Mennonites tarred and feathered. The refusal of Hutterites to be drafted, buy war bonds and give up the German language, subjected them to charges of being pro-German and to attacks by hostile neighbours. Some Hutterites were court-martialed and placed in barracks, while others were abused and publicly ridiculed. Their property was vandalized and their livestock stolen. The cruel torture of four forcibly drafted Hutterites and the resulting death of two of them motivated many of them to leave for Canada.

The entry of German-speaking conscientious objectors to Canada aroused a storm of indignation. The Great War Veterans' Association took up the battle against these religious communities and recommended that they all be expelled if possible. It urged that the Hutterites who had entered the country be deported and that any further immigration of non-resisters be prohibited. Under pressure from this organization, an Order-in-Council was passed on June 9, 1919, prohibiting the immigration of conscientious objectors. The immigration of citizens of the formerly hostile Central Powers was also prohibited.

The years of war and the ethnocentrism they fostered encouraged the government not only to bar the entry of enemy aliens but also to confine its immigrant recruitment endeavours primarily to British subjects. With this goal in mind, the Canadian government entered into the Empire Settlement Agreement with the British government, which encouraged British farm workers to come to Canada. This was complemented by the Empire Settlement Act in 1922, whereby the British government co-operated with the Canadian government and other colonial governments to recruit agriculturalists in Britain, and assist them in emigrating and making a new start in the colonies.[25] However, it was found that British immigrants were little inclined to farm. Nor could Canada's labour intensive industries depend on British workers to meet their growing labour needs. British immigrants were, by and large, not inclined to work in lumbering, railway construction, mining, or in unskilled urban jobs. The failure of British immigrants to meet the needs of the Canada's economy made its political leaders look elsewhere to meet Canadian labour demands.

In particular the railway companies lobbied for more relaxed immigration controls governing continental European immigration. More immigrants would mean an increase in traffic for their industry. Also, more immigrants would expedite the settlement of vacant railway lands. Mennonite leaders, in turn, hoped that emigration to Canada might offer a solution to the plight in which their co-religionists found themselves in the Soviet Union. With this goal in mind, a delegation of Canadian Mennonites travelled to Ottawa in March 1922, where they received from Prime Minister King the promise that the restrictions that had been placed on Mennonite immigration in 1919 would be removed. They received a favourable response largely because of the generally positive attitude toward Germans of the Liberal Mackenzie King administration. This led to the resumption of German immigration in 1923.

General conditions of turmoil and social unrest in Germany and Eastern Europe encouraged emigration. This was especially true of

---

[25]   Jonathan Wagner, *A History of Migration from Germany to Canada, 1850-1939* (Vancouver: UBC Press, 2006) 165.

Germans in the Soviet Union. Even more so than in North America, in Russia the war against the Central Powers had been fought not only against Germany but against anything German. Germans in Volhynia were expelled to the east, an expulsion during which about a quarter of them died. Germans were at different times also threatened with being expelled from Russia. However, this did not seem to be the main objective of the Czarist government. Rather, its main objective was to destroy Germans politically and economically within the country. With this end in mind, partial expropriation of land held by people of German origin was decreed on February 2, 1915, and on December 15, 1915, the last and complete expropriation law was promulgated. It made all German land holdings subject to expropriation under conditions that equaled theft. All the property of the German element in Russia was to be liquidated by the spring of 1917. The German colonists were also not permitted to leave Russia but instead were to be dispersed among the Russians in order to work for them.

The Russian Revolution of 1917, while leaving the expropriation laws unenforced, inflicted even worse suffering upon the Germans in Russia. Being generally better off than their Slavic neighbours, Germans were objects of envy. This frequently led to their villages being attacked and plundered by the neighbouring Slavic villagers. When the communists came to power, a disproportionate number of Germans were typecast as kulaks, leading to their expulsion and death in the labour camps. Worse was the religious persecution Germans had to undergo as the communists sought to wipe out what they saw as the opiate of the people. Germans responded by seeking to flee.

Although not as drastic as in the Soviet Union, Germans in the newly formed states of Europe also saw emigration as an escape from the political and social discrimination they faced. In Germany itself, the economic handicaps placed on the country as a result of the Treaty of Versailles and its political and social ramifications brought hardship and uncertainty. The influx of nearly half a million refugees, for the most part from territories lost by the Treaty of Versailles, increased population density at a time when economic opportunities were shrinking. Civil unrest, unemployment, inflation and the severe devaluation of the German currency between 1919 and 1924 caused many Germans to lose faith in their country. At the same time, a chronic agricultural crisis in south-western and north-eastern Germany led to a steady migration from rural to urban areas. As a consequence, Germans in both rural and urban centres saw in emigration the possibility of improving their situation.

After World War I, the Canadian government put the immigration and settlement of "agriculturists, agricultural workers, and domestic servants" from non-preferred countries, from which most of the German immigrants came during the inter-war period, into the hands of the Canadian Pacific and the Canadian National Railways. In this situation, the federal government concerned itself basically with medical examinations and visa matters, leaving the recruitment and settlement of immigrants to the railway companies.

The railway companies began recruiting immigrants not long after the cessation of hostilities. To this end, Colonel John S. Dennis of the CPR took a lead in establishing the Western Canada Colonization Association in 1919. However, complaints regarding its operation arose soon after it was established. As a consequence, the Dominion Government withdrew from the undertaking. The two railways carried on another year, when the Canadian National abandoned the project to establish its own land settlement association, while the Canadian Pacific continued to operate the Western Canada Colonization Association on its own.[26]

To forward their immigration work, the Canadian National and the Canadian Pacific negotiated an agreement with the federal government in 1924 which allowed them to bring in more than 6,700 farm labourers from continental Europe. The following year they negotiated what came to be known as the "Railway Agreement," which authorized the CNR and the CPR to recruit *bona fide* agriculturalists and farm labourers in southern and Eastern Europe. Those who were not settled on the land or employed in farm work within a year could be deported at the cost of the transportation companies. The agreement ran until 1928 when it was renewed for an additional two years.

Immigrant recruitment was guided by Canada's labour needs, driven by employers making requests to the Canadian government for permits based on their employment needs. With the assistance of various ethnic organizations and immigrant aid agencies, suitable individuals were then

---

[26] James B. Hedges, *Building the Canadian West: The Land and Colonization Policies of the Canadian Pacific Railway* (New York: The Macmillan Co., 1939) 336-67.

selected abroad and brought to the attention of Canadian immigration authorities. If the individuals selected satisfied the employment requirements and successfully passed their medical examinations, they were issued visas, permitting their emigration to Canada.

To recruit German-speaking immigrants, the railway companies placed their agents in different parts of Germany. For example, while in 1925 the CPR had two agents working in Germany, by 1929 these had increased to fifty-one. Some two-thirds of them worked in either Baden/Württemberg (twenty-one) or Prussia (thirteen), areas from which most of Canada's immigrants from Germany originated. To guide the company in this work, the Canadian government informed the CPR Hamburg office of the number of farmers and female domestics that it desired, as well as of the date they should arrive and where they should be sent. The railway then went about recruiting the desired number.

The CPR also established relations with different German Canadian community organizations to recruit immigrants. Thus, it made arrangements with Lutheran synods to obtain from local pastors lists of friends and relatives of their parishioners living in the United States and Europe. Through the pastors, the railway planned to get in touch with people who wished to emigrate, with a view of locating them on its lands. The pastors, in turn, made an effort to locate their co-religionists near established churches in Western Canada, through this encouraging their growth and their ability to become self-supporting as soon as possible.

To help carry out this mutually beneficial work, the railway brought into its services T.O.F. Herzer, a Lutheran minister from the United States. He became so successful in placing members of his faith on Canadian Pacific land that he was appointed special agent of foreign colonies in the United States.[27] Later, he was appointed manager of the Canada Colonization Association, the main organization used by the CPR to carry out its immigration and settlement work.

To further forward its work in recruiting German Lutherans, the CPR encouraged German Canadian Lutherans to establish the Canadian Lutheran Immigration Board (LIB), with offices in Montreal and Winnipeg. In this case, the Canadian government let the railways know of the number of farmers, farm workers and domestics it wanted to be brought into the country. The railways would share this information with

---

[27]   *Ibid.* 286.

the LIB. Following this, the Lutheran Immigration Board worked closely together with Lutheran emigration missions in Germany and elsewhere to secure the appropriate immigrants. Working closely together with the CPR, LIB representatives negotiated travel rates from Europe to the place where the immigrant settled in Canada. After the immigrants arrived in Canada, LIB pastors met them at the train stations, helped them find temporary accommodation, as well as kept in contact with them to assure that their spiritual and economic needs were being met.[28]

Another organization with which the CPR co-operated was the *Volksverein deutsch-canadischer Katholiken* (VDCK). Organized in Western Canada in1909 to promote German Catholic interests, the VDCK extended its mission after World War I to include immigrant assistance. The work of recruiting Catholic immigrants from Germany, for example, involved a collaborate effort on the part of the CPR, the *St. Raphaels-Verein* in Germany and the VDCK in Canada. In this process, the CPR would let the VDCK know how many German Catholic immigrants the Government wanted to have brought over. The VDCK would put the person it sought to bring over in contact with the Hamburg office of the *St. Raphaels-Verein* through his parish priest. A representative of the *St. Raphaels-Verein* would provide for the emigrant's immediate needs and then passed the migrant on to the VDCK's network in Canada. The VDCK would help the emigrant obtain his train tickets, helped him find temporary housing, as well as aided him in finding farm work in a Catholic environment.

In its work with Mennonites, the Canadian Pacific became closely involved in particular in helping Mennonites come to Canada who were seeking to escape from the Soviet Union. A delegation of Russian Mennonites, consisting of A.A. Friesen, B.H. Unruh. C.H. Warkentin and J. Esau had come to North America as early as 1920 to explore the possibility of emigration. They recommended Canada as the preferred destination. However, emigration to Canada was impossible because of the Canadian Order-in-Council prohibited the entry into Canada of conscientious objectors. When this was lifted in 1922, other problems arose, making it difficult for Mennonites to enter Canada. One was the outbreak of a cholera epidemic in southern Russia. The Soviet government

---

[28]   Jonathan F. Wagner, *A History of Migration from Germany to Canada, 1850-1939* (Vancouver, 2006) 196-197.

refused to allow Canadian doctors to enter the Soviet Union to examine the health of prospective immigrants because a Soviet trade delegation had been refused entry into Canada. At the same time, the Soviet government refused to readmit to the Soviet Union any people who had been refused admission to Canada after they had been examined by Canadian doctors in Hamburg. The issue was resolved when the German government opened Lechfeld, near Augsburg, as a transit station for emigrants.

With this problem resolved, emigration could begin, in 1923. In Canada, the movement was organized by the Canadian Mennonite Board of Colonization. Initially established (in May 1922) to provide aid to starving Mennonites in the Soviet Union, it focussed on emigration when this became a possibility. To forward this, the Board of Colonization obligated itself to find temporary accommodation in Mennonite communities and to eventually settle the new arrivals as farmers. All Mennonites were to be collectively responsible for mentally and physically disabled persons. To aid the Board of Colonization in its work, the CPR extended to it a loan of about 2 million dollars, which was bonded by Mennonites already established in Canada.

Mennonite leaders further entered into an agreement with the CPR that would offer to refugees from the Soviet Union a reasonable rate from Libau, Latvia, to Western Canada. Between July and October 1923, some 2400 Mennonites had been brought to Canada by the Canadian Pacific.

Arrival of first group of Mennonite refugees in Rosthern, Sask., July 23, 1923. Courtesy of CMBS NP029-01-11

To help defray transportation costs, the Mennonite Colonization Association of North America was established, which raised the money needed for its work by selling fixed shares to Mennonites in both the United States and Canada. Beneficiaries of the plan were to repay the principal, with interest not exceeding 5 per cent.

To accelerate the process of settlement, a Mennonite Land Settlement Board was organized, consisting of three representatives from the Canadian Mennonite Board of Colonization, three from the Canada Colonization Association, and three representatives from among Mennonite newcomers. The Land Settlement Board found owners of improved land, as well as aided new arrivals in establishing themselves and in running their farms. Through such cooperation, some 21,000 Mennonites were settled in Canada by the time the movement came to an end, toward the end of 1929 and the beginning of 1930.

Of non-Mennonites, German Canadian Catholic, Lutheran and Baptist organizations were able to help some 10,000 of their co-religionists in the Soviet Union come to Canada. While in particular German Lutherans and Catholics were more numerous in the Soviet Union than the Mennonites, they were not as well organized. This was also true of the Church organizations in Canada working to bring Soviet Germans over. Furthermore, with most Mennonites in Europe being in the Soviet Union, Mennonites concentrated on bringing over their co-religionists seeking to escape from the Soviet Union. Non-Mennonites concentrated on bringing over their co-religionists west of the Soviet Union. Aiding their Soviet co-religionists was ancillary to their main immigration work, which no doubt influenced the number of Soviet German immigrants they brought to Canada.

Non-Mennonites who came from the Soviet Union followed essentially the same route as the Mennonites, leaving Russia by crossing the Latvian border. Those who did not receive permission to emigrate to Canada because of illness, stayed in Germany until they were free of their disease and then left for Canada. Then the different immigration societies availed themselves of the services of the railway and shipping companies to bring over their co-religionists. As with Mennonites, the movement ended soon after 1928, when Stalin disallowed further emigration.

Although not as extensively involved in immigration work as was the Canadian Pacific Railway, the Canadian National Railways also developed staffing and policies in the late 1920s to tap into the German emigrant pool. Lacking the CPR's shipping capacity, the CNR entered into an agreement with the North German Lloyd and the Holland American Steamship Lines to assure reasonable rates for its immigrants. From its headquarters in Rotterdam, the railway company supervised the work of its agents in Germany and other areas of Eastern and Central Europe to recruit immigrants for Canada. In its recruitment efforts, it used German and Canadian religious agencies as affiliates, founding, for example, the Catholic Immigration Aid Society in October 1928 and shortly after the Canadian Lutheran immigration Aid Society for recruitment purposes.

Departure from Bremen, 17-6-1930. Library and Archives Canada, PA-010397

Church organizations tended to be given considerable freedom in the selection of immigrants. For example, in regards to the Baptists, the selection of immigrants was first the responsibility of German Canadian Baptist Church officials. However, when problems arose over the acceptance of immigrants who were unable to sustain themselves due to insufficient funds, the Canadian National Railway took over the selection procedure. Also, Baptist Church officials had problems selecting immigrants because countries such as Poland didn't accept the Church's direction in emigration matters. This left the Canadian National Railway in the position of taking a greater part in the selection process while also acting as an arm of the Canadian Government's immigration authority. In this regard, the government stipulated that all families brought over would have sufficient money so that they would not become a burden to the Canadian taxpayer. Also, only bona fide agriculturists were to be brought forward.

Soon after the outbreak of the Depression in 1929, Canada terminated its immigrant recruitment program in continental Europe. Some of the people who had come during the 1920s, finding it difficult to adjust to Canadian conditions during a time of economic crisis, returned to Germany once employment conditions had improved there under the Nazis. At the same time, people leaving Germany, in particular those of Jewish faith, fled or were forced out by the Nazi regime. Canadian economic conditions, combined with prevailing attitudes, resulted in few of these coming to Canada.

However, Canada did accept some European refugees. In keeping with the Munich Agreement of 1938, Britain arranged a £10 million loan for the resettlement of 20,000 Czech and 10,000 Sudeten German refugees from temporary camps near Prague. Responding to British pressure, combined with the offer of a $1,500.00 grant per family, Canada placed somewhat over 1,000 healthy German-speaking families of this group on railway land. However, opposition from Canada's western premiers prevented the evacuation of most of these families until German troops occupied Prague in March 1939. Of the 1,043 Sudeten Germans who reached Britain, most were sent to Canada.

Some 2,300 of the 65,000 mostly Jewish refugees from Germany and Austria who resided in Britain after World War II broke out also came to Canada. They had been interned during the fifth column scare which swept through different countries following Germany's occupation of France, Belgium and the Netherlands in 1940. An invasion of Britain seeming imminent, the British government decided to send the internees to the dominions.

About 60% of Canada's 100,000 German immigrants between the world wars came from European countries east of Germany, with some 30,000 coming from the Soviet Union, 14,00 from Romania and Yugoslavia, 8,000 from Poland, 2,000 from Hungary, 3,000 from Czechoslovakia and 2,000 from Austria. Insofar as they could, in all these cases the German Canadian Church boards, co-operating with the railways, sought to co-ordinate their activities with emigrant aid organizations in Europe. Church organizations in Europe, insofar as they could, worked together with the Canadian religious organizations and with the transportation companies to arrange for passage, housing and jobs at the Canadian destination. Upon arrival in Canada, the immigrants were transferred to the care of their railway and Church boards, which guided the immigrants to their prospective employers and parishes.

Inter-War Settlement Patterns

While the federal government had taken a leading role during the pre-war years in both recruiting immigrants from Central Europe and settling them, after World War I the federal government left both the recruiting of immigrants and settling them to the CPR and the CNR. The railway companies, in turn, sought to involve the German Canadian community, in particular the churches, in the immigration and settlement work. Church leaders sought to direct the new arrivals into areas where their people were already settled, through this solidifying the membership base of their congregations. While encouraging this, the railway companies also sought to settle immigrants on land along its lines that, in many instances, had been abandoned.

Immigrants were generally directed to areas where their co-religionists had already established themselves. While some Germans, in particular immigrants from Germany, settled in urban centers, most went to different German rural settlements. Here, their co-religionists helped them find work and a place to stay. In particular, new arrivals were directed to congregations that had few members, through this helping the different Churches move their smaller congregations toward financial independence. In some instances, new settlements were also established. To help in this, the railways extended relatively inexpensive loans to settlers to help them make a start. Also, the railways kept track of the progress of settlers, on occasion helping settlers with loans when they encountered financial difficulties.

As a result of these efforts, a number of smaller German settlements were formed. One was the Schneider settlement outside of Winnipeg. Through the co-operative work of the Canada Colonization Association of the CPR and the *Volksverein deutsch-canadischer Katholiken*, some 30,000 acres of privately held land was purchased near Winnipeg. Recruited largely from the Black Forest and Westphalia through the initiative of Fr. Kierdorf of the *Volksverein,* some 100 German Catholic immigrants were settled on this land by the CPR.

In co-operation with the Department of Colonization of the CNR, German Baptist Church leaders established some smaller settlements, in this case on land that had for the most part been abandoned by returned soldiers to whom it had been granted after the war. One such settlement was located near Minitonas, Manitoba, where German Baptist families began to arrive in the spring of 1927. Another settlement lay between the Ochre River and St. Rose, Manitoba, some 180 miles northwest of Winnipeg. Both settlements consisted of fewer than a hundred families.

In the case of the Mennonites, Church leaders not only directed immigrants to existing congregations, but also to areas that had been or were being depopulated through the exodus of Old Order Mennonites. Objecting to being deprived of the control of their own schools, many Old Colony Mennonites had left or were eager to leave Manitoba and Saskatchewan to find new homes in South America. Not having the financial means to purchase the land being vacated, the Mennonite community turned to the government and the CPR to help them purchase the available land. In this situation, the Mennonite Land Settlement Board sought out land Old Order Mennonites wanted to vacate and, with the help of the CPR Canada Colonization Association, made arrangements for the purchase of this land by Mennonite refugees.

Similar arrangements were also implemented to establish new Mennonite settlements, such as the one established in Reesor, in northern Ontario. The settlement, named after the Old Order Mennonite, Thomas Reesor, was established by Mennonite refugees who had first settled in Waterloo, Ontario. Aided by loans extended by the CPR and through the help from the Mennonite community, the settlement developed rapidly. However, after reaching a high of 75 souls in 1932, the settlement declined during the Depression, when a combination of poor land and depressed economic conditions made it difficult for the new arrivals to sustain themselves.

Another group of refugees to form small settlements were the Sudeten Germans. Although the Sudetens were primarily tradespeople, the Canadian government required that they go into farming as a condition for their entry into this country. To help them in this, the Canadian government extended to them the financial aid it had received from the British government. The money was handed over to the colonization departments of the railway companies, which were responsible for settling the refugees. The CNR placed 148 Sudeten families on abandoned railway land near St. Walburg in northeastern Saskatchewan. The CPR settled refugee families in the Peace River District of northeast British Columbia. In case of the Tate Creek settlement, in B.C, the railway chose to relocate the settlers on what was formerly the "Gundy Ranch". It was an existing ranch, which consisted of 16,000 acres, but with additional purchases the total area increased to approximately 24,000 acres. By August 1939, 518 of the Sudeten settlers arrived at their new home here, where they were helped by the CPR and its agents to adjust to farming and Canadian life.

A considerable number of other Germans also settled in the Peace River District. Although settlement here began in the pre-World War I period, the far distance of the district from the main areas of settlement, as well as the difficulty people had in growing wheat this far north, caused many settlers to again leave. But then Herman Trelle,[29] a German American farmer, directed attention to the area by winning prizes for the strain of hybrid wheat that he had grown in the Peace River District. This popularized the area and led to the rapid inflow of settlers, including German immigrants, and contributed to the formation of a number of smaller German settlements in the district.

In summary, the co-operative work of the railway companies and the different German Church bodies resulted in the establishment of a few small German settlements during the inter-war period. At times established on marginal land, these sometimes had difficulty sustaining themselves. More important, through their work in directing German immigrants to existing urban and rural congregations, the Churches and railway companies helped to strengthen the most important German Canadian community organizations, the churches, thereby helping the community establish itself more firmly on Canadian soil.

---

[29]   Herman Trelle, a German American, started farming as a boy after his family left Idaho for Canada and settled in the Lake Saskatoon area, Peace River District. He enrolled at the University of Alberta in 1912, in engineering. Upon graduating, he returned to farming and at the same time opened a seed hybrid business. He first displayed his grain in the Chicago International Hay and Grain Show in 1923, where he won 3rd prize. In 1926, he captured his first wheat crown. In total, he won 135 International awards for Peace River grown grains, including field peas.

Post-World War II German Immigration and Settlement

Canada sought to recruit specialized Germans soon after the cessation of hostilities at the end of World War II. Also, as part of the war reparations program in which the victorious allies sought to strip Germany of its advanced technological and scientific know-how, Canada sought to bring German industrial equipment to this country. Bringing in scientists and skilled manpower was part of these endeavours. To forward these objectives, it launched the "1000 Scientists and Technicians from Europe" scheme as well as other similar programs. Unlike the American "Project Paperclip" and the different Russian programs, which resulted in these countries acquiring thousands of German scientists and technicians, Canada's programs had little success. In part, this resulted from Canada's launching its programs later than most of the allies. Also, Canada did not have a well-planned and efficiently executed strategy to forward its projects. As a result, Canada obtained only a small number of the scientists and technicians who had been behind Germany's scientific and economic success.

The attempt to recruit immigrants from Germany did not recommence until 1947. The initiative in this regard came, not from the Canadian government, but from different German Canadian organizations active in relief work in Germany. They saw emigration as part of the solution to dealing with the refugee problem following Germany's collapse and the Soviet Union's expansion into the heart of Europe. The collapse of Germany left the Allies with millions of foreign workers who had been brought to Germany as part of the Nazi war effort. Many of these, who had come from Eastern Europe, did not want to return. Other people had fled in front of the advancing Soviet armies. Still others, such as members of the Vlasov army, had fought against the Soviet Union as allies of Germany. The Soviet Union demanded the return of all peoples in zones controlled by its Western allies. At first, the Western powers complied. However, as relations between the Western allies and the Soviet Union worsened and it was found that the Soviets executed returnees, the West balked at giving in to Soviet demands.

This left the Western powers with an overpopulation problem in areas of Germany under their control. They responded by having these people emigrate. With this end in mind, the International Refugee Organization

(IRO) was founded. The IRO, however, excluded from its mandate some 10 million *Volksdeutsche* refugees in West Germany. Responding to the plight of these people, who at times were family members, the German Canadian community launched a relief effort. Established in 1946, organizations such as the Canadian Society for German Relief and Canadian Lutheran World Relief distributed food parcels, clothing and medical supplies. Simultaneously, the organizations explored the possibility of helping the refugees by having them emigrate to Canada.

While Canadian laws did not permit the immigration of so-called *Reichsdeutsche*, it did allow for the entry of *Volksdeutsche*, in particular those upon whom German citizenship had been forced by the Third Reich. At the same time, *Volksdeutsche* couldn't come to Canada because the IRO refused to process them. German Canadian community organizations dealt with this problem by establishing their own immigrant processing network. For this, they were well qualified as many of their Church organizations had been involved with either the CPR or the CNR in bringing members of their religious denomination to Canada during the inter-war years. Also, a member of the Lutheran Church, T.O.F. Herzer, had been head of the Canadian Pacific Board of Colonization. Among Germans, he took a leading role in organizing the different German Canadian religious groups as well as the Sudeten Germans who were interested in bringing over their relatives into the Canadian Christian Council for the Resettlement of Refugees (CCCRR). At the same time, he as well as other German religious leaders used their contacts with the railways as well as with government leaders to gain support for establishing an immigrant processing network independent of the IRO.

They were successful in this for several reasons. German settlers had been able to build a positive reputation that had made a greater impression on Canadians than the hostility evoked by two world wars. Thus, it was felt that German immigrants would make a positive contribution to the country. At the same time, the German community found able spokespersons in such people as Walter Tucker, MP for Rosthern, who spoke on its behalf in Parliament. Furthermore, German community leaders were able to use not only their connections with members of parliament, but also their contacts with different government departments and agencies to gain not only institutional but also financial support to establish immigrant processing centres through which immigrants would pass prior to coming to Canada.

The first processing centres were set up in Hannover, Karlsruhe and other cities close to refugee centres or seaports where representatives of the CCCRR could operate with limited restrictions. For the most part, names of potential immigrants were forwarded to the respective Church bodies by their members. The prospective immigrants were then contacted. Having been interviewed and deemed suitable by the representative of the CCCRR, potential immigrants were examined by a Canadian doctor and interviewed by Canadian officials to certify they were healthy and were not politically suspect. The government also provided financial support to the CCCRR to enable it to gain the services of a ship, the *Beaverbrae*, to transport the immigrants across the ocean.

As Canada was experiencing a post-war boom, it was in need of manpower. To recruit this, the government established different programs to draw workers to areas where these were needed. These include the "Domestic", "Farm Labour", "Bush Worker" as well as other schemes that served to channel new arrivals into the different areas. Recruited workers could then apply to bring over other members of their family under the "Family Re-Union Scheme."

To take advantage of these schemes, immigration workers in different organizations that made up the CCCRR would contact Canadian employers to determine what type and how many workers they needed. For example, the different churches contacted farmers who might want labourers. Lumber and mining companies were contacted to determine whether they might be in need of workers. The CCCRR then looked for people in Europe who might fit into these different categories and arranged for their emigration. Again, people were not only brought over: the Churches remained in contact with the immigrants, sought to integrate them into their congregations, as well as offered them advice and guidance when they encountered problems at home or at their place of employment.

These different labour recruitment schemes worked so successfully that by 1950 the CCCRR had brought over 15,000 German-speaking refugees. The organization found that many of the *Volksdeutsche* it had selected for emigration were rejected by Canadian authorities because they had taken on German citizenship. German citizens were not yet allowed entry into Canada. The issue was still more confusing in that it wasn't quite clear whether the *Volksdeutsche* had voluntarily accepted German citizenship at the time of the Third Reich or whether it had been forced on them. The rejections were interfering with the ability of the CCCRR to find enough passengers for the *Beaverbrae* to fill the quota required to qualify for government support for its work. It therefore requested that the Canadian Government loosen its restrictions regarding the admissibility of German citizens.

Although there was a lingering hostility toward Germans as a result of the wars, developments in Canada encouraged a positive government response to the request. One of these developments involved a change in public attitudes towards Germans. In 1945, a Gallup poll measuring Canadian attitudes showed that more than half of Canadians over 21 years of age were antagonistic towards Germans, with 14 % of the Canadian adult population showing a "raw hatred." However, poll results in 1947 showed that 28 % were unfriendly, while 41 % felt "friendly" toward Germans. By 1952, the situation had completely altered from 1945: over half (52 %) of Canadians felt friendly, while only 14 % felt "unfriendly" towards their former enemies.[30]

Also, Canadian attitudes toward German immigrants mellowed over time. Results of a poll in October 1946, placed German immigrants as third last, with a 34 % disapproval rating, ahead of Japanese (60%) and Jews (49 %). Attitudes softened by April 1950, when another poll disclosed that of the 38 % of Canadians who were in favour of immigration two-thirds supported the admission of Germans. Five years later another poll suggested that the public's rating of German immigrants had further improved.[31]

At the same time, Canada's rapid economic expansion during and after the war presented it with a pressing need for additional manpower. Some of this had been provided through the entry of displaced persons after the war. However, by the early 1950s this supply was drying up. Also, political leaders and leading members of the public service tended to be highly in favour of German immigration, essentially because of the positive contribution earlier immigrants were seen to have made towards Canada's development. This was true in particular of J.R. Robillard, who served as Canada's chief immigration official in Germany between 1951 and 1956.[32]

---

[30]   Ronald E. Schmalz, "Former enemies come to Canada: Ottawa and the postwar immigration boom, 1951-1957" (unpublished Ph.D. thesis, University of Ottawa, 2000) 46.

[31]   Ibid. 47.

[32]   Ibid. 79.

This led to Canada's lifting its ban on German immigration in late 1950. Following this, Canada opened offices in Germany to forward the flow of German immigrants into the country. These operated under the direction of Canada's chief immigration mission in Karlsruhe. Each year Ottawa set targets for the number and occupational types of immigrants it required and forwarded these to its overseas offices. Germans were also invited to write to the Canadian missions should they wish to emigrate. Following this, the chief mission in Karlsruhe either selected prospective immigrants from its store of applications or negotiated the German government's assistance in recruiting immigrant workers.

As in the case of the *Volksdeutsche*, the Canadian government had a number of labour schemes in place through which immigrant labour was recruited and placed. These included the "German Miner's Scheme," the "German Lumber Worker Scheme," the "German Farm Labourers Scheme," the "German Domestics Scheme," the "Skilled German Labourer Scheme," and the "German Professional Scheme." Different business sectors would contact the Canadian government, letting it know of their needs. Following this, the government would estimate Canada's labour requirements and the skills needed. It would pass this information to its missions in Germany. These would notify their officers so that the required people could be recruited.

The result was an immediate increase in the number of German immigrants to Canada, with the number increasing from 5,800 in 1950 to 32,000 a year later, with the influx peaking in 1953, at 39,000. There were a number of factors encouraging Germans to leave. Pressure to emigrate came from unsettled economic, social and political conditions in the early years of the decade and from people's despair about the future. This was encouraged not only by the past war but also by the proximity of the Soviet Union, people fearing that it might expand westward at any time. Having been deprived of the opportunity to travel for more than a decade, many Germans also simply wanted to see the world, learn English and gain whatever other experience travel offered. At the same time, with job opportunities waiting and untouched by the ravages of war, Canada seemed like an ideal place for a European who had just gone through a destructive conflict.

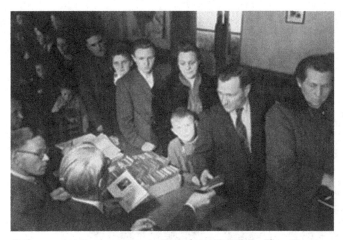

Refugees receiving passports to Canada at CCCRR offices, Bremen, 1950. Library and Archives Canada. PA 165211

Emigration was further encouraged through the aid extended by German Canadians to help their family members emigrate. Also, Canada's assisted-passenger scheme offered interest-free loans for immigrants whose skills were needed. In 1955, families of people brought over through government aid also became eligible for loans, which were to be repaid within twenty-five months after arrival in this country. This situation changed by the late 1950s, when increasing unemployment in Canada, coinciding with a shortage of workers in Germany, brought a decline in emigration, with a mere 5,000 German immigrants coming in 1962. That year also witnessed a return migration of 3,300 people.

Between 1960 and 1970, the number of immigrants of German ethnic origin fluctuated between 4,400 and 8,200, and during the 1970s and 80s averaged between 1,500 and 3,400 per annum. By then, of course, Germany had itself become an importer of people to operate its economy, and Canada had turned to countries outside Europe to feed its manpower needs. Nevertheless, some 400,000 German-speaking immigrants had come to Canada from the end of the war to 1994. Of these, about 10 per cent declared themselves as being of either Austrian or Swiss origin.

Immigrants crowd deck of S.S. Beaverbrae as moment comes to disembark at Port of Québec. Library and Archives Canada. PA 124423

Patterns of Settlement of Post-World War II Immigrants

Unlike prior to World War II, post-World War II German immigrants settled for the most part in the cities. While many of the earlier post-World War II arrivals started off in rural areas, working either for farmers, in lumber camps or in mining, well-paying work opportunities for them existed primarily in the urban centres. After having completed their compulsory work schedule as part of their immigration agreement, new arrivals tended to find work in Canada's major cities. This was true in particular for the *Reichsdeutsche*.

The settlement of Germans in the cities was facilitated by the work skills of the new arrivals. In particular prior to World War I, most German immigrants had been farmers or farm workers. After World War II, a much higher percentage of German skilled or professional workers arrived. From 1953 to 1963, over 19 per cent of skilled newcomers to Canada were of German origin, although Germans constituted but 13 per cent of the immigrants. Between 1954 and 1970, 45 per cent of German arrivals sought work in secondary industries, with 80 per cent of these being skilled craftsmen. Of post-World War II German immigrants who arrived before 1946, 55.9 per cent settled in urban centres; of German immigrants who arrived between 1946 and 1961, 83.5 per cent settled in urban centres. Combined with the increasing urbanization of the Canada-born, this saw a rapid increase of Germans in the different Canadian cities. The Canadian census for 1961 shows that 61.8 per cent of people of German origin lived in urban centres. Of these, 56.8 per cent were Canadian born. All the major urban centres give evidence of growth. For example, the German population of Toronto grew from 19,329 in 1951 to 80,300 in 1961, an increase of 310 per cent. The German population of Kitchener grew from 20,258 in 1951 to 50,450 in 1961, an increase of 170 per cent.[33]

---

[33] Other centres show similar increases. The German population of Vancouver grew from 19,328 in 1951 to 51,056 in 1961, an increase of 168 per cent. The German population of Winnipeg grew from 24,499 in 1951 to 50,206, an increase of 110 per cent. The German population of Edmonton grew from 12,762 in 1951 to 41,422 in 1961, an increase of 242 per cent. The German population of Calgary grew from 9,591 in 1951 to 31,760 in 1961, an increase of 232 per cent, and the German population of Montreal grew from 7,329 in 1951 to 27,837 in 1961, an increase of 280 per cent.

SURVIVING THE WARS

World War I

World War I, while fought by professional armies, involved the nation state as a whole in the war effort. This necessitated mobilizing the entire nation for the conflict. One means of affecting this was through legislation that served to encourage participation in the conflict by the larger society; other laws, in turn, served to restrain those interests that were deemed to threaten the war effort. Another method of encouraging society as a whole to be involved in the conflict was through the use of propaganda that, ultimately, served to mobilize the will of the people to sacrifice and fight.

No doubt, these methods would work well in a homogeneous society in which all segments of the nation identified with the power groups supporting the conflict. However, this can have a negative effect in a multicultural society comprised of a variety of ethnic and interest groups. It can have a disastrous effect on those groups in the nation who originate from, or have close ties with, the enemy country or countries. This may be observed when looking at the position in which Germans and German-speaking peoples originating from Austria-Hungary found themselves when war broke out in 1914.

On the one hand, German Canadians participated in the war effort, even though it was against their ancestral homeland. Some served directly in the Canadian military. Others served in a supportive role, as in the medical corps. Thus, 486 Waterloo County residents, many of them of German origin, gave up their life for Canada. Germans also participated in collecting funds to support the war effort. The first two months after the outbreak of war showed that the German community of Berlin, Ontario, had contributed $ 96,859.00 to the Patriotic Fund.

Loss of jobs

These contributions did little to protect German Canadians from the aggression that the larger society directed toward them as a result of the war. Such aggression affected German Canadians in a number of ways. The most immediate direct effect was the loss of jobs. Except in the present-day Kitchener-Waterloo area, where German Canadians controlled both the urban and rural economy, urban workers of German cultural origin tended to work for establishments essentially controlled by the English Canadian sponsor group. There were many incidents where English Canadians gave expression to their patriotism by dismissing workers associated with the enemy countries.

The German community responded to this problem by mounting a massive mutual aid program. In Winnipeg, for example, the local *Unterstützungsverein*, with the co-operation of German Canadian farmers, local churches and *Der Nordwesten*, helped the local unemployed find work on farms. Again, in Saskatchewan workers in urban centres were helped through the co-operative efforts of the German Canadian Association of Saskatchewan, working together with local churches, German farmers and *Der Courier*.

Despite community efforts, unemployment and the risk of being laid off haunted German and Austrian Canadians during the course of the war. For example, following the sinking of the Lusitania, in 1915, German miners at Fernie, B.C. were dismissed after miners went on strike, until the Crow's Nest Pass Coal Company agreed to dismiss all its German and Austrian employees. Unemployment and the threat of being laid off affected not only labourers but also professionals. The University of Toronto dismissed three German-born professors amidst much fanfare. In Toronto, also, naturalized senior municipal administrators, such as Dr. Erwin Kohlmann, lost their jobs. In London, Ontario, G.H. Glaubitz of the Public Utilities Commission, was forced to resign.

The war was no sooner over when demands arose that workers originating from countries with which Canada had been at war be replaced by returned soldiers. In early 1919, the British Columbia Employers' Association and the British Columbia Loggers' Association announced that their members were prepared to offer employment to returned soldiers by dismissing workers originating from enemy countries. Similar promises were made in northern Ontario and in the coal mining regions of Alberta. In cities such as Winnipeg returned soldiers took matters into their own hands and sought to force companies to dismiss workers originating from enemy countries and hire returned soldiers. The jobs of alien enemies, or those workers who came from countries with

which Canada had been at war, continued to be in jeopardy until the
employment situation improved in Canada during the 1920s.

The Threat of Physical Violence

Another problem faced by Germans and Austrians was the threat of
physical violence. This erupted immediately after the outbreak of war. In
Winnipeg, for example, war had no sooner been declared when rowdies
expressed their enthusiasm for the war by beating up German-speaking
citizens, breaking windows and doors of the German club on Heaton and
attacking the German and Austro-Hungarian consulates.

Following such initial outbreaks, the situation became calmer, but
rumours persisted that Germans and Austrians were spies. This, for
example, resulted in the search of German bookstores, clubs and churches
in Winnipeg, in case weapons had been hidden there. The sinking of
the Lusitania in 1915 brought a new outbreak of attacks. In Calgary, a
hotel and a restaurant that hired Germans were wrecked by a mob, and
local Germans feared for their life. In Montreal, a club was destroyed.
On May 8, a day after the sinking of the Lusitania, a mob wrecked
the Blanshard Hotel, in Victoria, which was owned by a naturalized
Canadian of German origin. The riot spread from the Blanshard Hotel
to the premises formerly occupied by the German Club, which had been
closed since the outbreak of war. It, too, was wrecked. The windows of
Simon Leiser and Co. and of Moses Lenz's establishment were smashed
and the premises looted. The premises of Carl Loewenberg, a nephew of
Leopold Loewenberg, who before the war had been German consul in
Victoria, was also attacked by vandals.

Anti-German riot in Calgary on February 10, 1916. Photograph shows the destruction to the Riverside Hotel in Calgary, caused by an anti-German riot. The riot supposedly started because the owner of the Riverside, located at 4 Street S.E. and Boulevard Avenue, was German. Glenbow Archives, NA-3965-11.

On Sunday night, trouble erupted again at the corner of Yates and Blanshard and moved down to the Phoenix Brewery where windows were smashed, and the mobsters helped themselves to beer. The premises of Hermann and Stringer, 848 Yates, a dry-cleaning establishment, were wrecked, but the worst looting of the night was at the premises of Schaper and Glass, where practically everything in the shop was carted away. Women were seen holding sacks for their husbands to fill, all the time keeping an eye out for the patrolling police and soldiers.

The mob then got the idea that Edward F. Geiger was a German, despite the fact that he had been born in Victoria, and they descended on his plumbing shop and wrecked it. That night Mayor Stewart stood on the corner of Yates and Government and read the Riot Act to the crowd, while 800 troops patrolled the streets. This, however, was not before an estimated $20,000.00 to $40,000.00 of damage had been done. In Berlin – now Kitchener -- rowdy elements broke the windows of the Concordia Club and smashed club furniture. People who were identified as being pro-German, such as Pastor Tappert, were beaten up. In Berlin, trouble arose not only because of the sinking of the Lusitania, but also by problems recruiters were having in recruiting soldiers for the war effort.

Acts of violence continued throughout the war. Germans and German-speaking Austrians responded by keeping their views to themselves and by isolating themselves in their own communities. This helped to keep the communities as a whole fairly safe. However, towards the end of the war and after the victory of the allies was assured, the problem became the returned soldiers. These went on a rampage several times. In Winnipeg, returned soldiers went on a two-day rampage against foreigners and socialists. The unrest began on January 26, when soldiers disrupted memorial services that socialists were holding in City Hall Square for Rosa Luxemburg and Karl Liebknecht. After attacking the headquarters of the Socialist Party, soldiers proceeded to the North End where soldiers and hoodlum elements looted and destroyed the property of German Canadian business establishments, such as Ert's auto accessory business, Riedle's Brewery, and a number of German restaurants. Soldiers and hoodlum elements broke into the German-Hungarian club, where they smashed windows and doors and threw the piano out of the second-floor window. German homes were broken into and their occupants forced to kiss the British flag.

Registration and Internment

Immediately after the outbreak of war, laws were put into effect to control the movement of aliens. Under these laws, some 80,000 aliens were required to hand in their firearms and register. After that, they had to report to the local post office or police station about once a month to give proof of their whereabouts.

In addition, laws were passed to intern enemy aliens. These laws tended to be very broad. Under the discretionary powers invested in the Canadian government, civilians could be interned if considered "agents" of enemy powers or persons whose activities might be of service to enemy powers during the war. Initially, these laws were intended to keep enemy alien reservists from crossing the border and joining the enemy side. However, the most determined of these aliens had already crossed the border by the time internment operations had come into effect and became operational. The result was that many of those who were interned were incarcerated for relatively minor reasons. This might include failure to report to registrars, walking along a railway line or uttering comments critical of the Allied cause. Others were interned because they found themselves being in the unfortunate position of being unemployed. This, however, tended to affect Ukrainians rather than German-speaking elements.

There were several reasons why such severe steps were taken against the enemy aliens. In regards to the unemployed, internment served as a means whereby local municipalities shifted the burden of looking after the unemployed from the local municipality to the federal government. Furthermore, the British element had always looked upon non-British peoples as somehow not quite having the right to be in the country. The war merely served to justify prejudices that were already there. Also, the outbreak of war was accompanied by an outbreak of hysteria and paranoia regarding peoples from enemy countries. The government was, as a consequence, continuously pressed to put people who may threaten the war effort behind barbed wire. Internment was its response to such pressure.

The internees were to be treated as prisoners of war, not as convicts and, as a result, the government was subject to the Hague Convention of 1907. This entitled the internees to the same standard of quarters, food and clothing as Canada's soldiers. When someone was arrested by the police, he was first sent to a receiving station where the initial paperwork was filled out and a decision was made as to the location where he was to be sent. Internees in Manitoba and Saskatchewan were first sent to the Brandon exhibition grounds, while those from Alberta were initially interned at Lethbridge.

By late 1915, the Brandon camp held between 800 and 1,000 internees. The internment facility, in the Brandon Winter Fair arena, was a one-and-a-half story building of frame construction, 256 by 500 feet, which covered an entire city block. It included dining, exercise, recreational, lavatory, sleeping, and hospital areas along with parallel facilities for the guards. Being located in an urban centre, there was no employment for the bulk of the internees. The only inmates receiving the 25 cents per day government wages were prisoners employed within the camp as barbers, tailors, hospital orderlies or in similar lines of work.

Mail to and from internees was censored, with outgoing mail being limited to eight letters a month per prisoner. Relatives and friends could visit once a month. The camp had no facilities for interning wives and dependents. A wife shown to be destitute as a result of the internment of her husband was eligible for government assistance, usually consisting of 20 dollars per month for a woman with one child.

After about two years the holding facilities in Brandon and Lethbridge were closed and the internees were sent to alternate work sites and internment camps across the country. This included camps at Spirit

Lake, Quebec, Petawawa, Kingston and Kapuskasing, Ontario, as well as camps at Banff, Jasper and in the interior of British Columbia.

Here, the internees were compelled to work for the Canadian government. This might include erecting and repairing buildings, building roads, clearing, stumping and draining land. They received 25 cents per day for their work, or the "working pay" supplement paid to Canadian soldiers for work done outside of their routine military duties.

Discipline was harshly enforced. For example, for refusing to work, an inmate might be punished by one day of confinement with bread and water plus eight hours of hard labour. For loafing in a latrine, an internee might be subjected to nine days confinement, three days alternate bread and water, plus eight hours per day hard labour. For loafing, insolence and interfering with other internees in their work, a person might be subjected to 15 days confinement, bread and water every third day, eight hours hard labour every day.

German Internees lined up for food within walls of Fort Henry, Kingston, Ont. [1916]. Courtesy of Fort Henry National Historic Site.

In total, about 8,579 men were interned. This included 817 merchant seamen transferred to Canada from the Caribbean and Newfoundland. 1192 Germans from within Canada were interned, as were 5,954 Austro-Hungarians. Although there is some evidence that women would be treated the same as men (correspondence from the British Embassy to the Governor-General of Canada dated March 13, 1918) only 81 women and 156 children were interned and these came with their husbands and fathers.

Of Austro-Hungarians interned, it is difficult to state what proportion was of German cultural background. Few of the available statistics break the Austro-Hungarian group down by cultural identity. A general survey of the list of names of Austro-Hungarian internees shows a good proportion of these internees to have German names. Nevertheless, the majority of Austro-Hungarian internees were of Ukrainian origin.

Most internees remained behind barbed wire until 1916. The massive flow of Canadian manpower into the armed forces had created a serious labour shortage in industry and agriculture, forcing the government to reassess its policy of "keeping thousands of harmless Austrians" forcibly idle or occupied "with deliberately non-essential work." Increasingly, large corporations and farmers turned to the internment camps to solve their labour needs, and by the spring of 1917 virtually all of the nearly 6,000 "Austrian" internees were released on parole. Parolees could not leave Canada without proper authorization while the war lasted, and were to report as directed by the police. Their certificates of release functioned as internal passports, to be used in travelling. This enabled internees to move to different areas of Canada to find work.

Of the remaining internees, most were Germans. The main holding points for them were Fort Henry (Kingston, Ontario), Vernon (British Columbia) and Amherst (Nova Scotia). Internees at Amherst consisted largely of interned German sailors who had been transferred to Canada from the Caribbean and Newfoundland. Most remained interned for the duration of the war. By December 1918, 2,222 aliens were still interned. Between 1919 and February 1920, over 1,800 internees were repatriated to Germany. In addition, 302 Austrians were deported. Altogether, 107 internees died in the camps. The majority succumbed to tuberculosis, pneumonia and heart disease, with a handful dying during attempts to escape and from suicide.

The war and enemy or enemy alien property

When someone was interned, they were required to deposit with the authorities everything that could facilitate an escape. This included not just maps and knives but also cash and jewellery. This was then deposited in a "prisoner of war trust fund."

The total deposited during the war was $329,153.17 with $298,015.44 returned upon release. Several thousand dollars of the money deposited, consisting of both cash and valuables confiscated from internees at the Toronto internment centre, had vanished without a trace and without anyone being charged with theft. This left some $31,137.73 still in the hands of the Receiver-General.

In July, 1920, the total balance that was placed in a special account totalled $94,112.75. As the prisoners had been earning some $.25 per day for their labour, this may well account for the difference between the two figures. By June 30, 1926, the ledger stated that $32,418.55 in earnings and $3,017.09 in cash was still unclaimed.[34] No provisions for the release of this money had been made during or after the war until P.C. 574 which was passed on March 17, 1920. In spite of advertisement and contacts with the Consuls Generals of the countries concerned, few claims were received.

Many of those arrested and detained also held real and personal property. In a January 26, 1916 memorandum to the Deputy Minister of Justice, the department was of the opinion that there were no provisions which obligated the government to protect an internee's property. However, the government also acknowledged that when it assumed control of the property of internees it was obligated to provide proper custody, in addition to assuming the responsibility for storage and other charges it incurred while it managed the property of internees.

In addition to managing the property taken from internees, the Custodian also managed the investments in Canada by people of enemy origin. To obtain information on such property, the "Public Custodian" of Enemy Property in Canada sent circular letters to banks, asking for statements under four headings:

Property, real or personal, in Canadian territory, belonging to enemy subjects.

Debts, including Bank deposits and Bank balances, due to, or held on behalf of enemy subjects resident or carrying on business in enemy territory, or due to, or held on behalf of enemy subjects resident in Canada.

Property, real or personal, in enemy territory belonging to British subjects resident or carrying on business in Canada.

---

34   Library and Archives Canada (hereafter LAC) RG 6,819. Report of A. H. Mathieu, Assistant Deputy Custodian.

Claims of British subjects resident or carrying on business in Canada against enemy Governments.

Records to November 30, 1918, show enemy alien holdings in Canada as following: First, real and personal property, Germany, $8,427,543.00; Austria $399,312.00; Turkey $350.00; Bulgaria none; debts and bank balances due to persons in Germany, $1,875,605.00; Austria 322,604.00; Turkey $550.00; Bulgaria $1,460.00. Third, real and personal property, Germany $96,816.00; Austria $434.00; Turkey none; Bulgaria none. Debts and bank balances due to persons in Germany $495,820; Austria $59,855.00; Turkey $9,084; Bulgaria none.

Canadian bonds held by citizens of enemy countries, as well as Canadian real estate owned by them, or companies operated by them in Canada, were sequestered by the Custodian of Enemy Property. Article 297 of the Treaty of Peace, signed at Versailles on June 28, 1919, provided that "the Allied and Associated Powers reserve the right to retain and liquidate all property, rights and interests belonging at the date of the coming into force of the present Treaty to German nationals, or companies controlled by them..." Article 297 (h), sub-paragraph (2), provides that: "The proceeds of the property, rights and interests, and the cash assets, of German nationals received by an Allied or Associated Power shall be subject to disposal by such Power in accordance with its laws and regulations and may be applied in payment of the claims and debts defined by this article..." [35]

This meant essentially that German properties sequestered during the war were transferred to the Creditor Governments. At the same time, the German Government "undertook to compensate its own nationals in respect of their properties liquidated abroad."[36] Allied powers took the right to sell property owned by German nationals within their borders to pay reparation and other claims made by their nationals against Germany. In accordance with this, the Canadian government proceeded to sell property in Canada owned by German citizens to pay reparation claims. This situation changed only in January 1930, when Canada entered into an agreement with Germany by which Canada "formally agreed to release and deliver to Germany" all such property, rights and

[35]   LAC. RG 117, vol. 3, file 9.

[36]   Ibid., p. 3.

interests of German nationals as were not already liquid or liquidated or finally disposed of by June 7, 1929.[37]

While some money was used to pay reparations to Canadian citizens, it is unclear how other money was spent. Thus, of the "money which remained in the hands of the Secretary of State of Canada as Custodian of Enemy Property, payments have been made by the Custodian to the Canadian Treasury to recoup a small portion of the expenditures authorized by the Canadian Parliament to defray in part the obligations of Germany under the Treaty of Versailles." For this propose 6 million dollars were paid into the Canadian Treasury on March 31, 1932, and 4 million dollars were paid into the Canadian Treasury on March 31, 1933, for a total of 10 million dollars.[38]

It is difficult to ascertain what proportion of the property sequestered by the Custodian of Enemy property belonged to citizens of Germany and what proportion to German immigrants to Canada who were still citizens of Germany, in particular to the some 1800 people who had been interned and were later returned to Germany. However, several comments could be made regarding these dealings. Firstly, being deprived of the control of their property had a negative influence on all those affected. This may be seen in the case of the German Canadian Farming Company, of Hussar Alberta, whose main shareholders were interned. Farm machinery owned by the company was stolen. Company shareholders had little control over the management of their company, which detrimentally affected their ability to hold onto their land, an attempt made more difficult by the vendor of the lands, the CPR, which sought to take possession of lands owned by enemy aliens resident in Canada.[39] Similar difficulties were encountered by German investors in the German Development Company.[40]

---

[37]   Ibid. p. 4.

[38]   Ibid. p. 6.

[39]   LAC. RG 6 H, vol 768.

[40]   LAC. RG 117, vol. 9, file 93.

Censorship and Propaganda

Censorship involved control by the Chief Press Censor of information that appeared in German language papers. It also involved regulating the entry into Canada of German language newspapers. Censorship did result in some friction between editors of German language papers and the Chief Press Censor. This was the case in particular in the relationship between the editor of the *Alberta Herold* and the Chief Press Censor's Office. In most instances, however, German language editors worked fairly harmoniously with the Chief Press Censor. They did so primarily because they were well aware that the country was at war and consequently were willing to accept restrictions on what was printed.

If censorship was merely an irritant during the war years, propaganda was to have a dramatic negative effect on German language peoples originating from Germany and Austria-Hungary. A propaganda campaign was launched almost immediately after the outbreak of war. Directed largely against Germany, this consisted of denunciatory articles intended to discredit the German national character, German science, and the German cultural heritage. Treitschke and Bernhardi were quoted to show that the war was an outgrowth of the German mind and of the German tradition. It was described as having inevitably evolved from the German cultural heritage. German achievements in the field of science were belittled and Germans were described as modern-day barbarians. So-called German atrocities in Belgian and northern France were compared at different times to the ravages of the Goths or Huns, the term Hun becoming the most popular characterization.

The suggestion that the German people were forced into the war by their military overlords, briefly considered, was dismissed during the early stages of the conflict because the German soldiers were seen to be fighting too keenly. Rather, both the Kaiser and the military were seen to embody the will of the German people, the war being a fantastic attempt by Germans, not only in Europe but also on other continents, to co-operate in an effort to conquer the world. Neither the Germans of Canada nor of the United States had left at home either their Hun-like mentality or their aspiration for world conquest. They were not to be trusted. The role of the allies was seen, at different times, to perpetuate the cause of democracy, bridle the Kaiser or teach a lesson to the German people.

The propaganda drive was initiated in either Britain or Ottawa. Stories were fed to the press, which was free to either accept or reject them. In most instances, the English-language press followed the lead of the government and published articles prepared through government initiatives. Such propaganda appears to have had several effects. Among Anglo-Canadians it fed hostility towards anything German, which expressed itself in laying off people associated with the enemy, interning enemy aliens for the slightest reason, or in outbreaks of violence against German Canadians. In February 1916, the Anti-German League in Toronto dedicated itself to eliminating German products, immigrants and influences from Canada, including driving naturalized Canadians of German origin out of the public service. Signs advertising German beer brewed in Berlin, Ontario, were prohibited, and street names associated with Germans were changed. Place names were changed in Western Canada, where Coblenz, Kaiser, Prussia, Waldorf, Carlstadt, Wittemberg and Düsseldorf were renamed Cavell, Peebles, Leader, Béthune, Alderson, Leedale and Freedom. At the same time, in all of Canada, German had virtually disappeared as a subject of study in schools and universities. Commenting on this situation, Helling writes: "The behaviour against enemy aliens in World War I can be best explained in terms of scapegoating. War-time propaganda was developed to a high degree and used for political purposes, yet the actual enemy was several thousand miles away. Other outlets for aggression had to be found and immigrants became the victims by proxy."[41]

Propaganda also had an effect on German Canadians. Most German Canadians responded to the anti-German propaganda with disbelief and bewilderment, in particular the caricature of the German as the ferocious Hun. This was true in particular of the adult generation who still recalled the homeland. Among people born here, and students who were required to write exams on causes of the war, the result appears to have been somewhat different. This may be observed to some extent in Berlin, Ontario where allied propaganda contributed largely to banning the teaching of German in Berlin's schools. The measure was successful in 1915 in part at least because of the measure of support the ruling received

---

[41]   Rudolf Helling, Bernd Hamm, et. al., *A Socio-economic history of German Canadians: They, Too, Founded Canada: a research report* (Wiesbaden: F. Steiner) 55 and 56.

from local German Canadians. The same can be said of the change in the name from Berlin to Kitchener Waterloo. While the name change was in large part initiated by the local German business community to protect its economic interests, intimidation, including physical force, were used to bring about the change in name. Concluding her study on Germans in Kitchener (Berlin), Mckegney states: "With the end of the war, the propaganda ended, and no mention of its influence in Kitchener (Berlin), or in Canada has been revealed. The tremendous power that it gave to those who supported the war faded away. The disgrace and bewilderment it brought to German Canadians remains".[42] This would include German Canadians not only in Kitchener-Waterloo but German Canadians anywhere in Canada.

The World War II Experience

Unlike World War I, the war against Nazi Germany tended to be viewed as an ideological conflict. Thompson makes reference to this when he states that during the First World War every German, from the Kaiser to the most humble peasant, had been a "Hun." Guilt for World War II was not collectively attached to the German nation but was personified in Adolf Hitler and the Nazi hierarchy.[43] The Canadian government's propaganda campaign in support of the war effort, therefore, tended to target this leadership, rather than the German people as the enemy.

Despite this, a number of Germans again lost their jobs immediately after the outbreak of war. This was not enough to please certain patriotic associations, in particular veteran associations, which demanded that Germans be replaced on jobs by British boys. This happened in 1940, following the fall of France, the Low Countries and the German march into Norway. It is difficult to ascertain how many German or Austrian Canadians were affected by this. Commenting on this situation in September 1940, the Under Secretary of State, E. H. Coleman, comments that a number of German Canadian families found themselves in a

---

[42] Pat McKegney, *The Kaiser's bust: a study of war-time propaganda in Berlin, Ontario, 1914-1918* (Bamberg, Ontario: Bemberg Press, 1991) 196.

[43] John Herd Thompson, *Ethnic Minorities during Two World Wars* (Ottawa: Canadian Historical Association, 1991) 12.

difficult position because the breadwinner had lost his position because of his nationality. He adds that the position of these people was exacerbated in that certain provinces were refusing to provide relief to them.[44]

As during World War I, German organizations sought to provide relief to people who had lost their jobs as best they could and there is little evidence of people having been interned because they couldn't find employment and, as a consequence, were destitute.

Also, immediately after the outbreak of war, the German press was censored. In September1939, about 16,350 enemy aliens were required to register, consisting of German nationals or German-born British subjects naturalized after September 1929. Through a new Order-in Council in 1940, registration requirements for enemy aliens were expanded. From June 1940 all residents from countries dominated by Germany and Italy, who had become British subjects after September 1, 1922, had to report to registrars of alien enemies. By March 1941, a total of 82,500 were registered in Canada, including 30,000 German-born, as well as 21,500 Czechoslovak and Austrian-born persons. Of these, 21,000 were granted exemption certificates.

Naturalized German Canadians were freed of the duty to report to Registrars of Enemy Aliens in December 1942, because of their "exceptionally good behavior" since the war's beginning. By mid-1943, most of the administrative restrictions against Germans and German Canadians were also lifted; at this time, furthermore, enemy aliens of German or Italian background were permitted to join the Canadian armed forces if their application for naturalization had been accepted by the government and they passed security clearance. Records show that by the summer of 1944 an estimated 36,000 members of the Canadian military service had German as their mother tongue.[45]

As during World War I, German and Austrian Canadians were interned. Internment began even before Canada went to war. In the early morning of 4 September, six days before Canada went to war, police squads swooped down and arrested 303 Germans and German Canadians. Subsequently others were arrested as well. About thirty-five of those arrested were members of the National Socialist Workers Party in Canada (NSDAP), about 200 were in the DAF (*Deutsche Arbeitsfront*), and

---

[44]   LAC. RG 6, vol. 806.

[45]   LAC. RG 26, vol. 13/A.

approximately sixty were in the Canadian Society for German Culture, or Bund members. Of course, all these organizations had existed and operated legally in Canada before the outbreak of war. People had joined them for a variety of reasons. There is little evidence showing that they saw a conflict between membership in these cultural, social or fraternal organizations, which were legally registered in Canada, and their loyalty to Canada.

German civilian internees, Fredericton, May, 1943. Gunzel, K., Library and Archives Canada, Accession number 1985-34, PA-139350.

Nor did the police have solid evidence that the people arrested in any way threatened Canada. Rather, during the 1930's the RCMP were absorbed with averting a threat from the communists and tended to ignore rightist elements in society. When war approached and the government pressed the RCMP to present a list of people who might actually present a danger to Canada and should, therefore, be interned, they had essentially only membership lists of organizations that were branded as subversive because of the outbreak of war. The government accepted organizational affiliation as the criteria for suspicion and loyalty, and recommended the internment of people so defined because it was under tremendous pressure from the Canadian public to do something to counter any possible hostile acts from those elements that were in any way associated with National Socialist Germany.

Similarly, it was also public pressure that was behind the wave of arrests of Germans and Austrians following the sweep of Hitler's armies through the Low Countries and France in 1940. The speed of the German conquest tended to be attributed to the activities of fifth column elements in the conquered countries. It didn't take long, therefore, for people caught up in the war effort against Nazi Germany to also point to the danger posed by fifth column elements in Canada.

Public pressure exerted through letters, speeches and massive petitions, demanded that anyone identified with the enemy be effectively dealt with, and led the government to close down all Nazi, Fascist, and also radical left-wing organizations. The RCMP Commissioner called for new lists of subversive Nazi agents, requesting his local commanders to send him names of fifth columnists and persons making utterances prejudicial to the safety of the state or attempting to impede the war effort.

The government advisory committee overlooking internment made little attempt to have the police justify the reasons for interning the people whose names were brought forward. As a result, numerous Germans were interned essentially on the strength of local denunciations to the police. To help them in their search for subversives, the RCMP even placed newspaper ads seeking anonymous denunciations of fifth columnists. Registrars of Enemy Aliens added their suspicious candidates for internment. By the end of 1940, the number of civilian internees had quadrupled. About half of the 1,200 internees were Germans and German Canadians; the remainder were Italian or Canadian fascists or Canadian left-wing radicals. Commenting on the state of affairs, Norman Robertson admitted that the real reasons for the arrests were local and social rather than political and subversive.[46] This was also admitted by a local RCMP commander who stated that the effect of periodical internments is very beneficial in stabilizing public feelings.[47]

As during World War I, the Canadian government also took control of property owned by foreign nationals and internees. Unlike during World War I, this tended not to be extensive. Reparation payments and

---

[46]   LAC. RG 24, DND, vol. 4-1-5 (1), file 6585, Robertson to Min. of Justice, July 5/40.

[47]   LAC. RCMP, Record, vol. 1, file C 11-19-4. 2. Assistant Commander F Division to Commissioner, Aug. 15/40.

the economic turmoil in Germany after World War I meant that German industry and the German population in general had little capital for investment abroad. Internees, for the most part new immigrants, hadn't been here long enough to build up sizable assets. This was made still more difficult by the Depression, during which many of the new arrivals lost their jobs.

The fifth column scare, which encouraged the internment of enemy aliens, began to dissipate in 1941. By mid-1941 the number of interned Germans and German Canadians reached its high point and then declined as the government began to shift its attention towards the Japanese. Italians began to be released from internment in large numbers in 1941 and 1942. Gradually the number of interned German Canadians fell as well. By the end of 1942, 491 Germans and 94 naturalized German Canadians were still interned. A year later, 449 were held in camps, the number falling rapidly in 1944 until by January 1945 only 103 remained. At the end of the war in May 1945, 89 Germans were still incarcerated.

Commenting on motives for the internment, Keyserlingk states that as far as the possibility of Nazi subversion was concerned, the RCMP and government had been unprepared to deal with the problem in 1939 and 1940. To cover this unpreparedness, they took arbitrary actions against individual Germans and German Canadians to demonstrate to an irate public that they were in control of the security situation. Furthermore, politicians called upon bureaucrats to immediately present them with a list of "agents within the gates."[48] However, these bureaucrats possessed too little hard information and were given too little time to respond properly. Therefore, they threw together haphazard lists of hundreds of Canadian residents of German origin, without much chance of turning up truly dangerous agents. The hundreds of German Canadians arrested for organizational reasons or general suspicion were mainly farmers or workers, often denounced by other Canadians.[49]

---

[48] Robert H. Keyserlingk, "Agents Within the Gates: The Search for Nazi Subversives in Canada during World War II," *Canadian Historical Review* (LXVI, 2, 1985) 237.

[49] *Ibid.* 237.

The same may be observed from the files of the internees themselves.[50] The sources suggest that the internees were bewildered by what was happening to them. Some felt they had been interned because of the jealousy of neighbours. Others questioned the rationale of using their membership in social organizations that had been legal prior to the outbreak of war to make them targets for internment. Of the interned, most were released after three years of internment. One person, John Hilmer of Toronto, who remained interned until the end of the war, felt he had been interned because the company for which he worked didn't want to pay him the workman's compensation owed to him following an accident. He remained interned until the end of the war, he felt, because he had protested vociferously against the injustice of his internment. His wife had protested as well, only to find herself interned, while their children were placed in an orphanage.[51] Justified anger and outrage at unfair treatment were viewed as a sign of guilt by a system that branded one as guilty merely because of one's organizational affiliation and one's ethnic background.

Conclusion

Looking at the German and Austro-German experiences during both World War I and World War II, the following may be concluded. In both World War I and World War II, Germany was perceived as the main enemy by the larger Canadian society. The propaganda effort of both the government and the popular media was directed against it. During World War I, this propaganda effort targeted all Germans; during World War II the Nazi regime was targeted as the main enemy.

World War I propaganda especially affected Germans in Canada in a disastrous way, causing them to give up their ethnic identity and

---

[50]   Barbara Lorenzkowski provides some insight into the views internees had regarding reasons for their internment in her study "'Spies,' 'Saboteurs,' and 'Subversives,' German-Canadian Internees and the Wartime Discourse at the Canadian home front, 1939-1945." Also see Martin, Friedrich (MG 30, C 154) and Holtmann, Heinrich (MG 30 C 153). Library and Archives Canada.

[51]   John Hilmer, *Ein deutsches Schicksal in Kanada: Einwanderung, Internierung, Ringen um Rehabilitierung*. Ed. and compiler, Lothar Zimmermann (Toronto: German-Canadian Historical Association, 1996).

assimilate into the larger society. This was not quite the same during World War II when the targeted enemy was Nazi Germany rather than the German people.

Also, there was a significant difference in the treatment of Germans in Canada during the wars. During World War I, all Germans and citizens of countries allied with it were under suspicion and liable to be interned, essentially because of their nationality. During the Second World War, the groups especially targeted for internment belonged to what were seen as pro-Nazi or pro-Fascist organizations.

During both world wars, the people who had been interned were assumed to be guilty and were not given a fair trial to prove their innocence. They were interned, it was said, to protect the nation from saboteurs and spies. Little evidence was ever found, however, to prove that any of the people interned were involved in spying or sabotage. Rather, it was the suspicion that these people might become a danger to the allied cause which led to their internment.

Internment affected a small segment of the German community and, in a sense, was a short-term consequence of the war. The war propaganda and the image it created of Germans had a much more profound and long-lasting effect. Commenting on the situation of German Canadians during World War II Gerhard Bassler states that for "the second time within the lifespan of one generation, German ethnicity was singled out as suspect and undesirable in Canada and German Canadians had the experience of being a helpless minority within a hostile society. In the face of this experience the recovery of ethnic confidence... seemed problematic enough without the post-war discoveries of the atrocities committed by the Nazi regime. These revelations perpetuated the wartime stigmatization of Germans everywhere regardless of their involvement in Nazi crimes. They also delayed... the restoration of respect for [the] German identity, and of confidence in its cultivation among all generations of German Canadians."[52]

---

[52] Gerhard P.Bassler, *The German Canadian Mosaic Today and Yesterday: Identities, Roots, and Heritage* (Ottawa: German-Canadian Congress, 1991) 28.

INSTITUTIONS ESTABLISHED

Soon after German immigrants arrived in Canada, they sought to establish social organizations that would serve their needs and attain their goals. The most important of these institutions were the churches, touching on the most important aspects of people's lives. They performed baptisms, marriages and burials. They were the centre of sacred festivals, marking different times of the year. Often, because of the emphasis on raising children in the faith, schools were closely associated with the churches. They taught the German language, the language in which religious services were conducted. In many instances, passing on the German language was part of an overall endeavour to pass on to the child values that fostered his or her intellectual and moral development. [53]

In particular in urban centers and among people for whom the church no longer served as the focal point of their life, secular social organizations were established. These included clubs, which served to celebrate secular festivals brought from the homeland. In particular prior to the arrival of Medicare, they served a social welfare function, providing sickness insurance in case of illness, or death benefits to cover funeral costs. In some instances, fire or crop insurance co-operatives were established, in particular in rural areas, helping people deal with the vicissitudes of pioneer life. Later, as the community became more urban centered, profession organizations emerged, keeping engineers or lawyers in contact so that they might aid each other to meet the challenges of the new environment.

---

[53] See, for example, G. Henkelmann, Brüderfeld, 20 Mai, *Der Nordwesten* (Mai 30, 1901), 4. Henkelmann wrote: "Sind wir ja unseren Kindern schuldig dass wir uns bemühen ihnen die Muttersprache zu erhalten und die gute alte deutsche Sitte, deutsche Treue, deutsche Einfachheit, deutsche Zuverlässigkeit zu lehren." For similar views, see R.A. Steffan, "Erhaltung des Deutschtums," *Der Nordwesten* (Februar 21, 1912) 14, and "Lerne Englisch und Pflege das Deutsche," *Der Nordwesten* (Mai 31, 1894) 1.

Newspapers were established, helping Germans in different areas keep in contact with each other, and also informing Germans of international, national and local events. They helped local businesses advertise their wares, as well as notified people where they might purchase the items they needed. In addition, they permitted local congregations and clubs to advertise their meetings. Once the technology evolved, newspapers were supplemented or replaced by radio and television, serving entertainment needs and helping community members remain in contact.

Primarily because they were organized to serve community needs and attain community goals, social organizations altered as these needs and goals changed. The immigrant generation, often arriving in their youth, aged in time and died off. New generations born in Canada matured. New waves of immigrants arrived, sometimes settling in areas where the old immigrants had settled and community organizations had to alter to meet their needs. More often, they settled in new areas, where they established their own social networks.

People who had grown up in Canada often weren't sufficiently proficient in German to function effectively in the language. This meant that they could no longer understand German well enough to function effectively in the social organizations that had been established by the immigrants to serve their needs. Nor could they communicate effectively with new immigrants.

All these influences affected the German community and German community organizations as they evolved in this country. Community organizations had to adapt to these changes. Those that couldn't alter sufficiently died. Others, in particular the churches, gradually gave up German as the Canadian-born generations increasingly replaced the foreign-born in a congregation. With this, churches ceased to be German community organizations and in many ways became part of the broader organizational network of the larger society, serving, not a particular ethnic community, but Canadian society in general. In other instances, as in the case of newspapers, these ceased publication as a result of the language loss among the immigrant offspring. Clubs, in turn, generally declined as a result of a loss in membership as children of immigrants were absorbed into the larger society, but then found new vitality through the arrival of new immigrants. As such, they often served as a sort of half-way house, serving community members before they were integrated into the larger society.

In the following, I will examine the German community in the light of these changes, concentrating on the effect of language change on the German community in Canada and its community organizations. To explore this change, I will focus in particular on the churches, tracing their evolution from the time when they were essentially immigrant churches to the point where they gave up the German language and essentially ceased to be institutions serving a particular linguistic community. At the same time, I will look at schools, clubs, the German language media and other institutions established by Germans to serve their needs and attain their goals.

I will concentrate on language transition in the churches because, of institutions established, only the churches kept a fairly reliable record of the language transition from German to the dominant languages. Furthermore, with churches being the most important organizations in the German Canadian community, one can very well argue that language transition in the churches reflects the language transition in the German Canadian community at large.

Churches

The Church spelled out people's place in time and eternity. It offered solace at times of difficulty. At the same time, it was an integral part of people's life cycle, marking important events in their life from birth, through to marriage, into adulthood, old age and then death. In addition, it also served an important social function in relating one to other people who were significant in one's community. This was true of all German language churches, no matter whether they were Catholic, Lutheran, Mennonite, Baptist or any other. In the following, I will briefly look at the development of German Church life in this country, from its beginning to the point where congregations no longer made use of the German language in their services. I will look at the role of the German language in the church, examining those factors that contributed to its usage and, as well, will examine the influences leading to its decline.

Language plays a significant role in the maintenance of a religion and its transference to the next generation. Language is a vehicle through which religion is perpetuated. Because a person grows up practicing his or her religion in a certain language, an emotional bond develops between a person, the language used, and his or her religion. The religion means the old songs, the familiar prayers. These are what bind the person to his or her past and future. Defining and sharing sacred symbols, language serves to establish boundaries of group identity.

Members of German churches originated not only from Germany but also from Austria, Switzerland and other areas of Europe where Germans had settled. In fact, most of the members of German churches in Western Canada originated, not from Germany, but from the different small German enclaves that had emerged in Eastern Europe over the centuries. Often they had little more than the German language to bind them together.

Almost all religious communities that emerged in German-speaking territories in Europe are represented in Canadian society. As in Germany, the majority of Germans in Canada are Lutheran or Catholic. Mennonites are more numerous in Canada than in Germany because most Mennonites had left German-speaking lands over time, settling in Russia or the United States, from where they came to Canada. In addition, a considerable number of Germans in Canada are members of the Baptist denomination, in large part because of the evangelical work Baptists carried out among German-speaking groups. The German Canadian community also includes Moravians, Hutterites, Pentecostals, as well as members of other faiths.

The following section will look at the main German religious communities, tracing their beginnings in this country, analyzing in particular the influences that led German congregations to eventually become absorbed into the larger society, which saw them primarily using the English language in their religious services. While some of them retained segments of their religious tradition, they had now become, no longer German churches, but English-or French- speaking congregations that had their roots in a German past. I will begin by looking at German Catholics, Lutherans, Mennonites and Baptists. As other German language denominations followed a similar pattern of transformation, I will mention some of these denominations without discussing them in detail.

Catholics

Members of a universal Church, German Catholics had little other than language differentiating them from other Catholics in Canada.

Nevertheless, convinced that Catholics were threatened by the larger Protestant majority in North America, German Catholics focused on language preservation and even group settlement in an effort to preserve their religious identity in Canada. Also, Canadian Catholic leaders saw group settlements as necessary to provide different language groups with their own priests so that they wouldn't be assimilated into the larger Protestant milieu.

German Catholic settlement in Waterloo County, where the major German Catholic settlements were first formed, began in the mid-1820s. Settlers were dependent upon lay leaders to fulfill their spiritual needs until 1834, when the first travelling missionary, Johann L. Wiriath, arrived from Germany. He was soon followed by others. Eventually Bishop Armand de Charbonnel, stationed in Kingston, succeeded in recruiting German Jesuits for the Catholic work in Canada, many of whom were forced to leave their homeland as a result of the rise of Liberalism. The first two, Lucas Caveng, of Switzerland, and Bernard Fritsch, from Bavaria, arrived in St. Agatha, Upper Canada, in 1847. The German Catholic population of Waterloo County at the time was estimated to be between eight and ten thousand. The Jesuits played an important role in organizing and vitalizing German Catholic life in Waterloo County. Centred in villages such as St. Agatha, Neu Deutschland, St. Clements and New Prussia, where they held Mass almost every Sunday, they organized smaller congregations in different Catholic centres. New churches were constructed and old ones enlarged. Local schools were organized and staffed with teachers.

After 10 years of labour, the Jesuits ceased their work in Waterloo County. Some succumbed to ill health from the strain of the work; others were recalled to Europe as the influence of Liberalism gradually waned to make way to a new Conservatism, while still others were transferred to the United States. This left Waterloo County desperately short of priests.

In 1857, Bishop Armand de Charbonnel, the second Bishop of Toronto, went to Rome to find more missionaries for his diocese as well as for the dioceses of Hamilton and London. In particular Waterloo County, with some 12,000 German-speaking Catholics, was short of priests. When he heard of a new congregation of priests being formed to serve emigrés, he approached them with his problem. Unknown to him, however, was that this community, the Congregation of the Resurrection, was composed largely of Polish priests dedicated to serving that community. It is understandable, therefore, that the community was reluctant to accede to Bishop de Charbonnel's request. However, it did offer him Brother Eugene Funcken, a German member of the Order, as well as Father Edward Glowacki, a Silesian, both of whom arrived in St. Agatha, Ontario, in 1858. Soon after his arrival, Father Funcken endeavoured to recruit others to join the Catholic work in Ontario, including his brother Louis, who arrived in St. Agatha in September 1864.

Noticing the sorrowful lack of priests as well as the generally low level of education among his Catholic parishioners, Father Louis Funcken, with the encouragement of his brother Eugene, decided to open a college, which would train not only priests for the German Catholic work in Ontario but would also help raise the educational level of German Catholics of Waterloo County in general. With this end in mind, Father Louis opened St. Jerome's College in January, 1865. Beginning in a small rented cabin in St. Agatha, St. Jerome's was moved to Berlin, Ontario, then a town of some 2,000, where it could hope to draw on a larger student population. Opening in 1866, it played an important role in supplying needed priests to German and other Catholics as well as providing Catholic lay leaders for Waterloo County. By 1915, almost every priest of the Hamilton diocese was a St. Jerome's graduate.[54]

To serve the spiritual and social needs of the community, the priests organized churches and parochial schools. In the latter, different orders of nuns, such as the Sisters of Notre Dame from Milwaukee, were active. In St. Agatha, for example, the sisters were responsible for both the separate schools, as well as the orphanage, the latter having been organized by Father Eugene Funcken in 1868. The priests organized men's and women's associations, choirs and other organizations to centre the organizational life of their parishioners around the church. When in the 1860s many of their parishioners were looking for new areas of settlement because most of the good land had been taken up in Waterloo County, the priests formed a settlement society to organize group settlements. However, the society dissolved once people sent out to locate land didn't find any area suitable for the settlement of a large number of Waterloo County Catholics.

---

[54] James A. Wahl, "Father Louis Funcken's Contribution to German Catholicism in Waterloo County, Ontario," *CCHA Historical* Studies 50 (1983) 529.

Nevertheless, the departure of many German Catholics to Saugeen weakened their churches in Waterloo County. The declining membership in their congregations brought them into greater contact with English and Irish Catholics. While in the early years of settlement they had received many of their priests from Europe, after 1860 many of their priests were graduates of St. Jerome's. This all resulted in a situation where by the end of the 19th century Catholics of Waterloo County were becoming increasingly anglicized.

As in Eastern Canada, priests also took a very active role in the life of German Catholics as these began to settle in Western Canada. The first German Catholics arrived here in the 1890s, primarily from Austria-Hungary and Russia. In 1893, a missionary was sent out from Montreal to hold services for German Catholics of Winnipeg, who were thereupon invited to organize themselves into a congregation. There were too few of them, however, for such an undertaking. Their essential needs were met by Father Woodcutter, who at first served them from St. Boniface and, later, from Gretna, a rural Manitoba community in the Mennonite settlement where a few German Catholics had settled. To serve Catholics from continental Europe on a regular basis, the Bishop in St. Boniface thereupon invited the Oblates of Mary Immaculate from Europe. The first to arrive was Father Albert Kulawy, a Polish priest who spoke German. He started his work in 1898, to be joined by his brother several years later. At Holy Ghost Parish, Winnipeg, they served both German and Polish Catholics. When the turn of the century brought a considerable influx of German Catholics into the city, Father August Suffa arrived from Europe to work among them. He was joined by Father Joseph Cordes in 1901, who in 1904 organized the German Catholic parish of St. Joseph's.

To establish the parish, the Oblate fathers purchased twelve blocks of land in an as yet unoccupied area of the city. Lots were then sold to German Catholics, no matter what their area of origin. To prevent land from falling into the hands of non-Catholics, and also to avoid speculation, buyers who wished to resell their land had to sell it to the Fathers. In this way, they established a fairly contiguous small German Catholic settlement in the city.

Of course, the Oblates could not have purchased this land without the support of the local Church hierarchy. The Catholic Church had a long tradition of ethnic parishes. To meet the spiritual needs of Catholics of different linguistic backgrounds, and to prevent them from being swallowed up by the largely Protestant majority in North America, the Church had decided to establish ethnic as well as territorial parishes in different centres where there was a need for them. This might involve providing priests and a place of worship for parishioners of a specific linguistic background. In some instances, as in the founding of St. Joseph's parish in Winnipeg, the Church also provided the resources for the creation of a small block settlement in an urban centre.

This points to one advantage that German Catholics had in the organization of their religious life that was not available to most other German religious groups. Catholics came to a territory where their Church was already well established. This made it possible for German Catholics to draw on the support of their co-religionists in the larger society to establish themselves and build their community.

The Oblates, who were the main religious order working among continental Europeans in Western Canada, worked under Superiors in St. Albert or St. Boniface. Ethnic parishes had no sooner established themselves in Winnipeg when priests there expanded their mission work to include German Catholics further west. Thus, Father August Suffa helped open the first parish for German-speaking immigrants who had settled in Regina while he was stationed in Winnipeg. In 1902, Father Schulte used his base in Winnipeg to work among German Catholics in Edmonton.

Oblates served in particular the different German Catholic settlements that emerged in and around Regina, be this St. Mary's in Regina, or German Catholic settlements in Balgonie, Odessa, and neighbouring areas. Once the parish of a particular settlement had grown large enough, priests were stationed there to minister to locals as well as to Catholics in smaller settlements in the surrounding area. Parishioners were encouraged to build a church and become independent as soon as possible.

Oblates were also involved in establishing rural block settlements, as for example St. Joseph's Colony, within the boundary of the Diocese of St. Albert. It was also the Oblates who took on the responsibility of caring for the settlers there. While the Catholic Colonization Society, with F.J. Lange as president, and F. Bens as secretary, carried out much of the advertising and the work to bringing in the settlers, the project was carried out under the spiritual guidance of Oblate priests, Fathers J. Laufer, A. Suffa, and W. Schulte.

Of course, the Oblates weren't the only Catholic order working among German Catholics in Western Canada. When German Catholic settlers in Minnesota were looking for new land where they might establish themselves, they approached the Rt. Rev. Peter Engel, OSB, Abbott of St. John's Abbey, a Benedictine abbey in Collegeville, Minnesota, to provide them with priests for their new settlement. The Abbot was sympathetic. Following this, Father Bruno Doerfler and three prominent German Catholic laymen went to Western Canada to seek out suitable land. They settled on land near Saskatoon. At the invitation of Abbot Engel, Prior Alfred Mayer, OSB, moved his community from Cluny Priory to Canada. In the meantime, Abbot Engel contacted Bishop Pascal, OMI, in whose territory the new colony was located and whose permission and that of the Holy See had to be obtained for the founding of the monastery which would serve the new settlement. Permission for both was granted.

St. Peter's Cathedral, St. Peter's Abbey (today), Muenster, Sask. Public Domain.

When the settlers recruited by the Catholic Settlement Society arrived in St. Peter's colony, named in honour of Abbot Peter Engel, the Benedictines were there to serve them. They worked to establish not only their monastery but also laboured to serve the spiritual needs of the settlers. They offered mass, visited the settlers in their homes, performed marriages, baptisms and burials.

While concentrated in their main centre in Muenster, the Benedictines served German Catholics all over the new settlement. They organized congregations and encouraged them to build their churches and establish parochial schools to teach not only religion but also the

German language. In fact, as other German Catholic religious leaders, they did their best to organize the life of their parishioners around their church. Within each parish, they organized men's and ladies' auxiliaries. As the Oblates, they established a religious press. For the Oblates, it was the *West Canada,* which was founded in Winnipeg under the direction of Father Cordes, in 1907. The Benedictines, in turn, started the *St. Peter's Bote,* in 1904, to help keep in contact the German Catholic communities which they were serving.

One of the major areas in which Western Canadian German Catholic leaders took a role was in German language instruction. They not only encouraged their parishioners to establish schools, but taught in such schools themselves, when necessary. They also did their utmost to attract different orders of nuns to take up teaching positions for schools that had been organized. An example is Leipzig, in St. Joseph's Colony. Soon after the completion of the church in Leipzig, Father Kirst, pastor at the time, set up a building fund for the establishment of a convent school. This goal was taken up by other Church leaders. In order to find teachers for the undertaking, Father Kierdorf, OMI, visited the Notre Dame Sisters in Munich, Bavaria, to interest them in coming to Western Canada. Following this, a delegation of three Notre Dame Sisters arrived in Saskatchewan, in 1926, to explore the situation. In August of the same year, the first four Sisters arrived from the Canadian mother house in Hamilton, Ontario. In December, 1927, the Notre Dame Convent was opened in Leipzig, Saskatchewan, providing instruction to some 56 children.[55]

Similar negotiations had led to the transfer of Ursuline Sisters to St. Peter's Colony. In April 1913, the Rev. Abbot Bruno Doerfler had travelled to Germany to discuss the possibility of transferring Ursuline Sisters in Winnipeg to St. Peter's Colony. Mother Xaveria Loens, superior of the Ursuline Convent at Cologne, came to Winnipeg and then to Muenster to make the necessary arrangements. In September 1913, the first Sisters arrived, both from Germany. Soon after, they were followed by others. The Sisters' home was no sooner completed when a new modern school was joined to the Sisters' house. Although in the 1930s

---

[55]   Oblate Priests (Compilers). *Pictures and Pages of the Silver Jubilee of St. Joseph's Colony.* Trans. Lambert and Tillie Schneider (Battleford, Sask.: Marian Press, 1930) 66.

the different parish schools were changed into public schools, the Sisters continued to offer instruction in them.

One of the major organizations established by German Catholics in Western Canada was the *Volksverein deutsch-canadischer Katholiken*. The *Volksverein* was apparently the brainchild of Father Bruno Doerfler, who conceived of the idea of inviting all German Catholics across the country for a gathering patterned after the great conventions held in Germany and the United States. Muenster was the scene of the first *Katholikentag* in Canada, with speakers coming from such centres as Winnipeg, Regina and Minnesota. At the next *Katholikentag,* held in Winnipeg, 1909, the *Volksverein* was organized. Its main goal was Catholic action, to instill Catholic values in adherents and to represent Catholic interests in the broader community.

In particular during the inter-war years, the *Volksverein* became extensively involved in immigration work, co-operating with the railway companies in recruiting and settling German Catholics in Western Canada. Immigrants were generally settled in existing Catholic settlements. New settlements, such as Little Britain, near Winnipeg, were also established. This work came to an end with the outbreak of the Depression.

In the meantime, despite the new immigrants and the efforts of the Sisters to offer the children of settlers even a rudimentary knowledge of German, younger Catholics in Western Canada were losing the language. With the outbreak of World War II, they were often also unwilling to speak it. Already prior to the war, German had become less and less important in German Catholic community life. Many of the pioneers who spoke and read German gradually passed away. The younger generation was not sufficiently conversant with the language of their forefathers. As a result, during World War II the *Volksverein* ceased operating in Catholic communities, being replaced by the Catholic Immigration Aid Society. In Muenster, the St. Peter's Bote ceased publishing in 1947 because it had lost most of its readership, to be replaced by the *Prairie Messenger.*

By the end of World War II, German Catholics in Western Canada were well on the way to losing their language, as had the earlier Catholics in Ontario, when a new wave of Catholic immigrants began arriving. Brought over through the work of the Catholic Immigrant Aid Society in co-operation with the railways, some of the post-World War II immigrants settled in rural areas where most German Catholics had previously settled. However, there weren't enough of them to influence the language transition in the congregations they joined.

The vast majority of the new arrivals settled in urban centres, in particular in the major cities such as Toronto or Vancouver. This was true even of those who started out working in farming, the lumber industry, or the mines. They ended up moving to urban centres, where the wages were better and there was greater opportunity for advancement.

Although Catholic territorial and national parishes had existed side by side for some time in Canadian urban centres, the ability of German post-World War II immigrants to have their own national parish, and with it, services in their own language, differed from situation to situation. That was because the papal constitution, *Exsul Familia*, which had been designed to regulate the right of migrants to receive religious services and comfort in their mother tongue, tended to be ignored by local Canadian bishops. That meant that local conditions had an important influence on determining the nature of the service provided to the new arrivals. For example, until 1975 national parishes in Toronto were considered to be of little significance, with the bishops going so far as urging an end to the establishment of such parishes altogether. But then, in 1975, a reversal occurred. With Canadians gravitating towards the suburbs, Toronto came to be seen as a prime centre for immigrant communities, and Roman Catholic immigrants, including their churches, were placed under an auxiliary bishop, who himself was an immigrant.

The diocese of Hamilton tended to give little consideration to non-English services. Perhaps that was because the Church hierarchy expected ethnic parishes to have a short life. A German Catholic parish had been established in the city in the 1870s, but then had declined as parishioners either left or joined English-language parishes in their neighbourhood. Nevertheless, when the new German Catholic arrivals took the initiative in Hamilton and proceeded to organize their parish, they were eventually supported by the hierarchy.

In Kitchener, German Catholic immigrants revived German services at St. Mary's church once again. The congregation had been established in 1854 by German-speaking Catholics. By 1903, all sermons were in English. After World War I, German services were re-introduced in the basement of the church as new immigrants started arriving. These services ceased during World War II, only to be started again in 1948, as a new wave of immigrants settled in the city. Other dioceses in Ontario also offered German language services, some occasionally and others on a more permanent basis.

The situation was similar in Western Canada, where almost all parishes were organized on a territorial basis by the end of World War II. However, some ethnic parishes were still in existence, an example being St. Joseph's, Winnipeg, which served the German parishioners in the city. In some centres, such as Vancouver, new German parishes were established to meet the needs of the new arrivals.

Immigrants, no matter in what urban centre they settled, tended to settle relatively close to their church where they were most often served by priests speaking their language. Here they found the companionship of other immigrants, with whom they could share their experiences. The parish provided for more than their spiritual needs; the priest and members of the congregation helped the new arrival find employment, and frequently the parish set up language schools to help the new arrivals learn English. All in all, the parish did its best to help the immigrants adjust and find their place in the new environment.

Urban German Catholic parishes initially tended to undergo a period of rapid growth, followed by a decline. They thrived as the immigrants arrived and adjusted to Canadian life. As an example, St. Patrick's parish, Toronto, was established prior to World War II by *Donauschwaben*, who had originated from Hungary, Romania and Yugoslavia. The parish had a credit union that helped parishioners with major purchases. It had a funeral society that helped with burial costs. The parish's Catholic Settlement House provided for children during after-school hours, as well as functioning as a neighbourhood social and cultural centre.

The new arrivals after World War II brought a new vitality to St. Patrick's. The parish credit union expanded to 800 members. English classes were in demand as they had been when the parish was founded in the 1920s. The combined number of baptisms and marriages climbed from about 80 in 1950 to 660 in 1957. Parishioners report that it was common for 300 young people to be at the church hall on Saturday evening – dancing, playing table tennis, billiards or bowling. After that, they walked home, for they lived within walking distance of the parish hall.

New organizations were also established to meet needs and interests particular to the new immigrants, including, in the case of St. Patrick's, the *Kolping* Society and the *St. Michaelswerk Verband katholischer*

Donauschwaben. Founded in 1954, the *Kolping* Society was modelled after its German counterpart. Originally a society that provided lodging for travelling journeymen, in Toronto it helped newcomers find housing and jobs, and offered them advice on how best to adjust to the new land. Founded in 1949, the *St. Michaelswerk Verband* helped *Donauschwaben*, whose lands had been confiscated in their homelands in Europe, obtain compensation for their losses under Germany's indemnification laws. At the same time, it served to foster the cultural heritage of *Donauschwaben*.

The late sixties and the seventies witnessed the gradual decline of St. Patrick's German-speaking congregation. Some of the original members had begun to leave the area near the church on McCaul Street to purchase homes in the city's outskirts. The new immigrants started to leave the inner city for the suburbs in the late 1960s. Rather than travel downtown, they attended the English-speaking parishes in their neighbourhoods. While St. Patrick's continued to exist, the number of baptisms and marriages performed greatly declined. Organizations such as the credit union, the funeral society, *St. Michaelswerk Verband* and the *Kolping* Society continued. However, they no longer attracted many new members, particularly not young members. Most of the post-World War II German immigrants, having become well off and acculturated, were no longer in need of the mutual aid provided by these organizations and their function now became largely social. Organizations that continued to maintain a benevolent function began to direct their activities to helping people in other countries. The Catholic Settlement House, while continuing its day-care services for the neighbourhood, started providing these services essentially for non-German speaking children, as Germans had been replaced in the neighbourhood by new arrivals from different parts of the world.

This transformation was even more pronounced in St. Joseph's Church in Winnipeg. Founded at the turn of the last century for German parishioners, by the year 2000 about two-thirds of its parishioners as well as its priest were of Philippine origin. German services continued to be provided, but these were provided by a Philippine priest who spoke German for the mostly elderly German immigrant parishioners who still attended the church.

This pattern is also evident among German Catholics elsewhere in Canada, as, for example, in Vancouver. Looking not only at German Catholics but also at German Baptists, Mennonites and Lutherans,

Beatty and Ley found that German immigrant churches went through a
cycle. First was a period of growth as new immigrants arrived to enhance
the membership of established churches or to start new congregations.
At this stage, the church served not only the spiritual needs of the
congregation but also became a home away from home. The congregation
responded by establishing an institutional network to meet people's
needs. This might include choirs, young peoples' groups, men's clubs and
other organizations.

Beatty and Ley found that in Vancouver German churches
established by post-World War II immigrants attained their high point
in the 1950s and the early 1960s, essentially during those years that the
immigrants arrived and adjusted to Canadian life. Significant changes
occurred in the late sixties.[56] One was the cessation of immigration,
with fewer Germans entering the country, because of improving
economic conditions in Germany and also because changes in Canada's
Immigration Act in 1967 removed the policy of European preference. At
the same time, Germans had participated in Canada's boom in the 1950s
and 60s, many of them moving from their basement suites in South
Vancouver into new suburban homes. Many of these people chose to
attend English-language churches in their neighbourhood rather than go
to their ethnic church in South Vancouver. Thirdly, during this time their
children were growing up. Not having the experiences of the immigrant
generation, these didn't share the values of the immigrants. Nor did they
have the same attachment to the German language. Of course, in some
instances the parents also didn't have an attachment to the German
language, but rather the opposite. Burdened by the history of the Third
Reich, they discouraged their children from learning German. The result
was that many of the younger generation often didn't have a good enough
knowledge of German to be able to benefit from a German language
service.

In time, this brought about a decline in church attendance, which
left the existing German congregations in the inner city with a problem.
While some churches followed their membership to the suburbs, the

---

[56]   Laura Beattie and David Ley, "The German Immigrant Church in Vancouver:
       Service Provisions and Identity Formation" *Vancouver Centre of Excellence:
       Research on Immigration and Integration in the Metropolis. Working paper Series
       no.01-19* (October 2001) 1-25.

majority remained in the inner city, where Germans were being rapidly replaced by new immigrants from China, India and elsewhere. German churches responded in different ways to meet this challenge. Some gave up the language and focused on the use of English, both to retain their own young people who still came to church and to encourage outreach to the neighbourhood community. In other instances, this was combined with the endeavour to make the church building available to the newcomers. In all these cases, the need for German language services was greatly reduced, leading to a point where German services essentially served old survivors of the immigrant generation.

In this regard, an identifiable pattern is observable among German Catholics, no matter when they arrived in this country. German Catholic parishes were established by German immigrants to serve their needs. Different sub-organizations were established to meet these goals. Change came once the immigrant generation began to die off and their children and grandchildren took control of the parish. One of the changes was the loss of the German language by succeeding generations. The priests responded by giving up German and making English the main language of communication.

In rural settlements, this change was slower than in urban centres, tending to take place when the second or third generation reached adulthood. In urban centres this transformation tended to take place when the people who came over as children or the first generation born in Canada reached adulthood. In all these instances, language change was motivated by language loss among the parishioners and the desire by the priest to serve his flock in a language that they best understood. This led to a situation where by 2010 rural German Catholic parishes had essentially disappeared in Canada. Such parishes that existed were located primarily in urban centres. Parishioners in these parishes consisted for the most part of older members of the immigrant generation. Unless a new wave of German immigrants arrives, such parishes will disappear once this generation dies off.

Lutherans

As with the Catholics, German Lutheran church life started in Eastern Canada, in this case Nova Scotia. Unlike German Catholics, German Lutherans did not find an existing Church in the territory where they settled that might help them establish themselves. This presented some difficulties, in particular as the Anglican Church, the Establishment Church, sought to interfere with the endeavours of the Lutheran Church to take a foothold in the country.

Lutherans faced several problems upon arrival in Canada. Most of them were poor, with few means at their disposal. Furthermore, they came from territories where pastors had been supported by the state. This meant that they didn't have a tradition of financially supporting their pastor and Church. Combined with their general poverty, this made it difficult for them to obtain pastors and keep them after they arrived. Added to this was an overall paucity of pastors.

Nevertheless, soon after the first German Lutheran immigrants settled in Canada, they endeavoured to assure that their spiritual needs would be taken care of. German Lutherans had no sooner arrived in Halifax in 1749 when they sought to organize a church. Plans had been made prior to their arrival by local officials for the building of a Church of England edifice for them, which was to be named St. Paul's. Little attention was given to the fact that the Germans were Lutheran rather than Anglican. The Germans were expected to contribute and conform to the state Church. Having been taught Luther's Catechism and being familiar with the Augsburg Confession, Lutherans insisted on abiding by their faith. To demonstrate this, they organized an Evangelical Lutheran congregation and laid plans to build a Lutheran church.

However, they encountered difficulty in having their needs served. Their church services were irregular. Rene Christian Burger, their first pastor, eventually went to England to be ordained as an Episcopal minister. When he returned with a large number of German Bibles and prayer books, his boat likely sank, for he was not heard of again. Following this, the church was on occasion served in German by a Reverend Slater (Chaplain of the troops). Services became more regular in 1760 when Johann Gottfried Jorpel took up his duties as schoolmaster for the children of the congregation. In addition, he also conducted religious services. However, this brief period of fairly regular services came to an end when Jorpel died, in December 1761.

This was followed by further attempts to absorb Lutherans into the dominant state Church, at first by Anglican ministers who on occasion served the congregation; then by the Lutheran minister Bernard Michael Houseal. He came to Halifax in 1784, along with other refugees during the American Revolution. Within a year of his arrival, however, he set sail for England, where he applied to the Bishop of London for Deacon's orders in the Church of England.

On his return to Halifax, he became minister of St. George's congregation, where he remained until his death in 1799. During this time, the last of the immigrant generation died off. The younger generation, no longer speaking German fluently and, not firmly indoctrinated in the Lutheran faith, was less resistant to Anglican influences. Although the congregation voted for another German minister to replace Houseal, this ran into some opposition, and the congregation eventually settled on the Reverend George Wright, an Anglican. Under him, St. George's Lutheran congregation eventually passed out of existence, and the "Little Dutch Church" in Halifax became the property of the Anglican Church.

Little Dutch (Deutsch) Church, Halifax, Nova Scotia.
Author: archer 10 (Dennis), CC BY-SA 2.0.

Similar difficulties with the Anglicans were encountered by other early Lutheran churches. To preserve the German language for their children after their arrival in Lunenburg, German Lutherans were concerned with opening a school. This they established in 1760. At the same time, they brought a teacher, Gottlob Neumann, from Germany, to instruct the children. Neumann also conducted religious services in the homes, using devotional booklets of the day. Although the influence of the Anglicans led to German being greatly restricted in the instructions offered by Neumann, he continued his work as teacher and with his sermons for the larger community.

In 1770, Lunenburg Lutherans began with the construction of a church. However, they didn't have a minister. Largely as a result of the appeal of a Mr. Kaulbauch, who was in New York on a business trip, Pastor Friedrich Schulz accompanied Kaulbach back to Lunenburg. Under Schulz, Zion Lutheran Church was built, with some seventy-five families forming the congregation.

After Schulz, the congregation again had difficulty attracting a pastor. Often they had to wait several years before attracting a new one, with many staying a short period before moving on. The exception was Carl Ernst Cossmann. As most pastors serving Lunenburg Lutherans, Cossmann had studied theology in Germany. He began his service in 1835. As instruction in the German language tended to be brief and intermittent in the schools, most of the people who had grown up in Lunenburg were beginning to have but a rudimentary knowledge of it. Cossmann was therefore required to appeal for an English-speaking Lutheran minister to aid him. This led to disputes between Cossmann and his English-speaking aids as they served Zion Lutheran, as well as Lutheran congregations in Bridgewater and Mahone Bay. With the retirement of Pastor Cossmann in 1876, German language services were terminated in Lunenburg and the surrounding area.

The German Lutheran work in Nova Scotia had not yet ended when it began in Upper Canada as an increasing number of Lutherans settled there. Some of the first of these were Loyalists who had come to Upper Canada following the American Revolution. They had first settled in the vicinity of Bath and Ernesttown but then had left because they found the soil unsuitable. They then settled in the area of present-day Morrisburg. In 1784, they organized a Lutheran congregation in Williamsburg. In 1791, Pastor Samuel Schwerdtfeger, one of the founders of the "New York Ministerium," left the United States to serve the congregation as well as Lutherans in the surrounding area. During his fourteen year service Schwerdtfeger also established Lutheran congregations in Osnabrück (Aultsville) and Mathilde, churches that were later lost to either the Anglicans or the Presbyterians.

After a brief service by Pastor Friedrich August Meyer, Pastor J. G. Wiegandt took over as pastor of Salem Lutheran Church in Williamsburg. In large part to care for his financial needs, because of the irregular support he received from his parishioners, Pastor Wiegandt joined the Anglican Church and took his church with him. This led to a feud between those who didn't want to join the Anglicans and those who had joined the Anglican Church. After three years without a minister, Williamsburg Lutherans called Pastor Friedrich Meyer, who had served them earlier, to be their minister. He, however, also joined the Anglicans, leaving them without a minister.

Eventually, in 1826, Pastor Hermann Hayunga took up the work of serving Lutherans along the St. Lawrence. As the younger generation had by now either lost the German, or spoke it poorly, Pastor Hayunga preached in English and the German work along the St. Lawrence essentially ended.

Forces at work among German Lutherans along the St. Lawrence are also evident among German Lutherans in Vaughan and Markham townships. At first, German Lutherans there were served by Pastor Liebig (or Lewich), who appears to have accompanied the settlers to the United States and from there to Canada. After a brief service by a certain Pastor Andrich, Pastor John Dietrich Petersen, who had come from Pennsylvania, took up service in the townships. Under him, three churches were constructed. However, as Petersen received part of his income from the Anglican Church in return for eventually bringing the Lutherans into the fold, opposition to him arose and in 1829 he resigned. Following this, Pastor Jakob Hüttner served the congregations for ten years. After this, the congregations were served only irregularly by a pastor, resulting in the loss of members to the Presbyterians and other denominations.

Under these circumstances, Adam Keffer, a member of Zion Church in Vaughan, set out in the winter of 1849 to go to Pittsburgh to plead that a pastor be sent to them. The Pittsburgh Synod responded and sent out Pastor E. F. Diehl, who took up his position in Vaughan and Markham in 1850. Pastor Diehl at first presented his sermons in German. However, he discovered shortly after his arrival that most of his parishioners spoke English better than German, and so found it necessary to deliver his ministry in the English language.

The rapid language change among Germans along the St. Lawrence and in Vaughan and Markham can be attributed in part at least to the sparse nature of German settlement in these areas. The change to English appears not to have been as rapid in Waterloo County, where Germans had settled in a larger block.

The first major settlement of Lutherans emerged with the mass inflow of settlers from Germany, the first Lutherans arriving in the 1830s, primarily from Hessen, Württemberg and Alsace. However, there were few pastors to serve them. Among the first to arrive was Friedrich Wilhelm Bindemann. Of Reformed background, and at the same time a rationalist and universalist, he was not quite acceptable to the conservative farmers and tradespeople who had settled in Waterloo County. Nevertheless, he was indefatigable and in 1834 founded, among others, St. Paul's Church in Berlin, St. Peter's in Preston, Zion in St. Agatha, Trinity in New Hamburg. At the same time, he served the Lutheran church in Sebastopol, that had been founded in 1832, as well as preached in Heidelberg and other areas where Lutherans had settled.

In the meantime, H. W. Peterson, the founder of the *Canada Museum*, who also served as a lay minister, performed burials and baptisms. Opposed to the liberal-minded Bindemann, he turned to the German Evangelical Lutheran Ministerium of Pennsylvania to request a pastor. Responding to Peterson's invitation, Pastor J.H. Bernheim arrived in August 1835 to serve Lutherans in Waterloo County.

Although aided by Peterson in whose newspaper he could advertise, Bernheim found himself forced to discontinue his work after some ten weeks because of Bindemann's influence among the parishioners. The next pastor was obtained from Buffalo through a newspaper advertisement. He, however, turned out to be a Presbyterian who attempted to win Lutherans for his Church. At the same time, Baptists as well other denominations carried out missionary work among the Lutherans in an attempt to win them away from their faith. It was under these circumstances that Adam Keffer of Vaughan Township walked to Pittsburgh to plead with the Pittsburgh Synod to send them pastors for the Canadian work. In response, the Pittsburgh Synod sent out several missionaries during the following years to organize Lutherans of Waterloo County into congregations. In 1853, these pastors organized the Canada Conference of the Pittsburgh Synod. To help it in its work, the Canada

Conference received an annual support of $400.00 from the Pittsburgh Synod and $200.00 from the Pennsylvania Ministerium.

In 1861, at a meeting in Vaughan, the Canada Conference re-organized itself to become the Ev. Lutheran Synod of Canada. After 1868, the Synod published the *Kirchenblatt der Ev. Lutherischen Synode von Canada*, which in 1910 merged with the *Deutsche Lutheraner*, brought out by the General Council of North America.

Although this regulated the organizational structure in which pastors worked in Upper Canada, it did not solve the ever-present problem of the lack of pastors. To deal with this difficulty, the General Council established relations with seminaries in Berlin, Basel, Bremen, Kropp and other centres in Europe. Increasing Anglicization, however, made it imperative that a seminary be established in Canada, which brought about the establishment of Waterloo Seminary in 1911-12. This, combined with pastors coming from elsewhere, at last provided the Synod with the spiritual leaders it needed.

Official opening of Waterloo Lutheran Seminary, Berlin, Ontario, 1911. Courtesy of Laurier University Archives

The shortage of pastors was further rectified when other synods from the United States also entered the field. Of prime significance among these was the Missouri Synod, which began its work in the 1860s and laid great stress on preserving what it perceived as being the true Lutheranism. At the same time, it stressed the importance of retaining the German language and German customs. To realize these objectives, it placed utmost importance on religious education and parochial schools.

Although the immigrants and in particular pastors coming from Europe placed great importance on preserving the German language, among the children of the immigrants, the desire for English-language services gradually emerged. Responding to this, St. Peter's in Berlin introduced English-language services in 1884, and churches in Preston did the same in the 1890s. In 1912, St. John's, Waterloo, introduced an English Sunday school to retain its youth. The drive for English-language services intensified with the outbreak of World War I and the propaganda against anything German which arose from it. The move away from German in church services continued during the inter-war years, encouraged by the continuing antagonism toward Germans. At the same time, a new generation was emerging within the churches that had received little instruction in the German language. This led to the situation where by 1939 German Lutheran churches in Waterloo County had to a large extent abandoned German language services.

Similar processes were underway in other areas of Ontario where Germans settled. German settlers took up Canada Company land in the Zurich area of Ontario in the 1840s. St. Peter's Lutheran Church, organized in 1861, was the first Lutheran church established in the little hamlet of Zurich. Services were at first in German. As the immigrant generation died off and the Canada-born generation grew into adulthood, the often divisive process of language transition began. English-language services were introduced between 1908 and 1913, and by 1921 the church was bilingual. In 1929, the Ladies' Aid of the church discontinued the use of German at its meetings. In 1930, the church constitution was translated from German into English. In 1937, revisions were made to the constitution stating that German services would be continued as long as 25 per cent of the members insist on it. In 1940, the German morning services were discontinued for the duration of the war, and with this German services came to an end altogether.

The mass migration of Germans to the Ottawa Valley began in the 1860s. Zion Lutheran Church of Pembroke was organized in 1883 by Lutherans in the Upper Ottawa Valley. Until 1921, all regular church services were conducted in the German language. Then the need arose for the introduction of English services for members who were no longer conversant in the German language. In November of that year, the congregation decided to conduct the evening services on the first and third Sundays of the month in English. With the outbreak of World War II, German services were withdrawn, but were re-introduced in November 1940. At the same time, the pastor of the church was engaged by the government to conduct German language services at the Prisoner of War Camp at Centre Lake. In 1948, the congregation decided to hire two pastors, one for the German work and the other for the English work. English-language services were at 9:15 a.m. and German language services at 11:00 a.m. In 1954, this order was reversed so that the German service was at 9:15 a.m. and the English-language service at 11:00 a.m. Following a poll in 1956, the German service was moved to the afternoon, with English-language services being presented in both the morning and the evening. German services were held primarily for the older members of the congregation and ceased with their deaths.

Similar forces influenced the language transition of St. John's Evangelical Lutheran Church of Petawawa, which was organized in 1867 by German Lutheran immigrants from Prussia. German reading and writing were taught by the pastor of the church until the mid-1920s. Nevertheless, in 1930 the pastor was required to preach one English sermon per month. In 1939, English services were presented every second Sunday. German services were discontinued in the early 1940s. At the same time, when new immigrants arrived in the area in the late 1940s, the church's pastor conducted German services for them every second Sunday.

Writing of Grace Lutheran Church, Locksley, in the Ottawa Valley, the Reverend Kenn Ward states that up to 1929 "the services in the congregation had been conducted almost exclusively in German. However, the congregation now felt that there should be some English. A resolution was passed to have one English service a month whenever there should be an afternoon service." He adds that the change "to English met with a great deal of resistance. Not all congregations were as slow at adopting English as Grace, Locksley. For instance, English began to be used at Zion, Pembroke, in 1921 and at St. John's Petawawa, in 1928. As congregations found their younger members were leaving to go to churches where English was used, they, too, began to make the change. In 1975, monthly services in German were still being conducted at St. John's, Augsburg, but the use of German (in the Upper Ottawa Valley) has now all but died out."[57]

In the city of Ottawa, similar forces were at work in churches that had been established by immigrants who settled in the Ottawa Valley

---

[57]   Rev. Kenn Ward, *A Brief Historical Account of the Lutheran People in the Upper Ottawa Valley of Ontario.* Unpublished paper (May, 1976) 7-8.

before the turn of the 19th century. St. Paul's Evangelical Lutheran Church in Ottawa was organized in 1874 by Lutherans from Pomerania who had emigrated after the Franco-Prussian War (1870-71). A school which offered German, as well as religious instruction, was organized soon after. While English services were occasionally conducted, a demand for regular English language services arose only toward the end of World War I. These were then held twice a month. At the same time, regular confirmation classes in English were organized. Also, a decline in the knowledge of German made English-language religious instruction imperative, and in March 1922, the congregation resolved to establish a regular English Sunday school for children who were unable to attend German language religious instruction. In 1932, a full English program was inaugurated, with regular English services being presented every Sunday evening. Heretofore they had been held on alternating Sundays. At this time, attendance at German services outnumbered the English attendance about two to one. German religious instruction and German language services were discontinued between 1939 and 1946, essentially during the years of World War II. However, occasional German language services were held again after World War II, essentially to serve German immigrants who arrived after the war.

Similar trends are evident in Lutheran churches in Western Canada. The first attempt to organize German Lutherans in Western Canada was made in 1872, in response to an appeal by members of the Church who had come up the Red River from St. Paul, Minnesota. After several meetings and baptisms, the group disintegrated when most of its members returned to the United States. Responding to the missionary work of F. Petereit, of the German Baptists, to win converts to his faith, some 40 Lutherans who had settled in Winnipeg in the 1880s requested that the Canada Synod send them a minister to strengthen local Lutherans in the faith. In response to the appeal, the Reverend H.C. Schmieder arrived from Philadelphia to serve as Lutheran missionary for Manitoba and the Northwest.

Other Synods soon followed. Responding to rumours that German Lutherans had settled north of the American boundary, Reverend H. Brauer, of the Missouri Synod in North Dakota, in 1890 undertook an exploratory journey to the Northwest. Following his trip, he recommended the Synod send a full-time missionary to develop the new field, and in 1891 the Reverend H. Buegel arrived to serve Winnipeg and the Northwest. The Ohio Synod, in turn, entered the Northwest following a split in Trinity Lutheran of Winnipeg, in which members of the congregation that had separated from the old church turned to the Ohio Synod to send them a minister.

Once established, the different synods competed with each other for the allegiance of Lutherans in Western Canada. New ministers were recruited, both from the United States and from seminaries in Germany. Following this, the different churches joined the largely German American synodical bodies that had organized them. Because of the distance from established centres to the east and to the south of the Canadian border, these synods established local, semi-independent bodies as soon as possible. At the same time, these retained their connection to the larger synodical bodies centred in the United States.

Despite the general dispersion of Lutherans across the West, the relatively intensive work of different synods active among them made these less vulnerable than Lutherans in Eastern Canada had been to proselytizing Churches that sought to win their membership. At the same time, it put the different synods into a good position to establish seminaries to train pastors. Thus, the Missouri Synod established Concordia College to train pastors for its ministers. Similar training institutions were also established by the Ohio Synod and by the Synod of Manitoba and the Northwest, which was part of the Canada Synod.

As most Lutheran immigrants in Western Canada had arrived later than those in Eastern Canada, the war propaganda did not affect their churches as much as it did German Lutheran churches in Eastern Canada. That is, the churches were still very much under the control of the immigrant generation.

The Canada-educated generation had not yet reached the stage where they held important decision-making positions in the different congregations. In time, however, influences that brought about language loss in Eastern Canada were also to affect German religious groups in Western Canada. One such influence was the educational system. Bilingual education was abolished in Manitoba in 1916. Further west, no bilingual educational system was ever established. Whatever bilingual education existed was abolished or circumscribed during the war. The Saturday schools that were established to teach children German did not offer students sufficient knowledge of the language so that they could use it effectively. As a result, children growing up in the Anglo-Canadian milieu were often unable to follow a German sermon.

Some congregations sought to counter this by starting classes in which children were taught German. Such efforts tended to be short-lived. To certify that children would understand the lessons, Lutheran churches then started teaching lessons in Sunday school in the English-language. This, however, did not solve the language problem because the children who couldn't follow the Sunday school lessons in German also had difficulty understanding the German language sermons once they had reached adulthood. To deal with this problem, churches started to introduce English-language sermons.

Writing of the language transition at Immanuel Lutheran, in Landestreu, Saskatchewan, Norman Threinen states that the introduction of English was considered necessary because, being educated in English public schools, many young people no longer had a good understanding of the German. Simultaneously, intermarriage outside the community meant that one partner didn't understand German. To serve these people, some English services were introduced.[58] This observation is supported by Gilbert Johnson, in stating that English was introduced into St. Paul's Evangelical Lutheran of Langenburg, Sakatchewan, "due to the intermarriage between Germans and members of other ethnic groups, as well as to the decreasing use of German among the young people...."[59]

The English-language service, when introduced, tended to be attended by a minority of the congregation. Eventually, more and more church members attended the English-language service. In time, the English-language service was placed on an even footing with the German language service, eventually replacing it as the main service. As time went on, the older generation died off, to be replaced by more and more of the Canada-born. Eventually, German services were performed largely for older people, many of whom had difficulty with the English language or felt more comfortable with the German language services in which they had grown up.

---

58 Norman J. Threinen, *Immanuel Evangelical Lutheran Church, Landestreu, Saskatchewan, 1895-1970.* Ms. N.p., [1970] 18.

59 Gilbert Johnson, *"In His Service" 75 Years St. Paul's Evangelical Lutheran Church at Langenburg.* [Langenburg, 1965].

This progression of English gradually replacing German as language of the church services is most clear in the case of churches that received few immigrants. Thus, St. Paul's Ev. Lutheran, Langenburg, which received few new immigrants either after World War I or World War II, sought to introduce alternate services in German and English in 1936. This proved unsuccessful because the pastor didn't have a sufficient command of the English language. This changed when the existing pastor retired, in 1943, and a new bilingual pastor took his position, in 1944. With this, English language services were introduced. German language services ceased in 1965. A similar pattern of transition is evident at Immanuel Lutheran, Landestreu, Trinity Lutheran, Lemberg and Christ Lutheran, Neudorf, all of which introduced English-language services in the1930s or 1940s and ended their German language services some 30 years later.

The language transition from German to English, which was well under way in German Lutheran congregations by the time World War II broke out, slowed somewhat with the influx of new immigrants following the war. This strengthened the immigrant element, notably in the urban centres where the majority of immigrants settled, contributing to a prolongation in the use of German in the churches they joined. This was the case in particular where a church received a heavy influx of new arrivals. At times this also led to divisions within a congregation and the departure from the church of Canada-born members.

Despite the arrival of new immigrants, churches that received the new arrivals in time either gave up the German services or limited them to the older immigrant generation. This was the case, for example, with Trinity Lutheran Church, Regina. The church was organized in 1906, by the Reverend George Gehrke, who, stationed in Winnipeg, served as travelling missionary for the Ohio Synod of the Lutheran Church. The congregation grew rapidly and in time had some 10 per cent of Lutherans living in Regina associated with it. It received additional members after both the First and the Second World War and by 1950 had just under 3,000 members. In 2003, its membership expanded still further when it merged with St. Paul's Lutheran of Regina, which had been founded by post World War II German immigrants. Starting out as a unilingual German church, by 2003 St. Paul's, as Trinity, provided both German and English-language services. In 2010, Trinity Evangelical Lutheran was the only Lutheran church in Saskatchewan that still provided a regular

German service, a service to meet the needs of the older immigrant generation.

Other urban German Lutheran churches underwent similar developments. Trinity Lutheran, Winnipeg, which was founded in 1888, introduced English language services in 1929. Although still bilingual by the time World War II ended in 1945, English had become the predominant language, in particular for the Sunday school and youth groups. However, with the arrival of the post World War II immigrants, a German Youth Group was organized in 1954. The new immigrants also revitalized the regular German services. By 2010, however, the church no longer had German services.

The Evangelical Lutheran Church of the Cross, Winnipeg, was organized in 1905. Until 1921, church services were only in the German language. Then, teaching children the "Word of God" became difficult because many of the youngsters had difficulty understanding the German. To rectify this, a school was started to teach children the German language, but the school closed two years later when the pastor retired. English services were then held occasionally. In June, 1921, bi-monthly English services were introduced Sunday evenings for children speaking only English. However, in 1922 English services were dropped, due to poor attendance. Attempts to reinstate English in 1925 and 1926 were defeated by the congregation. In 1929 a German school teacher was hired. However, the school was closed that same year because of poor attendance. In 1930, English services started to be held regularly. English and German services continued during World War II, with the German services expanding in particular after the arrival of new immigrants after the war. German services were still being held in 2010, but by then the main service was in the English language. German services were attended primarily by the older generation of immigrants.

St. Peter's Lutheran Church, Winnipeg, was founded in 1930 by former members of the Evangelical Lutheran Church of the Cross. English had become the only language used in its Sunday school by the time of the Second World War. To deal with its financial problems, the church contemplated uniting with First English Lutheran Church in the summer of 1944, provided that First English Lutheran was willing to introduce a bilingual service. This option ceased to be an alternative when the latter refused to introduce a bilingual service.

The situation changed for St. Peter's with the arrival of post-World War II immigrants, these being attracted to St. Peter's by the fact that it was bilingual. The membership of St. Peter's grew rapidly, with as many as forty souls at one time being received. The church helped the new arrivals find jobs and housing. An English language school was opened for the new arrivals. A German young people's society was started, with as many as sixty people or more attending. In addition to an English Sunday school, there was a German Sunday school. On special occasions the church became overcrowded, and the debt that had burdened the church for some time was rapidly being paid off.

The arrival of post-war immigrants didn't radically alter the overall pattern of language transition. At first, English tended to be offered primarily to the children of these new arrivals, who were starting to have difficulty comprehending Bible lessons in German. The problem arose, first, in Sunday school, then in regular services. English services at first tended to attract a minor portion of the children or grandchildren of the new arrivals. As more and more of the older generation, who also tended to be the immigrant generation, died off, attendance at English-language services increased, while attendance at German language services decreased. Eventually, only the old and recently arrived attended the German language services.

Rural German language congregations in Manitoba that had been established by pre-World War I immigrants in such areas as Steinbach, Broken Head or other areas of Manitoba no longer had German services in 2010, essentially because they received few immigrants. The only rural Lutheran churches outside of Winnipeg, Manitoba, that still had German language services in 2010, had been established by newly arrived Russian-German immigrants who had come to Canada after the 1980s.

German Lutheran churches in Alberta and British Columbia followed a language transition similar to that found in provinces to the east of them. For example, Immanuel Lutheran, founded in 1909 in Lethbridge, Alberta, had only German services until the mid-1920s. English services were introduced in 1926 because many members of the congregation no longer had a good command of the German. Gradually the German was given up. German services were reinstated in 1950 when the Federal government brought in immigrants as beet workers. In 1951, regular German services were offered twice a month. As the number of new arrivals increased, attendance at German services began to outnumber that at English services. By 1956, however, attendance at German services began to decrease and that at English services to increase. This led to a decline in the number of German services being offered by 1958.

Founded in 1904, St. Peter's Evangelical Lutheran Church, Edmonton, introduced English-language evening services in the 1920s to meet the needs of members of its congregation who no longer had a good command of the German. In 1933, the congregation decided to move English to the main 11:00 o'clock service, and the German service was moved to 9:30 a.m. In 2010, the church no longer had German language services. St. Paul's Lutheran Church, Edmonton, was founded in 1951 by German post-World War II immigrants. For about 25 years services were in the German language. Gradually the need for English language services made itself felt as children of the immigrants gradually lost command of the German. With this, English-language services were introduced. By 2010 English had become the main language in the church service, with German services being held at 9:30 for the immigrant generation.

St. Paul's Lutheran Church, Rosenthal, Alberta, offered English services on the fourth Sunday of each month in 1952. From 1963 to 1967, a bilingual English and German service was given every Sunday during the summer months. In 1967, an English service was introduced every Sunday. German services were reduced to two services a month plus festival days. In 1968, the church changed its name to Rolly View. All congregational meetings were held in English, with minutes of the meetings being recorded in the English language. At St. Peter's Lutheran, Scapa, Alberta, English services were inaugurated in 1937. In time, attendance at English-language services increased, bringing a corresponding decline in attendance at German language services, which were discontinued in 1961. German Lutheran immigrants in Calgary founded Resurrection Lutheran Church in 1965. The congregation maintained German services for a number of years, but by the mid-1970s the language used in Sunday school services and youths programs of the church had changed from German to English.

Similar developments are evident in British Columbia. In Vancouver, for example, three churches still had German language services in 2010. All Sunday morning services were either at 9:00 or at 9:30 a.m., with the main Sunday morning church service, at 11:00 a.m., in the English language. One of these churches, St. Martin Luther Church on Fraser

Street, was built in 1947. Its membership reflects the German immigrant community that lived in the area in the mid-1960s, their ages in 2010 ranging from the 60s to the 80s or older.

While German Lutheran churches were giving up the language of the founding immigrant generation, the central organizations of Lutheran churches were replacing German with English. For example, minutes of the Evangelical Lutheran Synod of Manitoba and other Provinces were at first entirely in German. In the early 1940s, more and more reports were submitted to the Synod's head office in English. By 1949, the minutes of the Second Biannual Convention of the Evangelical Lutheran Synod of Western Canada were published only in English.

When in 1955 the Synod explored the reasons for the language change, it found Lutherans born in Canada preferred a pastor who spoke English well, while more recent arrivals preferred a pastor who was fluently conversant in German. More students were entering the Seminary who had either an inadequate knowledge of German or no knowledge at all. These changes all pointed toward German decreasing and English becoming the language used in the German Lutheran Church and its different organizational structures.

By the end of 2010, the bulk of what had at one time been German Lutheran congregations in Canada were using only English or using English as their main language of service. Where German survived, it essentially served the ever-shrinking number of seniors of the immigrant generation.

Mennonites

The Mennonite Church had its beginning in 16th century Switzerland. While Martin Luther and John Calvin set out to reform the Catholic Church, more radical elements during the Protestant Reformation maintained that Calvin and Luther hadn't gone far enough. They challenged practices such as infant baptism, the unity of church and state, and the authority of priests. In 1525, radicals who called themselves Swiss Brethren re-baptized each other to publicize their conviction that Church membership should be voluntary and the Church distinct from the remainder of the world. They won others to their beliefs, who came to be known as Anabaptists (re-baptizers).

Persecuted for their beliefs, with many of them dying a martyr's death, Anabaptists fled Switzerland to seek refuge in surrounding states. Here, they won more converts. In 1563, the Dutch priest Menno Simon joined the movement and soon assumed a leading role in ministering to congregations and articulating the theology that guided them. Under his guidance, Anabaptists came to be known as Mennonites.

Anabaptists refused to partake in military service and swear oaths of loyalty to temporal rulers. Acknowledging the rights of the state in civil matters, they also maintained that the Christian's primary loyalty was to Christ. They also insisted on a strict separation of Church and state. To this end, they stressed codes of behaviour that served to separate adherents to the faith from the outside world. Differences of opinion regarding these codes at times led to splits among the Anabaptists. Thus, in 1693, disagreements arose among Swiss Brethren Anabaptists in Alsace over Church discipline and nonconformity to the world. Jacob Ammann, a leader of the group insisting on strict discipline, left the Brethren and established a new Church. His followers came to be known as Amish Mennonites or Amish.

Anabaptists continued to face persecution in the environment in which they found themselves. To escape this, beginning in the 1540s, Dutch Mennonites sought refuge in Poland and, later, in Prussia. In the late 1780s, many of the Mennonites that had settled in Prussia took advantage of Catherine the Great's offer of freedom from military service and control over their own schools and took up land in southern Russia.

Other Mennonites left for North America, the major migration beginning in 1683, when Mennonites in Krefeld, Germany, accepted William Penn's invitation to settle in Pennsylvania. They established Germantown, where they founded the first Mennonite congregation in North America. They were followed by some 4,000 Swiss and South German Mennonites, as well as 200 Amish Mennonites.

Mennonites planted their religious communities in Canada following the American Revolution. They established their first community in Canada in the Niagara Peninsula, in 1786. This was followed by the formation of a larger community in the Waterloo region, and the establishment of smaller settlement in the Markham area and elsewhere.

First Mennonite church in Ontario. Artist's rendition of Benjamin Eby's Meeting House, 1813. Courtesy of J.M. Snyder/Mennonite Archives of Ontario.

Mennonites who left Russia in the 1870s and 1880s organized their religious communities on the East Reserve and the West Reserve, in Manitoba. Other Mennonite reserves were established in Assiniboia and further west as land here opened up for settlement and a land shortage developed on the East and West reserves. Mennonites also streamed in from the United States and Russia. The next major waves of Mennonites entering Canada came in the 1920s and after World War II. Unlike earlier arrivals, these seldom established new rural settlements but rather settled in existing Mennonite settlements or in Canada's developing urban centers.

Mennonite religious communities differed in one major way from most other religious communities established by Germans in Canada. More than any other German religious community, except the Hutterites, Mennonites had, through their years of spatial withdrawal from what they saw as "the world," established a close link between religion and rural settlement. That is, they identified the rural life as a way of life that was pleasing to God. This caused them to strive to make their rural community as independent as possible, and at the same time encourage codes of conduct to reinforce their isolation from the outside world. The use of the German language was one means used to isolate the faithful from the outside.

In this context, language loss was not merely the replacement of one language of communication by another, as in most other German religious communities. Rather, it tended to be part of a larger pattern of transformation that saw Mennonites give up their tradition of spatial withdrawal from the world. Different Mennonite groupings went through this transformation at different rates. In the following, I will look at different Mennonite sub-groupings, exploring changes within their communities as they let down their barriers against the world and, in the process, replaced German with English in their church services. As language change among all German religious groups was influenced by generational influences, and Mennonites made a more detailed analysis of this change than did other German groups, the findings of Mennonite scholars may help shed a light on changes that affected all German religious groups discussed in this study.

Conference of Mennonite Brethren Churches

Of the major Mennonite sub-groupings, the Conference of Mennonite Brethren churches moved the furthest from giving up German and adopting English as their language of communication. The Mennonite Brethren Church emerged in Russia in 1860, at a time when a renewal movement swept through the Mennonite settlements there. Encouraged by the preaching of the German Pietist Eduard Wuest, people converted through his work felt that the established Mennonite Church was stifled by formalism and spiritual stagnation. They began to meet separately for Bible study and prayer. In January 1860, they withdrew from the established Church and formed the Mennonite Brethren Church, with emphasis on baptism by immersion following conversion.

From 1874 to 1880, Mennonite Brethren left Russia for America, where they settled in the Midwestern United States. Soon they were involved in missionary outreach. In 1883, two Mennonite Brethren went to Manitoba to seek converts among Old Colony Mennonites settled there. Converts established the first Mennonite Brethren church in Canada, in 1888, near Winkler, Manitoba. American Mennonite Brethren also moved to Saskatchewan, where they established several congregations after 1895. The Church organized itself into a conference in about 1910 when representatives of different Mennonite Brethren congregations met to form the Northern District of the North American Mennonite Brethren Church.

The Church expanded rapidly in particular after the arrival of some 20,000 Mennonites from the Soviet Union between 1923 and 1927, with about one-quarter of the new arrivals being Mennonite Brethren. It was strengthened further with the arrival of more refugees after 1945, many of whom were Brethren. Further expansion by the Mennonite Brethren Conference came about with its absorption of the *Allianz Gemeinde* and the Krimmer Mennonite Brethren Church. The *Allianz Gemeinde* had been organized in Russia in 1905 to bridge differences between Mennonite Brethren and the larger Mennonite Church. The Krimmer Church, which emerged from the *Kleine Gemeinde* in the Russian Crimea (Krim) in 1869, merged with the Mennonite Brethren Conference in 1960.

The Mennonite Brethren Conference has much in common with mainstream evangelicalism. It emphasizes adult baptism following the confession of faith. With its focus on seeking to build the Church through a spiritual rather than a spatial withdrawal from the world, it emphasizes the moral separation between the Church and the "world." It is the most urban of Mennonite churches, with the highest percentage of university educated members.

Except in instances where these serve older members, most Mennonite Brethren churches abandoned German for English between the 1940s and the 1970s. In 2007, they ended publication of their German language periodical, which had been founded in 1880, and had served as a Mennonite Brethren magazine since 1945.

Insight into this process may be obtained by looking at the language change examined by Edinger, who sees this change among Mennonite Brethren as having been initiated by generational influences. Language change in the different churches began when a generation emerged that could no longer benefit from the German language service. The initial response of churches was to focus on the use of German language schools, usually Saturday schools, to counter this trend. This tended to work for a short period, but after some time the children lost interest in the schools and failed to attend. By this time, the parents were making little effort to speak German in the home and depended upon the school to pass a knowledge of German on to the children. The result was that Sunday school teachers began to use English to assure that everyone understood the lessons. By this time, the teachers tended to have grown up in Canada and were more familiar with English than German, encouraging them to teach in English rather than German.

The change from German to English was also encouraged through intermarriage, to keep married couples in the church rather than having them attend English churches. Language change was encouraged by endeavors at church outreach. With their emphasis on adult conversion, Mennonite Brethren placed great emphasis on mission work and vacation Bible schools for the children. In particular the vacation Bible schools sought to attract as many neighborhood children as possible, so conducted Bible instruction in English. The question then arose as to what to do with English-speaking children who converted during the course of these meetings. The same problem arose when conversions accompanied evangelical meetings sponsored by churches in the English language so as to attract as many people as possible in the neighborhood. In these situations, the German language stood in the way of disseminating the Good News and integrating non-German speaking converts into the congregation.

Edinger describes these influences on language change as it occurred in the Mennonite Brethren church in Vineland. The Vineland Mennonite Brethren Church was founded in 1932 by 27 members who had left the United Mennonite congregation in Vineland. In time, new members were attracted and the congregation grew. Services at first were strictly in German. Not only that, from the very beginning of the Mennonite Brethren Church, its members maintained a very close connection between religion and language. This was especially true of Russian Mennonites who had arrived in Canada between 1924 and 1927, encouraged by the many years that German-speaking Russian Mennonites had lived as a separate community, which had led to the merger of their ethnic and their religious identity. Also, in particular many of the 1923 to 1927 refugees had received a good education in German while in Russia, which had imbued them with a strong love for the German language and German culture in general. This was further encouraged by German aid provided to Mennonites when they sought to leave the Soviet Union and emigrate to Canada.

This encouraged the refugees who started Vineland's Mennonite Brethren congregation not only to have their services in German but also seek to ensure that such services would continue for their children.

Thus, not long after it was organized, the church not only expanded its programs to include a youth society, a choir and two women's missionary societies, but also placed a great emphasis on the education of its young, establishing a German language school for this purpose.

Despite these efforts, it was found in 1950 that after 20 years of operation of the language school, children in Sunday school answered more and more in English. By then, the majority of the Sunday school staff had been educated in Canada, which made it difficult for them to instruct in German. Without church sanction, Sunday school instruction gradually changed to English.

Although still strongly committed to the German language, during the 1950s the congregation permitted an increased use of English, in particular for the young. In 1951, the youth group was given permission to purchase English hymnals at its own expense. In 1953, a special English language week-night program for youth was started to encourage faith formation. In 1959, the church granted ministers permission to use English for the annual baptism classes, if necessary. In 1959, the church council granted permission to purchase one hundred English translations of German hymnals generally used by the congregation.

During all this time, the German language school was operating. The increasing necessity to use English, despite the school, suggests that a considerable number of the children were not attending language classes, or that the school wasn't providing children with a sufficiently good knowledge of German so as to benefit from religious instruction during Sunday school or church services.

This problem was related to a broader issue, namely evangelical outreach of the congregation, which arose in 1959 when the congregation participated in the planning and execution of an area-wide evangelical campaign conducted by the English-speaking Swiss Mennonite evangelist, George Brunk. Less problematic for the congregation was the Vacation Bible School mission begun by its young people in the Stoney Creek-Hamilton area. In this case, there was less possibility for English-speaking converts joining the Mennonite Vineland church. At the same time, young adults in the church were given the opportunity to practice their faith and mission in English.

In the meantime, in the early 1950s, attendance in the German Saturday school was sharply declining. An appeal by church leaders for members not to neglect the study of German by the young reversed the decline in attendance temporarily, but by the end of the 1950s school attendance was again in decline. The question of whether or not to continue the German language school was debated by the congregation in 1959, with 28 members voting to continue the school and 10 voting for its termination. This indicates that the congregation itself was becoming ambivalent about the school's continued existence and usefulness.

The 1960s brought further changes that encouraged the decline of the German language in the church. One was the decision by the congregation to engage a full-time pastor. Until the mid-fifties, pastoral care had been provided by ministers largely without remuneration. In 1960, the congregation completed the construction of a new church and hired a professional pastor. Although they knew German, pastors were trained in Canada and had received much of their training in the English language. Consequently, they were more comfortable in that language. At the same time, they tended to see the German language as hindering their outreach into the larger community. They therefore discouraged its usage.

Records of a church council meeting in September 1960 noted a marked decline in attendance at the Wednesday night Bible study and prayer meeting, all still in German. This caused the church council to raise the question whether the time had arrived to introduce a fully bilingual Sunday service. The pastor, youth leader and Sunday school superintendent were requested to explore the matter. The week following the council meeting, the congregation recommended the appointment of a committee to prepare a plan for the introduction of bilingual worship.

In his appeal to the congregation, the pastor and his committee stressed that many youth members could no longer follow the German language service. The congregation voted on the issue, with 63 members voting for the introduction of an English-language service, none against, and one-fifth of the assembled members abstaining. Soon after, the congregation voted for a bilingual worship service, with the English service lasting fifteen minutes, and the German service, thirty. At the same time, parallel bilingual prayer meetings were proposed. These measures were approved at the church's annual meeting that was held in September 1960.

In this way, during his first year of service, the pastor had moved the congregation into greater congruence with its English-speaking members and with the larger community. The gradual loss of commitment to a unilingual German service in the fifties was gradually making way for the unilingual English service. Children who were introduced to English Sunday school in the mid-forties were becoming members of the congregation. Young adults who had participated in running the summer Bible school and mission Sunday school were now young parents and both groups had an important influence on shaping the language policies of the congregation.

This could not fail to affect the fate of the German language school. At the September 29, 1960 general meeting, which saw the provisional implementation of the bilingual service, voting members also decided to continue the German school, with 24 voting for the school, six against, and the remainder abstaining. Although the vote carried, the motion showed that fewer than half of the members present were in favour of its continuation. This did not bode well for its existence. Its demise was further encouraged by the decline in student attendance, despite exhortations by church leaders that parents send their children to the school. On December 7, 1963, after thorough discussion, the congregation voted 42 to 14 to close the school. Of the total 63 members who attended the meeting, seven abstained, showing that two-thirds of the members present voted to close the school.

The demise of the school happened in the context of new programs that the church was interested in pursuing. Throughout 1962, pressure had been growing in the congregation to begin a children's Wednesday evening recreational and religious instructional program in November. Its purpose was religious nurture of the congregation's evangelical outreach among children in the larger community. This occurred at a time when a growing number of parents were no longer interested in sending their children to a German school, but interested in mid-week religious training for them. This was further encouraged by the belief of many in the congregation that the church should give real meaning to its weekly invitation, as spelled out in its bulletin; that everyone was welcome. The drive to give real meaning to this invitation was supported in particular by the younger segment of the congregation. Thus the German language school was replaced by a community outreach program directed at children.

This was followed by the attempt of the congregation, directed in large part by its pastor, to further expand its outreach into the larger community. Not only children were targeted, but also younger members of the congregation who had married non-Mennonites and all non-German speaking families in the larger community. English became increasingly vital to the congregation's activities. In 1964, by a unilateral decision, the pastor and council decided on having baptismal service only in English. The formal reception of baptismal candidates as members of the church was also to be conducted in English. In 1964, while annual meetings did not deal with language related issues, a recording secretary for membership meetings was elected who decided to perform his duties in English. From this time on, pulpit committee minutes and council minutes were also recorded in English.

1966 witnessed the final stages of the transition to English unilingual services. In a council meeting on December 6, 1966, in preparation for the coming annual meeting, the pastor gained permission from the church council to present the congregation with a proposal to separate the German and English service, with the German service being conducted during part of the Sunday school hour, and the English service being presented 11:00 to 12:00. Initially, this proposal did not obtain enough support by attendants at the annual meeting to pass.

However, the pastor persisted. In preparation for the annual meeting in 1967, he raised the "Language and Worship service Problem" in an agenda for the board of elders. Three alternatives were drafted, each featuring a separate English service from 11:00 to 12:00. These were ultimately accepted for presentation to the congregation. Members of the church council were not allowed to argue against the proposals on the church floor. On January 11, 1968, the congregation voted to conduct German Sunday school and a German worship service from 10:00 to 11:00 during English Sunday school hours, with the English worship service presented after. After that, it was inevitable that the German language services would disappear completely. Within a little more than a generation, this Mennonite Brethren congregation had given up German as the language of service for its church, replacing it with English.

Edinger found similar patterns evident in Mennonite Brethren churches he looked at in Winkler and Winnipeg. Here he found that the Mennonite Brethren church in Winkler and the Mennonite church in Elmwood, a suburb of Winnipeg, had made the transition to English as the language of their major service in the 1960s. Also, by 1965 English had become the official working language of the Canadian Brethren Conference and the language of one of the official Mennonite Brethren publications.

Edinger sees language having become an issue for Mennonite Brethren as early as 1910, when Mennonite Brethren who had come to Canada in the 1870s appeared ready to begin the transitional process. This did not happen because of the massive inflow of immigrants, many of them Brethren, in the 1920s. Highly educated, many of them soon took a leading position in Mennonite society. At the same time, the newcomers took immediate steps to protect their heritage of *Deutsch und Religion*. However, their children did not accept the argument that the German language and the Mennonite Brethren religion were indelibly linked. This eventually led to the loss of the German language among them and the replacement of German by English in Mennonite Brethren church services.[60]

Edinger sees a number of significant influences leading to this outcome. He considers the educational system as having had a prime influence on the language transition. Mennonites did not have control of their schools (in particular after World War I.) This made it difficult for them to pass on to their children a good knowledge of German and an appreciation of the link between German and the Mennonite Brethren faith. A further important influence contributing to the language transition was the emphasis on crisis conversion, "occasioned by a profound sense of personal sinfulness, leading to a daily life of ethical purity and public witness...."[61] This encouraged the desire for outreach and mission, in particular among the idealistic young.[62] Another important influence leading to the language transition was leadership. The failure of the Church educational system had produced religious leaders who, in time, were not fully functionally bilingual. This, combined with the extra work to serve a bilingual congregation, encouraged ministers (particularly once churches had moved to hiring professionals) to press congregations to move to a unilingual service. This was further encouraged by the desire of ministers to reach the young,

---

[60] Gerald C. Edinger, *Crossing the Divide: Language Transition Among Canadian Mennonite Brethren, 1940-1970* (Winnipeg: Centre for Mennonite Brethren Studies, 2001) 192-199.

[61] Ibid. 201.

[62] Ibid. 201

many of whom had difficulty understanding German, as well as the larger English-speaking community.[63]

Mennonite Church Canada

The Mennonite Church Canada, founded in 1999, represents a union of three historic streams of Mennonite immigration: Swiss, Amish and Russian Mennonite. It also represents the union of earlier mergers, including two Ontario-based conferences that had integrated with Russian Mennonite sister conferences in Ontario in 1888. This integrated body, with about 14,000 members and 90 congregations, called itself the Mennonite Conference of Eastern Canada. This conference had its roots in the first Mennonite immigration to Canada, in 1786, with settlers coming from Switzerland and southern Germany via Pennsylvania. This group established the first Mennonite church in Canada, in 1801, in Vineland. Ministers of the different congregations established began meeting in about 1810 to decide on a common policy and lay the foundation for the conference. This was made difficult when conflict arose regarding modernization and change, which eventually led to a division of the churches, with those who chose to remain with the traditional form of worship and lifestyle becoming known as the Old Order Mennonite Church. Those who embraced modernization and change eventually established the Mennonite Conference of Eastern Canada.

The Western Ontario Mennonite Conference had its roots in the Amish migration from Europe to Canada, in 1822. In the 1880s, the Amish in Ontario divided into the "House" and "Church" Amish. Thereupon the "House" group became known as the Old Order Amish and the "Church" Amish organized themselves into the Amish Mennonite Conference. In the 1960s, "Amish" was dropped from the name and the group became the Mennonite Conference.

The Conference of United Mennonite Churches, the third partner in the Mennonite Conference of Eastern Canada, was organized by Mennonite immigrants from Russia who arrived in Ontario in the 1920s. This group was the provincial body of Conference Mennonites in Canada, founded in 1903 by Russian Mennonites in Western Canada. This conference had its beginning in Manitoba and Saskatchewan. The

---

[63]   Ibid. 201-202.

first Mennonites from Russia, including the whole colony of Bergthal Mennonites, arrived in Manitoba between 1874 and 1876. In the 1890s, Mennonites from Russia, Prussia, and the United States settled in Saskatchewan. The Manitoba group formed the *Bergthaler Gemeinde*. The Saskatchewan group formed the *Rosenorter Gemeinde*. Deciding to work together, leaders of the two groups, at a meeting in 1902, laid the groundwork for the Conference of Mennonites in Central Canada. All these different groups uniting led to the formation of the Mennonite Church Canada.

As the Mennonite Brethren Church, most congregations of the Mennonite Church Canada had replaced German with English in their services by the end of the twentieth century, with the same forces at work in Mennonite Church Canada congregations as in Mennonite Brethren congregations. Yet, the time and manner of change differed somewhat for the groups involved. This is true in particular of the Amish.

The Amish who continued to worship in meeting houses eventually became differentiated still further from their Old Order brethren. In 1923, these five congregations united to form the Amish Mennonite Conference. Although the Conference had no authority over the congregations, which jealously guarded their autonomy, annual meetings were held to discuss matters of common interest. Changes in the 1960s resulted in Conference Amish, in contrast to Old Order Amish, adopting a typical form of church leadership, including church councils, elders and pastors. In 1988, the Amish Conference united with two Mennonite groups to form the Mennonite Conference of Eastern Canada.

By this time, services in Amish churches that had joined the Mennonite Conference were largely in English. Language change in the different congregations tended to be gradual. Even though the Amish did not object to English being instructed in public schools, they were at first opposed to the use of English in their worship services because the English language was identified with being worldly and proud. English was first introduced into the religious service of these congregations as part of the Sunday school movement, with the first Amish Sunday school being held in Wellesley Township, in 1884. All teaching was at first in German. At this time, a German ABC reading book was introduced to teach German, serving most congregations until about 1930. Thus, Sunday school was seen as ideally suited to teach the children German as well as the faith of the fathers.

Gingerich observes that the Sunday school, "even though it started out as a German language school...ended up being the door through which the English language became acceptable in Amish worship."[64] Still, the change to English came gradually, spearheaded in particular by the young people. This is reflected in the hymnals used by the congregations. English hymns, which had been collected over time, were at first used by the young people at their "singings." They were included in the required church hymnal, thereby encouraging the language change that was occurring.

Originally, English hymns were at the back of the book; however, in the hymnal acquired in the 1930s, this order was reversed. English hymns, with musical notations, were in the fore-part, and German hymns, without musical notations, were in the back part of the hymnals.[65]

Similar patterns are evident in the general use of the German. Even after Sunday schools became acceptable, they operated under certain restrictions. All teaching was to be in German, including instruction in German reading for the children. Instruction was to be strictly from the Bible. "Lesson helps" for instruction were not sanctioned until the 1920s. Some ten years later, English-language instruction was introduced in the Sunday school. Not too long after, an occasional service was preached in English.[66] The result is that by the 1970s the only German used by Conference Amish congregations was perhaps the occasional hymn. With this, also, came further accommodation by the group, which eventually led to the replacement of German by English.

The "Church" Amish were, of course, only one group that eventually made up the Mennonite Church Canada. Looking at the language transition in the Mennonite Church Canada as a whole, Ens points to a number of influences leading to the language transition. He sees the change in the churches as part of a larger change in Mennonite society. The use of English came gradually, initially for those who needed it for business and official contacts. World War I increased the pace of change in that it increased the animosity toward Germans during the war. At the same time, it deprived Mennonites of their control over their schools, decreased the teaching of German and made the schools a vehicle for the assimilation of minority groups into the larger Anglo-Canadian milieu.

---

[64]   Orland Gingerich, *Amish of Canada* (Newton, Kansas: Herald Press, 1979) 69.

[65]   *Ibid.* 80.

[66]   *Ibid.* 95.

The arrival of some twenty-thousand Mennonites after World War I slowed the rate of change somewhat. Still, the influence of these arrivals was mitigated in that they did not form group settlements but rather scattered in small groups in different areas. They learned and adopted English faster than had the immigrants of the 1870s. In the churches, children and young people made the switch to English sooner than their parents. Congregations sought to counter these trends by establishing German Saturday schools. Also, members of congregations lobbied to ensure that a significant part of school programs in Mennonite Bible schools was in German to assure that future church leaders, and the young in general, would have a good knowledge of German. Furthermore, the *Mennonitische Verein zur Erhaltung derDeutschen Sprache* was founded to encourage the preservation of German.

However, such actions did little to counter the increased usage of English among the young. During the 1950s, Sunday school and youth meetings in Mennonite Church Canada congregations shifted to English, and by 1966 some 70 per cent of Sunday school classes were in English, compared to 30 per cent a decade earlier.[67] Baptismal services, which often followed the conversion of young people,also increasingly involved the use of English.

While the language change differed in the different churches, dependent to some extent on the number of new immigrants in a particular congregation, the overall transition of the Conference was to English. This was the case in 1956 when the move to a board structure brought a considerable number of younger members into official positions. As these were more comfortable in English, this led to an ever-increasing use of English in Conference meetings. In 1964, the Conference Chairman presented his report in English. In 1966, the entire *Yearbook*, published after each summer's annual session of Conference delegates, was published in English. At the ministers' conference, which had been held on the day prior to delegate sessions since 1927, German was used exclusively until 1965. Two years later the minutes of the meeting were published in English only.[68]

---

[67] Adolf Ens, *Becoming a National Church: A history of the Conference of Mennonites in Canada* (Winnipeg: CMU Press, 2004) 101.

[68] *Ibid.* 106.

About two third of Mennonites in Canada belong to the Conference of Mennonite Brethren Churches and the Mennonite Church Canada. Nevertheless, disagreement in the different churches over religious, social and economic matters led to numerous divisions among Mennonites. Usually, the sub-groupings that emerged tended to be small. As the language transition often differed for the different grouping, looking at some of these may provide further insight into the forces contributing to language change in the Mennonite community and among German Canadians in general.

Old Colony Mennonite Church

The Old Colony or *Fürstenland* Mennonites were part of the migration from Russia to Manitoba in the 1870s, along with the *Bergthaler* Mennonites. Both *Fürstenland* and *Bergthal* were daughter colonies of the "Old Colony" of Chortitza, the first Mennonite colony established in Russia. In Russia, the Chortitza or Old Colony Mennonites were poorer, less educated, and more conservative than the Mennonites who came to Russia later. This was to influence the evolution of their social and religious beliefs in Canada. Old Colony Mennonites could be compared to some extent to the Hutterites, or to the Amish, although more conservative than these. Their entire life, including language, clothing, education, furniture, self-government, mutual aid, village pattern, and all forms of custom, is shaped by their church concept. They observe the most extreme form of separation from the world and practice church discipline through the ban and avoidance. Contact with the outside world is kept at a minimum.

In 1895, to escape the possibility of having English-language schools imposed upon them, some Old Colony Mennonites left Manitoba for Saskatchewan, where another reserve had been set aside for Mennonites. Others left Manitoba for Saskatchewan in 1905 to take up land near Swift Current. In the 1920s a considerable number of Old Colony Mennonites left Manitoba for Mexico so as to be better able to retain their way of life. In 1936, the Old Colony Church was officially recognized.

The Church was strengthened significantly after World War II by the return of thousands of Old Colony families from Mexico, settling primarily in Ontario, Manitoba, and Alberta. Those settling in Ontario organized a congregation in the 1960s, with the aid of Church leaders in Western Canada. The Ontario congregation has evolved into having more members than any other Old Colony church in Canada. Canada's only Low German radio station, started in 2003, is located in Aylmer, Ontario, a centre of Old Colony settlement.

The Old Colony has resisted cultural assimilation and has remained separate from other Mennonite groups. While Old Colony members in Mexico and Bolivia have resisted technology, churches in Canada permit the use of cars and technology in general. Women wear dark print dresses and a black kerchief. Members have retained the German language (primarily Low German) for worship, although some English is used. Hymn singing is in unison. They are served by lay ministers, with the different congregations being loosely organized as a religious body.

Church of God in Christ, Mennonite

In 1859, John Holdeman, a Swiss Mennonite from Ohio, left his Mennonite congregation because he felt it was too formal, lacked spiritual vitality, and didn't sufficiently strive to strictly separate itself from the "world." His goal was to organize what he called "the true church which began with the Apostles".

The Church of God in Christ, generally known as the Holdeman Church, focused on rigorous church discipline and nonconformity and emphasized repentance followed by conversion. The movement attracted some followers among the Amish in Ontario, who later moved to Michigan to join a congregation there. Holdeman had greater success among Mennonites in Western Canada. In 1881, the bishop of the *Kleine Gemeinde* in Manitoba, Peter Toews, invited Holdeman to conduct services in Manitoba. Impressed with Holdeman's message, Toews joined the Holdeman Church, drawing one-third of the membership of the *Kleine Gemeinde* with him. With this, the Holdeman movement took root in Canada.

In 1902, several Holdeman families of Swiss origin from Oregon settled in Linden, Alberta, where they were joined by Russian German co-adherents of the Holdeman movement from Manitoba. Beginning in 1928, Holdeman Mennonites from Linden and Manitoba established a congregation in the Peace River area of northern Alberta. In the 1940s and 50s, Holdeman families spread to BC and Ontario, where they established congregations.

The Holdemans began their annual revival meetings in the 1920s and their mission work in the 1930s. They have mission programs in different provinces, as well as voluntary service units in Newfoundland and Quebec. In addition, they carry on missionary work in Spanish America, India, Nigeria, and in Europe. In 2005, their worldwide membership stood at about 20,600, with 18,130 in North America.

Concentrating on tracts and books, publishing is a priority for them. Their Church periodical, *Messenger of Truth*, was started in the early 20th century. The Holdemans emphasize self-sufficiency and separation, including separation from other Mennonite groups. Virtually every congregation operates its own elementary school. Modest in clothing and lifestyle, the men have beards and the women wear black head coverings. They worship in plain buildings. In the U.S., the membership still reflects the church's beginnings among Mennonites of Swiss-German and Kansas-Prussian ancestry. In Canada, the membership is derived primarily from people of Russian Mennonite background.

The language change from German to English was more rapid in Holdeman churches than in other Mennonite churches in Canada. Thus, in the 1950s, Russian immigrant communities used German as primary language in church life, both in worship and in official conferences. The only exception at that time was the Church of God in Christ, Mennonite, among whom English-language services were beginning to predominate.

Like the Old Colony Mennonites, the Church of God in Christ emphasizes spatial isolation from the "world." However, language has ceased to be criteria for defining separateness. Rather, the Holdemans use rural settlement, dress and other things to define their separateness. The absence of language to define the in-group, in this instance served to encourage the language transition from German to English.

Old Order Amish

The Old Order Amish emerged in the 1880s as Ontario Amish divided over the decision to build meeting houses for worship. Those who continued to meet in homes – the House Amish – emphasized traditional ways and came to be known as Old Order Amish.

From 1953 to 1969 Old Order Amish from Ohio established settlements at Aylmer, Chelsea and other parts of Ontario. The Old Order Amish are the most traditional of all Mennonite groups in Canada.

Members worship in homes and still use the *Ausbund,* an Anabaptist German hymnal dating back to the 16th century. Pennsylvania Dutch is the main language of their homes and in their church services, as well as some High German. In their dress, the men wear clothing usually fastened with hooks rather than buttons. Also, the men have beards but not mustaches. Like the Old Order Mennonites, the Amish have their own schools and teachers, children being taught from grades 1 to 6. Higher education is forbidden. They use horses for farming and horse-drawn buggies are their main means of transportation. For longer trips, they hire vans and drivers or take public transportation. Rules regarding technology, such as the use of electricity or telephone, are different for different communities. The group has its own publishing business, Pathway Publishers, in Aylmer.

Old Order Amish horse and carriage in Oxford County, Ontario, 2006, CC BY-SA 2.5

Summary

The largest Mennonite Churches, the Mennonite Brethren and the General Conference, have given up German or are on the way to giving it up for their services. German is retained by Mennonite groups that still focus on spatial withdrawal and separateness. As the Holdeman case illustrates, it will be retained by these groups as long as it remains part of the criteria used by them to differentiate between the in-group and the "world."

Hutterites

As the Hutterites have been more successful than any other German religious community in preserving the German language, it is important to also look at them. The Hutterite Church grew out of the Anabaptist movement in 16th century Europe. As the Mennonites, Hutterites believe that the major Protestant Reformers, such as Luther, Calvin, or Zwingli, had not carried the Reformation far enough. As well as advocating adult baptism, they want greater separation of Church and state. In keeping with Jesus's teaching against resolving conflict through violence, they refuse to bear arms. Also, Hutter's followers hold their property in common.

Whereas the Anabaptist movement that evolved into the Mennonite Church had its beginning in Switzerland, the Anabaptist movement that led to the establishment of the Hutterite Church had its beginning in the Habsburg province of Tyrol, in present-day Austria and northern Italy. As Anabaptists elsewhere, Anabaptists in Austria, then under the rule of Charles V, were severely persecuted in their homeland. In 1529, a Tyrolese Anabaptist leader by the name of Jacob Hutter decided to take his followers to Moravia, to where other dissenters from different parts of Europe had fled. Although Roman Catholic, local nobles were opposed to the Habsburgs and welcomed the refugees.

The Hutterites prospered during their early years in Moravia, in the second half of the sixteenth century. During what came to be known as the "Golden Years" of the Hutterites in Moravia, some fifty to sixty communities developed, with a membership of twenty to thirty thousand. In addition to agriculture, they produced ceramics, created handicrafts, as well as gained expertise in herbal medicine, with their medical advice being sought by the neighbouring communities.

Their situation altered when war broke out between the Habsburgs and the Ottoman Empire, in 1593. As the Ottomans pushed into southern Moravia, Hutterite communities were devastated. Those who didn't flee were killed or enslaved by the Ottomans. The Ottomans had no sooner been defeated when the Thirty Years War between Catholics and Protestants erupted, in 1618. During the war, which marked the pinnacle of the Catholic Counter-Reformation, the Habsburg emperor ordered his Moravian nobles to expel the Hutterites.

By 1622, the year of the expulsion order, a third of Moravian Hutterites had been killed or had succumbed to the plagues that accompanied the periods of unrest. Expelled from Moravia, the Hutterites sought refuge in Transylvania, where the ruler, a semi-independent Hungarian Protestant prince, was opposed to the Habsburgs. In Transylvania, the Hutterites re-established their communal lifestyle, only to abandon it after 1690. They revived it in Walachia, present-day southern Romania, the next area where the Hutterites sought refuge.

Following this, the Hutterites moved into north-central Ukraine, where they settled in Radichev. Life being difficult during the next seventy-some years, from 1770 to 1842, Hutterites were again forced to abandon communal living. They restored it when they moved to the Molotschna region of southern Russia. By this time, they depended almost exclusively on agriculture to make their livelihood. They had been in the Molotschna region for just three decades, when they decided to emigrate to North America, in 1874. As the Mennonites, they left following the Russian government's ukaz, in 1871, which introduced compulsory military service for all its male citizens. They were also unhappy with the Russian government's introduction of Russian language instruction in elementary schools, in 1864. Until then, Mennonites and Hutterites had used German exclusively.

At the time of their departure for North America, in 1874, Hutterites, with a membership of about 1,200, were divided into two groups. The *Dariusleut*, the followers of Darius Walter, had re-established a communal farm at one end of Hutterdorf, the village in the Molotschna region where they lived. The followers of the blacksmith Michael Waldner in Hutterdorf, or the *Schmiedeleut*, had not taken up communal living.

Communal and non-communal Hutterites, a total of 1625 people, emigrated from Russia between 1874 and 1879. About half established themselves in three *Bruderhofs*; the remainder took up homesteads. Of the latter, generally known as the *Prairieleut*, most eventually joined the Mennonites. Of the group that took up communal living, the *Schmiedeleut*, Michael Waldner's group, established their "mother colony" in Bon Homme County, South Dakota, along the Missouri River. Followers of Darius Walter, the *Dariusleut*, established "Wolf Creek," their first settlement, in 1875. Followers of the teacher Jacob Wipf, or the *Lehrerleut*, who arrived in 1877, established the colony of Elmspring that same year, in South Dakota. As these settlements expanded, Hutterites began to look for land to the north, both in North Dakota and Manitoba. In the 1890s, some Hutterites took up land in Manitoba, but soon after moved south again.

Hutterites began to look North again with a view of settling there when their situation worsened in the United States after the country entered the war on the Allied side in World War I. As the American Selective Service made no provision for conscientious objectors, Hutterite young men were incarcerated for refusing to enter the service after they were called up. Here, they were often mistreated, with some of them dying as a result. Hutterites were forced to buy liberty bonds and had their property confiscated when they refused. Also, they were forbidden to use the German language in their schools.

As a result, members of all Hutterite colonies, with the exception of the Bon Homme colony, moved to Canada within one year. The *Schmiedeleut* established six colonies and the *Dariusleut* five colonies in Manitoba, while the *Lehrerleut* established four colonies in Alberta. Although a few of the group returned to the United States after the war, in particular during the Depression, the remainder remained in Canada.

In North America, communal Hutterites have grown from some 500 individuals in three colonies to 35,000 in 368 colonies. While most *Schmiedeleut* moved to Manitoba in 1918, today they have colonies in North and South Dakota, Minnesota, as well as in Manitoba. All the *Dariusleut* came to Canada in 1918. Alberta, today, has the largest number, while others established communal farms in Saskatchewan, Montana and Washington State. In total, Alberta has the largest concentration of Hutterites, with about 130 colonies, followed by Manitoba with 85 colonies.

New Hutterite Colony, CC BY-SA 3.0

Hutterites differ from other Anabaptist groups through their emphasis on communal property, basing their belief on Acts 2:44, which states: "And all who believe were together and had all things in common; and they sold their possessions and goods and distributed them to all, as they had need." Except for brief periods, Hutterites have sought to live according to this exhortation for some 500 years. The attainment of salvation, for them, includes subjecting all aspects of life, including one's economic life, to the discipleship of Christ.

The Hutterite community, as such, has two main goals. One is to meet the needs of community members, be these social, economic, or spiritual. Another is to create boundaries to regulate the community's relationship with the outside world, in this regard creating a structure that helps the community meet its needs through its contacts with the outside, while at the same time serving to separate the community sufficiently so as to certify that contacts with the outside do not become a snare directing the community away from its main purpose, which is to serve Christ and lead the godly life.

Although today Hutterites are looking beyond farming as a means of making their livelihood, until the beginning of the 21st century Hutterites in North America have made their livelihood from farming. To assure that they would have sufficient land to support the members of a colony, a colony tends to have from 75 to 150 people, about half of whom are adults and the remainder children. When a colony reaches the upper limits of its membership (about 150 people), it subdivides, which in the 1950s occurred every fifteen years. Keeping the membership fairly low serves to maintain primary relationships, discourages bureaucratization, and helps to avoid exorbitant land purchases in the future.

Colonies are hierarchically organized. The minister is the head. Beneath him comes the colony manager, who looks after the colony's financial affairs. Then come the German language teacher and the directors of the different departments, such as crops, hogs, cattle, chickens. All positions are filled by males. A woman might be chosen as head cook. She might also supervise the gardening operations of the colony, which she generally carries out in co-operation with a male.

The minister, colony manager, German language teacher, and some additional elected members constitute the council of the colony. Meeting frequently, it plans the overall activities of the colony. All leaders are voted in by the baptized males of the community, thereby assuring that they reflect the ideals and goals of the community as a whole. This is further assured through meetings to discuss overall concerns.

To ensure separation from the outside world, colonies are generally located at some distance from towns and main roads. Contact with the outside world is maintained in several areas. One is the English-language teacher, who tends to reside in a town near the colony. Other contacts tend to be of an economic nature. This might include lumber yards or implement dealers. Hutterites generally operate the most modern farming machinery, be this for harvesting and seeding or raising hogs, cattle and poultry. They have their own shops to repair tractors and trucks. Generally, these also serve neighbouring non-Hutterite farming communities. To keep abreast of the most current farming techniques and enable them to operate and repair the most current farm machinery, Hutterites maintain contact with the department of agriculture at the local university, as well as subscribe to the latest agricultural and automotive journals.

Another area of interaction with the outside is in the area of politics, which, perhaps, is logical because the Hutterite community is a product of persecution at the hand of government. They were forced to move from place to place because of outsider intolerance of their beliefs and practices. This has generally made Hutterites suspicious of government. Suspicion was further encouraged by the Hutterite belief in the separation of Church and state, which includes the attempt to avoid the worldly power insofar as possible.

In Canada, Hutterites found it necessary to take cognizance of those in power when the Canadian government passed an act in 1919 which barred Hutterites from coming to Canada. Of course, by then most of the Hutterites who had left the United States to escape persecution had already settled in Canada and taken up land here. Hutterites were required to take further notice of the state when, in 1942, the Alberta government passed the Land Sales Prohibition Act, which prevented the transfer of land to "enemy aliens, Hutterites and Doukhobors," restricted Hutterite land purchases, as well as regulated the distance between a mother colony and a newly established daughter colony. Although the law was eventually repealed because it was found to be discriminatory, it nevertheless caused Hutterites to be aware of the attitude of others towards them.

To help sustain group solidarity and restrict contact with the outside, interaction is insofar as possible restricted to the Hutterite community. More than this, it generally takes place within the same sub-grouping, with *Lehrerleut, Schmiedeleut* and *Dariusleut*, for example, intermarrying within the group.

Hutterites set themselves off from the outside world through their attire, with clothes serving as symbols separating them from the non-Hutterite world. The same is true to some extent of their language. In their everyday conversation, Hutterites speak "Hutterish," which is similar to the German spoken in Carinthia, southern Austria, yet includes non-German words picked up as Hutterites migrated through Central Europe, into Russia and then to America. High German is used in their German language schools and religious services. English is used in the regular school and to communicate with non-Hutterites, usually on business matters.

German being important to perpetuate their religious heritage and for purposes of boundary maintenance, Hutterites do their utmost to maintain it. This is made possible through the control they have over their schools and the education of their children. At age three, children are sent to *Klein-Schul*, or kindergarten. About the age of 5, they enter the *Gross-Schul*, or German language school. Instruction here is offered by a married man selected by the colony. Children generally attend before and after they have attended the English-language school, where the teacher is usually an outsider. Children might also attend the German school on Saturday, where they practice writing and learn to read the German medieval script. They also study Bible stories and Hutterite history. Children attend Sunday school until they are baptized. Here the German language instructor teaches them songs, encourages them to memorize Bible verses as well as discusses subjects to help them better understand the Sunday sermon. In many respects, the Sunday school is an extension of the German language school, serving to instruct children in the group's heritage and tradition and to pass on its beliefs and approach to life.

More than any other German religious community, Hutterites have established a way of life that helps them not only to sustain and perpetuate their existence as a separate people but also serves them well in relating successfully to the world around them. Their emphasis on maintaining and perpetuating the German language is part of this strategy of survival. The language records their religious heritage and helps them define themselves as a people. At the same time, it serves as part of the social structure the community has established to separate the "Church" from the "world."

Baptists

Unlike most Christian denominations in Canada, which had their beginnings in Europe and then established themselves in Canada, the German Baptist Church had its beginnings in North America. It emerged during the anti-immigrant period in the United States, at a time of massive German immigration. Feeling threatened by this influx of non-English-speaking immigrants, many Americans felt that the way to deal with these people was to assimilate them as rapidly as possible. One way to do so was to expose them to the religious beliefs of the American majority. Conversion, from this perspective, was the Anglo-American means used to assimilate new immigrants.

One means of achieving this was through missionary work among recently arrived German immigrants, the majority of whom were either Lutheran or Catholic. To this end, the Baptist Home Mission Society supported the work of Konrad Anton Fleischmann and Joseph Eschmann. Both had been exposed to the influence of the Swiss Separatist Movement, which encouraged adult baptism. Fleischmann, who arrived in the United States in 1839, and Eschmann, who arrived in 1843, began their work among German immigrants with the support of the American Baptist Home Mission Society. It did not take long for their work to bear fruit, with converts establishing churches in different parts of the United States. At the first conference of German Baptists in North America, in 1851, pastors from New York, Philadelphia and Buffalo participated.

By this time, the German Baptist work was already expanding beyond the eastern American seaboard states, as well as into Upper Canada in British North America. In the case of the latter, the work here had its beginnings with August Rauschenbusch, who was to become an instructor at Rochester Theological Seminary and whose son, Walter, became one of the main spokespersons of the Social Gospel Movement in the United States. Informed that some forty thousand German immigrants, many of whom were neglected by their own denominational clergy, lived in Waterloo County, Rauschenbusch visited the county in 1847 on behalf of the American Tract Society to ascertain whether it would be advisable to employ a German colporteur there.[69] Encouraged by his success, in the summer of 1851 Rauschenbusch took three months leave from the Tract Society to conduct evangelical services in Canada. This resulted in the baptism of a number of people, who in 1851 organized the Bridgeport German Baptist congregation. Soon after being organized, the congregation had about 40 members.

Similar success was achieved in other areas, and by 1852 three more churches had been organized in Upper Canada, one in Berlin, another at Wilmot and the third at Woolwich, which in 1853 recorded a membership of 31, 40 and 21 respectively.[70]

It appears German Baptists established themselves only in the Waterloo area of Upper Canada at that time. Church membership grew gradually in the congregations established, dependent in large part upon the ability of a minister to win new adherents, in particular among new arrivals. Thus, the Baptist church in Berlin, with some 88 members shortly after it was founded in 1848, in 1904 had a membership of 200.[71]

In the meantime, the German Baptist work in Western Canada had begun, largely at the initiative of English-speaking Baptists in Manitoba. J. B. Eschelmann had moved from Berlin, Ontario, to Winnipeg, where he became a member of First Baptist Church of Winnipeg. Encouraged by the Manitoba Baptist Convention, he began gathering together a small group of Germans in Winnipeg. When the Bible class he taught reached about thirty members, he let his provincial Baptist Convention know that additional manpower would be required to adequately nurture his flock.[72] He also contacted the German Baptist Convention in the United States. In response, the Reverend J. C. Grimmel, who had joined the Baptist Church as a result of the missionary work of Oncken in Germany, was sent out in 1883.

---

[69] Frank H Woyke, *Heritage and Ministry of the North American Baptist Conference* (Oakbrook Terrace, Illinois: North American Baptist Conference, 1979) 71.

[70] *Ibid.* 72.

[71] *Ibid.* 72.

[72] Edward B. Link, "North American (German) Baptists," in *Baptists in Canada*, ed. Jarold K. Zeman (Burlington, ON: GR Welch, 1980) 91.

Grimmel reported that the few German Baptists in Western Canada, "ein zerstreutes Häuflein," should be visited from time to time. However, the Reverend F.A. Petereit, who made his first visit in 1884, in 1886 decided to stay in Western Canada.[73] Here he served as German Baptist missionary for Winnipeg and the British North-West. Almost from its beginning, Petereit's work was supported both by Canadian Baptists and German Baptists of the United States, with the first two hundred dollars coming from the Women's Missionary Society of the Manitoba Convention.[74] However, the promised four hundred dollars from the Dominion Board of Eastern Canada never arrived, eastern leaders apparently finding it difficult to respond to the needs of foreigners in the West.[75] However, in 1888, German American Baptists committed themselves to providing the four hundred dollars. This initiated a cost-sharing principle, systematized in 1902, in which Western Canadian Baptists co-operated with German Baptists in the United States and Ontario in supporting the missionary work among Germans in Western Canada.[76] In addition to helping to provide financial aid to the German Baptist venture in Western Canada, the German American Baptist Conference also supplied pastors for the Canadian field.

The work in the West expanded gradually. Several years after F.A. Petereit's arrival, C. Poehlmann, who had been serving a German Baptist church in Ontario, was sent to Western Canada. F. A. Mueller started his work in Alberta, primarily serving parishes in Rabbit Hill and Leduc. Parishes were also started in Souris, in Manitoba, and in Ebenezer and Edenwold, in Assiniboia. In 1889, Pastor Petereit formally organized the first German Baptist church in Winnipeg.

---

[73]   *Ibid.* 91.

[74]   *Ibid.* 91.

[75]   *Ibid.* 91.

[76]   *Ibid.* 92.

First German Baptist Church became McDermot Avenue Baptist Church as part of the language change from German to English. Public Domain.

As the Canadian churches were very poor and thus found it difficult to attend sessions of the Northwest Conference, which included Michigan and southern Illinois, of which they were a part, the Northwest Conference recommended, in 1901, that the Canadians form their own conference. With this, the Northern Conference was organized. At its first meeting in Leduc, Alberta, in 1902, some 14 churches with 394 members were represented.[77] By 1900, the combined membership of German Baptist churches north of the American border numbered 1,406. Strengthened by immigration, in particular of German-speaking Baptists from Poland and Russia, as well as by missionary work among German-speaking immigrants already settled here, Baptist membership in the Northern Conference increased to 36 churches by 1918, with a membership of 2,948.[78]

World War I, which had broken out in 1914, brought into focus the issue of language use for German Baptists. American Baptists had initially supported the German work in the hope of helping to Americanize the immigrants. This included encouraging Germans to give up their mother tongue and adopt English as their main language of communication. That is, they saw the organization of the German

[77] Woyke, *Heritage and Ministry of the North American Baptist Conference*, 263-264.

[78] *Ibid.* 271.

conference as a temporary phenomenon that would cease to exist once the immigrant generation had disappeared and their offspring had sufficient knowledge of English to be able to join English-language congregations. With the cessation of German emigration to the United States and Eastern Canada, an increasing proportion of the membership of German Baptist churches in these areas consisted of the second generation. Growing up in North America, many of them had an insufficient knowledge of German to be able to follow German language services. This put these churches in a dilemma. It had been tacitly agreed upon that the German Conference concentrate on presenting its services in the German language. Yet, young people in many of the churches found themselves more comfortable in the English language and preferred English language services. The problem became still more acute when, during the First World War, some states, such as Iowa, forbade the use of the German language in public, including in Sunday church services.[79] At the same time, some member churches of the Conference, as those in Lycoming County, Pennsylvania, had become entirely English-speaking, already by 1895. This encouraged some churches to respond to the anti-German hysteria during the war by withdrawing from the German conference. At the same time, young people, although remaining loyal Baptists, demanded English-language programs of their own.[80]

Similar changes were at work in Canada, in particular Eastern Canada. With the opening of the Canadian West, when the majority of immigrants began moving to Western Canada, Ontario churches found that the immigrant generation of their membership was dying off and that an inadequate knowledge of the German language was being passed to the second generation. To deal with this problem, the church in Berlin, Ontario, for example, found it necessary by 1907 to present evening services in the English language.[81] This trend was accelerated by the anti-German feelings generated by the outbreak of World War I. In 1918, all church services in the Berlin (Kitchener after 1916) Baptist church were conducted in English.[82]

---

[79]   *Ibid.* 282.

[80]   *Ibid.* 293.

[81]   *Ibid.* 73.

[82]   *Ibid.* 73.

As the German Conference continued to use the German language, churches that had switched to English, such as the German Baptist church in Kitchener, were put in a difficult position. To deal with this problem, the Kitchener church transferred its affiliation from the German Conference to the English-language Ontario and Quebec Convention. With the loss of Kitchener, German Baptist churches in Ontario were reduced from a membership of 932 to 732.[83]

The German Conference did the best it could to deal with these changes. Rather than give up the German, pastors of the German General Conference maintained that they would continue their work in the German language. They felt that although some second-generation members of their churches would leave, others would stay and help to bridge the gap between new immigrants and North American society, thereby facilitating the integration of new arrivals into American society. This change would be slow, necessitating that their churches remain bilingual for many years.[84]

At this time, the Missionary Committee of the General Conference in the United States became self-supporting. Similar developments were afoot in Canada. In 1920, the co-operative agreement between German pastors and the Baptist Union of Western Canada (originally the Manitoba Baptist Convention) was terminated. Concerned with the integration of German Baptist churches into its fellowship, the Baptist Union of Western Canada, which had been fostering the Baptist work among Germans, demanded closer co-operation with them, requesting that the German churches in Canada become full members of the Union. Northern Conference leaders, however, chose to remain with the German American Conference. With this, the Baptist Union of Western Canada fully recognized that the German Baptist churches were no longer part of its fellowship. The German churches were now dependent upon themselves to carry out their work.

These changes could not help but affect German Baptist congregations in both Canada and the United States. As German immigration declined considerably after World War I, the establishment of new churches decreased. Churches that gave up the German in their services transferred to other conventions. This included a number of

---

[83] Linke, "North American (German) Baptists," 96.

[84] Woyke, *Heritage and Ministry of the North American Baptist Conference*, 294.

churches in Canada. Thus, the German Baptist church in Vancouver left the German Northern Conference and joined the English Pacific Conference. It was followed by the Prince George church in 1935 and by the church in Kelowna, which joined the Pacific Conference in 1936. Similar changes were evident elsewhere, resulting in a decline in the total number of churches in the Conference. Numbering some 289 churches in 1919, these fell to 266 churches in 1931.[85] After this, the number of churches remained fairly steady. In this situation, congregations that insisted on the exclusive use of the German generally disbanded once a few elderly members were left. Gains in the number of churches came from the division of congregations, with those wishing to use only English in their services forming their own congregations. These increasingly remained with the Conference rather than joining English-language fellowships.[86] Also, as families became smaller and transportation improved, smaller rural churches tended to merge into one congregation, thereby reducing the number of churches.

Losses and gains generally kept the number of churches steady. However, church membership increased during this period, encouraged largely by the inflow of immigrants coming primarily from Eastern Europe. Although this led to the establishment of few new churches, the new immigrants strengthened many of the existing churches that were still bilingual. The membership of Conference churches continued to grow, from a total of 31,758 in 1919 to 38,710 in 1946. [87] When the German language Conference was first established, it had been assumed that the mission work of the Conference would be restricted to the use of the German language, with the Conference ceasing to exist once this mission had been fulfilled. The churches no longer using the German language would automatically join an English-language convention. This would, no doubt, have led to a rapid demise of the German language Conference, with its work ceasing first in the United States, where immigration was less pronounced and the German language tended to be given up more rapidly.[88] However, the decision to continue the German

---

[85]   *Ibid.* 363.

[86]   *Ibid.* 363.

[87]   *Ibid.* 303.

[88]   *Ibid.* 359.

language work in bilingual congregations changed all that. At the same time, the Conference increasingly focussed on a bilingual rather than on a strictly German ministry, with leaders advocating greater use of the English. In 1923, the Conference began publishing *The Baptist Herald*, which was directed particularly at young people, who were becoming increasingly less familiar with German. By 1940, General Conference sessions were conducted in English, and two years later the Conference changed its name to The North American Baptist General Conference.[89]

At the same time, the focus of German Baptists in North America altered. The mission that had involved bringing "the gospel to German immigrants in North America," was increasingly altered to bringing "the gospel to North America, regardless of language."[90] This, of course, meant that a German-oriented Church body had to find a place for itself in the larger institutional framework of Baptists in North America. In this regard, several influences encouraged the Conference to remain separate. German Baptist leaders felt that both the heritage of German Baptists and their experience in North America had led to their developing distinctive worship and fellowship patterns.[91] Also, in regards to theology, the German Conference tended to be more orthodox than its English-language counterparts. Although this did not pose a problem for English-language churches, German Baptists and their leaders were apprehensive about the liberal stance of many English church leaders. This encouraged the Germans to remain within their own Conference rather than become a sub-group in the larger English-speaking conferences.[92]

The focus on ethnicity encouraged the German Conference not only to concentrate its work on German immigrants but also to direct its attention to Central Europe. This was true in particular following World War I and World War II, when the Conference became extensively involved in relief work, in particular among the many refugees. Following this, the Conference became involved in immigration work. As emigrating to the United States was extremely difficult because of strict security regulations, the Conference sought to encourage

---

[89]   *Ibid.* 294.

[90]   *Ibid.* 362.

[91]   *Ibid.* 362.

[92]   *Ibid.* 362.

its co-religionists in Europe to emigrate to Canada. With this end in mind, the German Baptist Immigration and Colonization Society was established after World War I. Co-operating with Canada's major railway companies, the Society helped screen immigrants in Europe and aided them on their arrival in Canada. At the same time, it helped to steer them to areas where German Baptists were already settled and then helped them integrate into German language churches.

The work of the immigration society essentially ceased with the outbreak of the Depression. However, it was revived again after World War II under the name "North American Baptist Immigration and Colonization Society." In co-operation with the Canadian Christian Council for the Resettlement of Refugees, of which it was a member, the Colonization Society extended loans to the impoverished to help them emigrate and collected payments on transportation loans. Church leaders welcomed the immigrants, distributed Bibles, and informed new arrivals of the conditions they could expect here. They directed immigrants to German Baptist churches in the country as well as helped them find employment. Although the German Conference had taken the initiative in beginning this work, it was supported, in particular financially, by the Baptist World Alliance Relief Committee and the World Council of Churches.

The inflow of German Baptist immigrants after World War II continued to about 1955 when improving economic conditions in West Germany reduced the influx to a trickle. By then, the Conference had helped some 6,200 people, for the most part co-religionists, settle in Canada. The arrival of so many immigrants in a short period could not help but have an unsettling influence, in particular in Western Canada. Conference leaders welcomed the newcomers, in part in the hope of strengthening the existing churches, many of which were still bilingual. To encourage this, the Mission Society sought to discourage the formation of new congregations, except in areas where no German Baptist congregations existed. As the flow of immigrants increased, problems arose. Some bilingual churches introduced so much German into their programs that English-speaking members left.[93]

Nevertheless, the arrival of so many immigrants strengthened the German Conference's base. For example, the inflow of Baptist

---

[93]   *Ibid.* 433.

immigrants during the 1950s re-Germanized the three oldest Baptist churches in Alberta, those of Edmonton, Calgary, and Medicine Hat. In addition, twelve new churches, with 1,250 members in all, were organized by the immigrants. The arrival of so many immigrants also helped to revitalize the German language publications of the Conference. It gave new life to *Der Sendbote*, which increased in size and together with the *Baptist Herald* came out monthly. In the early fifties, a pressing need arose for a German hymnal. To meet it, the General Council reprinted 2,000 copies of the *Neue Glaubensharfe*.[94]

Just as the increase in German immigration immediately after World War II strengthened German Baptist churches, the decline in the flow of immigrants strengthened the forces of assimilation. With the decline of immigration, local churches became increasingly dependent upon attracting the young people in their church community or upon mission work in their immediate neighbourhoods to encourage church growth. As these neighbourhoods tended to be largely English-speaking, outreach meant making use of the English language to win converts. At the same time, although bilingual churches and churches that used only the German language often introduced Saturday German language classes to help pass the German to the next generation, this did not provide the children with a knowledge sufficient for them to follow sermons in that language.

Assimilation also had another effect. While the inflow of immigrants strengthened in particular German Baptist urban churches, as most of the immigrants settled in urban centres, relatively few of the new arrivals settled in rural areas or in the small towns. Rather, these areas lost population, with most of the young people there finding work in the major urban centres. Few of these arrivals still spoke German well enough to be able to follow the German service. They tended to join English-language churches. This meant that if the North American Baptist Conference did not want to lose these people, it had to provide for their needs. German American Baptist leaders became aware of this already prior to World War II, and became acutely aware of the language change in their congregations once war broke out. It was this change that caused the General Conference of German Baptist Churches in North America to remove the reference to ethnicity in its title and change its name, in 1942, to The North American Baptist Conference.

---

[94]   *Ibid.* 410.

Assimilation was also encouraged by other factors. Intermarriage generally resulted in both partners opting for an English service rather than a German one which only one of the partners understood. Social mobility within the city as people moved from less desirable to more desirable parts of the city or to other cities where they may have found jobs often resulted in people joining non-German churches in their locality rather than a German church some distance from them. The language shift was further encouraged by a radical change in the media. Television and radio were largely in the English language, and, unlike the more traditional media, had access to every home. Also, finding and maintaining one's employment meant perfecting either one's English or French. All this resulted in a situation where German meant less and less as people went about living their everyday life. To this were added the forces of secularization. These forces not only drew people away from religion; they also offered to people new foci for their loyalty. Under these conditions, religious leaders who wanted to counteract these influences were required to strip religion of its non-essentials, which encouraged dropping the ethnic language and concentrating on disseminating the Gospel. This all served to de-emphasize the use of the German in church services and encouraged the use of English.

Under these conditions, bilingual churches frequently dropped the German, replacing it with English. Older members in this situation frequently left the church and joined a church that still presented German language services. Unilingual German churches, established for the most part by post-World War II immigrants, became bilingual. In this situation, young people were generally attracted to the English-language services while the older people continued to attend the German services.

An example of some of these influences affecting language change may be seen in the case of Central Baptist Church, in Kitchener-Waterloo. The church was founded in 1953 by post-World War II German Baptist immigrants attending Benton Baptist Church.[95] At first, services were solely in German. In 1972, Central Baptist had its first pastor, Pastor Grams, who was more fluent in English than German.

---

[95]   Benton Baptist itself was founded as a German church in 1848. It retained German language services for about 70 years. At first it became bilingual. In 1916, in response to the anti-German war hysteria, it dropped German altogether.

Pastor Grams concentrated on the youth, who were less fluent in German than their parents. Under him, meetings of the church youth group switched entirely to English. On November 1ˢᵗ, 1976, the first English service was held at Central Baptist and soon after English-language services became regular, with Pastor Grams serving the congregation in both languages. After that, in particular the English congregation continued to grow, and the church hired both a German and an English pastor. By 1984, the majority of the congregation attended the English-language services, with German language services being attended primarily by the older people. With the church being bilingual, at first congregational meetings were held in both German and English, but by 1985 German was dropped and congregational meetings were conducted in English. As this trend continues, it is only a matter of time, as the older people die off, that German language services will end and church services will be entirely in English.

The language shift was equally rapid elsewhere. Thus, for example, none of the four German Baptist churches organized in Winnipeg by post-World War II immigrants any longer offer German services. The only Baptist church in Winnipeg offering German language services is McDermot Avenue Baptist.[96] Four of the post-war German Baptist churches that had been established by immigrants in Alberta are already extinct, (three in Edmonton, and one in Lethbridge), as is also the re-Germanized church in Medicine Hat. What remains are their surnames, the dishes brought to church suppers, and the sparsely attended German worship service preceding the English service each Sunday.

The more than forty new churches organized by the former German North American Baptist Conference since 1960 today concentrate on winning membership in their neighbourhoods, rather than seeking to serve any specific ethnicity. Insofar as they concentrate on winning non-English speaking members, they seek to win members among the new waves of immigrants entering the country, all of them not of German descent.

---

[96] It is rather ironic that one of the new immigrant churches, Mission Baptist Church, was formed by members who wanted only German services. About this time, also, another group separated from McDermot Avenue Baptist because they wanted only English services.

Other Churches

Other German language churches went through a transformation
similar to that of the four largest denominations among German
Canadians, the Lutheran, Catholic, Mennonite and the Baptist.
That is, they gave up the German and gradually accepted English as
the main language of their church services. This was true no matter
whether their congregations were Seventh Day Adventist, Reformed,
Pentecostal, Church of God, or any other. Without going into detail, I
will briefly look at this transformation in two of these denominations, the
Evangelical Association and the Moravian Brethren.

The Evangelical Association (*Evangelische Gemeinschaft*) was
organized in 1803 as a result of the activities of Jacob Albright, a German
Lutheran convert to Methodism, who in 1796 had begun missionary
work among Pennsylvania Germans. Methodist in policy and doctrine,
the Evangelical Association concentrated on serving the German element
in both Canada and the United States. It established German language
congregations in both Eastern and Western Canada.

Language use became an issue for the Evangelical Association during
its early years. For example, in the Annual Conference of the Canada
Conference of the Association, held in Mildmay, in 1890, the Hespeler
Mission sent a petition signed by 40 members requesting the right to
have morning and evening services in English and German services in
the afternoon. They argued that these changes were necessary if they were
going to keep their young people. Language use was a problem not only
for the Hespeler mission. As Getz states: "The problem (of language use)
was not actually settled for the churches of the (Canada) Conference until
the war years of 1914-18 when as a product of the war, the work began
to move forward in the English language and continued to do so ever
after...."[97]

The language change may be observed by looking at Zion Church
of Crediton, Ontario, which had been one of the major congregations of
the Evangelical Association in Canada. The congregation was founded

---

[97]   Henry Getz, editor, *A Century in Canada: the Canada Conference of the
      Evangelical United Brethren Church* (Kitchener: Committee on Centennial
      Observance and the Historical Society of the Canada Conference of the
      Evangelical United Brethren Church, 1964) 14.

in the early 1850s as a result of the missionary work of circuit riders of the Evangelical Association among German Lutheran immigrants. At first, services were solely in German. In 1923, it was suggested that some English be introduced into the congregation's services for the benefit of the younger members. This was not acted upon. However, the next year it was decided to have English-language services the first two Sundays of the month. In 1924, 18 members of the congregation still subscribed to *Der Christliche Botschafter* and 31 members subscribed to *The Evangelical Messenger*, the publications of the Association. By 1931, only 9 homes still subscribed to the German language publication. By 1929, English was extended to the first three Sunday services of the month, if there were five Sundays in the month. In 1932, the language question was voted on by the congregation for the last time in the church's quarterly conference. Fourteen voted to hold services entirely in English and one voted to retain some German. With this, German disappeared from the congregation's services.[98]

In 1946, the Evangelical Association merged with the United Brethren in Christ Church, to form the Evangelical United Brethren Church. The Brethren in Christ were also known as Tunkers in Canada. The Church, strongly influenced by the Baptists, Presbyterians and Methodists, emerged among Germans in Pennsylvania in the 1770s. Tunkers started coming to Canada in the 1780s, following the American Revolution. They appear to have been bilingual already when they came. In 1967, the Evangelical United Brethren Church merged with the United Church of Canada.

The Moravian Brethren Church was organized among German immigrants following the arrival in Canada of German-speaking Moravians from Volhynia in the 1890s. Church life was first organized under the leadership of Andreas Lilge. By 1896, three congregations had been formed: Bruderheim (1895), Bruderfeld (1895), and Heimthal (1896). In 1896, the first minister arrived from the United States, who served the German congregations and at the same time preached among the English in the neighbourhood. However, the English settlers were unresponsive to his message. Nevertheless, at different times attempts were made to introduce English into the services of the German

---

[98] Zurbrigg, Howard G. "*Songs of Zion: the Story of Zion Church, Crediton, Ontario* [1969] 30.

congregations to help disseminate the Gospel. Throughout the years, also, ministers provided English-language services on a "wanted" basis, at least every three weeks. In 1926, an attempt was made by the minister, for example at the Heimthal congregation, to make English services more regular. However, this did not succeed. But in time, language change became more and more inevitable so as to serve younger members of the congregation and also English-speaking visitors. The change came after World War II, with the language transition from German to English coming to completion in the Heimthal church in 1958.[99]

Summary

Looking at the language transition in churches established by Germans on Canadian soil, the following generalizations may be made. Churches were organized essentially by the immigrant generation. Insofar as possible, immigrants sought to perpetuate the beliefs and practices they brought from the homeland. The use of the German language was one of these practices. Generally, other influences also nourished the desire to plant and perpetuate the use of the German language by the congregations established. In many cases, immigrants believed that perpetuating the German language would help their advancement in the larger society and in the world at large. Also, at times, a moral quality tended to be attached to the language. In particular prior to the revelation of Nazi excesses, a frequent justification for retaining the German language was that, as the bearer of German culture, the language reinforced the values and ideals inherent in the Christian message.[100]

Language change came after the immigrant generation no longer controlled the affairs of the congregation. Usually, this occurred when the Canadian-born offspring no longer had sufficient knowledge of the German to follow the church services. In all situations under study, language change in the churches was accompanied by a degree of conflict, with the older generation wishing to keep the German and the younger generation wishing to introduce English. This was especially the case

---

[99]   Kurt H. Vitt, *Heimthal Moravian Church: An Evangelical Community Church Founded in 1896* (Edmonton: Heimthal Moravian Church, 1971) 14.

[100]   See, for example, Grenke, *The German Community in Winnipeg 1872-1919*, 125-126.

where church policy was decided by members of the congregation rather than by the Church hierarchy. In these instances, except in churches where language was used successfully to separate the community of believers from the outside world, the language conflict tended to be reduced to the following question: Is it the purpose of Christ's Church on earth to perpetuate the Christian message of salvation or a certain cultural tradition? In all instances where the question was raised, the answer tended to be the same: the purpose of the Church is to proclaim Christ's message of salvation.

The end result was the introduction of English into the church service. This tended to be done gradually, with English being introduced, but German being retained for the main part of the service. Generally, the minority of the congregation, usually consisting of the younger generation, at first tended to attend the English services. In time, more and more people attended these services, with the German language service eventually being switched to a less important time, while the English-language service became the main service. In time, the number of German services tended to be reduced, being offered as long as enough older people were present to benefit from them.

While the language transition occurred during the entire period under examination, the war years appear to have helped to accelerate this transition. The wars and the propaganda produced to encourage people to fight, denigrated the German nation, the German national character and the German language. It divided the world into white and black, good and evil, with the German language associated with evil. All this contributed to accelerating the process of language change, in particular in situations where congregations were under the control of the Canada-born, who had been educated in English-language schools. Furthermore, the wars encouraged antagonism against anything German, and even anything foreign, motivating the host society to implement laws that restricted the ability of Germans to transfer their linguistic heritage to their children.

The prevalence of immigrants in a congregation influenced the language transition. Thus, the influx of immigrants after World War I helped keep alive the German language services, in particular in Western Canada, where the community had not been as extensively assimilated as in Eastern Canada. The influx after World War II helped keep alive the German services in particular in many of the urban churches, where most of the immigrants settled. Rural settlements that received very few immigrants at that time were little affected by the new arrivals.

In areas where the immigrants settled, the new arrivals had varying effects. They tended to have the least effect on Catholic parishes. Here, the tradition of the ethnic parish had a long history. Furthermore, the parish was established by the Church hierarchy and the priests were provided by the same hierarchy, making it more difficult for any faction to break away from a particular parish and establish its own. Furthermore, appointed by the Church hierarchy, the priest was less dependent upon the congregation and thus in a better position to mediate between different factions that arose. In Protestant congregations, the arrival of the newcomers tended to be more divisive. This was especially the case in instances where the influx overwhelmed the existing congregations. Coming from different areas of Europe and having different experiences, the immigrants were often at odds with parish leaders who had been in power when they arrived. When this involved language use, it might cause the group that had been most committed to language change, prior to the arrival of the newcomers, to leave the congregation and establish its own church. In the meantime, with the new influx, the use of German became more important in the church. At the same time, immigrants often established new churches, thereby strengthening the German religious community in general.

The language transition from German to English varied from denomination to denomination. Thus, the language transition tended to take longer for denominations that used language as a means of separating the community of believers from the "world". Thus, the language transition was slower among Mennonites and Hutterites than among Lutherans, Catholics or Baptists, who did not use language to separate themselves from the larger society. In the Mennonite community itself, the language transition was faster among the Holdemans, for example, who dropped language as a means of separating themselves from the outside world, than it was among the Old Colony Mennonites, who retained the German as an important feature of their religious identity.

Language retention was also influenced by settlement patterns. This becomes evident not only in case of the Mennonites and Hutterites, who focused on establishing self-sustaining communities, which contributed towards maintaining their linguistic identity. It is also evident when one looks at other communities, such as the Lutherans. Lutheran settlements, such as the Loyalist settlements, where Germans tended to be broadly distributed among a larger English-speaking population, lost their linguistic identity much sooner than did Lutherans in German block settlements that were established in Waterloo County.

The language transition was influenced by the educational system set up by the different religious groups. The greater control the community had over the teaching of German and using it in the everyday environment, the slower was the transition from German to English. The educational system further affected the language transition in that, generally, it did not provide students with a solid enough grounding in the German language to permit students to use it effectively in their church setting and in their everyday life. As will be seen in the next chapter, that is because German was often taught as an ancillary subject. The teaching of it was often haphazard, with significant breaks occurring in its instruction.

The language transition, where it occurred, had different effects on the different Churches. Among Catholics, for example, it meant the decline, and in some instances the demise, of the ethnic parish and the growth of the territorial parish. Ethnic parishes had been set up by the Church hierarchy to serve the different linguistic groups that settled in North America. Such parishes were no longer necessary in instances where a group had lost its ethnic identity. In such instances, a priest might be appointed to serve the people in a particular area rather than a particular language group. At the same time, consideration was given to the fact that older members of the parish still felt more comfortable with the language of their homeland. The Church sought to meet their needs. In other instances, in cases where a new group of immigrants with a different linguistic background replaced the original members of a particular ethnic parish, consideration was given to having a priest who could serve the new parishioners and at the same time provide services to meet the needs of the older parishioners. This was the case, for example, with St. Joseph's, Winnipeg, where the Philippine priest serving the latest wave of immigrants that settled in the vicinity also presents services in German for the old parishioners of St. Joseph's.

Among Lutherans, the language change led to increased Lutheran convergence. In particular in Western Canada, Lutherans were divided into a number of national groups. While most Lutherans were German, the Canadian West also attracted a considerable number of Lutheran

Icelanders, Danes, Swedes, Norwegians as well as Lutherans of other national backgrounds. Like the Germans, other Lutherans had been served by state Churches in Europe and found it necessary to look to their own support in North America. They did so by organizing themselves into synodical bodies. Thus, the Swedes were organized into the Augustana Synod and the Norwegians into the Norwegian Lutheran Church. As among Germans, synods helped to preserve the doctrinal purity of the faith. They helped to train pastors or brought them from Europe to serve the different congregations.

Although the synods of the different national groups worked independently of each other, there was some co-operation. This was the case, for example, with the Lutheran Immigration Board of Canada, which brought all Lutheran bodies together, regardless of language spoken. Co-operation was also encouraged in the area of theological education. As some of the non-German groups had a small membership in Canada, they turned to the more numerous German Canadian Lutherans to help them train pastors. Thus, the Swedish Augustana Synod arranged for the training of its pastors at Lutheran College and Seminary, which had been established by the largely German Manitoba Synod of the ULCA. Further co-operation was encouraged through American influence, where the union of several Lutheran synods led to the formation of the American Lutheran Conference. This encouraged co-operation of Canadian branches of the new organization.

As churches of the different synodical bodies assimilated, ethnic isolation gradually decreased. This was further encouraged, for example, in the American Lutheran Conference, by different ethnic groupings interacting with each other on the Commission on Canadian Affairs and on the Home Mission Council. In this instance, ethnic boundaries were also bridged through the *Lutheran Voice*, which spoke for the American Lutheran Conference. When World War II broke out, co-operation was encouraged as the different ethnic synods co-operated in serving Lutherans in the armed forces. Also, urbanization was bringing an increasingly large number of Lutherans to the cities, thereby expanding the contacts between members of the different synods.

Furthermore, demands of the post-World War II refugee period, which led to the formation of Canadian Lutheran World Relief and the National Committee for Canada of the Lutheran World Federation, forced the different Lutheran synods to co-operate to meet these challenges. This was facilitated by the language change from the mother tongue to the common language of English that the different ethnic communities were experiencing.

Once ethnicity had a decreasing importance in dividing Lutherans, theological and confessional differences emerged to take a dominant influence in dividing Lutherans from each other. These influences also brought into focus common confessional and theological influences that united Canadian Lutherans. This, in turn, fuelled the drive to overcome divisions among Lutherans and work toward the establishment of a united Lutheran Church in Canada. However, despite such efforts, differences have persisted. Caused largely by the Missouri Synod's insisting on doctrinal differences it saw separating it from other Lutherans, this led eventually to the emergence of two larger Canadian Lutheran Church bodies.

Among Baptists, the decline of the use of German in their churches led to a reorganization of the North American German Baptist Conference, and its de-emphasis on its ethnic background. To justify its further existence, it differentiated itself from the larger body of English Baptists by emphasizing its conservative nature.

Among Mennonites, the language change had varying effects. Among Mennonite Brethren, it essentially led to the rejection of the values that had caused Mennonites to withdraw from the world. These were replaced by a focus on transforming the world, a goal that had inspired Anabaptists when they first appeared on the scene in the early 16th century. It had a less profound effect on General Conference Mennonites, who sought to combine the focus on revival with a stress on values that had motivated communities to withdraw from the world. It had still less an effect on Mennonites who chose to retain their focus on separating the rural community of God from the world. In some instances, German was retained as a means of separation. In other instances, German was given up, with greater emphasis being placed on other customs that helped believers maintain the separation they saw existing between them and the "world." At the same time, the general de-emphasis on language use has had a negative effect on the sense of peoplehood that Mennonites had developed in particular in Russia.

The general loss of, or de-emphasis on, ethnicity also had another effect on the different German religious communities. Prior to this, much energy of the different Church groupings was expended on fighting to retain their ethnic identity. In all instances, language change involved separating what was seen to be the cultural dimension of the belief system from its core Christian message. It involved a re-definition of what it means to be Christian. This new focus encouraged all the groups under discussion to focus on outreach. This might involve sending out missionaries to convert non-believers. It might involve extending aid to people outside Canada or within the country. It also might involve outreach in the communities where the churches found themselves.

In summary, German churches started out seeking to preserve the language and religious traditions immigrants brought with them from Europe. They were able to do this as long as the leadership drew on the German language and old country traditions to build and preserve the particular religious community. These efforts were challenged once a generation arose in the Church that no longer had a good command of the German language. This happened at different rates in the different congregations, depending upon the ability by a parish to perpetuate the German language among its offspring. In almost all churches a common pattern emerged: that is, a generation emerged that no longer had sufficient command of the German to be able to follow the service in German. At that stage, the congregation generally introduced English-language services. The only situation where this did not arise is in religious communities in which German was seen as a means of separating the community of believers from the outside world. In all other situations, English gradually replaced the German, with German services eventually being provided essentially for the older members of the congregation that still had a good comprehension of the language. It will cease to be used once this generation dies off.

As the church had always been the centre of social life in the German Canadian community, the language transition in the churches reflects changes, not only in German Canadian religious life but also in the German Canadian community at large. It indicates the demise of the element in the German Canadian identity that most clearly differentiates it from most other communities and thereby marks an important step in the community's integration into the larger Canadian society. This may be observed when looking at other aspects of German Canadian life.

Schools

The school is the main means through which a community passes on its language, traditions and beliefs. That is why Germans, no matter of what background, sought, insofar as possible, to set up their own schools. At the same time, they sought to make use of the Canadian public school system to help perpetuate in particular their language. In this, they achieved their goals only to a limited extent. This may be observed by looking at the different schools German-speaking immigrants sought to establish. Their success in attaining their goals through the schools very much influenced the extent to which they were able to transfer their cultural traditions, in particular their language, to their offspring.

The first attempt to establish a school for German-speaking children in what was to become Canada was made in Nova Scotia with the arrival of the foreign Protestants. In 1759, German Lutherans in Lunenburg appealed to the House of Assembly that the government provide them with a pastor as well as a schoolmaster. However, their request was ignored. The parishioners thereupon decided to search for a teacher without government aid and secured a schoolteacher in 1760. The school started with a large enrolment of students. Then the English missionary brought the teacher under his direction by arranging that he should be paid 5 pounds in addition to the salary he received. Thereupon German language instruction was abolished. As the teacher knew little English, he lost his position and the school was closed.

In Upper Canada, all schools in the German settlements were at first confessional. At the time of the passage of the Common School Act in Upper Canada, in 1842, there were 13 schools in Waterloo Township, 7 in Wilmot and 3 in Woolwich. The Common School Act divided townships into school districts and, as well, sought to regulate taxation in support of schools. Up to mid-century, German Catholics, Lutherans and Mennonites supported their own schools, with German serving as the language of instruction. At the beginning of the 1850s separate schools were subjected to the same conditions as public schools regarding language use and school attendance. In 1851, the Council for Public Instruction permitted French or German to replace English as the language of instruction. This meant that where Germans were the majority of ratepayers in Upper Canada, German could be used as the language of instruction in both public and separate schools. Although the exact number of German schools operational in Upper Canada is unknown, in 1851 the Township of Waterloo and North Dumfries, the townships where Germans were concentrated, had 79 schools with 81 teachers, and a student population of 5,250.[101]

Schoolchildren and teacher, Noah Martin, at Rummelhart School S.S. #9 Waterloo Township, Sept. 1899. Kitchener Public Library, Waterloo Historical Society, P-00789.

German parents, while supporting German language instruction, also insisted that their children obtain a well-functioning knowledge of English so as to prepare them for life in the larger English-speaking society. Although this was difficult at first, because few of the teachers were bilingual, in time teachers graduated who were capable of teaching in both languages. By 1854, German and English were taught in both public and separate schools. At the same time, pressure arose in the larger society that sought to abolish German as a language of instruction, because it was seen as interfering with the emergence of a homogenous nation. This, in turn, affected the ability of Germans to use the public school to perpetuate their linguistic identity. Concentrating on the public schools of Berlin, Ontario, the following will examine the process through which the Anglo-Canadians used the public school in Ontario to absorb the German Canadian minority linguistically.

The school was seen as playing a central role in absorbing linguistic minorities into the larger Anglo-Canadian society. Working through

[101]   Gottlieb Leibbrandt, *Little Paradise: Aus Geschichte und Leben der Deutschkanadier in der County Waterloo, Ontario, 1800-1975* (Kitchener, ON: Allprint Company Ltd., 1977) 116.

the Department of Education, which was founded in the mid-1870s, Anglo-Canadian administrators of the Department began their attack on bilingual schools with the insistence that English be adequately taught in bilingual schools. To achieve this, in 1885 the Department of Education made English compulsory in every school where it was not already the language of instruction. The Department required every school to teach English writing, spelling, composition, as well as translation into English. While enacted as a regulation, school inspectors at the local level certified that the regulation was implemented.[102] Other regulations furthered English-language instruction. In 1889, the then Minister of Education, George William Ross, introduced a regulation which stated that no teacher in the province can receive a permit to teach in a public or private school unless he or she passes an examination in English in every subject on the curriculum. Regulations introduced in 1890 required that the mastery of the English language by students in bilingual schools be the same as that of students in English schools. Another regulation passed that year required that French or German be taught in addition to English, thereby altering the 1885 regulation that merely added English to the curriculum of French or German schools.[103]

When the conflict between French and English Canadians regarding linguistic and religious rights led to the appointment of a commission to inspect French schools to determine the qualification of teachers and the students' knowledge of English in the province, a similar commission was also authorized to study German schools. The report of the German Commission, covering German schools of the counties of Waterloo, Perth and Bruce, shows that in 1889 all but two German teachers had regular certificates, indicating that they were well-qualified. German schools were found to be almost English schools, with German not being used as the language of instruction in any of them. In the majority of schools, German was taught only to the 2nd, 3rd, and 4th classes; all beginners were learning only English.

The Commission further concluded that learning German did not interfere with the acquisition of English by students and that no special

[102] Benjamin Bryce, "Linguistic Ideology and State Power: German and English Education in Ontario, 1880-1912," *The Canadian Historical Review* 94:2 (June 2013) 217.

[103] *Ibid.* 217.

corrective measures were required for German schools. Furthermore, qualified teachers who could teach both German and English were easily obtainable. The commission also noticed that in a large number of schools in Waterloo County in which there were German students no German was taught. By 1889, there were only 10 German schools in Waterloo County. Of the 2,332 students in these schools, 1,905 were of German descent. Of these, only 307 were studying German.

McKegney blames the first Waterloo County inspector, Thomas Pierce, who regarded the teaching of German as a threat to professional standards, for this decline.[104] However, Pierce was merely assuring the implementation of policies that had been initiated by the Department of Education in Toronto. The position of county inspector was created by the Ontario School Act of 1871 to bring the licensing of teachers more under government control and to help standardize the quality of education in different provincial schools. The example of Pierce shows that the Department of Education and its local inspectors co-operated quite effectively in encouraging the advancement of English and the decline of German in the Ontario school system.

When Pierce assumed his position in 1871, Waterloo County had 96 schools for a population of 40,251. Of these, 89 were elementary schools, 2 high schools, and 5 Roman Catholic separate schools, with a total student population of 12,445 and 152 teachers. In his report of 1872, Pierce stated that at least three quarters of the inhabitants of Berlin, Waterloo, Preston and New Hamburg spoke a foreign language and that 50 to 75 per cent of children made their first attempt to speak English when they started school. He further reported that in Waterloo County German was taught in 31 schools; in 8 schools all students learned German; in 14 schools 10-15 students learned German from one to three hours per week, in eight schools only a nominal amount of German was studied, and that in New Hamburg 120-150 students had no English-language instruction.[105]

To deal with this matter, Pearce introduced a system that certified that children learned English as soon as they started school. Also, he suggested a revision in the manner in which German teachers were examined. According to this new system, German teachers would be

---

[104] Patricia McKegney, "The German Schools of Waterloo County," *WHS* (1970) 54.

[105] Leibbrandt, *Little Paradise,* 120.

required to be fluent enough in English to cope with the same English examination paper as other teachers, and be competent in German as well. Their certificates would, however, still permit them to teach only in German language schools.

Germans of Waterloo County objected to this solution. To register their protest, a committee of citizens requested a meeting with the Inspector of the German Departments of all Ontario public schools. In this they followed the example of the *Deutsch-Canadischer Nationalverein* of Bruce and Grey that, a year earlier, had drawn up a petition requesting that in Ontario counties where German-English schools existed or were yet to be established, the county council appoint a commission or board of professional educators with authority to examine German teachers and grant certificates. Furthermore, it asked that one member of the board visit, with the county inspector or alone, all such schools in which German is taught, and that he be given the same power regarding the method of teaching and the general government of such German schools as the county inspector.

Responding to German pressure, the Council of Public Instruction ordered that county councils, within whose jurisdiction there were French or German settlements, be authorized to appoint one or more persons (who in their judgment may be competent) to examine teacher candidates in the French or German language at the semi-annual examinations. Furthermore, provisions were made to appoint a competent person to examine pupils in German, and that he report to the county inspector. A further regulation regarding German schools, in 1874, empowered county councils to appoint inspectors for forty of the municipalities in which French or German was the prevailing language.

Reports of the Public Schools of the Waterloo County, 1872-81, show that the total number of schools in which German was taught over the years was thirty-nine. The report also suggests, according to McKegney, that as the hiring and dismissal of teachers was controlled by the county inspector, County Inspector Pierce was using his power to discourage the teaching of German.[106]

Despite the findings of the German commission, Inspector Pierce complained that in particular at Berlin high schools the students' reading knowledge in English was sorely inadequate. He attributed

---

[106] McKegney, "The German Schools of Waterloo County," 54.

this to the fact that children had to spend their time learning German in the lower grades. In December 1899 school authorities for public schools set the period during which German would be taught from 8 to 9 a.m., beginning in January 1900. Germans objected to Pierce's claim that German language instruction interfered with the acquisition of English by students, and established the German School Society for the maintenance of German instruction. They saw in Pierce's assertion nothing less than an attempt to abolish German from their schools.

The creation of the German School Society not only stemmed the attempt by school authorities to phase out German as part of the school program but also encouraged parents to have their children learn German. From 1906 to 1909, the number of students studying German in Berlin rose from 800 to 1,029.[107] At the same time, English elements in the community insisted that if Germans wanted German in their schools, they should pay for it out of their own resources, rather than having it provided by the public purse in public schools. In the meantime, the number of students in German language classes steadily grew. For example, in 1913, the number of students studying German in Berlin public schools reached 1,459 out of a total of 1748.

While these changes increased the number of students exposed to German, one may question their effectiveness on the long-range preservation of the German language in the German Canadian community in Ontario. As Bryce makes abundantly clear, the school books made available by the Ontario Department of Education for teaching German were inadequate for preparing a person to function in both German and English on a bilingual basis. Too few teachers were made available for teaching German, essentially because, rather than an important subject, school officials saw it as equivalent to Art and penmanship. Furthermore, not enough time was allowed for teaching German wherever it was taught to prepare the child to use the language effectively once he or she grew to adulthood.[108]

German language instruction ceased altogether with the outbreak of World War I. In 1915, it was reported that 397 students in Berlin public schools had stayed away from German language classes without reason. Following this, school authorities abolished German language instruction

---

[107] Leibbrandt, *Little Paradise*, 133.

[108] Bryce, "Linguistic Ideology and State Power," 228-231.

in Berlin schools. By this time, of course, Berlin public schools no longer offered to students sufficient instruction in German that would allow them to use the language effectively in the everyday working world.

German language instruction fared no better in Catholic parochial schools in Ontario than it did in the public schools. In particular the Jesuits placed great attention on the religious schools, seeing these as the "foundation for a good and progressive parish."[109] They organized churches and schools wherever possible during the nine to ten years they laboured in Waterloo County. One of these schools was the Berlin Separate School, organized in 1859. The school from the beginning "taught in English." That is, classes were always "taught in English, except for German."[110] This, however, was not the case in all German Catholic Separate schools. Writing of German Roman Catholic Separate schools in Waterloo County, Inspector Cornelius Donovan writes, in 1887, that the teachers, "while instructing in reading, spelling, Christian doctrine, and sometimes other subjects in the mother tongue of their pupils, faithfully follow the departmental programme of English studies."[111] By 1916, however, the situation had completely altered. Writing of German language instruction in Catholic parochial schools in 1916, Theobald Spetz noted that there were hardly any German Roman Catholic parishes in Waterloo County where German was still taught. Although he regretted this loss, he nevertheless saw it as part of the natural process of assimilation.[112]

Similar patterns are evident in German Lutheran parishes that made the effort to establish parochial schools. Of German Lutherans, particularly the Missouri Synod placed great stress on the Christian Day School (*Gemeindeschule*), seeing it as an indispensable part of preserving and perpetuating the basic tenets of Lutheranism. At the same time, the Synod viewed maintaining the German language as equally important and saw English as threatening "the pure doctrine and polity" of their

---

[109] Spetz, *The Catholic Church in Waterloo County*, 195.

[110] *Ibid.*, 125, 127.

[111] Cited in Bryce, "Linguistic Ideology and State Power," 227.

[112] Spetz, The Catholic Church in Waterloo County, 43.

Church.[113] Christian Day Schools and German language instruction were seen as an important part in preserving and perpetuating the basic tenets of Lutheranism in the New World.

In Ontario, attempts were made by Missouri Synod Lutherans to establish Christian Day Schools in various localities, including Humberstone, where a school was started before 1860. In Fisherville, the school was founded under Pastor W. Linsenmann (1872-81). It was taught by the pastor until the first regular teacher was installed, in 1892. In Elmira, a Christian Day School was organized in 1894. Except for Fisherville, these first attempts failed. Part of the problem was the competition between the different Synods. This became problematic in particular in the smaller centres. In some areas, two or even three congregations were established where one would have sufficed to serve the local Lutheran population. Schools necessitated a financial outlay involving building costs, paying a teacher, etc., costs difficult to meet by small congregations. Thus, few Missouri Synod Lutheran congregations had a fully functioning Christian Day School. They couldn't afford it.

The 1912 Statistical Yearbook of the Missouri Synod shows that its Canada District, essentially covering Ontario and Quebec, served some 55 parishes, most of which were quite small, with under 200 members. Many also had fewer than 100 members. Of the parishes belonging to the Synod, 30 had a Christian Day School. Of these, one had one teacher. One school, in Ottawa, had three teachers. Of the remainder, the pastor served as teacher. Of schools in which the pastor served as teacher, 13 remained open 5 days a week. Thirteen of the remaining schools offered religious and German language instruction by the pastor on Saturdays, with students attending the public schools during the week.

Although a Christian Day School opened in Berlin, Ontario, it lasted but a short period. The most successful Christian Day School in the Canada District was opened by St. Paul's Ev. Lutheran Church of Ottawa, in 1871. The pastor served as teacher until 1885, when the congregation decided to hire a teacher. Most teachers remained a few years, but some, as H. C. Bruer, remained 30 years. By 1901, school enrolment had climbed to 124, and in 1903 a second teacher was hired.

---

[113] Robert M. Toepper, "Rationale for Preservation of the German language in the Missouri Synod of the Nineteenth Century," *Concordia Historical Institute Quarterly* vol. XLI – no. 4 (November, 1968) 165-167.

As in other Missouri Synod Christian Day Schools that operated 5 days a week, the teacher taught all the subjects of the public school, as well as German and religion. In fact, before World War I, "when the services in most congregations were predominantly in German, much time and effort in the schools of the congregations were spent teaching the children to read and write in German."[114]

However, the focus on German language instruction in school did little to stem the pressure of Anglicization in Missouri Synod congregations. From about 1915 onward, confirmations were no longer performed in German in most Missouri Synod churches of the Canada District, essentially because of the inadequate knowledge children had of the German language.[115] In St. Paul's church itself, the first confirmation classes in English were organized towards the close of the war, when also the demand arose that regular worship services in English be introduced.[116]

Similar developments are evident in Western Canada. Here, of German groups, Mennonites made the most concerted effort to establish an educational system that would help them perpetuate their beliefs and identity. Not knowing that education was under the jurisdiction of the provinces rather than the federal government, prior to their emigrating to Canada, Mennonites had signed an agreement only with the federal government which gave them a right to establish their own schools. As soon as villages were laid out on the Mennonite East and West Reserves in Manitoba, schools were established in each village. The purpose of these schools was to prepare students for their future role in the church and the local community. An extra incentive in this regard was the Mennonite practice of electing ministers, bishops and deacons from among the church membership. Every youth could potentially become a leader, so education was seen as necessary to certify that the person had the required reading and writing skills if elected.

---

[114]   Rev. Frank Malinsky, *Grace and Blessing: A History of the Ontario District of the Lutheran Church – Missouri Synod* (Elmira, ON: Lutheran Church – Missouri Synod, 1954) 37.

[115]   Ibid., 37.

[116]   ----- *Kept by His Power, 1874-1974: The Evangelical Lutheran Church of St. Paul Wisconsin Synod - Ottawa, Ont.* (1974) 7.

The educational curriculum in Mennonite schools concentrated on grammar and religious studies. As church services were in High or Low German, courses tended to be taught in German, usually High German. English was also introduced, at first as a second language and then as a language of instruction in some subjects.

When Mennonites established their schools in the 1870s, the Manitoba Department of Education was divided into a Roman Catholic and a Protestant Board, with Mennonite schools organized under the Protestant Board. This changed in 1890 when denominational schools were abolished in favour of a Board that was intended to be secular and non-denominational. Thereupon, the Liberal Government appointed H.H. Ewert of Kansas to persuade the Mennonites to adopt the public school system and to supervise schools that they might establish under the 1890 School Act. He was generally successful in this. However, when the Roblin Government introduced the Flag Policy in 1907, which required that public schools fly the Union Jack, a number of schools withdrew from the public school system and reverted back to become private schools.

In the meantime, Roman Catholic leaders protested against the provision of the 1890 School Act. The so-called Manitoba School Question raged for a number of years, reaching its height during the Dominion election in June 1896. In November of that year, the Laurier Liberals and the Manitoba government reached an agreement that stated that where 10 pupils spoke French or any other language other than English as their mother tongue, the teaching of such pupils should be in their mother tongue and English on a bilingual basis.

In particular the German-speaking Mennonites sought to take advantage of these provisions. In the lower grades of their bilingual schools, German was the first language of instruction and English was taught as a subject. In the upper grades, English was the language of instruction and German was confined to language lessons and religious education. In 1897, there were fifty German-English schools in Manitoba based on the Act of 1897, forty-nine among the Mennonites and one in the German Lutheran settlement of Hiebert.

Among Germans, primarily Mennonites were in the position to take advantage of the bilingual system, because only they were able to supply teachers from within their own ranks. To forward this goal, they founded two teacher training institutes - one in 1891 in Gretna by the *Bergthaler* community and the other, founded in 1907, by the *Sommerfelders*, in Altona. More recent arrivals such as the German Lutherans were still too poor to financially support a teacher training institute, which very much hampered their ability to have bilingual schools. Also, Lutherans felt ambiguous toward public schools. For example, Pastor George Gehrke, of the Ohio Synod, was of the opinion that bilingual schools could be of help to German Lutherans, and that it was important to get trained people from their congregations into positions teaching in the German-English system. He also was convinced that the ultimate goal of the Ohio Synod was the *Gemeindeschule* (parish school), for the future of Lutherans in this country would depend on this institution.[117]

Furthermore, German Lutherans had no block settlements and tended to be scattered among other linguistic groups in Manitoba, which would have made it difficult for them to establish bilingual schools. Therefore, they were much more dependent on the *Gemeindeschule* to pass on their linguistic identity to their children. Many of their congregations, therefore, had parochial schools. For example, in Winnipeg, which had the highest percentage of Lutheran parochial schools in the province, most congregations had, or sought to have their own parochial school. When first organized, the schools concentrated on teaching German and religion. The teaching of English tended to be neglected, in part because of the lack of instructors, and also because it was felt that the children would pick it up on the street. Once organized on a regular basis, the schools offered German and religion within the broader framework of the public school curriculum.

The one German Catholic parish in Winnipeg, St. Joseph's, also had its parochial school. Although the first teachers at St. Joseph's were secular, teaching after 1905 was largely the responsibility of the nuns. As the Lutheran schools, St. Joseph's parochial school offered German and religion within the broader framework of the public school curriculum. Other German religious communities in Winnipeg, such as the Baptists, did not have parochial schools but offered German language instruction either in the summer or on Saturdays to pass on the language.

The problem with parochial schools was that the parish often had difficulty supporting them. This was the case in particular among

---

[117] John Cobb, *German Speaking Lutherans in the Prairie Provinces Before the First World War.* (Ph.D. thesis, University of Manitoba, Winnipeg, 1991) 334.

Lutherans. For example, among Lutherans in Winnipeg, every family, regardless of how many of its children attended, were required to pay one dollar per month toward the support of the day school. The remainder was paid by the respective synod to cover expenses such as heating and lighting the classrooms or paying salaries. Despite the relatively low cost to each family, most Lutheran congregations found it difficult to keep their parochial day school. This was especially the case during periods of economic depression. This meant that the education of children was often interrupted.

Of Mennonites, only the two most conservative Mennonite religious groups, the Old Colony and the *Sommerfelders*, opted to stay with the purely private school system rather than join the public one. By 1912, there were sixty German-English public schools. Shortly before they were abolished in 1916, there were sixty-one German-English public school districts in Manitoba, with seventy-three teachers and 2,814 students. Of these, the vast majority were Mennonite. Lutherans, the other major group of Germans, tended to send their children either to English public schools or to parochial schools.

The bilingual public school system came under attack in Manitoba especially prior to World War I. In 1912, the Winnipeg Free Press argued that unless Canada wished to become another Austria-Hungary, bilingual schools had to be abolished. On other occasions, it argued that bilingual schools need not be abolished, but that the teaching of English at such schools needed to be improved.[118] The issue came to a head during the election campaign in 1915, which brought the Norris Liberals to power. Following this, the Liberals abolished Clause 258 of the Manitoba School Act, which had provided for bilingual instruction.

When some Mennonite schools withdrew from the public system following this, the government passed the Compulsory School Attendance Act, which forced children to attend public schools. When a large number of Old Colony and *Sommerfelders* resisted the closure of their private schools and refused to send their children to the newly set-up public schools, they were fined, which gradually broke their resistance. Rather than accept this situation, some six to seven thousand Old Colony and *Sommerfelder* Mennonites left Canada for Mexico or Paraguay. Those

---

[118]   For a discussion of this, see Arthur Grenke, *The German Community in Winnipeg, 1872- 1919* (New York: AMS Press,1991) 145-149.

Mennonites who remained accommodated themselves. At the same time, they worked out an agreement with the government that allowed them to use public school facilities to provide German language and religious instruction for their children outside of regular school hours.

A similar evolution emerged in the teaching of German in public schools in the Territories. When Germans first settled in the Territories, there was no provision in the Territorial legislation that provided for German language instruction. To teach their children, many Mennonites, Lutherans and Catholics set up parochial schools. It was largely through the work of David Toews of Rosthern that German language instruction was eventually introduced into public schools in the Territories. On January 1, 1901, a petition, written by him, appeared in *Der Nordwesten*, which requested that the North-West Territorial Assembly in Regina permit the teaching of German in public schools. After this, Toews met with Premier F.W.G. Haultain as well as with other government officials to forward this goal. Haultain agreed to support Toews' petition if it were changed to request that the government support the teaching, not only of German, but of "foreign languages". Through legislation introduced by F.W.G. Haultain on June 11, 1901, the teaching of German or any other "foreign" language was allowed in Territorial public schools for one hour per day.

Germans realized that if they were to take advantage of this government legislation, they would have to have qualified teachers. The Mennonites were the first to take the initiative in this regard. In January 1903, Elder Peter Regehr of Tiefengrund met with others to begin planning for a teacher training centre. On March 7, 1903, an organizational meeting in Eigenheim agreed to proceed with the establishment of a school to train teachers. The school opened in November 1905, with an enrolment of six students, and in 1909 the German-English Academy of Rosthern was incorporated by the Government of Saskatchewan. Enrolment increased gradually and in 1919 it stood at an all-time high of eighty-two students.

While the impetus for such an undertaking came from the Mennonites, it was also supported by other German religious groups, with *Der Nordwesten* seeking to spur them on in this regard. German Lutherans were the next to introduce training centres, one in Melville and the other in Saskatoon. The Evangelical Lutheran Synod of Manitoba and other Provinces first opened Lutheran College and Seminary in Spruce

Grove, then moved it to Edmonton and by 1914 found it a permanent home in Saskatoon. Its prime purpose initially was to provide pastors. A more immediate goal, however, was to provide guidance for talented young people in a Lutheran bilingual setting. Courses offered served to prepare the students for university and to provide them with a teaching certificate. In addition, the college served to prepare pastors for churches of the Synod. It sought to provide them with a good knowledge of both German and English, thereby enabling them to effectively serve their parishioners in either language.

The Canadian District of the Ohio Synod opened Luther Academy in Melville in 1913. It was intended to serve, in part as a Normal School, and in part as a Pre-Seminary. It would teach religion, German and other subjects at a more advanced level and would prepare its graduates to teach in the Ohio parochial school system or in local bilingual public schools. At the same time, graduates could go on to study in a seminary of the Ohio Synod.

While Lutherans sought to take advantage of the public school to perpetuate their religious and cultural identity, their prime interest was the church school, or the *Gemeindeschule*, with in particular the Missouri Synod paying great attention to using the parochial school to perpetuate, not only the religious but also the linguistic identity of children. As teachers for Missouri Synod schools were prepared in St. Louis, Missouri, the Missouri Synod lagged behind other German Lutheran synods to establish a seminary or teacher training institute in Canada. At the same time, at least in its earlier days, the Missouri Synod sought to establish a parochial school with every congregation that it organized.

In 1892 there were more Missouri schools than pastors and more schools than congregations (officially) connected to the Synod. The nineteenth century Missouri Synod saw the parochial school as fostering the best in the German language and culture and the noblest ideals of Lutheranism. While the Ohio Synod gave less emphasis to the establishment of parochial schools than the Missouri Synod, both synods had a strong commitment to the *Gemeindeschule*. Of the three main Synods working in Western Canada, the Synod of Manitoba and Other Provinces was most ambivalent in its stand regarding parochial schools. Debates in the General Council, the parent body of the Manitoba Synod, were both critical and supportive of parochial schools. Some saw it as promoting parochialism and through this fostering intolerance, both of which were seen as interfering with the emergence of a strong American identity. Others saw parochial schools as necessary if the German language and culture, in fact Lutheranism, was to be fostered in the American environment. This ambivalence resulted in the Manitoba Synod's establishing fewer parochial schools than did other synods.

By 1913, the Ohio and the Missouri synods had over eighty *Gemeindeschulen*, varying from larger full-time schools in places such as Winnipeg, Calgary and Stony Plain, to more part-time arrangements in the smaller congregations. The Synod of Manitoba and other Provinces, on the other hand, had an estimated 10 to 15 such schools. Taken as a whole, only about one-third of German Lutheran congregations in Western Canada had parochial schools in the proper sense of the word. It was usually the larger parishes that had them, so that the influence of these schools was likely greater than the "one-third" would suggest. Unfortunately, the conflict between the different Lutheran synods kept many Lutherans away from Lutheran congregations. This meant that the children of many Lutherans did not attend parochial schools. Even congregations that had a parochial school were often poorly served by them. Parochial schools were all too often short-lived. People were divided as to their usefulness. Instructors were transient. All too often parochial schools, once started, had to be shut down, to be replaced by Saturday schools that taught German.

German Roman Catholics in Western Canada established a college to train educators only in June 1920, when the cornerstone of St. Peter's College was laid in Munster, Saskatchewan. They did not have as pressing a need as German Protestants to train teachers because during the beginning years of St. Peter's Colony and St. Joseph's Colony, the Benedictine Monks and the Oblate Fathers taught German as well as catechism. Later, they were assisted by the Ursuline Nuns from Germany and by the Notre Dame Sisters from the Ursuline convent in Waterdown, Ontario. Of course, for both the Monks and the Sisters, the parochial school existed primarily to teach religion. While German language instruction tended to be offered an hour a week, by 1910 most Catholic children attended schools taught entirely in English.[119]

---

[119] Clinton O. White, "Pre-World War I Saskatchewan German Catholic thought concerning the perpetuation of their thought and religion," *Canadian Ethnic Studies*, 1994, vol. 26 Issue 2, pp 15-30.

Germans also took advantage of government endeavours to help non-English groups perpetuate their identity. With this end in mind, the Government of Saskatchewan established the Regina Training School for Foreign Students in 1909. Thirteen of the fifty students enrolled at the school during the 1915-16 academic years were German.

Such an accommodating attitude by the larger society changed over time. While continuing to support "foreign" language instruction in the public schools, the increasing influx of "foreigners" to Western Canada after the turn of the century raised concerns among English Canadians as to how to assimilate these different peoples. As elsewhere, the demand arose in the Territories that the instruction in "foreign" languages be abolished in public schools and replaced by instruction in English only. In particular the chauvinistic patriotism evoked by the outbreak of war in 1914 strengthened the demand that bilingual instruction be abolished, and in 1917, the clause permitting the teaching of languages other than English was abolished in Alberta as well as Saskatchewan.

The provincial governments in both provinces also demanded that the curricula of the private schools be coordinated with those of the public schools. Prior to this, private schools were virtually free to determine their own curriculum. In addition to sufficient instruction in the German language and religion, private schools provided fairly extensive English-language instruction, with the exception of the strictly conservative Mennonite schools. Furthermore, the government demanded that an English public school be established in all school districts that previously had a private school, with the objective of making it more difficult to support a private school financially. In any case, as the private school had to follow the curriculum of the public school, people had no incentive to establish a private school. With very few exceptions, examples being some German Catholic parishes of St. Peter's colony, private schools in German settlements in Saskatchewan and Alberta eventually closed down.

Although such actions made German language instruction extremely difficult in Alberta and Saskatchewan, it did not completely prevent it. Providing parents defrayed the cost, the new School Act permitted the instruction of German in classrooms, occasionally even during regular school hours, unless such instruction, in the opinion of the teacher, interfered with other work. In particular Mennonites, whose schools tended to be almost exclusively staffed by members of their religious community, used this opportunity to provide their children with German language and religious instruction. The same was true to a large extent of German Catholic parishes, where schools were in many instances staffed by German-speaking sisters. However, in these schools German tended to be taught as a subject.

In other instances, Germans resorted to legal action to reopen their parochial schools. Such schools were not officially prohibited. Rather, they had been closed on the ground that they were inefficient from a pedagogical point of view. The Missouri Synod, which of Lutheran synods had always been most committed to parochial schools, took the government to court to reopen its former private school in Stony Plain, Alberta. Parents had taken their children out of the public school that had opened during the war and had sent them to private school. The Missouri Synod sought to sue the government for closing the school, arguing that its curriculum was entirely in accord with that of the public schools, with the exception that it also offered German language instruction and religion. However, the case of the German parents was dismissed when it reached the Supreme Court of Canada. When the members of the Stony Plain congregation threatened to emigrate, and the Missouri Synod threatened to move Concordia College, the Synod seminary, out of Edmonton, the Alberta government changed its mind and declared the school in Stony Plain "efficient," thereby permitting students to attend. Following this, the Missouri Synod encouraged its ministers to set up private schools in their different parishes, and by 1936 it had fourteen private schools in its German language parishes in Western Canada. However, German language instruction occupied a minor part in the curriculum of these schools. For example, in a school week of 1,650 minutes at St. Matthew's parochial school in Stony Plain, Alberta, only a few minutes were given to German language instruction.

Parochial schools were also established, and in fact became especially popular, among the Mennonites. The initiative for such schools came largely from the Russländer Mennonite immigrants who arrived during the 1920s. Convinced that the Mennonite religion and the German language could best be preserved if they established their own schools, they took the lead in establishing Bible schools. The main drive for these schools came from the desire to meet the needs of their children who were attending high school and going on to higher education in ever greater numbers. The best way to deal with this situation was to imbue them with a solid background in their own religion. The schools would also teach the German language and thereby perpetuate language and religion, the two pillars upon which they saw their separate identity being based. To pursue these objectives, Mennonites established Bible schools in different centres, including Leamington, in Ontario, Gretna and Winnipeg, in Manitoba, Rosthern, in Saskatchewan, Coaldale, in Alberta, as well as in Clearbrook, British Columbia.

Germans also organized other schools during the inter-war period to perpetuate their identity. While some used the vacation school, run during the summer months, the most popular school was the Saturday school. German Baptists had always sent their children to the public school and used the Saturday school to perpetuate their linguistic identity. German Lutherans organized Saturday schools to teach the children German whenever a congregation didn't have the resources to support a *Gemeindeschule*.

During the inter-war years, local German clubs, as well as organizations such as the *Deutscher Bund* and the German Canadian Association of Saskatchewan began to organize Saturday schools and vacation schools to teach German. The same was the case with some churches. For example, the Evangelical Lutheran Church of the Cross, in Winnipeg, found that teaching children the word of God was problematic by 1921, as many of them had difficulty understanding the German language. The pastor suggested having English sermons, but this was rejected by the congregation. In 1925, a school was started in which children were taught German on Saturday and in the evening.

Saturday schools were especially suited for urban centres. Here, Germans were dispersed over a fairly compact locality. Being immigrants, they tended to have few financial resources. This made it difficult for them to have an influence on any particular public school, and public schools did not provide German language instruction in the lower grades. Saturday and vacation schools to teach the German language seemed a logical answer to the problem of passing a knowledge of German on to the children.

German Saturday schools became especially popular after World War II, fuelled by the desire of some 400,000 German immigrants who entered Canada after the war to pass their linguistic heritage on to their children. On arriving in Canada, the immigrants found that in public and private schools there was hardly any German language instruction at the primary or secondary school levels. The immigrants didn't want their children to lose the language of their ancestors. They therefore decided to tackle the problem of language transmission themselves. Having German language instruction on Saturday seemed suitable for this purpose, as the children had no school that day, and school classrooms were empty Saturdays.

German language Saturday schools in Western Canada during the post-World War II period were started primarily by the different religious denominations, with clubs also participating. In Quebec, as long as it was still active, the Trans-Canada Alliance of German Canadians took a leading role in organizing German language Saturday schools. In Ontario, about half of German language schools were started by German clubs, school associations and private individuals, while the other half were operated by the churches.

At first, these schools were financed through the contributions of individuals or through the help of organizations that sponsored them. Soon, the German Federal Republic provided school books free of cost to the schools. In time, German consulates helped to provide some financial support.

Children, ranging mostly from five to 15 years of age, were taught basic grammar, reading and writing. The schools operated out of churches, German clubs and anywhere else where parents could rent suitable space. While some of the teachers were professionals, in most cases anyone who had a good knowledge of German and was willing to give up their Saturday morning for this purpose could serve as a teacher.

About half of German language schools were established in Ontario, with Ontario schools serving as a model for other provinces. The schools grew gradually. At the peak of the post-World War II German Saturday school development, 12,000 students received instruction in 106 schools from coast to coast. Although the schools were private or organized by the local church or club, the overall administration was carried out by the Trans-Canada Alliance of German Canadians (TCA), which, founded in 1951, served as an umbrella organization for many German organizations in Canada. The TCA also organized annual meetings for the teachers, providing them with the opportunity to exchange ideas on how best to carry out their work.

The TCA provided this service as long as non-professional teachers made up most of the teaching staff. However, by the end of the 1960s the student body of children who could speak a fluent German gradually decreased. It was found that while the first child in an immigrant family often spoke a fluent German, the second or third child often did not. Second-generation Germans, who didn't speak the language at home and depended on the school to pass it on, sent their children to these schools, as also did non-Germans. This meant that new pedagogical methods had to be applied to teach these children. The TCA did not have the qualified staff to deal with this situation. Also, by the late 1960s, the TCA was undergoing internal strife that was eventually to lead to its demise.

Meanwhile in Germany, the responsibility for foreign language schools was transferred (in 1970) from the Foreign Office to the *Bundesverwaltungsamt, Zentralstelle für das Auslandsschulwesen*. From then on, it was the latter organization that provided financial support and the necessary literature for the schools. Headed by professional language teachers, it concentrated, not on teaching German grammar to children who already knew the language, but on teaching German as a foreign language to students who had no knowledge of it.

To advance this goal, German Saturday schools received literature suitable for teaching German as a foreign language. Preparations were also made to train teachers in the proper and most effective use of this material. Until 1960, most Saturday school teachers had been new arrivals, who earned a little extra income from what they saw as a community service. After 1965, most teachers were young Canadian graduates of teachers' colleges and universities, whose mother tongue was German. While familiar with the Canadian environment, such teachers required instruction in how to teach German to students who had little knowledge of the language. This consisted largely of an internship with established schools.

To help German Saturday school teachers teach German according to this new method, the *Verband Deutsch-Kanadischer Sprachschulen* (Association of German Canadian Language Schools) was organized. It sponsored meetings for teachers to discuss problems they encountered. It certified that the necessary teaching material was at hand to help instructors best carry out their work. Training schools were set up. In Ontario, the two most important training schools were the German language school of Club Harmony, while it existed, and the German language school in London. Since 1964, special courses were also offered to teachers, first at the Goethe House in Toronto, and in 1971 and 1972, in Gummersbach, Germany.

During this time, also, the Canadian and provincial governments started to take an interest in ethnic language schools. The federal government took the lead, giving notice in June 1977 that it would spend over one million dollars for its so-called "Multicultural Program." As education was a provincial responsibility, provincial governments felt threatened by this initiative. They therefore launched their own programs. In July 1977, for example, the Ontario government launched its "Heritage Program," with one of its objectives being the support of ethnic Saturday schools. As part of this program, the Ontario government helped to finance German Saturday schools, which included the payment of teachers. It also made it easier to recognize the credits earned in Saturday schools as part of the regular educational program for children.

While German Saturday schools had an important role especially in providing immigrants with the opportunity to pass the language on to their children, they gradually declined as the children and grandchildren reached adulthood. The new generations did not have the same attachment to the German language as did their parents or grandparents. In addition, many of the churches that at first had taken a leading role in establishing Saturday schools gradually became bilingual, or switched entirely to English, resulting in the closure of their Saturday schools. As a consequence, the Saturday schools gradually lost their importance as a vehicle for passing on the linguistic heritage in the German Canadian community.

Summary

German immigrants started schools and fostered German language instruction in the broader educational environment in order to pass on the German language. Language transmission was seen as important, not only to pass on the cultural heritage of immigrants but also to transmit the family's religious beliefs to the offspring. To do so, parents took advantage of whatever opportunities existed in the larger society to do this. At the same time, in particular the different religious communities started parochial schools to transmit both the language and religious heritage of the parents.

Countering these aspirations were efforts by members of the larger society to circumscribe the endeavours of the linguistic minority to use the school system to perpetuate its linguistic identity. They sought to use the educational system to assimilate the minority.

Germans sought to overcome the encumbrances the larger society sought to place in the way of their efforts to perpetuate their linguistic and cultural identity in a number of ways. Insofar as possible, they improvised ways of using the public school system that would help them teach their language and culture to their offspring. At other times, they established parochial schools, and vacation and Saturday schools, esssentially to teach the German language.

Despite these efforts, there came a time in the different German communities that emerged in Canada when the younger generation lost the ability to use the German language effectively. This change can be traced most readily in church records, the main social organization in the German Canadian community. By the year 2000, what had been German churches in Canada had given up their German services, or were in the process of doing so. Excluded from this were small religious groups, such as the Hutterites and conservative Mennonites, for whom maintaining the German was important, not so much to pass on a cultural or even a religious heritage, but because they saw it as an important part of the boundary separating the community of God from the "world." The vast majority of German Canadian children, however, no matter whether they attended public or parochial school, eventually lost the German. The schools they attended often did not imbue them with a knowledge of the language sufficient for them to use it effectively either in church or in their everyday life. Another reason for the language loss was the increasing lack of interest in learning German as the Canada-born generations became integrated into Canadian society. Both influences, working together, led to a situation where by the end of the twentieth century the central organizations established by German immigrants, the churches, had, for the most part, given up the German language in favour of English. Because the churches have always had a central role in German Canadian community life, it can well be argued that the language transition in them is indicative of the language transition among German Canadians in general.

SECULAR COMMUNITY LIFE

Clubs and other Secular Community Organizations

Unlike congregations, which were concerned with the whole life of the individual, secular organizations established by Germans concerned themselves largely with preserving and perpetuating cultural traditions brought from the homeland. In particular prior to the introduction of Medicare, they also served mutual aid needs, with club members pooling their money to cover the expense of paying a doctor or funeral costs. In addition, clubs offered the opportunity for people to get together and reminisce about old times as well as allowed for the celebration of festivals brought from the homeland.

These organizations were established by and served primarily the interests of the immigrant generation. This means that they followed the waves of German immigration, being established first in the east and then further west. At the same time, clubs had already declined or were in the process of decline in some centres by the time they were established in new centres. For this reason, I will look at these organizations as they were established and flourished during different periods of German immigration and settlement.

Secular Community Organizations Prior to World War I

The First Clubs in Eastern Canada

The first known secular social organization formed by Germans was the short-lived *Hochdeutsche Gesellschaft*. Little more is known about it other than that it was active in Halifax between 1786 and 1791. The next organization established was the German Society of Montreal. Founded in 1835, the Society was organized by Germans from the United States, Switzerland and Germany. Since its beginning, it has helped German immigrants in Canada. In fact, it was first organized to help several hundred German immigrants who arrived in the city who had been shipwrecked. After this, it continued aiding immigrants. It provided them with advice upon their arrival in Montreal; where necessary it provided them with material aid, in particular in cases where immigrants had arrived destitute or had lost their jobs. As part of this program, the Society supported the Protestant House of Industry and Refuge, to which it made an annual financial contribution, as well as the Montreal General Hospital. In the summer of 1864, it helped the survivors of an accident in which 97 immigrants, most of them German, had lost their lives as their train plunged into the Richelieu River at Beloeil. The Society's lawyer, J.C.S. Wurtele, also represented the interests of the survivors in their dealings with the railway company. Today, the German Society of Montreal still maintains a monument in the Mount Royal Cemetery for those who had lost their lives in this tragedy.

Scene of disaster as immigrant train of Grand Trunk Railway crossed Beloeil Bridge, near Montreal, June 29, 1864. Of the 97 immigrants who died, most were German. Public Domain.

The society also became involved in settlement work, when in 1872 it entered into an agreement with the federal government whereby it was granted a township in Manitoba on the condition that it settle German immigrants there. The agreement stipulated further that the Society was to bring over fifty families during the first year and one hundred families during following years, until all the land was taken up. The government cancelled the agreement two years later because the society had not fulfilled the conditions of the agreement. The society, however, had succeeded in bringing over a few immigrants, largely through the work of Wilhelm Wagner, who was active on its behalf in the Northwest.

As German settlement expanded into Upper Canada, German clubs also were organized there. They arose in all the major urban centres. Thus, the *Männerverein* 64, a glee club that eventually became the Germania Club of Hamilton was formed in Hamilton in the early 1860s. Similar clubs arose in Toronto and other areas of German settlement. This was true in particular for Waterloo County, which eventually became the centre of German organizational life in Eastern Canada before World War I.

As singing and musical presentations played an important role at family, church or school meetings, choral groups appeared in the different German communities in their early beginnings. Orchestral groups were established in Berlin in the early 1840s. Choirs were established in Bridgeport, Preston, Berlin and in other areas of Waterloo County since the mid-1840s, and in 1853 an umbrella organization was formed for German choirs in Berlin, Bridgeport and Waterloo to co-ordinate their activities.

In 1856, the first village band was organized in Berlin, soon to be followed by another, and in 1877, the two bands merged to form the Berlin Music Society. Similar bands also were formed in Preston, New Hamburg, Waterloo and other areas of German settlement. Especially the bands of Berlin and Waterloo were to gain considerable recognition, in particular under the leadership of George H. Ziegler. He also established what was to become a well-known women's orchestra, consisting of some 100 members.

In the 1850s, gymnastic associations arose in the larger villages. The first such association was established in Preston in 1854, to be followed by the organization of one in Berlin the next year. A *Turnverein* was established in Waterloo in 1861, and one in New Hamburg in 1863, with others being established in centres such as Elmira, Wellesley, Petersburg and New Dundee. Each gymnastic club had its own flag. Gymnasts wore white trousers and a white shirt. Gymnastic equipment included bars and the horse. The idea behind the movement was the belief that a healthy body constitutes an important part of one's general well-being.

The gymnastic association movement had become popular in Germany during the struggle against Napoleon. Some of its most prominent proponents in North America were the 1848 refugees, who had fled to North America following the suppression of the democratic movement in German-speaking lands that year. Thus, in Berlin the *Turnverein* was organized by the 1848er Eduard Lindemann, who was also secretary for the weekly *Der Deutschkanadier*. Beginning with some 30 members, the club, as other gymnastic associations, had as goal educating youth and nurturing them into vital and healthy manhood. Gymnastic instructions were held twice a week, beginning at seven in the evening. While at first each club tended to celebrate its own annual feast, after 1861 the various associations came together to hold their annual celebration together. These associations were especially active until the 1870s.

Theatrical groups were also organized by German clubs in the different centres. Generally they were formed within the confines of each local club, presenting plays on different occasions. As with other aspects of German social life in Eastern and Central Canada, the most active and vital theatrical groups arose in Waterloo County. In particular the gymnastic associations were active in organizing theatrical groups. Thus, both the gymnastic association of Berlin and Preston had its theatrical group. In addition, Germans in Preston had a children's theatre and the German Catholics of St. Agatha a boy's theatrical group. Historical dramas, and in particular comedies, formed an especially popular part of any venue.

Plays were often an integral part of special festivals. This may be seen, for example, in the case of the Gymnastic festival that took place in Preston in 1861. This included not only gymnastic presentations. Bands and choirs performed during the course of the festival. In addition, two plays were performed. A children's festival formed part of the event, with a major high point being the closing ball in which local bands provided the music.

The 1870s brought significant changes to the organizational life of Waterloo County. Immigration to the county had not only ceased, but there was also a sizable exodus, in particular of younger people moving to the Huron Tract and to the west. This made the gymnastic presentations less popular, which in turn also brought a decrease in the number of theatrical presentations. At the same time, German victories over France during the Franco-Prussian war and the formation of the Reich in 1871 awakened a certain degree of nostalgia for the old homeland. This strengthened the interest in particular in folk songs, which in turn encouraged the formation of choirs, preparing the way for the *Sängerfeste*, or song festivals, which became popular among Germans of Central Canada during the latter part of the 19th century.

Choirs were an important part of all German national associations. Thus, the *Männergesangsverein 64* continued to be an important part of the Germania Club of Hamilton even after the organization changed its name. The German Society of Montreal had choirs as subgroups, as did German national associations in Toronto or elsewhere. In addition, choirs such as the Teutonia Society of Montreal arose. Founded in 1880, it was independent of any national clubs.

In Waterloo County, choirs in the different villages visited each other and performed at annual festivals. In 1873, these locals, at the behest of H.A. Zöllner, of Berlin, organized themselves into the *Deutschkanadische Sängerbund* (German Canadian Choir Association). Many of these choirs, such as the *Männergesangsverein 64* in Hamilton, were also members of the *Peninsular Sängerbund,* in which German choirs from both Canada and the United States were represented.

These choirs organized *Sängerfeste* that became a central part of German Canadian social life in Central Canada during the latter part of the 19th century. Major song and music festivals (involving both vocal and instrumental music), which might last as long as three days, took place in centres such as Waterloo, Bowmanville, Hamilton, Bridgeport, Elmira, almost every or every second year from 1874 to 1907, and then again in 1912. In particular in German villages, the entire community participated, and in centres such as Berlin or Waterloo, the whole city was decorated for this festive occasion.

Interior of concert pavilion at the first German Canadian singers' festival in Waterloo, Ont., 1874. Canadian Illustrated News, Sept. 1874.

Just like at gymnastic festivals, the *Sängerfeste* included bands, theatrical groups, and gymnastic performances. There were plays, parades, picnics, with the *Sängerfest* generally concluding with a ball. Some of the major festivals, such as the 1875 festival organized by the Concordia Club of Berlin, attracted 15 choirs from Montreal, Toronto, London, Detroit, Chicago and elsewhere. It featured some 500 choristers, with both English and German singers participating, and drew an audience of 12,000 people. The 1886 festival, deemed to be one of the most impressive for North America at that time, presented five full concerts, including a performance of "The Creation."

The 1880s and 1890s in many respects saw the height of the *Sängerfest*. The gradual assimilation of community members led to the gradual decrease in attendance. The festivals were given a further blow by the outbreak of World War I, when the organizations sponsoring these events were forced to suspend their activities.

Western Canada

The first German clubs arose on the west coast where a small German community had arisen in the mid-1800s. In Victoria, they organized the *Germania Sing Verein* in early 1861. Drawing its membership not only from the German community but also from among English Canadians, the *Verein* not only lasted up to the start of the First World War but was also one of the leading cultural institutions in the city.

The major concentration of German organizational life, however, was to emerge, not on Canada's west coast, but on the prairies. Here, German clubs arose with the arrival of the first immigrants, in particular from Germany. Germans from outside Germany, in particular those from Russia, did not tend to form clubs, essentially because their social life centred around their church. German clubs tended to be formed primarily in the cities. However, German immigrants tended to remain in urban centres for only a brief period before moving to the land. This was to have a significant effect on German club life, for example, in Winnipeg, which was not only the major urban centre on the prairies during the early period of settlement but also was a major centre funneling settlers into the hinterland.

So the German Society which briefly appeared in Winnipeg in 1871 disappeared when many of its members moved to the land. The same fate befell the German choral group and the mutual aid society that emerged in 1878, and the German Society which existed in Winnipeg between 1884 and 1887. The problem was that, unlike congregations, clubs were able to recruit only a small number of Germans in the city. They arose when a sufficiently large number of Germans arrived and declined after many of them again departed for the hinterland. This situation changed only in the 1890's when, with increased German immigration, a larger number of Germans remained in Winnipeg. This is the main reason why the German Society, organized in 1892, did not immediately decline.

The society grew rapidly and by 1904 had some 190 members. It provided its members with sickness and death benefits. Its library had some 200 books by the turn of the centure, as well as German language newspapers. It had its own hall and offered bowling, the occasional dances, and the opportunity to take part in traditional celebrations such as the *Stiftungsfest, Fasching,* or *Maskenball.*

Similar organizations also developed in other urban centres of Western Canada where Germans settled, in particular among *Reichsdeutsche.* Thus, in Regina the *Deutsche Vereinigung* was formed in 1907, and the German Teutonia Club in 1908. Strassburg, which was settled largely by Germans from the *Reich*, had a gymnastic association, a choir and a literary club. In Edmonton, Club Edelweiss was founded in 1906, and clubs were also founded in Calgary and other urban centres, including Vancouver, where local Germans organized a chapter of the Sons of Hermann Lodge (*Hermannssöhne*) in 1892.

The organizations had no sooner been formed when splinter groups led to the emergence of new organizations. This happened in Winnipeg, where the majority of German clubs existed. In 1905, Germans from the *Reich* separated from the German Society of Winnipeg to establish the *Reichsdeutsche Verein* (Imperial German Society). That same year, Swiss members of the German Society formed the Swiss club *Helvetia*. The following year, Austro-Hungarian members of the German Society separated to establish the German-Hungarian Club.

A number of influences led to these divisions. The different national sub-groupings had remained members of the older German Society of Winnipeg as long as their own group wasn't strong enough to support its own club. Once they had what they considered a sufficient number of their own people in the city, different groups sought to establish their own organizations. This was encouraged by conflicts that at times broke out between different groups, encouraged by differences in origin. Also, different national groups celebrated different national festivals, with the Swiss, for example, celebrating Swiss Independence Day, Germans the *Sedanfeier*, and Austro-Hungarians the *Weinlesefest*.

As in Eastern Canada, clubs were also organized in Western Canada to satisfy the different interests of German immigrants. In Winnipeg, for example, the short-lived *Germania*, organized in 1878, was strictly a glee club. Another *Germania* glee club was organized in 1900 and not long after a similar group, the *Liedertafel Concordia* was organized. These music groups provided entertainment on special occasions, sponsored the occasional ball, presented concerts or performed at dances.

Germans also organized other types of organizations. For example, in Winnipeg they founded dramatic societies, gymnastic associations and literary groups. The gymnastic association *Turnverein Jahn* was organized in 1906, and later replaced by the *Turnverein im Grünen Kranz*. Offering their members the opportunity to keep fit through gymnastic exercises, they also sponsored dances and appealed in particular to the young. In 1909 a literary club was organized to meet the interests of community members wishing to read and discuss German literature and, about the same time, the drama group *Talia* was formed to present dramatic pieces.

Umbrella Organizations in Western Canada

In Eastern Canada, where local choirs found it necessary to co-ordinate their activities so that they could participate in the regional *Sängerfest,* in Western Canada, for example in Winnipeg, even as German organizational life in the city splintered into various national sub-divisions, efforts were made to bring about closer co-operation between the clubs. Simultaneously, efforts were made to interconnect local clubs with other clubs in the region. These objectives were pursued by the *Alldeutscher Verband,* organized by Rudi Klein to unite German clubs of Western Canada under an umbrella organization that would be tied to the *Hauptverband* in Berlin, Germany. This effort came to naught because the sponsoring organization was too weak to have much influence among Germans in the West. Also, it was felt that connecting any German national organization to Germany would rouse the ire of English Canadians. To be useful, any German Canadian organization should serve the interests of German Canadians rather than Germany.

To forward this goal, F. Liebermann, editor of the Conservative German language weekly, *Germania,* took the initiative to establish the *Verband deutscher Vereine, Sitz Winnipeg.* Organized in 1908, it sought to co-ordinate the activities of the different German local clubs. At the same time, it aspired to act as a pressure group to forward German goals, in particular in the city. Thus, it aimed at working toward introducing German language instruction in Winnipeg schools and uniting Germans behind aldermen or members of the legislature who would support German interests. The organization ceased its activities two months after it was formed, with the editor of the weekly *Der Nordwesten* accusing Liebermann of seeking to use the organization to forward Conservative interests. Liebermann, on the other hand, accused the editor of *Der Nordwesten,* Hugo Carstens, of having become too Anglicized to undertake anything in the interest of Germans in the West himself, and out of spite choosing to wreck initiatives of others.

The next effort to create an umbrella organization for Germans in Winnipeg and Western Canada came in 1912, when in November of that year the representatives of Winnipeg's German clubs met to discuss the formation of an umbrella organization that would help to co-ordinate the activities of the different German clubs in the city. On February 13, 1913, the clubs organized themselves into the *Bund deutscher Vereine Winnipegs.*

While organized to meet the needs of German clubs in Winnipeg, the club was also part of a more ambitious program of uniting German clubs in Western Canada.

The inspiration for this goal came from the example of German Americans. The German American *Bund* was viewed with admiration as a power that no government could ignore. Although German leaders in Western Canada considered it impossible to establish an organization equal in influence to the German American *Bund,* they felt that Germans could organize in the Canadian west an umbrella organization that would help them attain the position of influence to which they were entitled because of their number. As Germans frequently settled in small clusters in the west, often in groups of 12 or 13 families, they were considered too weak to form clubs at the neighbourhood level. They would, therefore, be unable to imitate the example of the German American *Bund,* which rested on the strength of the local clubs. To unite Germans in Western Canada, it was considered advisable, first, to form an executive body that could serve as an advocate for the interests of even the smallest German enclave. This goal was attained when in February 1913, the *Deutschkanadische Nationalbund* was organized, under the leadership of G. Maron, editor of the Conservative weekly, *Der Nordwesten.*

Sponsors of the *Nationalbund* felt that Germans were tolerated in Canada only because they were needed to build up the country. It was hoped that the *Nationalbund* could obtain from English Canadians more sympathy and understanding for the German way of life. It was also hoped that, through the *Nationalbund,* Germans could become sufficiently powerful to realize objectives such as the expansion of German language instruction in the public schools and the liberalization of Sunday laws. Although the *Nationalbund* did not object to the abolition of bars, it wanted restaurants where a family could enjoy beer and concerts. The *Nationalbund* also intended to foster an adequate representation of Germans at all levels of government and to work against the policy formerly pursued by the dominant English element, which was to unite a predominantly German district with a larger Anglo-Saxon one so as to render the former politically impotent. To elect Germans, the *Nationalbund* proposed that German political candidates be supported, no matter to what party they belonged. Its goal was to pursue German Canadian interests rather than follow any particular party line.

Regarding international policies, the *Nationalbund* aspired to construct a countervailing force against the English influence in Canada, thereby assuring international peace by preventing war with Germany. By explaining to English Canadians the German point of view regarding international issues, it intended to rectify the damage done by the jingo-English press in Canada, which had caused Canadians to view Germany as a perfidious, war-mongering nation.

The *Nationalbund* was unable to realize any of these objectives for it ceased to exist a month after being formed. A major cause for its demise was the bickering between the Liberal *Saskatchewan Courier* and the Winnipeg-based Conservative *Der Nordwesten*. The *Saskatchewan Courier* argued that since Regina was the capital of the province in Western Canada that had the largest German population, any German national or regional organization ought to have its headquarters in Regina. Proponents of the Winnipeg-centred *Nationalbund* argued that, unlike Regina, Winnipeg had shown itself capable of perpetuating German secular organizations; therefore it could better carry out the objectives of a German national organization. The *Saskatchewan Courier* argued further that *Der Nordwesten* would use the *Nationalbund* to forward the interests of the Conservative Party. In reply to the *Nationalbund*, centred in Winnipeg, the *Saskatchewan Courier* and other elements associated with Liberal Party interests in Saskatchewan set out to establish the German Canadian Association of Saskatchewan.[120]

With the demise of the *Nationalbund* efforts to establish a larger regional organization which would be representative of German interests in Western Canada essentially ceased. The main contribution of the *Nationalbund* was that it gave impetus to the formation of the German Canadian Association of Saskatchewan. Sponsored by the *Saskatchewan Courier* and its editor, Conrad E. Eymann, the organization was able to recruit some 4,000 members soon after it was formed. However, the *Nationalbund* was little able to pursue any of its political and social objectives.

Several causes contributed to the difficulty Germans in Western Canada had in maintaining a broad umbrella organization. One was the diversity of their community. They came from almost all the countries of Eastern and Central Europe and therefore had little other than language

---

[120]   For further information on this dispute, see Grenke (1991), 82-83, 218-219.

uniting them. Furthermore, in particular for Germans of Eastern Europe, secular organizations were of little significance. Their life was centred on the church. Most churches to which Germans belonged were little interested in the secular life of their members. Rather, they sought to involve their membership in the different religious organizations of their respective congregations, be these choirs, prayer groups or other similar organizations.

The main exception was the Catholics. This, perhaps, is why one of the most important secular organizations formed by Germans was established within the framework of a larger religious body. Organized in Winnipeg in 1909, the *Volksverein deutsch-canadischer Katholiken* served as an umbrella organization for German Catholics in Western Canada, who lived mostly in Manitoba (more specifically Winnipeg) and in the German Catholic block settlements in Saskatchewan. Although a lay organization, the clergy were always extremely active in it. It combined both secular and religious goals, especially in the area of education. As such it was a strong advocate of Catholic separate schools; at the same time, it encouraged the use of German as an integral part of the school curriculum.

While German secular social organizations that sought to co-ordinate the activities of the community as a whole had difficulty co-operating in normal times, this was less the case when the entire community came under attack, as occurred when war broke out in 1914. The community had already been put under pressure when the depression broke out in 1913, with many Germans losing their jobs. In Winnipeg, for example, the *Deutsche Unterstützungsverein* was organized to help the unemployed. This situation became much more grave with the outbreak of war. The proclivity of some English Canadian employers to display their patriotism by laying off their German workers brought a great increase in the number of unemployed. As a result, a major community-wide effort, spearheaded by the *Unterstützungsverein,* was undertaken to channel unemployed Germans into the hinterland.

Just as the Winnipeg *Unterstützungsverein* played an important local economic role in Winnipeg, the German Canadian Association of Saskatchewan played an important economic role among Germans in Saskatchewan. Thus, locals of the association, such as the one in the district of Disley, were active in organizing local farmers to undertake communal purchases. At the same time, the organization led to the formation of a German local of the Grain Growers Association, which worked to forward the communal interest of German farmers. Especially during the early years of the war, with the British population uneasy with their having so many foreigners in their midst, the Association represented Germans in Saskatchewan both with government and with other cultural groups so as to steer the community through this difficult time. Furthermore, it helped people who had lost their jobs as a result of the war find employment with German farmers, continuing this work until, like most German associations during the war, it essentially ceased its activities.

Although German secular associations had little difficulty surviving the early years of the war, the threat of attack from the majority population led to all German clubs eventually either closing or greatly reducing their activities. One of these activities was providing presents to people who had been interned during the war. The initiative for the campaign came from the Rev. F. Beer of Brandon, Manitoba, who argued that something be done to brighten the Christmas season for these unfortunates. Beginning in 1914, German-speaking women gathered every Christmas until the end of the war to collect clothes and money to purchase tobacco and other goods and to wrap presents for the prisoners. What started out as a local and regional initiative became a co-operative endeavour after 1916, when German clubs in Eastern Canada became responsible for providing gifts for inmates in camps in the East, while Western clubs provided gifts for internees in Western Canada.

The Inter-War Years

One of the first organizational efforts by German Canadians following the war was to collect money and material goods in aid of Germans in Europe. Through such endeavours, thousands of dollars were collected to aid relief organizations such as *Deutsche Kinder in Not* (German Children in Need) and *Ruhrhilfe* (Ruhr Relief).

However, much of this work was achieved outside the framework of German clubs. By the end of World War I, German club life had almost ceased to function in Canada. Fearing that they would become targets of attack, local clubs often shut their doors. Rather than seek to combine whatever influence they had in order to establish what they saw as their rightful place in Canadian society, German Canadians by the end of the war became interested primarily in safety.

Whereas German clubs had at one time attracted not only a German membership but also elements of the larger society who were interested in the recreational activities these organizations fostered, after the war German clubs had difficulty recruiting membership from their own community. The war propaganda, combined with the appeal of Canadian nationalism, made it increasingly difficult to recruit in particular members of the younger generation.

This was the case especially in Eastern Canada where many members of the German community had been born in Canada and were, in fact, second or third generation Canadian-born. The upheaval caused by the war as well as anti-German attitudes in the larger society caused many members of even the immigrant generation to stay away from German clubs. Thus, only a fraction of the old club members returned to the clubs after the war. This made it difficult for some clubs, as, for example, the Germania Club in Hamilton, to pay for the upkeep of its hall, forcing members to sell their hall and meet in rented quarters. In centres such as the former Berlin (Kitchener after 1916), German secular organizational life which was already very much weakened by the forces of assimilation, essentially died during or after the war. Only some of the major clubs, such as the *Sängerverein Concordia,* continued.

Of the German immigrants who came to Canada during the inter-war period, some thirteen thousand declared Eastern Canada as their destination. The German population of Eastern Canada was further augmented by some seven thousand of the new arrivals who, after seeking to make a start on the land in Western Canada, were forced by poor economic conditions to give up their farms and seek employment in Eastern Canadian urban centres. Persuaded by the relatively favourable economic conditions that existed for the wheat economy between 1925 and 1929, by railway companies eager to sell their land, and by different church leaders seeking to build up their congregations in the West, many of the new arrivals who had taken up land in the West found that, when the Depression erupted, they were unable to keep up payments on debts they had incurred to buy their farms. They were forced to give up their land and join the many unemployed seeking to find work wherever this was available. Many of these tried their luck in Eastern Canada and ended up in Toronto, Montreal and other centres.

In Eastern Canada, the new arrivals helped to revitalize German Canadian club life. For example, they founded the *Deutscher Verein Harmonie* in 1921, in Toronto. Branch organizations of the club included choirs and sports clubs, theatrical and cultural groups, as well as a German language school. In imitation of their co-religionists in Western Canada, German Catholics of Toronto organized their own club in 1929, the *Deutsch-Katholischer Verein,* which included a choral society and a sports club. Not long after the Nazis came to power, the *Deutsche Gesellschaft* was founded in Toronto to serve as a local of the *Deutscher Bund.*

In Kitchener, the *Concordia Club* gained new vitality with the new arrivals. In addition, new clubs were organized. The Danube Swabians, many of whom had come during the inter-war years, established the *Schwaben Club.* Transylvania Saxon immigrants organized a *Vergnügungsverein* in Kitchener in 1927. When it declined a year later, they established a sickness benefit society together with the Danube Swabians (in 1928), the *Siebenbürger Sachsen und Schwaben Krankenunterstützungsverein.* After the Danube Swabians left the *Verein* to found their own sickness benefit society, the Transylvania Saxons continued on, with the organization eventually evolving into the Transylvania Club, which was organized in 1951.

The new arrivals also revitalized or contributed to the formation of other clubs in Ontario. These included the *Verein Deutsches Heim,* formed in London in 1928, the *Deutscher Club,* organized in Woodstock in 1934, the *Deutscher Verein Teutonia* and the *Erster Sachsen Krankenuterstützungsverein,* in Windsor, as well as the *Deutscher Verein Frohsinn,* organized in Kingsville in 1931. In addition, the *Liederkranz* and the *Deutscher Club* were established in Ottawa during the inter-war years.

Following the example of Germans in the Prairie provinces, the different Ontario German clubs organized German Day celebrations. The first celebration, September 1-3, 1934, attracted over 3,000 people. Later celebrations led to the formation of the *Deutsche Arbeitsgemeinschaft von Ontario,* which included in its membership most German clubs in the province and served to co-ordinate the activities of the different clubs.

In Québec, where French Canadians had been less hostile toward the German minority during the war, German clubs were less severely affected than in English Canada. The German Society of Montreal, which had taken a leading role during the war in support of the internees, returned to its usual immigrant aid. Both the *Verein Teutonia* and the *Deutscher Verein Harmonia* regained some of their old vitality. In addition, new clubs were founded. These included the *Deutsch-Schwäbischer Verein,* founded in 1929 by German immigrants from the Banat. In 1931, German Hungarian members of the organization withdrew and founded their own club, the *Verein der Deutsch-Ungarn.* In addition, Montreal also had the *Edelweissverein der Deutsch-Schweizer,* as well as the *Sportklub Kickers,* which started out as a communist organization in 1932, but in 1933 purged itself of its communist members.

In Winnipeg, the only centre in Manitoba with a dynamic secular organizational life, one of the few German Canadian clubs to survive the war was the *Deutsche Vereinigung* (German Society). Reinvigorated with the arrival of new immigrants, it came to take an important role in local German community life. Another organization to survive the war was the *St. Josephsverein* (St. Joseph's Society), the men's club of the Catholic St. Joseph's parish. New organizations were formed, including the *Westfälischer Schützenverein von Little Britain,* organized by post-World War I arrivals who had settled just outside Winnipeg. Together with other societies, such as the *Deutsch-Kanadischer Kranken-Unterstützungsverein* and churches such as the Lutheran Church of the Cross, and Christ and Trinity Lutheran, these organizations united in 1930 to form the *Deutsch-Kanadischer Bund von Manitoba.* The main purpose of the Bund was to prepare for the *Deutsche Tage,* help people find work and represent the interests of Germans in the province in general.

In Saskatchewan, where Germans formed the largest percentage of the population, a number of German organizations were revitalized or emerged after the war. The *Volksverein deutsch-canadischer Katholiken,* with some thirty-six locals by 1937, gained new life, and became active both in immigration work and in general community life among German Catholics. The *Deutsch-canadischer Verband von Saskatchewan* (German Canadian Association of Saskatchewan), which had as well as ceased its activities during the war, was revived in 1928, and in 1934 had twenty-eight locals, in such areas as Edenwold, Herschel, Kelstern, Langenburg, Regina (3 locals), as well as in other areas where Germans were concentrated. It sought to promote German language instruction, German song and music, as well as the German language press. To promote the German language, it not only supported local Saturday schools but also offered prizes for the highest achievements in German language studies at higher educational institutions that offered courses in German, such as Luther College, the *Deutsch-Englische Akademie* in Rosthern, and St. Peter's College in Muenster.

*Meeting of German Canadian Association of Saskatchewan,
[1920s].* Library and Archives Canada, e011180498.

To co-ordinate the different activities of various local organizations in Regina, the *Deutsch-Kanadisches Zentral-Komitee* (German Canadian Central Committee) was founded in Regina in 1929. By 1934, two German Lutheran congregations, one German Baptist congregation, and two German Catholic parishes were members. In addition, the organization had as members the three locals of the *Deutsch canadischer Verband von Saskatchewan,* a local of the *Deutscher Bund Canada,* the *Deutsch-Canadischer Club,* the *Deutsches Haus,* formed in 1928 by Germans from Galicia, the *Deutsch-Canadischer Unterstützungsverein,* the *Deutscher Verein Germania,* and the *Deutscher Club Teutonia.* Both religious and secular organizations co-operated to represent and forward German community interests. In Saskatoon, as well, a co-ordinating agency for local organizations was created, the prime purpose of which was to prepare for German Day celebrations for Saskatchewan.

On the advice of Bernhard Bott, who then still worked for *Der Courier,* in Regina, the *Deutsche Arbeitsgemeinschaft Saskatchewan* (German Coordinating Committee of Saskatchewan) was formed in 1934. It included the *Volksverein deutsch-canadischer Katholiken,* the

Deutsch Canadischer Verband von Saskatchewan, the *Mennonitisches Provinzialkomitee,* the *Deutsch-Kanadisches Zentralkomitee,* the *Deutsch-Kanadisches Zentralkomitee* of Regina, the *Saskatoon-Deutscher-Tag-Komitee,* and the Saskatchewan district of the *Deutscher Bund.* By uniting all German organizations in the province under one umbrella, the *Arbeitsgemeinschaft* sought to enhance the influence Germans might have when seeking to forward German interests in the province.

In Alberta, the *Edelweiss* club, which had been founded before the war, was revitalized by the new arrivals. New organizations were also founded, including the *Deutsch-Canadische Vereinigung* and the *Turn-und Sportsverein Jahn,* both of which were founded in Edmonton in the early 1930s. During the same period, the *Vergissmeinnicht Club* and the *Harmonie* Club, as well as a local of the *Deutscher Bund,* arose in Calgary.

It was also in Alberta that the first attempts arose after the war to organize Germans at the national level. With the encouragement of *Der Nordwesten,* a Missouri Synod pastor working in Edmonton, Alberta, Alfred Martin Rehwinkel, took the initiative to revive the *Deutschkanadische Nationalbund* that had collapsed in 1913. As the founders of the *Nationalbund* prior to World War I, Rehwinkel felt that Germans could gain the political and social prominence in Canada to which their numbers entitled them only if they organized themselves as a pressure group. The best way to achieve this was through co-ordinated activity at the national level. With this end in mind, the *Deutsch-Canadischer National-Verband* (German Canadian National Association—DCN) was organized in 1926.

However, the DCN was unable to attain any of its political goals. Rehwinkel's own attempt to garner the support of the *National-Verband* when he ran for municipal office in Edmonton ended in failure when he went down to defeat. The *National-Verband* itself collapsed in 1928, when Rehwinkel, its main driving force, left Canada for the United States.

Following this, Germans in Alberta organized the *Deutsch-Kanadische Zentralstelle für die Provinz Alberta* (German Canadian Central Agency for the Province of Alberta), in 1932. In 1933, the new organization took on the name of the former *Deutsch-Kanadischer National-Verband.* However, by 1934, the *National-Verband* survived merely as a local relief society in South Edmonton-Strathcona.

Although not as numerous as Germans on the prairies, Germans in Vancouver also brought back to life organizations that had become dormant or near to dormant during the war and organized new associations. This includes the *Alpenvereinigung*, a *Deutscher Schulverein*, a *Deutsche Frauenschaft*. As more Germans from the Reich lived in Vancouver than in other Western cities, the city also had a branch of the NSDAP (National Socialist German Workers' Party) and of the *Deutsche Arbeitsfront*.

German Day Celebrations

German Day celebrations came about largely through the initiative of Martin Rehwinkel. Together with Gustav Koermann, founder of the *Alberta Herold*, and Bernhard Bott, editor of the *Courier* in Regina, Rehwinkel was instrumental in organizing the first German Day celebrations, which were held in Edmonton on the 8th and 9th of August, 1928. Having their beginnings in Alberta, German Day celebrations soon spread to other provinces, including Saskatchewan, in 1930, and Ontario, in 1934. Celebrations tended to be held in the major cities, with special committees established to organize the events. In time, small regional German days were also held in different centres. This included St. Walburg and Barrhead, where they were organized by German farmers in these localities.

The German Day celebrations were the main events organized by German Canadians during the inter-war years, attracting between 3,000 and 8,000 people. They attracted people from all walks of life. Often travelling great distances, people used the occasion to renew old friendships and establish new contacts.

In time, German Days developed a recognizable pattern. They opened in a stadium or a large festival hall, with an official ceremony during which the major community organizers spoke and in which important resolutions were presented. After this came competitions between different glee clubs and members of athletic associations. Folk dance groups performed and prizes were handed out for academic achievements in German. Simultaneously, arts and crafts prepared by Germans during the winter months were exhibited.

The celebrations pursued fairly consistent goals. Primarily, they reminded Germans of the rights and duties which were theirs as a result of their background. They also encouraged the community to preserve its ethnic heritage. In particular, they encouraged Germans not to lose their language, the preservation of which was integral to retaining their cultural identity.

Furthermore, the gatherings served to remind governments of the legitimate demands of the German minority to have German language instruction in the public schools, in particular in school districts where Germans constituted a majority. Also, the gatherings sought to refute the biased view of Germany and of the German element in Canada that had arisen in particular during the war years.

Deutsche Tage, Edmonton, 1932. Glenbow Archives, D-3-6181

The Depression, Nazi Germany and the emergence of labour and ultra-nationalist organizations in the German Canadian community

The outbreak of the Depression in 1929 brought not only Canadian society into a crisis but also the German community. The severe drought that turned much of Alberta and Saskatchewan into a dustbowl had a drastic effect on German farmers, causing the most severely affected to leave their homes and seek their livelihood elsewhere. People were thrown out of jobs, with little prospect of finding new employment. This especially affected new immigrants, who hadn't been here long enough to establish themselves. People turned to all sorts of solutions to keep up hope. The most common of these had their roots in nationalism and/or radical socialism. This led to the emergence of extremist organizations that took their inspiration, not so much from local conditions, as from international movements of the Right and Left that affected the world at the time. As these movements, in particular the movement of the Left, have been given little attention in the German Canadian historical literature, I will discuss it in some detail.

From Dreams of the Worker State to Fighting Hitler: the German Canadian Left from the Depression to the end of World War II.

Unlike in the United States, where the German element played an important role in first organizing labour, Germans in Canada only gradually became involved in the labour movement. From the mid-1700s to the early 1800s, most German immigrants who arrived in what today is Canada came from an essentially agricultural society. Being mostly farmers, they didn't see themselves as members of the working class. They had come to America to own their own plot of land, and often remained in urban centers only long enough to earn enough to establish themselves on the land.

Despite the strong rural orientation of early German-speaking immigrants, the labour movement gained some support among them. Thus, the Socialist Party of Canada had a German language section which together with the Jewish, Ruthenian and other language sections broke with the party in 1911 to form the Social Democratic Party of Canada. However, unlike many other language affiliates of the Socialist party, the German language section was small and short-lived.

There were a number of changes in the 1920s that were to make the socialist movement more attractive to German immigrants. One involved a change in the type of immigrant. Of some 100,000 German immigrants to Canada during the inter-war years, a sizable number came directly from Germany. Furthermore, by the 1920s the number of wage earners had increased substantially in the different smaller German enclaves in Eastern Europe. This meant that the German immigrant from these areas during this period was not as strongly oriented towards rural settlement as earlier immigrants. Also, many of those who came in the 1920s, unlike earlier arrivals, had already been exposed to Social democratic or communist influences prior to coming to Canada.

By the 1920s most of the good land in Western Canada had been taken, making rural settlement more difficult. Also, when the Depression broke out in 1929, it had a disastrous effect on both the urban and the rural economies. This meant that escape into the hinterland once one lost one's job was less of an alternative for the urban worker than it had been previously. Organizing themselves to protect their interests was, therefore, the only alternative for German immigrant workers forced to deal with the conditions into which the Depression had placed them. These conditions were to influence not only the type of organizations which German immigrants established but also the life span of these organizations and the membership they attracted.

Ushered in by the Wall Street stock market crash in 1929, the Depression led to tens of thousands of workers losing their jobs. Immigrant workers were especially severely affected, not only because of low wages and irregular work that made saving difficult, but they were also often burdened by travel loans, and handicapped by the difficulty of establishing themselves in a country where they didn't speak the language. Their situation was made worse by the fact that the few jobs available tended to be offered to Canadians, especially veterans. Furthermore, immigrants could not afford to become public charges. Sections 40 and 41 of the Immigration Act made it obligatory for all public and municipal officers to report immigrants who had become dependent on public relief. The deportation of immigrants for this reason rose from 430 in 1928 to 2,106 in 1930 and peaked in 1933 with 4,916 deportations.

To deal with this situation, German Canadian labour first organized itself in Winnipeg, Manitoba, with the formation of the German Workers Education Society. The initiative for forming the Society came from Jacob Penner, one of the founders of the Communist Party of Canada. Also, in 1929, the Association of German-Speaking Workers was formed in Edmonton. Unlike the Winnipeg Society, which had a strong ideological base, the Edmonton association stressed practical concerns. It offered legal advice to workers who had been incarcerated while seeking work or while taking part in demonstrations protesting against poor wages and working conditions. It offered to help them find work and gain memberships in unions that would aid them in protecting their jobs. As far as possible, it provided them with sickness insurance and also helped them cope with other day-to-day economic problems.

Soon after the formation of labour organizations in Winnipeg and Edmonton, German Canadian labour also organized itself in Regina, Calgary, Vancouver and Toronto. In 1930, the executives of these organizations met to establish the *Zentralverband deutschsprechender Arbeiter* (Central Association of German-Speaking Workers) to co-ordinate the activities of the locals. Differences soon arose, however, regarding the purpose of the central association. The Edmonton local, led by Walter Widmer, was Social Democratic in orientation, with an emphasis on serving the everyday needs of workers and the unemployed, and it sought to direct German Canadian labour in that direction. The Winnipeg branch, on the other hand, sought to integrate German Canadian labour into the larger communist movement in Canada and the world.

Central to the dispute between the Edmonton and Winnipeg organizations was the question of whether German Canadian labour should take a gradualist approach to social change and concern itself essentially with pragmatic matters, or should align itself with the Communist Party and its struggle for the radical alteration of society. The Winnipeg local won out in its competition with its more moderate socialist rival, in part because that local's control of the *Deutsche Arbeiter Zeitung* put it in a better position to influence the opinions of members of the movement, but also because, in a period when capitalism was in crisis, the Winnipeg local was more in tune with the times. Members of the Association of German-Speaking Workers were, for the most part, recent immigrants. They looked to Europe for guidance, where they had often been involved in the Social Democratic movement. Few of them, however, could draw inspiration from the problems that Social Democrats were having in dealing with the Depression. Workers in the Soviet Union, by contrast, were seen to be creating a new society under the direction of the Communist Party. It was therefore not unnatural for unemployed German Canadian workers to look to the Communist Party and the Soviet Union for a way out of their own difficulties.

As a result, the Edmonton local found little support in the broader German Canadian labour movement, which eventually led to its demise. The Winnipeg local, on the other hand, no longer restrained by Edmonton, became more pro-communist in orientation. Even its choice of a new name for the organization, German Workers and Farmers Association, reflected the communist influence. Although it was recognized that poorer Canadian farmers were also suffering from the Depression, members of the German working class had tended to see farmers as part of the bourgeoisie. Lenin, however, had succeeded in bringing about the revolution in Russia by uniting both urban workers and rural peasantry under the Bolshevik banner. By uniting both farmers and workers in their organization, German Canadian labour was acknowledging the relevance of the Bolshevik precedent: if the labour movement was ever to bring a Communist worker-controlled government to power in Canada, it would have to seek support among farmers as well as workers.

A main goal of the German Workers and Farmers Association was to educate German Canadians as to their true interests. The Association sought to explain to them, chiefly through the *Deutsche Arbeiter Zeitung*, that the Depression was capitalism's death agony, with the workers being forced to bear the brunt of suffering, caused by the system's painful demise. The Association declared itself a member of the united front of the international proletariat. In practical terms, this involved implementing policies and programs as they had been spelled out by the Communist International. This meant essentially carrying out policies as they had been formulated by Stalin and thereafter imposed upon the Communist International during the Sixth Congress, in 1928, and upon communist parties in Europe and North America. As viewed by Stalin, capitalist countries were increasingly approaching the proletarian revolution. In order to forward this process, communists had to intensify their efforts to win the working class away from socialist groupings and organize them in truly revolutionary organizations dominated by the communists. One way of doing this was by organizing workers in trade unions dominated by the communists. Another was to intensify communist propaganda against the established order and, in particular, intensify their attack upon the socialists who were seen to be compromising with the capitalist system and thereby perpetuating the life of this moribund structure.

In order to further these objectives, the German Workers and Farmers Association sought to encourage Germans to join communist-dominated trade unions. German farmers, in turn, were encouraged to join rural pro-communist organizations, such as the Farmers' Unity League (FUL). Working together, urban labourers and rural farmers would turn any attack upon them and their interests into a victory against the bourgeoisie.

The German Workers and Farmers Association also sought to involve German workers in labour holidays, in particular the annual

May Day festivities. It supported organizations of the unemployed sponsored by the Communist Party, such as the National Unemployed Workers' Association (NUWA) or the Relief Camp Workers' Union, the activities of which culminated in 1935 in the On-to-Ottawa-Trek that marked the "climax of the struggle by the Communists on behalf of the unemployed". The Association also sought to involve Germans in local labour protests and encouraged them to throw their moral and material support behind strikers, such as those at Estevan in 1931, who were described as forwarding the goals not only of their unions but of the entire labour movement. In addition, the Association threw its support behind labour organizations such as the Workers International Relief (WIR), which supported strikers both through financial aid and other means.

Although cynical about the "bourgeois" democratic process, which it saw as being essentially a means whereby the possessing class maintained control over the workers, the German Workers and Farmers Association supported Communist Party representatives when they ran for political office. For example, it supported Jacob Penner, one of its members, when he ran for Alderman in Winnipeg. However, the ballot box was not seen as a means through which the workers could attain power. The political process was to be used primarily to reveal the suppressive nature of the existing political and social structures.

The Association saw all German Canadians, with few exceptions, as belonging to the working class. The goal of the German Workers and Farmers Association was to make it clear to German Canadians that their ethnic interests corresponded to their class interests, and that only by eradicating the class problems of capitalism could the problems of the German ethnic minority in Canadian society be eventually resolved.

Besides seeking to involve Germans in what it saw as the class struggle, the German Workers and Farmers Association sought to help its members meet their everyday needs. To meet the health insurance needs of its members, for example, the Association joined the Independent Mutual Benefit Federation (IMBF) to obtain health insurance for its members. Each local of the German Workers and Farmers Association also offered a meeting place for club members and their families. As far as possible, the worker clubs had theater and song groups, as well as bands. These permitted members both to develop their talents as well as offered entertainment to the German community at large. Almost every local had its library of Marxist literature, and some had schools that offered German language instruction to the children of both members and non-members. In many ways, these locals were like all other German clubs; but whereas most German clubs emphasized cultural and recreational events, locals of the German Workers and Farmers Association stressed social action to win adherents among German Canadians.

The drive by the German Workers and Farmers Association to forward its goals and win adherents to its cause among German Canadians was to be radically affected by the rise to power of Adolf Hitler in Germany. Prior to his achieving power, Hitler had been viewed by the *Deutsche Arbeiter Zeitung* with a certain degree of condescension and derision. Attitudes changed radically, however, once Hitler took power. He was considered to have seized power with the help of the big capitalists and, as their agent, to be using terror to interfere with the capitalist system's logical evolution toward the worker state. Surprise and anger greeted the Nazis' rapid consolidation of their hold on Germany, together with outrage over their use of terror to suppress the German working class movement. The German Workers and Farmers Association encouraged its members to participate in mass demonstrations directed against what was happening in Germany and also appealed to German Canadian workers to support the German proletariat through financial help and other means.

Hitler's rise to power and the ascendancy of fascism in Germany sensitized the German Workers and Farmers Association to what it saw as the fascist threat in Canada. It saw signs of fascist terror in the treatment of labour during strikes and regarded Canadian governments from coast to coast as steering towards fascism in the various measures that they took to deal with radical labour. In particular, it saw evidence of Hitlerism in the policies of the Bennett Conservatives. Both Hitler and the Bennett Conservatives were seen as being the tools of big business, using similar tactics of incarceration, police brutality and murder. The Conservatives were also perceived as exhibiting a certain type of silk glove British fascism. Instead of Nazi terror, they were using legal means and a fake democracy to maintain the possessing class's control over the workers.

The German Workers and Farmers Association began to watch for the dissemination of Nazi propaganda in Canada. It criticized speakers sent out by the New Germany, claiming that they were nothing but representatives of the hooligans who were using terror to further the interest of German capitalists. Associations such as the Friends of the New Germany were criticized as doing nothing more than spreading falsehoods about the true situation in Germany; German consuls, such as Consul Seelheim of Winnipeg, were criticized for misusing their position to disseminate Nazi propaganda in Canada.

In its effort to fight the dissemination of National Socialist views and attitudes in the German Canadian community, the German Workers and Farmers Association sought particularly to counteract the propaganda of the *Deutscher Bund Canada*. *Bund* leaders like Karl Gerhard, Franz Straubinger or Bernhard Bott were described as Nazi agents seeking to indoctrinate German Canadians with National Socialist ideology. The worker's association challenged the *Bund* to stop its pretence of being non-political and interested merely in carrying on cultural work, when it was really a political organization spreading Nazi propaganda. Such propaganda was described as consisting, in essence, of two elements: encouraging hatred of the Jews and preaching national chauvinism.

To counter the spread of Nazi fascism both in Canada and abroad, locals of the German Workers and Farmers Association (for example the Windsor branch in 1934) became involved in the League Against War and Fascism. With Adolf Hitler's rise to power, the danger of an imperialist war was increasingly seen by communists as coming, not from some vague capitalist threat, but from Nazi Germany. At first, communists had believed that Hitler's hold on power would be brief. It was thought that once "Nazifascism" proved itself incapable of dealing with the problem of the Depression, it would be overthrown and its fall would usher in the proletarian revolution. Instead, the National Socialists were putting Germany back to work. Simultaneously, through the use of force, they were bringing labour peace to the country and by their example were inspiring similar reactionary forces outside Germany.

To oppose the Nazi threat, the Association called for the establishment of a united front against Fascism. Efforts to bring about a united front of working class parties were seen as necessary in order to pave the way for the eventual triumph of the proletarian revolution. As part of this endeavor, the *Deutsche Arbeiter Zeitung* rid itself of its cynicism regarding bourgeois democracy, and its criticism of the bourgeois political parties lessened. Rather than drawing a close parallel between the European fascists and Canadian bourgeois parties such as the Conservatives and Liberals, the German Workers and Farmers

Association now endeavored to differentiate between German fascism and Canadian political parties. It identified the National Socialists not with any particular Canadian political party but rather with Canadian capitalists, who were seen as being behind the forces of reaction in this country. Any criticisms of the political parties now tended to be of a practical nature rather than being cast in the traditional Marxist ideological framework. This altered stance was encouraged when the King Liberals replaced the Bennett Conservatives in 1935 and, in 1936, struck Clause 98 from the criminal code, a provision that the hated Bennett government had used to incarcerate communist leaders.

In pursuit of the united front, the German Workers and Farmers Association recommended to its locals to rid themselves of their sectarian approach to the class conflict and strive to co-operate with as broad a spectrum of German clubs as possible. At the same time, the German Workers and Farmers Association fought the spread of Nazism in the German Canadian community. It warned local German clubs that since the *Bund* was having difficulty spreading its Nazi propaganda openly in an essentially unsympathetic German Canadian community, it was doing so surreptitiously under the guise of carrying out cultural work.

The German Workers and Farmers Association also continued its efforts at clarifying Nazi ideology, not only for German Canadians but also for the wider Canadian community. For example, it explained the role that anti-Semitism served in a reactionary ideology such as fascism, and advised German Canadians to not let themselves be confused as to who was the real enemy. The Association stressed that there was a difference between Hitler fascism, which was reactionary and led to war, and German culture, a culture of progress based on service to all humankind, and it repeatedly warned that Hitlerism meant war, advising German Canadians not to support it if they wished to avoid the antagonism of other groups.

Evidence of the antagonism it warned about was seen in the objections Mayor J.A. Clarke of Edmonton made to having propaganda literature distributed and having the Swastika flag prominently displayed during the German Day celebrations in that city in 1936. Equally antagonistic attitudes were seen in criticisms expressed by dailies such as the *Daily Mail* or the *Winnipeg Free Press*, which were reacting to attempts made by German Canadian supporters of Hitler to justify his policies. The German Workers and Farmers Association warned fellow

German Canadians that Nazi activities in Canada, including their use of the *Deutsche Tage* for propaganda purposes, aroused hatred towards them by other nationalities, which could only be exacerbated by the growing distrust provoked by Nazi Germany's aggressive moves on the international scene.

With the fascist victory in Spain, the German Workers and Farmers Association became increasingly convinced that, if fascism was to be stopped, efforts had to be intensified to strengthen the alliance of all groups opposed to fascism. In order to appeal to as large a segment of the population as possible, the Association dissolved itself and, in November 1937, re-emerged as the *Deutschkanadische Volksbund* (German Canadian League). As part of this change, the name of the organization's newspaper, the *Deutsche Arbeiter Zeitung,* was changed to the *Deutsch-Kanadische Volkszeitung.* Justifying these changes, the *Deutsche Arbeiter Zeitung* argued that the example of Spain showed that all nations were threatened by the imperialist fascists. Furthermore, Nazi activities in Spain had harmed Germans abroad who sought to live in co-operation with other people. Nazism also had to be opposed to protect German character formation, culture and to avoid a war. As such, the *Volksbund* would serve as a refuge for all Germans who espoused these goals.

To advance its anti-Nazi work, the *Volksbund* (League) invited to Canada refugees from Nazi Germany, such as Ludwig Renn, Tony Sender, Paul Tillich and Joseph Ostermann, to give public addresses to English-speaking as well as German-speaking audiences. One of the largest of the anti-Nazi rallies sponsored by the League attracted some five thousand people to the Montreal Forum. A meeting organized by the League in Toronto to protest against Nazi persecution of the Jews attracted some two thousand people.

The League also held memorial services to commemorate the victims of Nazism, such as Ernst Thaelmann and a German Nobel prize winner, Carl von Ossietzky. Its publicity denounced the persecution of the Jews in Germany, and in both Kitchener and Calgary it sponsored mass meetings to protest against such persecution. In addition, it co-operated with the Canadian Jewish Congress to investigate pro-Nazi activities in Canada. The League also made representations to the Canadian government requesting that Jewish refugees be permitted to enter Canada, and condemned the deportation of refugees who had arrived. It also sought to persuade the Canadian government to conduct an official inquiry into

Nazi activities in Canada, in order to put an end to the often-repeated
rumor that German Canadians were pro-Nazi. At the same time, the
League deplored signs of discrimination against German Canadians as
a result of Nazi excesses. Although it never failed to stress that Nazi
agitators were active in the German Canadian community, the League
reassured the Canadian government and the Canadian people that the
vast majority of Canada's half a million German Canadians supported
the democratic system and were loyal to Canada.

When war broke out in September 1939, the League supported
Canada's declaration of war against Germany and called on other
German Canadians to do the same. Some co-operated with officials
to arrest members of the Bund. Despite this, the League's executive
buried its records immediately after the outbreak of war for fear that
they would be seized by the Canadian government, which would use
them to incarcerate pro-communists in the League. A major problem
for the League was the Ribbentrop-Molotov Pact that served to divide
Eastern Europe between Nazi Germany and Soviet Russia. As a corollary
of the pact, the Soviet Union denounced the war, which it branded as
an imperialist war that communists should oppose. This was too much
for some of the League's members. When Otto Kerbs, a leading member
of the Montreal branch of the League, was invited by Fred Rose of the
Communist Party to condemn the war publicly, he refused to do so.

The outbreak of war and Soviet neutrality also subjected members
of the League to the threat of internment. Soon after war broke out,
the Canadian government began interning not only pro-fascists but also
communists, including members of foreign language organizations under
the control of the communist party. Members of the German Canadian
League did not find themselves in quite the same position as the other
pro-communist language groups, essentially because it had attracted
considerable middle class support since it was founded. This becomes
evident in discussions involving security officials debating whether or not
League members should be interned. The RCMP, who considered the
League to be a communist organization, recommended that members
thereof be interned. This was opposed by Norman Robertson who,
essentially on the basis of his contact with middle class Jewish members
of the organization, disputed the RCMP view, stating that the League
was essentially an anti-Nazi organization which fervently supported

the war effort and therefore should be left alone.[121] Robertson's support overrode the RCMP recommendation. This did not, however, prevent some German members of the League from being interned, as for example, Jacob Penner, a declared communist in Winnipeg, or German miners in Nova Scotia who were members of the Independent Mutual Benefit Federation.

Once the war broke out, League members who had joined strictly because of its anti-Nazi activities became directly involved in the war effort. This left some four hundred communist and pro-communist members of the League in awkward suspension until July 1941, when Nazi Germany attacked the Soviet Union. With this, communist hesitancy to become involved in the war effort ceased. Shortly thereafter, the left-leaning section of the League began organizing itself again and, largely through its efforts, the German Canadian Federation was founded in 1942 and the Co-ordination Committee, German Canadian Federation, was set up in June 1943.

To achieve its goals in the German Canadian community, the Federation sponsored meetings in which anti-fascist films were shown or in which Allied goals in the war were explained. It stressed that it would give German Canadians a working class view of events as they unfolded in Europe, because the "middle class press provides only one-sided information." It also criticized people such as Emil Ludwig, who advocated the imposition of draconian peace terms on Germany. The ideological orientation of the group becomes particularly evident in instances such as its drive to collect clothes and other items for the Soviet Union and Tito's partisans, causes which were also espoused by Ukrainian Canadian communists. In its reports on the war's progress, too, it tended to emphasize Soviet successes rather than Western advances.

In pursuit of its objectives, the Federation co-operated with the Free Germany Movement (consisting essentially of groups of refugees from Nazi Germany who were working for the liberation of their homeland). In particular, it co-operated - for example in Mexico - with the communist element in the Movement. The Federation had reports

---

[121] LAC, W.L.M. King Papers, MG 26, J 1, vol. 273, 231077-89, microfilm reel C-3746. Memorandum: For the Prime Minister's Office. Re. Internal Security Measures taken on Outbreak of War, 2 December, 1939.

on its activities printed in the publications of the Movement, and it also received propaganda material from various segments of the Free Germany Movement - for example, from Mexico (*El Libro Libre*); the United States (*The German American*); and Moscow (The Publishing House for Foreign Language Literature); and it regularly received copies of *Freies Deutschland*. In addition, it donated money to the activities of the Free Germany Movement. The Federation, as such, left little doubt that its goals were the goals of the Free Germany Movement dominated by the communists.

In spite of its propaganda work, the Federation had little success in recruiting German Canadians as members and little influence among Germans in Canada. It failed to bring religious or cultural groups into the Federation, and even German Canadians opposed to Hitler - apart from those with a communist political affiliation - were wary of it. Among refugees from Nazi Germany, it found only Sudeten Germans amicably disposed to it and willing to become active in the organization.

The Federation's strong advocacy of the Soviet Union and its policies eventually led to extensive loss of membership and its demise in 1949. It blamed the West rather than the Soviet Union for problems that arose between the victors after the defeat of Nazi Germany. It justified the expulsion as well as the mistreatment and killing of Germans by the Soviet Union and its client states toward the end and after the war. At the height of its activities during the Depression the radical labour organization had a membership of about 2,000. Membership gradually dwindled as the organization altered from being an advocate of radical social change to being a mouthpiece of Stalin and the Soviet Union.

Deutscher Bund Canada

While some German Canadians turned to communism to answer the problems they faced during the Depression, others turned to National Socialism. Like the people who turned to communism, people who turned to National Socialism tended to belong to a similar socio-economic status. For the most part, they consisted of immigrants who had not yet established themselves in the new country.

The *Deutscher Bund Canada* was organized in January, 1934, by Ernst Knopf, Otto Geisler, Georg Messer, Paul Lechscheid, and Karl Gerhard. This was not the first attempt to organize a pro-Hitler movement in

Canada. Friends of the New Germany, an American organization, had established branches in Canada a year earlier. However, pressure from Washington led to the disintegration of the organization in late 1933. The *Deutscher Bund Canada* was determined to avoid a similar fate by having its leadership consist of German Canadians. Publicly, it also sought to be less pro-National Socialist than the Friends had been, with its leaders insisting that their organization was not national socialist in nature. The organization's goals, they maintained, were social and cultural rather than political.

The *Bund* insisted that it was established to unify Germans from coast to coast. At the same time, it sought to integrate Germans in Canada into a larger pan-German world-wide movement. It stressed that every German, regardless of the country in which he or she lived, who resolved to remain totally German, could belong to the organization. At the same time, it endeavoured not to become a mass organization. Rather, it sought to enlist a group of reliable members that would imbue the remainder of the German community with German *volkisch* beliefs and attitudes.

To carry out this task, the *Bund* established an elaborate national organization, organized in a pyramidical fashion modelled on the party structure of the National Socialist party in Germany. The national leader and his executive occupied the highest rank. Three district leaders (*Gauleiter*) came under the leader or *Fuehrer*. One of these was responsible for the eastern *Gau* (the Maritimes and Quebec); the other was responsible for the central *Gau,* and the third was responsible for the western *Gau,* (the western provinces). The *Gaus* were subdivided into *Kreise,* each of which was headed by a *Kreisleiter,* who was responsible for looking after *Ortsgruppen* or *Stützpunkte,* the local units of the *Bund,* in his area.

Attendance at *Bund* meetings was mandatory, as was also the acceptance of decisions made by the *Bund* leadership. As the *Bund* membership included people from many religious backgrounds and political leanings, *Bund* leaders prohibited religious controversy and the discussion of Canadian politics. The Bund stressed that members propagate the "German cause" among fellow Germans, which involved supporting German schools, German cultural events, as well as combating Bolshevism and anti-German propaganda.

To disseminate its message and attract fellow Germans to the organization, the Bund showed films from Germany at group events or in local theatres. It became extensively involved in *Deutsche Tage* (German Days), with the intent of using the occasion to disseminate its message in the German Canadian community.

Despite such effort, Bund membership never exceeded 2,000, even at the height of its popularity, during the 1937/38 period. As its sister organization on the Left, it had to compete with traditional German Canadian organization for members. German Canadians who had been in Canada for several generations and no longer spoke German were not interested in events occurring in Germany. Whereas the German Canadian pro-communist organizations attracted labourers and semi-skilled tradespeople from primarily the immigrant community, German pro-fascist organizations attracted farmers, skilled and semi-skilled workers and some business people from the same community. Both organizations tended to attract essentially marginalized people, who had been severely affected by the downturn in the economy during the Depression.

The *Bund* ceased its operation when war broke out in 1939, which saw its leading members being interned. Its long-range effect on the German Canadian community has tended to be negative rather than positive. Through its activities it roused the suspicion of the host society as to German Canadian loyalty. Worse, by seeking to identify German culture with the Nazi cause, it painted German culture in a negative light, causing community members to turn away from it, through this encouraging the very process of assimilation that the Bund sought to discourage.

Post-World War II

During the war, many German Canadian secular social organizations closed their doors. Some members left because they didn't want to arouse the antagonism of the larger society while Germany and Canada were at war. Others left because they wanted to leave behind their German identity or found the social organizations of the host society more attractive. By the time the war ended, German secular community organizations were in a sorry state. Their membership had shrunk. Community networks that had supported them were in disarray.

The organizations revived again once the new wave of immigrants arrived, blossoming as never before. There were several reasons for this. One was the large number of new arrivals, some 400,000 of them. More than previously, many of them originated from Germany and Austria proper, which were much more secular than German communities of Eastern Europe, from where many of the previous immigrants had come. Unlike post-World War I immigrants, many of whom arrived not long before the outbreak of the Depression, and therefore were plagued by employment difficulties, post-World War II immigrants experienced the economic boom in Canada following the war. After they established themselves, many of the new arrivals, who were largely tradespeople or professionals, also had the skills and leisure time to operate the new organizations. This contributed to the revival and growth of the old German social organizations and the emergence and growth of new ones.

The first major organizational effort by German Canadians following World War II was undertaken on behalf of German and Austrian relief. Reports from Europe, including letters from relatives, spoke of starvation, people without shelter and short of clothing, in particular winter clothing. Different German congregations, be these Catholic, Lutheran, Mennonite, Baptist, or any other, started delivering relief supplies soon after hostilities ceased. People also sent parcels to their relatives in need.

The Canadian Society for German Relief was launched in Kitchener in December, 1946, to broaden the relief base outside the churches. Soon after, the organization established branches in Guelph, Hamilton, Montreal, Toronto, and as far west as British Columbia. Local groups collected money, clothing and other essentials. These were cleaned, sorted, packaged by volunteers, and then sent across the ocean to be distributed among the needy.

By the summer of 1947, the efforts at relief had turned to encouraging the emigration of Germany's surplus population, resulting in an extensive influx of Germans into the country. Saskatchewan, which had become a major focus of German Canadian life during the inter-war years, received few immigrants. As a result, its importance as a German Canadian centre greatly diminished as the immigrant generation died off and their children were increasingly absorbed into the larger society. The situation was quite different in Ontario, Alberta and BC. The expanding industrial base in all these provinces attracted in particular the different skilled immigrants who entered the country, including Germans. This brought a resurgence and expansion of German secular community life in the major urban centres of all these provinces to serve the different needs of the immigrant communities that emerged.

This increase had a dramatic effect on the secular German community life in all these provinces. Prior to World War II, the province of Alberta had about two dozen German secular organizations. With the arrival of the new immigrants, these expanded to over a hundred. New secular social organizations were organized especially in the major urban centres, in particular Edmonton and Calgary. New clubs were also established in centres such as Lethbridge, Medicine Hat, Lloydminster and Grand Prairie. While most of these organizations sought their membership among all Germans, others organized Germans from a particular region. This included the Sudetenclub and the Canadian Baltic Immigrant Society, both in Edmonton. The members of one organization originated largely from the Sudetenland and those of the Canadian Baltic Immigrant Aid Society consisted of Germans from the Baltic region. Once organized, the different clubs provided activities appealing to certain segments of their membership, such as choirs, sports organizations, or dance groups.

While German national clubs tended to celebrate German popular culture, other organizations focussed on celebrating and perpetuating certain aspects of the German cultural tradition. These included book clubs, such as the *Bücherstube Edmonton*, which was established to provide German reading material for its members. Theatre groups such as the *St. Bonifatius Theatergruppe* in Calgary were organized to provide entertainment for the local German-speaking community, which included performances at the dinner theatre of the local German TV show *Telle-Treffpunkt*.

Organizations were established in support of German language and bilingual education. These included associations such as the German Bilingual Parents' Association of Edmonton and the German-English Education Society of Calgary. Organizations such as the German Cultural Exchange Association of Edmonton were established to build closer cultural contact between the local German community and the old homeland.

As in all situations where Germans settled, the arrival of the new immigrants saw a great expansion in the number of choirs. In Alberta, these include the Edmonton *Männerchor Liederkranz*, the Calgary *Singgemeinschaft*, the *Deutsche Frauenchor* Calgary, or the Medicine Hat German Canadian Harmony Choir. Choirs performed locally, took part in regional song festivals and organized tours of German-speaking countries of Europe.

As many of the new immigrants were young men, soccer clubs proved popular among the new arrivals. In addition, handball, volleyball, and bicycle clubs were organized, as well as dance groups. Clubs such as the Edmonton *Karnevalgesellschaft Blaue Funken* served to keep alive the Carnival tradition.

The new arrivals organized consumer societies, such as the *Deutsche Konsumgesellschaft* in Edmonton. Business organizations such as the German Canadian Business and Professional Association were established in major Alberta centres. Mutual aid associations, such as the *Deutsch-Canadischer Hilfsausschuss*, Edmonton, helped individuals or families in instances where the breadwinner had fallen sick.

The influx of new immigrants affected the organizational life of Germans not only in Alberta but also elsewhere. German voluntary associations, which numbered about two hundred in 1957, increased to 500 in 1974 and to over 600 20 years later. Most of these organizations tended to be concerned with preserving the secular rather than the religious aspects of the German cultural tradition. This led to the formation of essentially new German communities. In Ottawa, for example, the local German community that had been established largely by 1860s immigrants who had settled in the Ottawa Valley was in its final stages of assimilation when the new immigrants arrived. Their churches, the main social organizations of the earlier immigrants, were in their final language transition from German to English.

The new arrivals established a multitude of social organizations in Ottawa that hadn't existed before. As many of the new arrivals were young men, one of the first organizations to be established was a soccer club, the S. C. Victoria, in 1952. In 1955, the Germania Club was founded with a goal of helping the new arrivals adjust to Canadian life as well as to preserve the cultural heritage they brought from Europe. That same year, the Ottawa Mutual Aid Society was organized to help new arrivals adjust to Canadian life.

In 1955, a folk dance group, the *Gebirgs-Trachten-Erhaltungsverein-D'Gamskofler* was formed. In 1963, the Almrausch dancers, as the dance group eventually came to be known, united with the Maple Leaf soccer club to establish a new organization. The club expanded still further when in 1964 it was joined by a Bavarian folk dance group from Hull, which consisted mostly of Franco-Canadians. In addition to a soccer group, the club organized a marksman section, chess and *Skat* groups, and angler and hunter sections.

The community created musical societies and choirs. One of the earliest of these was the mixed choir *Melodia*, founded in 1956, and the male choir Concordia in 1958. Preoccupied with household chores and raising their families, the women only organized a female choir, the Concordia *Frauenchor*, in 1975. Both choirs attained some degree of recognition, in both the German immigrant community and in the larger society. This is true in particular of the Concordia Male Choir, which has become well known for its polished original presentations. In 1980, the Johannes Brahms choir, a mixed choir, was organized, which under the direction of Dieter Kiesewalter attained some note with its presentation of classical and semi-classical pieces.

Post-World War II immigrants organized a German Canadian Business Association in Ottawa in 1970. For years, it printed a telephone book consisting of the names and phone numbers of local German Canadian businesses. It invited Canadian community leaders, including former Prime Minister John Diefenbaker, to its meetings, both to make them aware of the German Canadian community and to help acclimatize local German business leaders to the Canadian environment.

A Saturday German language school taught the German language to future generations. In 1947, the community established the German language Club, affiliated with Carleton University, to provide students studying German with the opportunity to practice the language. In 1970, an umbrella organization was formed to help co-ordinate the activities of the different associations, especially in the sponsorship of community events such as musical presentations, lectures, and dances.

The German community has long been served by a radio program several times a week. The popularity of television brought a program to serve local German viewers at least once a week. Programs and reports have tended to concentrate on local news, music, as well as news from the homeland. Local news has focussed on reports on community events;

lectures, musical presentations, or seasonal festivals such as *Karneval* or Christmas. The German community's network of social organizations, in many ways, has allowed it to function as an organism that is separate and yet part of the larger society.

Few German communities were as radically altered by the new arrivals as the one in Ottawa. Yet all of them were affected by the new immigrants. Theatre groups emerged in Montreal, Toronto, Winnipeg, Vancouver and other urban centres to present performances in the German language, providing an outlet for immigrant talent. Societies of hunters and anglers arose in different centres, bringing together people interested in taking advantage of the abundance Canada had to offer in these areas. Strictly cultural associations were formed, including German language clubs, or clubs such as the Vancouver *Kulturkreis,* dedicated to encouraging the appreciation of the German cultural heritage.

Centres such as Toronto, Hamilton, Winnipeg and Vancouver organized business and professional associations to support their members and advise new arrivals wishing to explore business or other opportunities in Canada. They have long provided scholarships, in particular in the area of German language studies, and also have raised funds to support local community events.

Strictly professional associations arose, for example, the Association of German Engineers, Toronto, or the Canadian German Lawyers Association, a Canada-wide organization, which was incorporated on November 20th, 1992, in Germany, to bring together Canadian lawyers who act on behalf of German-speaking clients. Established in 1961 to promote the study of German at Canadian schools and universities, the Canadian Association of University Teachers of German (CAUTG) has long served as a forum for the discussion of professional and administrative matters relating to German language instruction in Canada. It has structured course outlines, prepared and circulated teaching aids and sponsored student and professor exchanges. In addition, the conferences it has organized over the years have permitted scholars to critically examine their findings in different areas of German literature. The Historical Society of Mecklenburg Upper Canada has for many years brought together scholars working in the field of German Canadian history. For a number of years, it published the *German Canadian Yearbook* as well as other publications to inform German Canadians and the broader Canadian community of the German experience in Canada.

The arrival of the new immigrants also brought a revival of song festivals. The arrivals not only formed new choirs but revitalized old choirs such as the *Gesangverein Concordia* in Kitchener-Waterloo. In 1958, the *Deutsch-Canadische Sängerbund* was formed, not only to co-ordinate the activities of the different choral groups, but also take a leading role in organizing German Canadian song festivals. Since its beginning, the *Sängerbund* has also made arrangements to have German Canadian choirs tour Europe and German or Austrian choirs tour Canada.

People dedicated to fostering different German folk dances started and/or expanded their network of organizations. Folk dance groups such as the *Schuhplattlergruppen* had already been popular during the inter-war period, in particular in centres such as Montreal and Vancouver. The popularity of *Schuhplattlering* led to classes for instruction in the dance, which, in turn, led to the formation of the Alpen Club in Vancouver. In 1936, Alpen Club *Schuhplattlers* won the trophy for best folk dance group at the local Canadian Folk Festival. In 1937, a members of the Alpen Club, Karl Bauer, left Vancouver and settled in Montreal. Together with Annie Bauer, who eventually became his wife, he performed the dance at various events. By 1952, he had brought together 6 couples, who organized themselves into the Montreal *Schuplattlergruppe Alpenland*. In time, *Schuplattlering* dance groups also emerged in other centres, such as Calgary, Edmonton, Toronto and Winnipeg. For years, their yearly *Gaufest* has offered dancers not only the opportunity to compete with each other, but also has provided entertainment to a wider audience, both German and other.

Regional and National Umbrella Organizations

The arrival of new immigrants after World War II also encouraged the growth of umbrella organizations that served to unite and act as spokespersons for immigrants originating from a certain area of Europe. One such organization was the Sudeten German *Zentralverband*. Efforts to unite Sudeten Germans under their own umbrella organization first emerged with the arrival of Sudeten German refugees prior to World War II. Their firm anti-Nazi stand at a time when most German Canadians sought to ignore the gathering storm in Europe provided them with a feeling of having a separate identity. This was further cemented by their common experiences as refugees and settlers. Furthermore, the endeavour by the West German government to compensate people for the suffering they had undergone at the hand of the Nazi regime encouraged Sudeten Germans to organize themselves so that they could take a common stand in their negotiations with West Germany. This led to the formation of the Central Organization of Sudeten German Clubs in Canada, in 1957.

Among Danube Swabians, the Alliance of Danube Swabians was organized on October 23, 1960, at a meeting of representatives of five local Danube Swabian organizations. Its objective was to advance good citizenship, encourage Danube Swabian immigration, and foster the preservation of Danube Swabian customs, religion, and art. At the same time, as in the case of the Sudeten Germans, it aided people who sought compensation from the West German government for losses they had suffered during World War II. The organization sponsors the Danube Swabian Day, which brings Danube Swabians together in celebration of their common heritage. In addition, it publishes a monthly, the *Heimatbote*, which not only helps to bind Danube Swabians together, but also serves to communicate their views and interests.

The Canadian Baltic Immigration Aid Society (CBIAS) was established in 1948 to help German Balts emigrate to Canada and aid them upon arrival in this country. Since the cessation of German Baltic immigration in the early 1960s, the CBIAS has served as an umbrella organization for clubs established by German-speaking Balts in Montreal, Toronto, Kitchener-Waterloo and in other centres across Canada.

The Association of Transylvanian Saxons of Canada, founded by post–World War II refugee immigrants in 1960, serves as umbrella organization for local Transylvanian societies in Canada. With clubs in centers such as Montreal, Toronto and Kitchener, the organization, which is affiliated with similar organizations in the United States, Germany and Austria, speaks for about 3,000 members. Since its beginning, it has published its monthly *Heimatbote*, which serves as the voice of the organization.

Endeavors to Unite the German Canadian Community from coast to coast

The large influx of Germans following World War II, as well as the expanding opportunities in communication during the post-war years, brought renewed efforts to establish organizations that would help to unite German Canadians, regardless of origin, from coast to coast. The first post-World War II organization to attempt this was the Trans-Canada Alliance of German Canadians (TCA). The Trans-Canada Alliance evolved from the collective effort by German Canadians to aid war-ravaged Germany and Austria after World War II. Once the new immigrants started arriving, the idea arose that a larger organization may be helpful to aid these people adjust to Canadian life. The organization would also help Germans speak with a collective voice with government and with other organizations or groups. This led to the founding of the TCA in 1951 and its incorporation in 1952.

Founding Meeting of the Trans-Canada Alliance of German Canadians. Library and Archives Canada, e011180497.

Once established, the TCA organized itself provincially, with provincial branches being organized in Ontario, Quebec, Manitoba and other provinces. Its membership included clubs and churches and different cultural organizations. It also encouraged individual membership. Membership in the organization consisted mostly of immigrants and immigrant organizations, with Canada-born German Canadians having little interest in German Canadian organizational life.

For a number of years after it was founded, the TCA played an important role in the post-World War II German Canadian community. It co-ordinated the operation of German language schools from coast to coast. It promoted cultural exchange between Canada, Germany and Austria, including the arrangement of group flights in either direction. Also, it had an important role in representing local German clubs with both the federal government and with the governments of Germany and Austria. Unlike earlier national organizations, it made little effort to represent German Canadians politically. The German community was itself divided politically, and it would have rent the TCA apart had it sought to take a political stand in favour of one political party or another. However, the TCA's endeavor to call government attention to the anti-German bias still prevalent in the North American media tended to obtain general community support.

Still, largely because of conflict between pre-World War II immigrants and post-World War II arrivals, the TCA in time became increasingly ineffective in pursuing German Canadian interests. After the Trans-Canada Alliance had lost much of its influence, the German Canadian Congress was organized, in 1984, to represent German Canadian political and cultural interests with the government as well as with non-German community organizations. By 1993, the Congress had branches in Ontario, Manitoba and British Columbia, in addition to some 550 member organizations across Canada. Among these were 130 churches, 100 German language schools, 20 senior citizens' homes, art associations, museums, theatres, credit unions, as well as four types of smaller umbrella organizations: the provincial umbrella organizations in Saskatchewan and Alberta; those of the Transylvanian Saxons, Danube Swabians, Balts and Sudeten Germans; the Canadian Association of German language Schools and also the German Canadian Choir Association, with branches in Kitchener, London, Hamilton, Stratford, Ottawa, Montreal, Toronto and Windsor.

German Canadian Congress membership, reflecting the diversity of the German Canadian mosaic's denominations and national origins, included Mennonites and Hutterites, Austrians and Swiss, as well as a few Anglophone and Francophone Canadians of German-speaking background. In many ways, it continued the policies of the TCA. In the area of German language instruction, it sought to use the German Canadian experience as a base for providing reading material for German language schools. It helped older people who had worked in Germany complete the necessary paperwork to obtain their pensions. At the same time, it made an effort to counteract the negative stereotype of Germans that often appeared in the media.

Despite its rapid growth, the Congress had difficulty sustaining itself, primarily because of conflict within the leadership of the organization, which was exacerbated by a cut in government funding in the early 1990s. This led to a closing of the National Office in Ottawa in 1995. Although the Congress has continued functioning at the national level, its activities have become very much circumscribed.

The Nature and Evolution of German Secular Voluntary Associations

When looking at the different secular formal voluntary associations that emerged in the German Canadian community, several generalizations may be made. Local clubs first were organized to meet in particular the needs of the new arrivals. They provided the opportunity for people speaking a different language to discuss many of the common problems they were facing as beginners in a new land. Clubs offered them the opportunity to meet and reminisce about the world they had left behind, as well as to enjoy the dances and sports activities of the homeland.

Once organized, clubs established sub-groupings to meet the variety of needs and interests of their membership. These included choirs, dance groups and other organizations to satisfy the needs and interests of club members. Until the advent of Medicare, clubs also tended to provide sickness and death benefits, which served to help new arrivals cope with the expenses incurred through illness or a death in the family.

As the German population in a particular centre increased, the number of associations tended to multiply. Some arose as a result of differences within an existing organization. At times, people from a particular region might join a German club and then form their own regional organization once enough of their people had settled in the community. Other organizations were formed to meet the interest of particular groups or to attain specific goals within the community. These included dance groups, choirs, mutual aid societies, or business and professional associations.

In essence, organizations increased so as to allow community members to participate in old country traditions and in the old country culture as fully as possible. At the same time, mutual aid organizations and business and professional associations emerged so as to maximize the economic and other benefits offered by the new environment.

Umbrella organizations first tended to be formed to permit local organizations to co-ordinate their various activities, thereby helping to certify that events sponsored by one organization would not conflict with those of another. This would allow people to attend as many functions in a particular community as possible; and would certify that the effort people had expended to put on a certain event would be of maximum benefit, financial or otherwise, to a sponsoring organization and to the community in general.

Provincial and national umbrella organizations that arose also served as liaisons with different levels of government and non-German community associations. They sought to realize the goals of their ethnic community within the larger society. In this regard, one finds striking differences in the goals pursued in particular by different German national organizations. During the pre-World War I period, German Canadian national organizations tended to make an effort to pursue what they saw as being German goals. This included broadening the opportunities for German language instruction. They sought, insofar as possible, to increase German membership in political bodies at the local, provincial and national levels. Also, they sought to shape the national environment so as to create social conditions, be this in the areas of Sunday laws, or alcohol consumption, that would help to make Germans feel at home in their new homeland.

The most important national organizations during the inter-war period, in particular Leftist organizations, were primarily concerned with the economic conditions in which German immigrants found themselves. Their focus was not so much on Canada. In fact, their hopes in this country had been destroyed by the shattering of their dreams as a result of the Depression. The German Canadian Left looked to Moscow and the German Canadian Right looked to Berlin to provide meaning and direction to their lives. Thus, both organizations in many ways acted as spokespersons for ideological movements in Europe from which they received inspiration and direction.

Post-World War II German national organizations were little interested in economic issues. They did not seek to become spokespersons for any ideological movement, either in Europe or Canada. Nor did they focus on advancing the position of German Canadians and enhancing their influence in Canadian society. Rather, both the TCA and the Congress focussed on the German Canadian community. In particular the TCA paid considerable attention to supporting German language schools and to cultural exchange with Germany. The Congress continued this tradition, in particular in its endeavour to use the German Canadian experience in this country to create instructional material for German language schools. Both the TCA and the Congress concentrated on combatting the negative stereotype of Germans that had developed during the world wars.

The survivability of clubs was influenced by their function in the community. Unlike the churches, which were concerned with the totality of a person's life and sought to prepare people for the afterlife, clubs were established to preserve the cultural tradition immigrants brought from the homeland. Their emergence and development was therefore quite different from that of the religious institutions. They didn't play a significant role among the mostly rural German immigrants who had settled on the land, whose social life centred on the church. The clubs were essentially an urban phenomenon, serving in particular those individuals or groups that no longer made the church the sole focus of their social life.

Less important to the life of the individual or the community than the churches, clubs tended to have a more precarious existence. Thus, the first German society formed, the High German Society, declined not long after it was established in the 1700s. Several German societies were established and again declined in Winnipeg before the German Society of Winnipeg, established in 1892, was to gain a firm footing. Churches, on the other hand, had a comparatively more stable existence after they were founded.

Although churches decreased in importance as the German community became more secular, in particular after World War II, churches are still the major community organizations among German Canadians. Some German groups, in particular evangelical groups such as the Mennonite Brethren or the Baptists, even view clubs as part of the "sinful world" that has to be avoided. German Canadian Catholics, while not seeing clubs as a "sinful" part of the world, have concentrated on integrating the individual into the larger church community by establishing organizations such as the *Volksverein deutsch-canadischer Katholiken*. National clubs totally independent of the church have been more important for groups such as the Lutherans who drew a sharper dividing line between the Church and the state, with the pastor essentially confining his work to the church. Clubs have been most important in helping to structure the social life of totally secularised individuals who didn't attend church or attended it only sporadically.

Concerned largely with the secular heritage rather than the total life of community members, clubs were affected differently than the churches by the community's process of assimilation. Whereas churches gradually changed the language used in services and church meetings as members of the congregation became assimilated, clubs altered in a different fashion. When first established, they helped immigrants continue the customs and folkways they brought from the homeland. They served as a sort of halfway-house for new arrivals, offering them a home away from home while they were being integrated into the larger society. Unlike the churches, which experienced the wars and the language transition with little loss in membership, clubs lost much of their membership during crisis periods. This was especially the case where the community was well on the way to being assimilated.

This raises the question of how German clubs will be affected by the extreme decrease in the flow of German immigrants to Canada that has occurred since the 1970s. To survive, choirs, clubs and dance groups have started to recruit not only German Canadians as members, but anyone interested in the activities they offer. The language of their business meetings is gradually changing from German to English. Clubs seek to emphasize programs such as *Oktoberfest*, for example, which appeals to a larger Canadian audience. In essence, as the community is being assimilated, its secular organizations are increasingly fitting themselves into the larger Canadian milieu, stressing that part of the German tradition attractive to the larger Canadian society and gradually divesting themselves of the remainder. Whether this assures their survival remains to be seen.

THE GERMAN CANADIAN MEDIA

The German Canadian media, consisting for most of the period under study of the German language press, came to life soon after the arrival of the first Germans in this country. The German Canadian media can be divided into two larger categories. One is the religious media. It consists of publications or broadcasts of different religious groups to keep members in contact with each other and disseminate a Church's message to its members and the wider society. The other category is the secular media. It consists, for the most part, of weeklies published by local or regional organizations that, among other things, inform their readership of local and international events. When radio and television appeared, these were put to the service of the community. The following presents a survey of the different types of media to provide the reader with an insight into the purpose these served in the German Canadian community.

The Secular German language Press

The first German language publication that came out in what was to become Canada was the *Neuschottländische Kalender* (1788-1801), published in Halifax by Anthony Henry (Anton Heinrich). Born in Alsace, he eventually became the "King's Printer" for Nova Scotia. A few issues of his *Kalender* can still be found at the provincial archives in Halifax and in the Library and Archives Canada, in Ottawa.

German publications were to appear again during the settlement of Germans in Upper Canada when Waterloo County became the centre of German Canadian public life. In his study of the German language press in Ontario, Herbert Kalbfleisch found that some 29 German language publications had made their appearance in Ontario between 1850 and 1900. This included the *Canada Museum und Allgemeine Zeitung* (1835-1840), and *Der Deutsche Canadier und Neuigkeitsbote*, published in Berlin between 1841 and 1865. The longest-lasting of these publications, the

Berliner Journal, was founded in 1859 and continued until it was closed down during the war, in 1918.

The period from 1900 to the outbreak of World War I saw a rapid reduction and amalgamation of German language publications in Ontario, reflecting the gradual assimilation of the community. Some newspapers ceased publication altogether, and others were absorbed into papers that had a larger circulation. Thus, the *Berliner Journal* absorbed the *Ontario Glocke,* which had previously come out as the *Walkerton Glocke,* which had gained considerable popularity in Bruce County through its publication of the Joe Klotzkopp Letters, published in the Pennsylvania German dialect.

Editorial Board of the Berliner Journal, [1885]. Public Domain.

Western Canadian German language papers made their appearance with the settlement of Germans in the Canadian West. The first German language publication was *Der Nordwesten.* Started at the urging of H.C. Schmieder, pastor of Trinity Lutheran, Winnipeg, and through the work of William Hespeler, the paper served to inform Germans of local and world affairs, as well as to help build a closer link between the various German settlements in Western Canada. Not long after it was founded, the newspaper fell under the control of the Liberal party. To counterbalance Liberal control of *Der Nordwesten,* Manitoba Conservatives helped establish the *Germania* in 1904. However, the *Germania* couldn't compete with *Der Nordwesten,* and in 1911 the Conservatives bought *Der Nordwesten* outright.

In the meantime, other German language papers appeared on the scene. In May 1903, the *Alberta Herold* commenced publication. It was brought out by Count Alfred von Hammerstein, an entrepreneur who learned about paper publishing from Frank Oliver's *Edmonton Bulletin* for which he worked for a brief period. Soon after the paper appeared, it was acquired by Gustav Koermann, an employee of *Der Nordwesten,* who took an interest in the paper while on a business trip to Alberta for the Manitoba-based *Der Nordwesten.* Politically Liberal, the paper concentrated on Alberta news. In 1908, a competitor for the *Herold* appeared, *Der Deutsch-Canadier.* Starting out in Edmonton as a pro-Conservative paper, it became pro-Liberal when it moved to Calgary eight months later. To broaden its appeal and define its field of operation, the paper started publishing a short-lived weekly supplement, the *Deutsch-Canadischer Farmer, w*hich concentrated on items of interest to farmers, the first German Canadian publication in Alberta to do so.

In 1910, a rival weekly, the *Alberta deutsche Zeitung* began publishing in Edmonton. It was brought out by Gustav Koermann after he sold the *Alberta Herold.* Professing to be politically neutral, the paper was strongly anti-Liberal and expressed pro-Conservative leanings. Experiencing financial difficulties, the paper began to appear irregularly. It was then sold to a German-Albertan consortium which expressed the desire to keep the paper free from any English-Canadian influence, despite the fact that some of its members were prominent German-Albertan Conservatives. The paper ceased publication in about 1913.

In the meantime, in 1907, the *Saskatchewan Courier* was started with the support of the Liberal party of Saskatchewan. With Saskatchewan's large German population, the paper grew quickly, becoming the main rival of *Der Nordwesten* not only in Saskatchewan but also in Western Canada.

In British Columbia, the *Westliche Kanadische Post* appeared in 1906. Founded by F.F. Blockberger, the paper sought to serve Germans in Vancouver and British Columbia in general. The paper folded after it was sued for having libeled Constantin Alvo von Alvensleben. When the editor lost the case, von Alvensleben won possession of the paper, which declined soon after. A second British Columbia paper was started in 1911 by Dr. Karl Weiss. Bilingual, the *Vancouver German Press* had a circulation of 8,400 by 1913.

The survival of German language papers was put to a severe test during World War I. The outbreak of war brought a drastic reduction in newspaper advertisements placed in the papers, making their operation difficult. Also, with the outbreak of war, German language newspapers were placed under the control of the Chief Press Censor, in Ottawa. Their reports, in particular on the war, were monitored. Some newspaper editors ran into difficulty. This was true in particular of the editor of the *Alberta Herold*. However, no action was taken against the paper, even though the editor's coverage of the war was overtly pro-German, in particular in its references to German victories over Czarist Russia. The provincial Conservatives introduced a motion in the legislature calling for its suppression and the persecution of its publisher for treason and sedition. The resolution was defeated by the Liberal-dominated legislature, which declared that only the federal government had the power to launch such action. The paper ceased publication before federally initiated steps were taken to censor and suppress the paper. Nevertheless, the endeavor by German language papers to confine themselves within the strictures laid down by the Chief Press Censor offended many of their readers, causing them to cancel their subscriptions. Other subscribers, in turn, cancelled their subscription because they did not want to be associated with a German language paper, which was the case in particular in Eastern Canada.

When World War I ended, German language publications were in a sorry state. Those that had not ceased publication were forced to publish in English. In Eastern Canada, German language weeklies disappeared altogether. Following the closure of the *Alberta Herold* and *Der Deutsch-Canadier,* German-Albertans remained without any press for at least a decade. In Saskatchewan, the *Saskatchewan Courier* was very much weakened. It was bought by the Western Printers Association Ltd., with a view of subsequently buying out the German Catholic *West Canada* and the German Protestant *Courier* and amalgamating the two to form a new and larger secular German language weekly, *Der Courier,* under Catholic direction. In Manitoba, the Conservatives had lost their interest in ethnic-language publications, and *Der Nordwesten* again came under Liberal control. The actual operation of the paper fell to the Frank Dojacek family, who looked after the daily operation not only of the German language paper but also several other foreign-language newspapers.

The inter-war period was not an easy time for German language publications. Immigration brought only some 100,000 German-speaking immigrants to the new country. These settled not only in Western

Canada but also in Canada's industrial centers in the east. The outbreak
of the Depression brought other concerns, which resulted in a drop not
only in subscribers but also in advertisements placed in German language
papers. At the same time, new competitors arose, including the *Deutsche
Arbeiter Zeitung* and *Die Deutsche Zeitung für Canada*, one a pro-
communist and the other a pro-Nazi publication.

The pro-communist publication ceased publication prior to the war
and the pro-Nazi publication ended publication with the outbreak of
World War II. With the outbreak of war, German language newspapers
again found themselves with a reduction of newspaper ads. They were
again placed under censorship.

The situation improved for them after the end of the war, which
saw the arrival of some 400,000 German immigrants. The number
of newspaper subscribers greatly increased. Unfortunately, most of
the increase was in central Canada, and in provinces to the west of
Saskatchewan and Manitoba, where Canada's major weeklies were
published. At the same time, most of the readership in places like
Saskatchewan was becoming assimilated and losing the ability to read
German. This meant increased shipping costs to get the newspapers
from where they were produced to the readership. Nevertheless, both
Der Nordwesten and *Der Courier* responded positively to the problem
by including regional issues in their publications. That is, each paper
had one main segment, dealing with the general news. Added to this
were special sections prepared for different provinces, be this British
Columbia, Alberta, or Ontario. Cities where Germans were especially
heavily concentrated, such as Toronto or Montreal, also tended to have a
section reserved for them.

The concentration of the readership in Eastern Canada and in the
westernmost areas of Western Canada also encouraged competitors
to emerge in areas where the new readership was concentrated. In
Montreal, in 1954, the *Montrealer Nachrichten* arose, seeking to appeal
to a Quebec readership. At the same time, it put out a publication, *Ihre
Brigitte*, which was devoted to women's issues. Seeking further support
for its undertakings by working for the recognition of the DDR by the
Canadian government, the publication lost clientele and was forced to
cease publication in 1975.

Started in 1978 as an information leaflet of the German Society
of Montreal, *Das Echo der deutschkanadischen Gemeinschaft* expanded

across the country as members of the German Canadian community left Québec following the "Quiet Revolution." In 1979, Paul Christian Walter, publisher of the newssheet, shortened its name to *Das Echo*. That same year, Walter turned the newssheet into a bimonthly newspaper and 2 years later it became a monthly serving the German Canadian community from coast to coast. With a monthly readership of about 100,000, the paper is one of the largest nationwide German language publications in Canada.

In 1953, the *Torontoer Zeitung* appeared. It sought to widen its appeal by also preparing issues for readers in Kitchener, Hamilton and Montreal. However, the paper had difficulty surviving and in 1980 was bought by the *Kanada Kurier*. Other southern Ontario publications were more successful. Published in Toronto since 1977, the weekly *Deutsche Presse* draws press reports from the *Deutsche Press Agentur*, the *Deutsche Welle* as well as uses its own correspondents in Canada and Germany to serve the local German Canadian community as well as German speakers across Canada and in the United States. With some 120,000 readers, the weekly is one of the largest German language publications in North America. Founded in 1990 as a bilingual publication, the monthly *Echo Germanica* serves the German-speaking communities in southern Ontario. Another bilingual publication published in southern Ontario since 1997, the monthly *Deutsche Rundschau*, draws its readership not only locally, but from some 140 countries. Local organizations based in southern Ontario also continue to bring out their publications, including the *Heimatbote*, published by the Alliance of Danube Swabians, as well as a publication with the same name published by the Association of Transylvanian Saxons in Canada.

Post-World War II immigrants in Ottawa published the monthly *Canada Herold* from 1970 to 1982. The monthly *Kontakt*, which served to represent the interest of the DDR, was largely the product of Horst Doehler of Toronto, who had been a former member of the *Deutsche Arbeiter und Farmer Verband*. It died with his death in the 1980s. In Vancouver, the *Pazifische Rundschau*, which occasionally appeared weekly from 1965, was for many years published by the post-World War II German immigrant, Baldwin Ackermann. Published in Williams Lake, British Columbia, by Krista Liebe and her husband, after she retired in 2002 from her job as broadcaster, *Die Kleine Zeitung mit Herz* serves German-speaking communities in British Columbia and Alberta.

All these publications essentially serve the immigrant community. As such, they all face the problem of declining readership as the immigrant generation dies off and the younger generation of immigrants and the first generation of Canada-born grow to adulthood. In Post-World War II Canada, this trend started in the 1970s and continued unabated after that. This forced a number of changes upon German language publications, as may be seen in the case of *Der Nordwesten* and the *Courier*. Having problems running *Der Nordwesten*, the Dojack family decided to sell the paper. In 1970 it was bought by the Western Printers Association Ltd., publisher of the *Courier,* which at the time was under control of Georg Scholtz. He decided to unite the two papers, to modernize them and make the print run more efficient. This new publication, under the title *Kanada Kurier,* had a circulation from coast to coast and was, for a period, the main truly trans-Canada German Canadian weekly. At the same time, he bought out papers such as the *Torontoer Zeitung* to establish himself more firmly in areas where Germans were concentrated.

The amalgamation of the *Courier* and *Der Nordwesten* helped briefly, but was not a solution to the problems faced by the German language press. Their competition was coming not only from Canada-based papers. The shrinkage of the global village was making it easier for readers in Canada to obtain German papers, and magazines such as *Der Spiegel.* To deal with this, Scholtz decided to become a distributor for publications from Germany, which tended to appeal more to the educated German readership than did small Canada-based publications. At the same time, radio and television were beginning to compete with the German language press. Television and radio broadcasts consisted of programs presented by local churches and clubs, as well as of radio broadcasts and television programs coming over specialty channels from Europe. These cut into the readership of the *Kanada Kurier.* The result was the demise of the *Kanada Kurier* in 2004.

What the community has been left with, primarily, are monthlies or regional papers, often published by two or three people who do this work essentially as a labour of love. Papers with a larger circulation, such as the *Deutsche Presse* and *Das Echo*, tend to be well connected with German language publications in Europe. In addition to the major publications, there are also publications of the various sub-groupings in the German community, published by their umbrella organizations, which are of interest to a community sub-group. Publications from German-speaking countries of Europe sold in Canada serve the needs of people requiring a broader knowledge of international business and political affairs, in particular as these concern the German-speaking countries in Europe.

The German language press in Canada offers, and has always offered, an important service to the German Canadian community. It connects with each other people in a particular area, city or province, and especially while the *Kanada Kurier* was distributed from coast to coast, served to bind together the different German communities across the country. Advertisements placed in the papers inform people where they might purchase necessities to meet their needs. The papers provide churches and clubs space to advertise their meetings, as well as inform people of different events of importance to the community. At the same time, the different papers provide space for locals to publish their work, which consists for the most part of poetry. This gives people so inclined a place where they might see their work in print.

The papers keep readers informed of the country in which they live, as well as makes them aware of the larger world. In particular, the papers keep them up to date on what is happening in the homelands they left behind. The control that political parties have over some of the publications, while adding another influence contributing to the various divisions in the community, also serve to integrate the German-speaking minority into the larger society.

The religious German language Press

All religious groupings in the German Canadian community had their own publications, including the Catholics, Lutherans, Mennonites and Baptists. Different sub-groupings within each religious community, such as the different Lutheran Synods, also had their own publications. These served the different religious communities as long as they used German as their main language of communication, with the publications declining as the churches gave up the German in favor of English in their services.

While Eastern Canadian German Catholics established a seminary in the 1880's to train priests, there is little evidence that they founded a major publication. However, in 1858 the *Katholisches Wochenblatt* began to appear in Hamilton for a brief period. In Western Canada, the

Benedictines of St. Peter's Abbey, in Muenster, Saskatchewan, brought
out the *St. Peter's Bote* in 1904 for Catholics whom they were serving.
Father Cordes, an Oblate who served St. Joseph's parish in Winnipeg,
founded the *West Canada* in 1907 to serve German Catholics under the
spiritual guidance of the Oblates. The *West Canada* ceased publishing in
1918. It was followed by *Der Katholik*, which was published in Winnipeg
between 1924 and 1931. The *St. Peter's Bote* ceased publishing in 1947,
because its German readership had shrunk. It was supplanted by the
English-language *Prairie Messenger*.

New German-Catholic publications appeared with the arrival of a
new wave of immigrants after World War II. This included *Der Katholik*,
which was published between 1960 and 1993 and served the German
language parishes that had been established after World War II. In 1994,
it was replaced by *Miteinander-Füreinander*, which ceased publishing in
2003, when the last editor resigned and no one could be found to carry
on the work.

The different Lutheran synods had their information bulletins. For
example, the Synod of Manitoba published the *Synodalbote* in Winnipeg,
which served synod members in different parts of Western Canada. After
1868, the Ev. Lutheran Synod of Canada published the *Kirchenblatt
der Ev. Lutherishcen Synode von Canada* which in 1910 merged with
the *Deutsche Lutheraner*, brought out by the General Council of North
America. Between 1933 and 1959, the Lutheran Missouri Synod
published the *Canadisch-lutherische Kirchenbratt*, which served as the
German counterpart of the *Canadian Lutheran*. It was formed through
the merger of the *Lutherische Herold* [1933] and *Unsere Kirche* (1924-
1933). All German publications declined as English replaced German in
Lutheran church services.

German Baptists were served by *Der Sendbote*. Founded in 1866,
in the United States, its popularity fluctuated according to the number
of German-speaking Baptist immigrants it served. In Canada, it did
quite well when the Baptist community was establishing itself prior to
World War I. However, it suffered with the outbreak of World War I,
when some of its churches gave up the German in favor of English in
their services. Although it grew in readership in Canada during the inter-
war years, it suffered from the relatively low number of immigrants who
came to Canada at this time. This was exacerbated as churches in both
Canada and the United States increasingly turned to English in their

services. It was in serious decline when the influx of new arrivals from Europe gave it new life after World War II. However, as more and more of the immigrant churches in Canada turned to English for their primary language of service after the 1970s, it found itself shrinking again in readership.

The same influences affected Mennonite religious publications. The *Mennonitische Rundschau,* founded in 1878 by Mennonite immigrants from Russia who had settled in the United States, in 1909 was transferred to Canada, where assimilation was less pronounced than in the United States. It continued publishing until 2007 when it was found that people had lost interest in it and were reading English-language publications. *Der Bote* came out 1924 to serve as a point of contact for German-speaking Russian Mennonites who had emigrated to Canada after World War I. In 1947, it merged with the *Christliche Bundesbote* and became the weekly paper for the General Conference Mennonite Church. It ceased publication in 2008, due to declining readership. Established in 1977, *Die Mennonitische Post* serves as communication link between Mennonite families in Canada and those in Mexico Belize, Paraguay, Bolivia and Argentina. It also serves as a mouthpiece for Old Colony Mennonites.

The above are only examples of some of the publications brought out by German language Catholics, Lutherans, Mennonites and Baptists. Other denominations had their own publications. German Pentecostals had the *Deutsche Pfingstgemeinde* and *Missionsnachrichten des deutschen Zweiges Pentecostal Assemblies of Canada* serving them, and the Evangelical Association was served by *Der Evangeliums Bote*, which during the general conference of the Evangelical Association, October to November 1893, even came out daily. No matter what publication, each spelled out the overall beliefs of the denomination publishing it, provided information relevant to its subscribers, as well as provided messages of inspiration, serving to keep readers strong in the faith.

Radio and Television

In the 1920s, when radio was becoming popular, many German language churches in North America were well on the way to giving up German as the language of their services. This was especially true in the United States. Radio broadcasts, when introduced, tended to be in the English language, directed both at a particular religious community and the larger society. Thus, one of the earliest radio programs launched by Mennonites was started in 1936 in Ohio, when the radio evangelist William Detweiler began "The Calvary Hour." Continued by his sons, the program could in time be heard on over 30 radio stations in both North and South America. In 1939, a former General Conference minister, Theodore Epp, founded "Back to the Bible, Inc.," a nondenominational ministry in Nebraska.

Among Lutherans, the Missouri Synod, with headquarters in that state, was one of the first to recognize the use of radio, both to reach out to its own membership and to the larger society. With this end in mind, members of the Synod, such as the Rev. Prof. J. H. C. Fritz and the Rev. Dr. Walter A. Maier of Concordia Seminary, in Missouri, established KFUO (850 AM) in October 1924. It presented sermons, programs on Bible study and biblical interpretation. In October 1930, KFUO-AM also began broadcasting The Lutheran Hour, dedicated to serving Lutherans not only in America but also worldwide. Today, the program is the oldest continually broadcast Christ-centered radio program.

In Canada, St. Peter's Church, Edmonton, began to broadcast its evening services over the radio in the 1930s to meet popular demand. In November 1934, four German language Lutheran broadcasts began to be offered over radio station CFCN, Calgary. CFRN, Edmonton, began broadcasting German language Lutheran radio programs on Sunday evening at 7:00 p.m. that same year. In 1937, CFRN also began broadcasting a Baptist German language Sunday evening program, 6:30-7:00 p.m.

St. Matthew's Lutheran Church in Kitchener inaugurated a German language broadcast, *Kirche Daheim*, in 1930, with the first sermon being presented on the 23rd of February of that year. At first, the congregation, which then was bilingual, intended to broadcast its evening English-language service, because it was believed to reach a greater number of people. However, as the 7 o'clock hour was not available to the church on the air, it decided to broadcast its German morning service. Here it was found that many of the aged and shut-ins, for whom the service was designed, preferred a service in their mother tongue. Not only that. It was found that the service also attracted listeners in southern Ontario in general, as well as in New York, Pennsylvania and Michigan.

The above examples tended to be the exceptions rather than the rule for German Lutheran churches. Of the 21 Lutheran churches in

North America offering regular radio broadcasts in 1930, only one, St. Matthew's, offered a regular German language broadcast.[122] For the most part, local German churches, no matter of what denomination, when making use of radio, did so on special occasions. Thus, Christmas or Easter special services might be broadcast over the radio. At times, radio was used when a special speaker spoke at a church service or during an evangelical revival meeting. On other occasions, different groups within a Church, such as the *Lutherliga* of the Manitoba Synod, made use of radio to popularize their message.

As in the case of the churches, radio began to gain some popularity in the secular German community in the 1930s. On some occasions, local choirs, such as the *Nord-Kildonan Männerchor*, Winnipeg, or the Morden-Winkler Symphony Orchestra, presented a music program over the radio. On other occasions, local church choirs such as the mixed choir of the Winnipeg German Baptist church presented songs that appealed to both a religious as well as a secular audience.

For the most part, these presentations tended to be short, one-time performances. It seems that one reason why German programs tended to be short and ran only for a brief period stemmed from the difficulty they had getting radio stations to give them more time. That was why the different advertisements for radio programs that appeared in the German language press generally asked readers to write the station concerned and request that the time period during which a program was presented be extended.

In Saskatchewan, the program *An der schönen blauen Donau* was broadcast on a fairly regular basis over a radio station in Regina. It presented popular music, in particular folk songs. It also offered special programs at Christmas and on other special occasions, which were well

---

[122] In its report on the radio program, the writer states that "in this district of Western Ontario (the Kitchener-Waterloo region) there are countless shutins, aged and infirm, and others who cannot go to church, whose mother tongue is German, but for whom no church service in that language is provided at all. Our Sunday broadcast enjoys, we believe, the unique distinction of being the only German service regularly on the air every Sunday on the Western Continent." See *Kirche Daheim: Church at Home – A Souvenir Booklet* [Kitchener, 1930] 16.

received by German audiences in the prairie provinces as well as by people in neighboring states south of the border.

In Alberta, German language newspapers mentioned German radio broadcasts intended for a general audience for the first time in 1929, when Edmonton's German South Side Band played over the radio. CFAC, Calgary, broadcast its first German show in 1932. On November 4, 1932, radio station CKUA started a German Hour, featuring in particular the *Schubertchor* (later renamed *Schubert-Gesangverein*), a choir especially assembled by the German Canadian community for radio broadcasts. In December of the same year, the program switched from CKUA to CJCA, apparently because the latter station was more powerful and could reach a broader audience.

Direct reception radio broadcasts via short-wave radio from Germany became possible in the early 1930s. Offering some six to eight hours of German language broadcasting a day, German radio broadcasts were accessible to anyone who had access to a short-wave radio. Advertisements in the German language press in Canada let people know what was being offered. Programs included radio dramas, musical presentations, news from Germany, as well as programs on different subjects that might be of interest to a general audience.

German language radio programming essentially came to an end with the outbreak of World War II. As with the German language press, the situation for German language radio altered radically after World War II. In Western Canada, in particular Saskatchewan, where a considerable number of subscribers to the German language press and listeners to German language radio had resided prior to the war, Germans had become increasingly anglicized. In fact, this was also true of German Canadians in general. The new wave of immigrants, therefore, became the predominant audience for the German language press and for German language radio. These had settled primarily in the urban centres. At the same time, they tended to be much better educated than previous immigrants. This influenced not only the German language press but also the electronic media serving the German Canadian community.

After World War II, Churches that used radio to broadcast their message did so primarily in the English language. The Mennonite Conference of Ontario began its broadcast of a "Mennonite Hour" in 1945. A Mennonite Brethren broadcast was started in Saskatoon in 1940, and a Mennonite Conference program in 1948. Mennonite broadcast activity expanded in the 1950s, with Bethel College, Goshen College and Eastern Mennonite College, all in the United States, operating their own FM radio stations. In both Canada and the United States, numerous local broadcasts were presented by the Mennonite Brethren Church, the General Conference Mennonite Church and by other Mennonite denominations. In cases where these denominations still made use of the German language, which was the case in many churches in Western Canada, broadcasts were at times in German.

At the same time, different branches of the Mennonite Church also developed special programs. Thus, Gospel Light (later known as Mennonite Brethren Communications) developed programs in English, German, Low German and Russian for adults and children. The General Conference Mennonite Church expanded a devotional broadcast in Newton, Kansas, to a conference-wide project in 1953. In the 1960s, this project was also expanded to television, with General Conference churches in local areas making use of different segments of this program to suit their needs.

Up to the 1970s, the different Mennonite conferences, especially when considering mission outreach, tended to create programs that would have domestic relevance and also could be used in mission outreach. Concerns about cultural imperialism and indigenous leadership, and increased sensitivity about exporting North American programs overseas, caused the different conferences to make use of local sources and talents. For example, in 1977 the *Europäische Mennonitische Radiomission* was formed to carry the responsibility for the German broadcasts conducted by the Mennonite Board of Missions.

In this situation, German became, not the language of the Church community, but rather a language of the foreign missions. Insofar as German was still used in Mennonite broadcasts, it was used primarily by conservative churches that still saw the use of the German language as a means of separating the community of believers from the "world." This was the case, for example, in the founding of the Low German Radio Station CHPD-FM, on 105.9 FM. Started in 2003, the station is owned and operated by the Aylmer and Area Mennonite Community Council. Broadcasting in German, Low German, English and Spanish, the station provides music, news reports, sermons and other information of interest to the Low German community that had left South America to settle in this area of Ontario.

As before World War II, the major Lutheran broadcasts, such as those over station KFUO of the Missouri Synod, were primarily in the English language. The same is true of programs when the Missouri Synod of the Lutheran Church ventured into television in 1952, with a dramatic series entitled "This is the Life." German programs came essentially from Germany rather than Missouri. For example, in 1952, Lutheran Hour was launched in German-speaking parts of Europe under the title *Lutherische Stunde.* At first, *Lutherische Stunde* programs were prepared in English and then translated into German. Since 1962, *Lutherische Stunde* prepared its own programs. These are accessible to anyone wishing to tune in on short wave radio in any part of the world. At the same time, during the period of massive German immigration following World War II, the Synod made use of shortwave radio to bring the Word of God to areas where Lutherans were sparsely settled.

For example, in 1955 and 1956, Lutheran church services in Northern Ontario were broadcast over a local radio station to serve the different Lutheran immigrant families that had settled there. This made it much easier to bring the gospel to believers than had been the case with the travelling missionaries, who often had to travel hundreds of miles a year to serve the small groups of Lutherans that had settled in Northern Ontario. At the same time, different local Lutheran churches at times presented special services directed at the immigrant community, be this on special occasions or to reach church members unable to attend regular services.

While German Lutherans tended to make use of radio to provide the Message to members of their own Church who, because of age, sickness or distance had difficulty attending regular Sunday services, German Baptists tended to direct their broadcasts to the larger German-speaking community. This was the case, for example, with Bethel Baptist Church of Prince George, B.C., which started a radio program in 1949, and the *Gnaden Baptisten Gemeinde* of Kelowna, B.C., which started a radio program in 1952. Bethel Baptist, which, as the only Baptist German language congregation in a 500-mile radius from Prince George, saw itself as especially obligated to bring the Word of God to German-speakers within the area.

As in the case of religious broadcasting, post-World War II broadcasts directed at the secular German Canadian community were also directed essentially at the immigrant community. These broadcasts expanded considerably after the war, and this for several reasons. One was the massive influx of German immigrants. These provided a ready audience for anyone wishing to start a German radio program, as well as made it worthwhile for radio stations of the larger society to offer programs directed toward German-speakers. At the same time, community members themselves saw the electronic media as a means of binding the community together.

Post-World War II German language programs addressed to the community as a whole tended to originate from several sources. A television or radio program might be presented by a major club or the *Stadtausschuss* of German organizations in a particular community. They might be financed by local businesses wishing to advertise their services to the German-speaking community. In the late 1960s, major German companies also sponsored such programs. These programs might include musical presentations, news on community, city, country and international affairs, in particular German or Austrian affairs.

By 1973, some sixteen local radio stations in Canada offered weekly broadcasts in the German language at least once a week. Most of these originated in major urban centers, such as Toronto, London, Kitchener-Waterloo, where most German immigrants had settled. Time of weekly broadcasting varied from 11.5 hours in London to one hour in St. Thomas or Midland. No matter where the programs originated, they all tended to concentrate on musical presentations, be these *Schlager* or folk songs, as well as on reports from local businesses and clubs. News from the homeland, in particular political news or news on sports events also received considerable attention.

By 1973, in addition to radio programs, German Canadians also tended to have access to fortnightly, weekly or monthly television programs. Often presented by the local community, they might show local dancers or musicians. They might also include discussions of issues of concern to the community, as well as reports on local, national and international events. They also showed films of interest to the community.

As in the case of the German language press, German language radio and television were influenced by the computer revolution and by globalization. In both instances, these weakened the local media and increased the influence of German language transmissions from Europe. Of course, Germans continued to some extent to be dependent on German language transmissions originating in Canada, in particular those originating from the multicultural stations such as CHIN.

However, as the 20thcentury came to a close, the most important transmissions came from Europe.

Radio Herz, based in Germany, established stations in different parts of the world, including Canada. In Canada, it is based in southern Ontario, but has connections to different centers. The station offers 24 hours of German language broadcasting, consisting for the most part of music. It can be heard via the internet through Bell Express Vu. On Bell Express Vu, for example, *Radio Herz* is on Channel 986. The channel is part of a "German Special" package, which also gives subscribers access, among other programs, to the radio and television service of the *Deutsche Welle*.

Deutsche Welle (DW) has served the German Canadian post-World War II community since 1953. It broadcasts through satellite and cable operators throughout the world, presenting news and information through shortwave, internet and satellite radio. It has a satellite television service *(DW-TV)* that is available in different languages. Among other programs, *DW* provides political talk shows, children's series and documentaries. It provides the latest in politics, business, the arts, sports, as well as presents language classes.

In addition, German television is available through programs such as BOXX-TV, a pay-TV package for households in North America. The program was launched with 7 TV channels on board, including family entertainment, *Volksmusik*, TV, TW1 and Euronews. Subscribers receive a package of programs under the title *Kanada Kurier* via the broadband internet through an IPTV compatible set-top-box that fits onto compatible television sets.

Globalization has transformed the German Canadian media. The German language media at one time developed almost totally in the Canadian environment. It received its support from the community, flourishing with the inflow of new immigrants and declining as the children of immigrants became increasingly absorbed into the larger Canadian environment. With increased globalization, German immigrants, or anyone else who has a knowledge of German, can live in this country and have immediate access to radio, television and other programs produced in Europe. While living in Canada, they can exist in an intellectual milieu in many ways divorced from their everyday life.

ENDOGAMY AND EXOGAMY

The alterations in the community life of German Canadians over time did not occur independently but were part of a process that saw the gradual integration of German Canadians into the larger society. A major area in which integration occurred was in family relationships, brought about through intermarriage. With the family being the core institution in our society, whom one marries will have a profound influence on the future society. Intermarriage will have an effect not only on the biological nature of the offspring but also on the beliefs and values passed on from generation to generation. Insofar as marriage is confined to the ethnic group, marriage will reinforce the ethnic identity of a particular individual. In the case of intermarriage, other strains are introduced, all of them serving to weaken the influence among the offspring of a particular identity, thereby encouraging assimilation.

Intermarriage has had an important influence on merging Germans into the larger society since the beginnings of German settlement in this country. This occurred in particular where Germans were sparsely settled. Some of the earliest soldiers and settlers who came to New France intermarried rapidly and were absorbed into the larger French Canadian community, with only their name at times suggesting their origin. The same was true of German settlers and soldiers who took up land throughout the Maritimes and in Upper and Lower Canada. Intermarriage tended to occur less frequently in areas of group settlement. Endogamy was also encouraged in instances where religion served to isolate a particular community from outside influences. Nevertheless, intermarriage was a constant factor affecting the German community, in particular in more recent times. This may be observed when looking at Canadian census data on this subject.

Census statistics provide an indication of intermarriage by ethnic communities in several areas. They provide information on marriage partners chosen by both male and female members of an ethnic community. They also provide insight into the extent to which different ethnic communities intermarry. Thus, in the case of Germans, they provide information on the number or percentage of Germans who chose a partner of the same background, or who chose partners of another background. They also show with which groups Germans tended to intermarry.

Thus, census statistics for 1921 show that 75.2 per cent of males of German origin married females of the same origin, and 72.6 per cent of females of German origin married males of German origin. Of the males who intermarried, 16.8 per cent married females of British origin, and 18.8 per cent of women of German origin married males of British origin.

The rate of intermarriage increased significantly by 1951. The 1951 census statistics show that 52 per cent of men and 52.3 per cent of women of German origin married a partner of the same origin. Again, the vast majority, or 32.5 per cent of men and 32.1 per cent of women of German origin married people who were of British origin. The next major group with which intermarriage occurred was the French. In this case, the 1951 census states that 3.9 per cent of German men and 3.3 per cent of German women married people of French origin, far fewer than chose British partners.

The 2001 census statistics illustrate a rapid integration of the German community into the larger society. They show that of 2,742,765 Canadians of German origin, 705,595 respondents had parents who were both of German origin. This suggests that in 2001 74 per cent of respondents of German origin were only partially of German background.

A number of influences encouraged or discouraged intermarriage. One of these was the availability of partners. This was particularly the case with auxiliary troops that had fought for the British cause in the New World and then had settled here rather than return to the homeland. Very often neither they nor their family had the means to pay the passage for a prospective bride for the bachelor. His alternative, therefore, was either to marry a local girl or remain single.

No matter what the religious group, immigrants themselves tended to marry within their community and encourage their children to marry within their ethnic community. Among regular immigrants, young unmarried men, who made up a major segment of the arrivals, often had left a fiancé or girlfriend at home. They tended to send for her as soon as they had established themselves. In other cases, they had their family or friends in the homeland search for a suitable partner for them. Arrangements would be worked out through friends or relatives, upon which the man would pay for the girl's passage over. At other times, a bachelor advertised in the homeland press to find a suitable wife.

Church membership had a profound influence on intermarriage. In particular prior to the middle of the 20th century, Germans tended to marry not only within their own ethnic community but also within their own religious community. Church membership also affected the intermarriage of Germans in other ways. Generally, intermarriage was influenced by the extent to which the community was isolated from other groups, with intermarriage being less prevalent in rural than in urban areas. This was particularly the case, as among Mennonites and Hutterites, where spatial isolation was reinforced by religious belief and language.

For the entire period under study, intermarriage was influenced by language loss in the ethnic community. Generally, this happened by the second or third generation. Language loss and its replacement by English and, in some instances, French, removed linguistic barriers existing between communities and encouraged the mingling of people and, with it, intermarriage.

A number of changes in particular following World War II brought about conditions that strongly affected the ethnic community and encouraged intermarriage. One of these was the closing of the frontier, which limited the possibility of the new generation to pick up land and make a living for themselves as farmers. Farming as a possibility of making one's livelihood was further limited by the rapid mechanization of the industry. The introduction of tractors, combines and other farm machinery meant that fewer people were needed to operate a farm. To pay for mechanization, farmers were required to expand their holdings. This, in turn, reduced the number of people working the land. This not only restricted the farm population but also the village population serving the farm community. This was further encouraged by the growing popularity of the car, which enabled farmers to go to the nearest city for their shopping, bypassing the merchants who had traditionally served them.

These changes were part of a broader change in Canadian society. The growing industrialization of Canada and decreasing opportunities for people to make their livelihood on the land meant that people starting out had to be trained in new ways of making their livelihood. This meant that often they had to leave their rural or village setting and go to the city to attend university or college, which led to the exposure to new ideas and mingling with people of other backgrounds.

Among the more liberal Mennonites, the decreasing opportunity to make their livelihood through farming, combined with urbanization, had a transformative effect on their beliefs. Rather than focussing on rural settlement as a means of separating the believer from the "world," in particular urban Mennonites returned to the traditional Anabaptist views that focussed on conversion, behaviour and belief as a means of separating the believer from the "world." At the same time, rather than withdrawing from outsiders, the Church increasingly focussed on converting outsiders and bringing them into the fold. With this, outsiders were no longer avoided, but were recruited to join the Church, through this encouraging intermarriage.

Among Lutherans, again, language loss in the different ethnic communities in Canada no longer made language spoken a factor influencing what church people would join. This encouraged the mingling of Lutherans, no matter what their linguistic background. This, in turn, encouraged intermarriage with non-German groups. The same forces influenced German Catholics once they left their ethnic church and joined a territorial congregation.

In many ways, urbanization, in particular in Western Canada, was occurring at a time when second and third generation German Canadians were losing their language. Rather than join an urban German church in which they had difficulty following the sermon, people joined an English church of their denomination, which encouraged intermarriage within the same church community.

There were also other influences that affected the German Canadian community that had an influence on their relationship with people of other backgrounds that encouraged intermarriage. In this regard, the emergence of a common Canadian identity had an important role. This was encouraged by the educational system. It was further encouraged by the growing influence of radio, television and the general communication media on peoples' lives. These not only discouraged the ethnic identity but also fostered the development of a common Canadian identity that eroded barriers between people and encouraged intermarriage.

These influences not only altered the ethnic self-identity of German Canadians, but encouraged the intermingling of people with different backgrounds. They encouraged the breakdown of traditional values and the evolution of new values. All these encouraged intermarriage and help to explain why, in particular after World War II, the majority of German Canadians had multiple ethnic origins in their background.

GERMAN PARTICIPATION IN CANADIAN ECONOMIC LIFE

Under economic life I include the different activities whereby people make their livelihood, in particular those areas that concentrate on the agricultural or industrial development of a country. While Germans participated in all segments of Canadian economic life, they were concentrated in certain areas. This is true in particular of agriculture, with many Germans coming here to satisfy their desire to own their own plot of land.

People without skills took jobs in different parts of the economy other than farming, with immigrants in particular after the end of World War II being selected for industries in which Canada had labour shortages, such as mining or lumbering. German professionals or tradespeople are represented in all occupations across the country. Frequently, people with a particular trade, rather than working for others, started their own business, in this case often hiring others of their national background to work for them. This not only helped to provide employment for members of the community but also encouraged the development of industrial enterprises serving not only the German community but also the larger society.

The following represents a brief survey of the different ways in which Germans participated in the economic life of Canada.

Pioneer Farmers

Germans played a significant role in the agricultural development of the country. As pioneers, they had an important role in turning woodland or prairie into farmland. In this way, German pioneers in the Maritimes were involved in developing the agricultural frontier in the St. John's River Valley. Germans in Lunenburg spread from their initial settlement in the Lunenburg area to take up land, and turn the forest into farmland in both Lunenburg County as well as in other areas of Nova Scotia. In

Upper Canada, Germans were among the first pioneers in the Niagara Peninsula, York County, Prince Edward County, and in particular in Waterloo County.

In Western Canada, German-speaking Mennonites from Russia were the first to develop settlements on the open prairie and show that it could be developed as agricultural land. German Lutherans, Mennonites and Catholics from Europe and the United States were extensively involved in helping to develop the prairie land in Manitoba, Saskatchewan and Alberta. They contributed to expanding the agricultural frontier in the poplar belt of the prairies. In the Peace River Valley of British Columbia, German pioneers not only turned woodland into farmland but helped to push Canada's agricultural frontier northward. In particular the German American farmer and agronomist, Herman Trelle, had an important role in this by developing seeds for different crops that would thrive in a northern climate.

As pioneers, German immigrant settlers faced numerous challenges. Of these, obtaining the land needed to make a beginning was probably the least daunting. Canada covered an extensive territory, most of it wilderness. To turn the wilderness into farmland, the government made land ownership as easy as possible. Settlers in Lunenburg County received 40x60 foot lots in the town, 70x160 foot garden lots at the east end of the town to grow their food, as well as 30 acres of farmland around the coastline and along the eastern bank of the LaHave River. In addition, at a later date, they received 300 acres of forest which they had to break to turn it into farmland.

In Upper Canada, the problems that led to the German Company purchasing the Beasley Tract from a land speculator raised the cost of the land. Around 1805, prices of land varied from $2.50 to $4.50 per acre. By 1815, the price of land had risen from $4.00 to $5.00 an acre in some of the older settlements of the township. By contrast, the Amish were granted 50 acres of free land per family in the 1820s in Wilmot Township, with permission to purchase additional land at reasonable rates.

In Western Canada, the government made available to pioneers 160 acres of free land, upon payment of a $10.00 registration fee. The settler could also buy adjacent railway land at very reasonable rates. He could only retain ownership of the free land grant if he cleared and cultivated a certain portion of the land within a specified time period.

In most of Canada, the land consisted of forest. Trees had to be cut and stumps removed before ploughing could begin. In the grassland, on the open prairie in Western Canada, clearing the land wasn't necessary and the settlers could immediately begin cultivation. However, before cultivation could begin, machinery and draught animals had to be

Clearing the land, Waterloo region. Courtesy of Joseph Schneider Haus

bought. Fodder for livestock and seed grain had to be acquired, and the settler needed to feed and clothe himself and his family, and ensure the necessary accommodation for his family and livestock.

A German settler breaking virgin prairie sod in Saskatchewan, spring, 1934. Used by permission of the American Historical Society of Germans from Russia.

Some of the beginners brought enough capital, livestock and the necessary machinery with them to start over without much difficulty. This was the case in particular for American settlers coming across the border to settle in Canada where the land was cheaper. Jacob Schneider had two four-horse teams pulling wagons loaded with his worldly belongings when he came from Pennsylvania to Waterloo Township in 1805. Christian Schneider, who accompanied him, had one four-horse team and one two-horse team, while Abraham Erb had one four-horse team pulling his Conestoga wagon carrying his family and goods. The goods included money needed to purchase land and other necessities required to make a beginning on the land.

Most new arrivals, however, arrived in Canada with very little. This was particularly true for immigrants from Europe. Most had incurred debts to pay for their trip over. New arrivals often stayed in cities such as Halifax, Montreal, or Toronto, in Eastern Canada, or Winnipeg, Regina or Calgary in Western Canada, to earn enough to pay off their travel loans and purchase the machinery needed to make a start on the land. Others worked as hired help for established farmers before settling on their own land. Still others settled on their own land, and when they had the opportunity worked for richer farmers in their neighbourhood to earn enough to purchase what they needed. Others worked their own land in the summer, but in the winter went to work for the railway to earn enough to cover their own needs and those of their family.

One of the first demands faced by the settler when he settled on his land was to build a shelter for himself and his family. In Eastern Canada, where wood was readily available, people built log cabins. Trees were felled and the branches removed. Logs were trimmed with a special axe and piled on top of each other to form the walls. Wooden spikes were used to hold them together. At the same time, the logs were notched to interlock at the corners. Frames were constructed in spaces left for doors and windows. On top of the log framework, beams were set at an angle to form the roof. Once the framing for the roof was completed, straw or turf were laid over it to keep out the elements. Once the house was built, tables, beds, chairs and other household furniture were constructed from the better lumber.

Wood was also the main building material in the poplar belt on the prairies. Here, the beams were much smaller than in Eastern Canada. In both Western and Eastern Canada, clay was used to fill the cracks between the beams so as to keep out the elements. While in Eastern Canada planks and beams were used to construct the roof, in the poplar belt of the prairies, three-to four-inch thick poles were cut to measure and then placed over the top beams of the walls. Willow branches were spread over the poles. Turf placed over top was obtained by ploughing up the soil in a moist, deep lying area, where the earth was less likely to crumble.

On the open prairie, where wood wasn't plentiful, the settler would often plough the ground and use the strips of earth and grass to build his house. These strips would be piled on top of each other, with frames marking areas for doors and windows. Once the walls were constructed, poles would be set at an angle to each other to construct the roof. Strips of sod and grass would be piled on top of these. In other instances, people would build their houses by digging holes in the ground. Poles would be set up to make the roof. Strips of ploughed grass and sod would be placed over these to keep out the cold and rain. Furniture for inside the house was handcrafted and rough. Stoves were generally made from baked clay. These would be used not only to prepare food but to heat the house.

German-speaking Lutheran settlers at Beresina, in present-day Saskatchewan, November, 1889. Francis F. Dixon. Library and Archives Canada. C 47333.

Sod house, with German settlers, St. Joseph's Colony, Saskatchewan, around 1900. Used by permission of the American Historical Society of Germans from Russia.

The most daunting task facing the homesteader was clearing the land and transforming the wilderness into farmland. This was especially the case in Eastern Canada, where the abundance of rainfall led to larger trees and thicker forest growth than on the prairies. All work was done manually by the homesteader with the help of horses or oxen if required. Lumber not used to build houses, barns, and furniture was pulled together by oxen and heaped into a pile. Once it had dried, it was burned. In time, the stumps were also removed, pulled together by oxen and burned. At times, they were also used as fences marking the owner's property.

Digging out stumps. Sketch by C. W. Jefferys. Library and Archives Canada. C-069998.

The same process was followed clearing the trees from the parkland of the prairies. With the trees being much smaller, this was a less daunting task. On the open prairie, except for the occasional shrubs, deforestation wasn't necessary. Still, it wasn't easy for man or beast to turn sod that had never before felt the plough, and the law required that the homesteader spend half a year each year of the first three years on his homestead and bring a certain portion of his land under cultivation.

Problems didn't dissolve once a farmer had cleared his land and built his house. One was the threat of fire, which might start with a strike of lightning. Once started in wooded areas open spaces funnelled the wind that fed the fire, directing it toward the farmer's house and barns. On the open prairie, the danger of fire arose especially in autumn. Having little use for the remaining straw after the threshing was finished, farmers burned it. A sudden shift in the wind or an unexpected upsurge of wind could readily send the fires out of control. To guard against this, farmers ploughed around their homes and barns to set up fireguards to prevent the flames from reaching their buildings.

Fires weren't the only danger facing the pioneers. They had to make sure they got their crops in on time. A wet spring might delay getting the crop in, resulting in the entire crop becoming cattle feed rather than a cash crop used to buy one's necessities. Another problem, on the open prairie, was sandstorms, in dry areas. A farmer might finish seeding when a heavy wind arose and blew away his seeds and precious topsoil. Another farmer might have seeded his grain, then no rain came, and whatever labour was invested in the land came to naught.

In such situations, it was only hope and the determination to go on that caused the pioneer not to give up on the land and find other means of making his livelihood. It was this perseverance of the pioneers that laid the basis for Canada's prosperity. Simultaneously, it laid the groundwork for the later industrial development of the country.

Industry and Business

While German immigrants came to Canada primarily to obtain their own piece of land, a fair number of tradespeople also emigrated. These came largely from smaller German rural centres. Other Germans left the farms to make their livelihood in the cities. This happened especially after the closing of the Canadian agricultural frontier, when land became unavailable or too expensive for a young family starting out. Many of these people moved to the cities or smaller rural centres, in particular to areas where Germans were already concentrated. This led to the development of many small business centres, the purpose of which was essentially to serve the agricultural hinterland.

German tradespeople settled in villages that emerged in areas where their fellow countrymen had settled in larger numbers. This was especially the case in block settlements. Thus, in Eastern Canada, small largely German villages arose in Lunenburg County. In Ontario, the second major concentration of Germans in Eastern Canada, small German villages arose especially in Waterloo County, with some also being formed in territories adjacent to Waterloo County. In Western Canada, Germans established towns in all areas where they settled in large numbers during the early period of settlement. This was especially true of Mennonites who settled in the East and West Reserves, in Manitoba, and in the Rosthern and Swift Current areas of Saskatchewan, as well as of Catholics who established the block settlements of St. Peter's and St. Joseph's.

In all instances, the villages served essentially the same function. In addition to providing services for farmers in the area, they became administrative centres for a particular region. This was where the smithy, grist mill, the general store and other businesses serving the farm community were located. Administrative offices for the locality might be located there. Also, the church or local school might be located there, serving the educational and spiritual needs of the farmers.

Serving the agricultural community and village formation

While most villages formed by German Canadians emerged to provide community services, some centres developed because they served military purposes. This is especially true of some of the earlier centres, such as Lunenburg. To establish it in 1753, the land was first surveyed by a British surveyor and then divided into small plots, which were given to the Foreign Protestants who settled there. Chosen for its strategic location, the town formed part of the military structure Britain established to protect its claim to the Maritimes against Catholic France.

Strategic purposes also played a role in the establishment of the different Loyalist settlements in British North America after the American

Revolution. Whether these settlers were of German or of British origin was of little relevance to the crown. It was of major importance that the settlers had fought against the rebellious colonists and, as such, could be depended upon to serve as a bulwark against possible American expansion into British holdings north of the former Thirteen Colonies.

Most German villages were established because of their location and because they met the needs of the surrounding rural area. Generally, villages emerged on major communication routes, be these rivers or roadways. When railways came to be built, they encouraged the development and expansion of towns near the railway and the decline of those that did not have railway access. Generally, early villages started to take form, for example in Waterloo County, in a location where a grist mill or sawmill was established. Soon after, a smithy and general store were built, as well as a hotel where people could stay while in town.

At times, local initiative had an important influence on where a town was established. Berlin (Kitchener after 1916) emerged when Benjamin Eby divided his land into small plots which he then sold to Catholic and Lutheran immigrants who arrived from Germany during the 1830s. He also provided land for industrial undertakings. Thus, when John Hoffman looked around for a place where he might locate his cabinet factory, he first went to people who had extensive holdings in Waterloo and Bridgeport to find a suitable location where he might establish himself. It was only after landowners in these areas had refused him that he approached Benjamin Eby, who provided for him the land he needed for his industrial undertaking.

Preston, which was largely populated by Germans, was at the end of the road from Dundas by which the first settlers arrived in the township. Important roads met here, which connected the village with Dundas, Woolwich Township, the Huron Tract and other areas of settlement. At the same time, Erb's mill, which served local farmers in the area, was located at the best local water site where there was room for growth on the south bank of the Speed River.

Another influence that encouraged the development of village and urban life, in particular of Waterloo County, was the abundance of entrepreneurial spirit. While Mennonite settlers and the German Company they formed made possible the emergence of a large German block settlement in Waterloo County, the development of the county was very much fostered by immigrants from Germany who had a trade. While many of these started out working for local Mennonite farmers, they also sought to make their livelihood through their trade. This led to the establishment of a great many small businesses. With many of the farmers in the area being of German background, entrepreneurs readily found purchasers, allowing them to get a solid footing before expanding into the larger society.

Influences operative in the formation of German villages in Eastern Canada also contributed to the formation of German villages in Western Canada. As in the east, German service towns emerged essentially in areas of concentrated German settlement. Soon after their arrival, Mennonites established their *Strassendörfer*, much as they had existed in southern Russia. That is, the community housebarns were arranged along the main street, with each household being provided with a certain quantity of land for the housebarn and a small garden plot. The village pastures and farmland surrounded the village.

The length of time a Mennonite community remained organized in this way depended upon its openness to outside influences. Some of the more conservative groups remained organized in this way for a long period and transplanted this pattern of settlement when they established daughter colonies further west. Villagers strongly influenced by the outside community started moving unto their own farms in significant numbers during the early part of the twentieth century. People remaining behind were largely involved in the service industry.

While many Mennonite villages were established on territory the community was able to reserve for their settlement, other predominantly German villages arose in areas where Germans had been able to populate a particular locality largely because of the generally slow rate of settlement. Such settlements included Lutheran settlements such as Langenburg, Lemberg and Edenwold, the largely Russian German Catholic settlements established in Saskatchewan, such as Odessa or Speyer, and the Moravian settlements of Bruderheim and Heimthal in Alberta. Villages in both the Catholic St. Peter's and St. Joseph's block settlements arose because of the rapid settlement of these areas through the concentrated immigrant recruitment work in particular of the Catholic Settlement Society.

As in Eastern Canada, no matter where German villages developed, they all provided services to the surrounding hinterland. The blacksmith was located there, as well as implement dealers and the general store. Medical services and schools tended to be located there. Often churches and other community buildings were located there. In many ways, such villages made the development of the agricultural hinterland possible. They helped the farmers to market their goods. At the same time, they provided the farmers with the necessities they needed but could not produce themselves.

While some of the villages organized by German immigrants declined with the advent of the railway and the car, others developed into important business or trade centres. Communication links, including closeness to a railway line, often influenced whether a village declined or grew. In particular with the advent of the automobile, the growth of a village was often determined by its closeness or distance from a major urban centre. In some instances, these factors, combined with local initiative, led to the growth of a village into a major centre. Four such centres might be mentioned: Lunenburg, in the Maritimes; Berlin (Kitchener), in Ontario; and Steinbach and Humboldt, in Western Canada.

Lunenburg

Lunenburg developed into an important regional centre essentially through its involvement in the fishing industry. Because of the good land in the area, Lunenburgers, unlike people in other outports in Nova Scotia, were at first loathe to turn to the fisheries. This was further encouraged by the proximity of Halifax, which offered a good market for Lunenburg agricultural products. By 1767, Lunenburg had only six vessels engaged in the fishery, which concentrated on providing fish and fish oil for local consumption.

By 1795, Lunenburg fishermen became quite extensively involved in the inshore fishery. They also became interested in the vessel fishery. In contrast to the inshore fishery, where the fish could be dried or pickled soon after being caught, in the vessel fishery fish were caught, cleaned, split and preserved in salt in the vessel's hold to be dried on her return to port. By 1829, Lunenburg County had a well-developed vessel fishery. Foreign Protestants who had come to the New World to take up land had largely turned to the sea for their livelihood, with Lunenburg becoming the hub of the east coast deep-sea fishery.

Lunenburg gained prominence after 1869, when its fishermen successfully introduce trawling or longlining. This, in turn, made offshore fishing profitable. In 1873, the *Dielytris,* a Lunenburg vessel, became the first vessel to spend the fishing season on the "banks" between Nova Scotia and Newfoundland, as well as off Labrador. This initiated the banks fishery, which at times saw as many as 150 Lunenburg fishing boats sail to the banks annually.

Simultaneously, Lunenburg established direct trade relations with the Caribbean and Europe. Founded in 1789, in particular Zwicker and Company became a pioneer in the transatlantic shipping trade. Zwicker ships carried lumber to England and returned with dry goods such as tea and hardware. They delivered lumber and salt fish to the Caribbean and brought back rum, molasses and sugar, which were sold in Halifax, Quebec and Newfoundland. Fishing and trade, in turn, encouraged the ship-building industry in the county. In 1861, construction was underway for 18 vessels in the building stocks in Lunenburg alone. In 1899, 15 vessels in total were in building stocks in LaHave, Lunenburg and Mahoney Bay.

While wooden shipbuilding declined in other parts of Nova Scotia with the arrival of the steamship, Lunenburg yards specialized in schooners, which, because of their speed and agility, were especially suitable for fishing on the "banks." Important shipbuilders include the Smith and Rhuland shipyard, which opened in 1900; Snyder's Shipyard, which opened on the east side of the LaHave River in 1876; and the Lunenburg Industrial Foundry and Engineering, a "world-famous" foundry since 1891. Although the Smith and Rhuland shipyard closed after the schooners became less competitive after World War I, the other two are still thriving.

Lunenburg, Nova Scotia, as seen from Common Range in the 1880s. Public Domain.

Berlin (Kitchener)

In Waterloo Township, all the villages started out essentially serving the rural hinterland. In some cases, the location of a particular village, as well as policies pursued by local town councils contributed to the emergence of important industrial centres. This was especially the case in the industrial development of towns such as Berlin, Waterloo or Preston. In Berlin, for example, industrial development was encouraged at first by the ready market that the rural Mennonite community offered to German immigrants who had come over with a trade. It was encouraged by the Berlin town council, with municipal assistance between 1874 and 1901 ranging from tax exemptions for a fixed number of years to allow an industry to expand without incurring extra costs to outright bonuses of up to $25,000.00 being granted to individuals who established a new company.

This contributed to the emergence in Berlin of a number of companies of national importance. This served the interests not only of the owners but also of the community at large. As McLaughlin states: "The sense of permanence and stability experienced by Berliners from the 1880s onwards had a profound influence on their perception of community life. In this, they were aided by the common Germanic identity of the factory owners and the factory workers.... Home-ownership and pride in Berlin and in its manufacturing prowess had certainly gone hand-in hand."[123] This pride and dedication helped enrich not only the owners and workers but also the local community.

Major industries established in early Berlin (Kitchener)

The history of Berlin's industrial development is largely the history of businessmen and tradespeople, many of whom learned their trades in the old country, applying their skills to build small enterprises into major companies. In this they were aided by a stable, fairly prosperous local market that helped them make a start without encountering major competition from long-established businesses in centres outside the county. Waterloo County also provided an industrious, reliable

[123] Kenneth McLaughlin, *Made in Berlin* (Kitchener, Ont.: Joseph Schneider Haus Museum), pp. 20-21.

workforce. This encouraged production without the concomitant strikes that often interfered with economic development. In this environment, a number of individuals turned smaller undertakings into major enterprises.

In 1849, Reinhold Lange founded a tannery which in its time became the largest in the British Empire. David Kurz started his business activities in Berlin with the manufacture of bricks. Then he turned to the manufacture of beer kegs. He brewed his own beer and eventually established a major brewery, which was amalgamated with Carling Breweries in 1936. Erwin Greb founded Greb Shoes Ltd. in 1912. When the company was sold in 1974, it was the largest independent shoe company in Canada. Wilhelm Hespeler started what under Joseph Galt became Seagram Brewery. Hartman Krug learned the art of furniture manufacturing in New Dundee from his father. Together with D. Hibner, he started a furniture manufacturing factory in Berlin. Becoming independent in 1887, he started his own furniture factory near the railway station in Berlin, building it into one of the largest business of this type by the turn of the century. Together with John Ahrens, Jacob Blaez, G. Lippert, and J. Kreiner, he was one of the most important of the 14 furniture manufacturers in Berlin. Alexander H. Welker helped manufacture Canada's first production car, the "LeRoy," for Milton and Nelson Good in 1901. He was co-founder of Electrohome Ltd; co-invented and built the Cyclecar at the Pollock-Welker Manufacturing Company and patented some thirty inventions in the mechanical field.

The insurance business had an important role in the development of Berlin. Of course, insurance had an important role in German Canadian community life. With little government support, people could be ruined should a member of their family suddenly fall ill or die. To assist people should unfortunate unforeseen circumstances befall them, the major German Canadian clubs offered sickness and death benefit insurance to their members. The different rural German settlements, such as Zurich and Neu Deutschland, in Ontario, and Langenburg, in Saskatchwan, established fire insurance companies, which came to the aid of people when fire destroyed their property.

Insurance companies began to flourish in Berlin and Waterloo County in the 1860s. Hugo Kranz, whose family arrived in Canada from Hessen in 1858, was one of the initiators of the Waterloo Mutual Fire Insurance Company. Other insurance companies followed, including

Mutual Life of Canada, North Waterloo Farmers Mutual Fire Insurance, Dominion Life, and the Economical Mutual Fire Insurance, which was founded by H. Kranz and Wilhelm Oelschlaeger. Berlin, and in particular its sister city of Waterloo, in time became what Hartford was for the United States, the insurance centre of Canada.

J.M. Schneider, an immigrant from Baden, who started his business selling sausages from door to door after he finished his regular work, eventually built a meat packing plant that made Berlin the meat sausage city of Canada. Georg Rumpel bought Jacob Y. Shanz's felt works and expanded it to the point where he became known as the felt shoe king of Canada. August John Kimmel was another industrialist who was active in the felt boot industry. Associated with the Berlin Felt Boot Company for 15 years, in 1900 he organized the Elmira Felt Boot Company. In 1907 he built the Kimmel Felt Company in Berlin. When the Canadian Consolidated Felt Company was formed in 1909, consolidating the Elmira company, the Kimmel company, and the Berlin Felt Boot Company, he became vice-president and general manager of the new organization. He also became associated with large rubber interests in Canada which later became the Consolidated Rubber Company Ltd. He became director of many industrial organizations in Berlin and throughout Ontario and Quebec. With T.H. Rieder he founded the Dominion Rubber Company, which became a very successful national organization. Emil Vogelsang arrived in Canada in 1867. In Berlin, he established the first button manufacturing factory in Canada. At different times, button manufacturing, which in time involved four factories, employed the most people in Berlin.

The outbreak of the American Civil War, 1861-1865, provided a strong stimulus to Canadian industry, resulting in the mushrooming of a whole number of new enterprises, leading to the establishment of small, medium and large industries in Berlin. Some of the largest construction companies in the city were run by people like Jacob Y. Shanz, Casper Braun, H.L. Janzen, and John Bramm, who was also active in the manufacture of brick. The steel industry prospered. Business people in the steel and metalware industries included such names as Boehmer, Hymmen, Moyers, Lautenschläger, Anthes, Ölschläger, Stäbler, Schmidt, Bauer and Kaiser. Family names of people in the textile and tailoring businesses included such names as Reiner, Böhmer, Gottlieb, Grebenstein and Stein.

Berlin became a major centre in the rubber industry. In the winter of 1898, Georg Schlee, whose father came to Preston 1853, studied the rubber industry in the United States. He interested Jakob Kaufmann, A. E. Breithaupt and Louis Weber in starting a rubber boot industry in Canada, which led to the establishment of the Berlin Rubber Co. Several years later, Jakob Kaufmann founded the Kaufmann Rubber Co., a massive work, which, among other things, helped to make Berlin the rubber centre of Canada.

Jacob Beck came to Waterloo Township in 1837. He operated a smelting furnace at New Hope (Hespeler) and later established ironworks on Spring Creek, Preston. He invented a turbine waterwheel and in partnership with John Clare and Valentine Wahn manufactured stoves at Preston. In 1854 he located a good source of water power in Spring Creek in Wilmot Township and purchased 200 acres. He erected a grist mill and foundry. In 1856, he subdivided his farm, sold lots and developed Baden.

Berlin benefitted not only from individual enterprise but also from initiatives it undertook in the area of public ownership. This led to Berlin's taking the city's waterworks out of private hands in 1889 and establishing a city waterworks, which led to a lowering of the city's water rates. In 1903, the city's gas-supply industry was taken over by the municipality, and in 1906, the city's streetcars were moved from private to municipal ownership. At a banquet of the Berlin Commerce and Trade Association, E. W. B. Snider suggested that the different communities combine to work toward harnessing Niagara Falls to supply electrical power to Ontario industries. This initiative was taken up by D. B. Detweiler, who established a one-man-committee that visited the different communities to interest them in the project. This led eventually to the establishment of a publicly-owned hydro-electric system and the establishment of the Hydro-Electric Power Commission, with Adam Beck as its first chairman. On October 11, 1910, Berlin became the first city in Ontario to be flooded with electrical light generated by the Niagara Falls.

East King Street, Berlin, Ontario, 1906. Public Domain.

Western Canada

As in Eastern Canada, some villages developed by Germans in Western Canada grew into important centres. While never attaining the importance, for example, of Berlin, they nevertheless attained a significant regional significance. As in the case of centres that grew in importance in Eastern Canada, they started out with a community base where they could readily market their products. This same market provided a source of labour from which entrepreneurs seeking to develop an industry could draw to forward their projects. Furthermore, they were part of a communication network that connected them to markets beyond their local community.

Steinbach

One of these centres was Steinbach, in Manitoba. Steinbach started out as a business centre in 1877 when Abraham Friesen built his first windmill there. Entrepreneurs started other businesses, helping to establish Steinbach as a regional service centre in the area. In 1912, Ford Canada opened a car dealership in Steinbach, the first in Western Canada. As the centre grew, trucking and retailing businesses opened, with the town prospering because of its automobile sales.

While Winnipeg was too far from Steinbach to comfortably allow for commuting, it was close enough for Steinbach to draw its clientele from that city. Having lower overhead costs, a Steinbach dealership could sell a car to a client coming from Winnipeg at a cost lower than what a car would sell for in Winnipeg and still make a profit. This led to Steinbach being labelled Manitoba's "Automobile City."

In time, Steinbach also developed enterprises in manufacturing, transportation, agribusiness, retail, and financial services such as the Steinbach Credit Union. Major industries developed or located there, including Biovail and Lowen Windows. Penner Foods, which was started in the 1930s and by 1998 had over 800 employees, had its beginnings there. Agriculture, the traditional industry in the region, continued to play a significant role in Steinbach's growth. Including large hog and poultry businesses, the area also has numerous family farms, which specialize in dairy, as well as in the growth of crops such as soy, canola, wheat, oats and rye. The prosperous hinterland helped to enhance the development of the urban centre, which in 1997 became the city of Steinbach. With a population of 13,500 in 1910, it had the third highest assessment value among cities in Manitoba, behind Brandon and Winnipeg.

East Main Street, Steinbach, Manitoba, 2011. Author: Krazytea. CC BY-SA 3.0.

Humboldt

Although established earlier, Humboldt started developing after the settlement of that area of Saskatchewan by German Catholics from the United States and Germany at the turn of the century. In its early years Humboldt was primarily German Catholic, as was the farm population surrounding the centre, and also the different nearby villages, such as Muenster, Fulda, Pilger, St Gregor and Englefeld.

Humboldt's growth was encouraged by the arrival of the Canadian Northern Railway in 1904. Its development was further stimulated by its being located in the Heart of the Safe Crop District, which meant that it was less influenced by the vagaries of the weather than many other areas of Saskatchewan. This affected the well-being of farmers in the area, and also meant that Humboldt, as their main service centre, could depend upon an affluent, reliable clientele for the services it provided. Its development was further abetted through the exploitation of oil, gas and potash reserves in the area.

Service industries that developed in Humboldt include trucking, financial management, wholesale trade and transportation. With a population of about 6,000, Humboldt became a city in 2000. The trading area of Humboldt and district has a population of about 30,000, establishing it as a major regional centre in Saskatchewan.

Humboldt's historic downtown, 2014, Humboldt, Sask. Public Domain.

German Workers in Major Urban Centres

German immigrants who settled in the major Canadian urban centres during the pioneer period tended to do so primarily to earn enough money to enable them to take up land and establish a farm. In the city, they tended to settle near their church or near where their relatives had already settled. Most of them were employed as labourers, in areas such as the building industry, the railway or in any other enterprises where they could find work. Thus, for example, in Montreal, Moellman found that many of the early immigrants worked on the railways or in the construction trades.[124] This was also true, for example, of Germans who settled in Winnipeg during the early period of settlement. Often working for the railway or in the building trades, they tended to remain in the city long enough to make sufficient money to establish themselves on the land.

German immigrants to Canada gravitated to the land until the Second World War, when most of the good and readily accessible land had been taken up. However, during the inter-war period, Germans increasingly remained in urban centres rather than move to often marginal land that was still not occupied, which offered little opportunity for making one's livelihood. As Canadian cities grew, they offered an increasingly greater variety of employment opportunities. At the same time, land shortages in particular among Germans in Eastern Europe forced an increasingly large number of them to take up a trade. This meant that more immigrants arrived equipped with skills that prepared them for urban life. This was the case even more often among German post-World War II immigrants. While many of these, through the agreement they had signed prior to their arrival in Canada, were required to find their first jobs in the mines or as farm workers, they soon moved to urban centres where they were in a better position to pursue their livelihood.

The reduction of opportunities on the land because of the closing frontier brought the children of farmers to the cities. Some of these were labourers. Others had acquired skills in Canadian schools that prepared them for making a living at a skilled trade or as professionals in the city.

The changing nature of work in which Germans participated in the larger economy is reflected in government statistics, which state that in 1921, 57 per cent of German men in Canada were employed in agriculture. German participation in the agricultural industry gradually declined. In 1931 and 1941, 55 per cent of German men worked in agriculture. According to the 1961 statistics, 21 per cent of German men in the labour force were still working as farmers or farm labourers. Of

---

[124]   Albert Moellmann, *Das Deutschtum in Montreal.* Schriften des Instituts fuer Grenz-und Auslandsdeutschtum an der Universitaet Marburg, No. 11. Jena: Fischer, 1937.

the Dutch, which included many Mennonites who during the war had assumed the Dutch identity, 22.5 per cent were working as farmers or farm labourers. However, the majority of Germans were active in non-agricultural work. 32.52 per cent worked as craftsmen and production workers. The next major category in which Germans were concentrated was the managerial one, with 8.29 per cent of German males occupying managerial positions. 6.9 per cent of Germans were in the professional and technical category. 6.37 per cent of Germans were employed in the service industry; 6.24 per cent were in the transport and communication industries, while 5.02 per cent were clerical workers and 4.4 per cent were in sales. Of the total, 5.59 per cent were employed as labourers.

Of German women in the work force in 1961, the majority, or 27.34 per cent, were employed in the service industry. The next major area in which German women were concentrated was in clerical work, with 25.36 per cent of German women falling in this category. 12.19 per cent of German women worked in the crafts or as production workers, while 11.57 per cent were active as professional or technical workers. 7.38 per cent were involved in sales, while 8.25 per cent worked on the farm.

Unlike with British Canadians (some 2.64 per cent of whom were listed as farmers and farm workers in the 1961 census), the census suggests that agriculture has always been an important part of the German Canadian's work life. One reason for this is the attraction to the land, which is strongly evident not only among Germans but also among other continental Europeans. Also, many Germans, such as Mennonites and Hutterites, associated agriculture with their religious tradition. This encouraged them to remain on the land rather than find work in the cities.

However, by the latter part of the twentieth century the large majority of Germans worked in urban centres. The 1971 census statistics give 14 per cent of German men and 9 per cent of German women working in farming, horticulture and animal husbandry. In the 1981 census this number declined to 12 per cent for men and 6 per cent for women. The 1971 census also lists 5 per cent of German men and 2 per cent of German women working in managerial and related professions. The 1981 census shows 11 per cent of German men and 5 per cent of German women working in the managerial professions and related areas, while in the 1986 census this percentage moved up to 13 per cent for German men and 7 per cent for German women. The next major area in which Germans were employed was that of sales, with 9 per cent of German men and 8 per cent of German women working in sales in 1971. Both the 1981 and 1986 census show 8 per cent of German men and 10 per cent of German women working in sales. The 1971 census shows 7 per cent of German men and 17 per cent of German women working in service occupations. The percentage remained the same for 1981 and 1986, except that for 1981 the percentage of German men working in service occupations stood at 6 per cent.

This shows that Germans gradually shifted from agricultural to urban work, in particular after the beginning of the twentieth century. This was encouraged by the rural to urban shift among Germans already settled in this country and by the type of immigrant Canada sought to recruit. As late as the early 1950s, Canada focussed on obtaining farmers and people who could be employed in other primary industries. By the latter part of the twentieth century, the number of German immigrants who came to farm greatly declined. For example, in 1991, 34 per cent of male immigrants from Germany worked in professional or management occupations. Also, German immigrant men tended to be concentrated in either construction or manufacturing. Of German women in the labour force in 1991, 57 per cent were employed in clerical, sales or service jobs.

Whatever occupation Germans found themselves in, they made a significant contribution in all areas of Canadian endeavour. In the area of agriculture, they helped open up the frontier and turned woodland and prairie into agricultural land. In their work as entrepreneurs in areas of German concentration, they helped to establish Canada's industrial base. They helped to establish villages and towns, in particular within the different block settlements. Some of these towns, such as Lunenburg, Berlin (Kitchener), Steinbach or Humboldt, became important centres in their particular area.

Entrepreneurs Outside Areas of German Concentration

When one looks at entrepreneurs and individual enterprises established by Germans in Canada, a highly visible difference is evident between enterprises established in centres of German concentration and those established outside such areas. One major difference is the great number of enterprises established by Germans within areas of German concentration. This is true in particular in the case of Berlin (Kitchener) and Waterloo County in general. This is not due to more Germans having settled in areas of German concentration. In fact, the opposite is true; most Germans, when they settled in towns or urban centres, tended to settle outside areas of German concentration.

The relatively large number of enterprises established in areas such as the former Berlin, in Waterloo County, must therefore be attributed to other factors. One is that many of German immigrants in the 1830s came with a trade on which they could build to establish their enterprises. Although arriving with little money, they were able to buy a small plot of land for self-sufficiency. Even though many worked for more wealthy farmers in the area, they had sufficient time to ply their trade in their spare time, helping them when first starting their businesses. At the same time, the local German community provided them with the opportunity to market their goods, with entrepreneurs often going from house to house to sell their products.

As their business grew, entrepreneurs had a considerable labour pool to draw on. The business owner and the workers being of the same national background encouraged co-operation between workers and management. Having no significant competitors in the area from people who had connections or a larger pool of capital to draw on, as was the case, for example, with English Canadians, offered the local German entrepreneur time to build up a financial base. Berlin in particular made a significant effort to help local entrepreneurs market their products outside the community. All these influences helped German Canadian businessmen in Waterloo County not only produce their products but also market them. This helped industries such Schneider Meats, the Lang Tanning Company and other companies in Berlin, Ontario, grow to become major industrial enterprises.

In Lunenburg, similar influences helped the community transform itself from what, at the beginning, was strictly a farming community, to becoming a major fishing and shipbuilding centre in the Maritimes. Later, in Western Canada, local enterprise, as well as the ready supply of relatively cheap labour, helped centres such as Steinbach become a major manufacturing and automobile centre in Manitoba.

There were no areas outside of Berlin, Ontario, or of Lunenburg, Nova Scotia, in which Germans, prior to World War I, demonstrated similar entrepreneurship. There were individuals, of course, who gained extensive wealth or established important industrial enterprises outside areas of German concentration. George Pozer (Johann Georg Pfotzer), who settled in Quebec city in 1785, succeeded in building a fortune through his grocery business and his money lending and real estate investments. His real estate investments included the Aubert-Gallion Seigneurie, where he settled 189 German immigrants. However, many of these died after a burn to clear the forest spread into a wildfire. Later, he gave land to the Archdiocese of Quebec to establish the parish of Saint-Georges. He is considered to be the founder of Saint-Georges-de-Beauce. The Steeves family played a major role in laying the foundation that led to Moncton's becoming an important centre in New Brunswick. The Loyalist John Walden Meyers had a major role in the founding of Belleville, Ontario. The Pennsylvania-German Samuel Zimmerman, who started out with little money, made his fortune building the Welland Canal in the 1840s and the Niagara Suspension Bridge, which was completed in 1855. Zimmerman owned hotels, steamers, banks, as well as extensive real estate in Toronto, Hamilton and Niagara Falls. At the time of his accidental death in 1857, he was the main promoter and contractor for the Great Western and other railways and was reported to be one of the richest men in the Canadas.

Samuel Cunard, son of the German American Loyalist Abraham Cunard, and a member of the Lutheran congregation in Halifax, was one of a group of twelve individuals who in his time dominated the affairs of Nova Scotia. His early ventures included co-founding the steam ferry company in Halifax harbour as well as investments in the pioneering steamship, the Royal William. To forward his career, Cunard went to Britain, where, together with his business partners, he was successful in winning a bid to operate the trans-Atlantic mail service between Britain and North America. The company operating this venture later became Cunard Steamships Limited, which was active in the passenger service. Winning a reputation for speed and safety, the company prospered and eventually absorbed many other steamship lines, to eventually dominate the trans-Atlantic passenger service.

Another person who became active in the trans-Atlantic service was the Montreal merchant Wilhelm Munderloh, who was instrumental in establishing steamship services between Canada and Germany. In this case, it was Munderloh's connection with German steamship lines that made the establishment of such services possible.

In 1890, the A. & S. Nordheimer Company, established by the German immigrants Samuel and Abraham Nordheimer, opened its factory in Toronto, manufacturing what quickly became one of Canada's best-known domestic piano brands. In 1928, the Nordheimer Company was taken over by the Heinzman Company. This company was founded by Theodor August Heinzman. Born in 1817, in Berlin, Prussia, Heinzman emigrated to New York in 1850, where he worked for a while for his fellow countryman Heinrich Steinweg, manufacturer of the world-famous Steinway piano. Heinzman eventually established his own firm in Buffalo. Financial difficulties caused him to transfer his business to Toronto. Concentrating on quality rather than quantity, his Heinzman piano eventually gained country-wide recognition, selling well in Canada as well as abroad. In 1876, the Heinzman Company won awards at the Philadelphia Centennial Exhibition, and, by 1879, it had built about 1000 instruments. During the 1880s, the company built some 500 pianos annually, which rose to about 1000 annually during the 1890s.

While most German immigrants who came to Canada during the settlement of the Canadian West prior to World War I came to pick up land, some came in search of business opportunities. This was the case with Werner Alvo von Alvensleben. Disgracing himself as a result of his escapades in the Prussian army, his father gave him the choice of either reforming or resigning his position as an officer. Von Alvensleben chose to leave Europe altogether. Arriving in Vancouver with four dollars in his pocket, he first made his livelihood at a variety of jobs. Soon after, he decided to become a real estate broker. Benefitting from Vancouver's boom in 1908 and from his connections with wealthy investors in the German Empire, he soon advanced to become one of Canada's foremost entrepreneurs. Counting among his clients investors such as Chancellor von Bethmann-Hollweg and Kaiser Wilhelm II, he reached the height of his career in 1912, when he feted the Vancouver elite with lavish parties. However, when World War I broke out, his enterprises went into rapid decline.

Another nobleman adventurer who became a successful entrepreneur was Alfred Freiherr von Hammerstein. Drawing on European as well as Canadian capital, he launched the Athabasca Oil and Asphalt Company in 1909, with a capital of 5 million dollars. One of the largest real estate holders in northern Alberta, Hammerstein, who died in 1941, promoted a rail link from the American border to Fort McMurray via Edmonton and the Peace River Crossing. Another German pioneer of the Alberta coal mining industry was Martin Nordegg. Arriving in Canada in 1906, he used the German capital of his *Deutsches Canada Syndicate* and of the German Development Company to develop Alberta's coal deposits. In 1910, he was decorated for his efforts by Kaiser Wilhelm II.

Fritz Sick arrived in the United States in 1883 with $5.00 in his pocket. Here he worked for a number of breweries before coming to British Columbia. In B.C., he established his first brewery, and then founded another at Fort Steele, during the construction of the Crow's Nest Pass Railway, and another at Fernie. In 1901 he sold out and went to Lethbridge, where he founded the Lethbridge Brewery. The Lethbridge Brewery became especially known for its old style Pilsener beer, which was first brewed in 1926 by Fritz Sick at his Lethbridge company. Sick Breweries Ltd. grew in the early part of the 20th century to include breweries located throughout Western Canada and the United States. In 1958, the enterprise was bought by Molson, Inc.

Henry Reifel was 17 when he left Germany for the United States in about 1886. He worked for a number of breweries before coming to B.C. in 1888. He started the San Francisco Brewery with his brother. When the operation failed, he again worked for different breweries in both Canada and the United States. In 1908, with associates, he founded the Canadian Brewing and Malting Co., which later merged with other companies to form Vancouver Breweries.

When in 1917 the temperance movement achieved its goal and the Prohibition Act banned the sale and consumption of liquor, Henry Reifel closed his Canadian operation and went to Japan, taking a considerable amount of brewing equipment with him. In Japan, he developed the technique of producing malt from rice and created the Anglo-Japanese Brewing Co. With the Japanese brewing venture successfully established, he sold his Japanese interests and returned to Canada. In 1924, he acquired the B.C. Distillery of Westminster, and later, the Pioneer Distillery of Amherstburg, Ont. The Reifel breweries were then amalgamated into the Brewery and Distillery Corp. Henry Reifel remained president of this enterprise until his retirement in 1933 when he sold his brewing interests.

Despite some successes, conditions were generally unfavourable for Germans wishing to establish business enterprises during the inter-war years. To launch a business successfully requires not only initiative, but a network one can draw on to produce and market one's product. Such an environment didn't exist for a German seeking to develop and market his products in a host society that had spent the war years demonizing anything German. The situation deteriorated still further with the outbreak of the Depression. Just surviving economically became a problem. New arrivals found themselves out of work or too busy seeking employment to support themselves and their families. That is, they had little opportunity or time for business undertakings. Furthermore, they had little opportunity to accumulate enough capital to lay the seeding groundwork for business enterprises. However, there were some successes. This included Zellers. Walter P. Zeller founded Zellers in 1931 as "stores for thrifty Canadians." The chain began with the purchase of the 14 Canadian locations of the bankrupt retailer Schulte-United. This was followed by an aggressive expansionist strategy so that within the next 25 years Zellers operated 60 stores and employed 3,000 people. Another company established at the time was Monarch Industries. Founded by John J. Klassen in 1935 to manufacture feed mills and then pumps for flood-prone regions of rural Manitoba, the enterprise expanded, in particular after World War II, to become a major manufacturer and distributor of pumps, hydrolic cylinders, mixers and custom metal castings. In 1995 Monarch Industries was recognized as one of Canada's 50 best managed companies.

It was only after the end of World War II that we again see Germans establish a good number of business enterprises. These were established, for the most part, outside of centres of German concentration. Several conditions favoured the establishment of these businesses. One was that many of the Germans who came to Canada came with a trade or other skills that they could exploit to establish themselves. Also, with the closing of the settlement frontier, rather than picking up land, German immigrants tended to settle in urban centres. Here they could readily be drawn on by entrepreneurs establishing their enterprises. For industries such as bakeries, or even in the building industry, the large wave of post-war immigrants offered entrepreneurs a market where they could sell their products. At the same time, with the massive influx of people, not only from Europe but elsewhere, the larger society became much more cosmopolitan. This created the possibility for Germans, often starting out serving their own community, to expand their services to the larger society, which led to the establishment of a great number of enterprises.

One was in the area of construction, with the establishment of German construction companies in the major centres across Canada, be this in Ottawa, Toronto, Winnipeg, or Vancouver.

Some of these companies and their founders deserve special mention. Paul Tuerr came to Canada in 1948 almost penniless and unable to speak English. A trained architect and engineer, Tuerr worked briefly as a labourer, bricklayer and carpenter to gain Canadian experience. In 1949, he started his own company, with $1,500.00 start-up capital. Due to Tuerr's creative designs and quality work, the company flourished. It employed 23 workers after three years, for the most part *Volksdeutsche* immigrants. As the company grew, Tuerr expanded from building houses to developing subdivisions, including residential as well as business properties.

While expanding his business, Tuerr was also active in German Canadian life, serving in various capacities with the Schwaben Club, the Concordia Club, the German-Canadian Business and Professional Association, as well as with the German Canadian Congress. In 2003, he initiated the founding of the German-Canadian Remembrance Society, to commemorate all who had fallen victim to genocide, expulsion and war. Part of this undertaking was the Anna Tuerr Memorial Park, dedicated to his wife, many of whose family members had been slaughtered in Yugoslavia by the Tito partisans. His interest in the German and German Canadian experience also led him to make a major contribution of $500,000.00 toward the establishment of the Centre for German Studies at the University of Waterloo.

Similar generosity and community support was shown by Rubin Spletzer, president of Crystal Developers, Winnipeg. While Crystal Developers isn't a major company, the financial contribution of its president helped establish the Chair in German-Canadian Studies at the University of Winnipeg in 1989. Scholarships funded by the Spletzer Family Foundation help to support scholars working in different areas of German Canadian history.

Born in 1921 in Conestoga, Ontario, Walter Hachborn purchased Hollinger Hardware in 1950 with two business partners. With him as president, the company (renamed Home Hardware) grew from 122 dealers to more than 1,100 stores. In recognition of his achievements the Retail Council of Canada presented him with the Distinguished Canadian Retailer of the Year Award. In 1999 he was also awarded the distinction of Retailer of the Century.

Another entrepreneur-marketer who has been even more successful than Hachborn is the German-born billionaire Tobias Lütke. With other innovators, he founded and is the CEO of Shopify, an e-commerce company serving as an online platform which allows users to set up an online store to market their products. Since founded in 2004, the company has become one of the most profitable enterprises in Canada.

An area in which a good number of major enterprises emerged was in the manufacture of meat and bread products. Starting out as local delicatessens, some of these enterprises grew into major companies, either at the regional or the national level. These include Bittner's Meat market in Toronto, Denniger's in Hamilton, Freybe's Sausage manufacturing of Vancouver, Dimpflmeier's and Rudolph's bakery of Toronto, and Bronson Bakery of Ottawa. Most of these were immigrant undertakings. For example, after graduating from the Handelskammer in Munich, Alfons Dimpflmeier emigrated to Canada in 1957. Baking at night and making his deliveries during the day, he quickly turned his one-man bakery into a bread-making enterprise. Today, Dimpflmeier Bakery delivers German-style baked goods to buyers all over the world.

Rudolf and Friede Denniger operated three food stores in the Black Forest region of Germany. They emigrated to Canada in 1953 and shortly after opened their first store on King Street in Hamilton. They quickly developed a reputation for producing high quality European style sausages, as well as fresh and smoked meats. To meet the demand, new stores were opened throughout the 1970s and 80s and Denniger's became an integral part of the shopping scene serving Burlington, Oakville and Stony Creek.

Gerhard Brandt followed in the footsteps of his grandfather and father, becoming a sausage maker and butcher. Coming to Canada in 1956, he and his wife, Ida, opened their meat and delicatessen business two years later in Toronto. With a focus on quality and service, Brandt Meat Products has over 100 employees and produces over 120 sausage and ham products, many of which won Gold Medals at international trade competitions.

Another area where Germans started a number of enterprises is in manufacturing. Born in Tiengen, Germany, Klaus Woerner trained as a tool-and-die maker in Switzerland. He came to Canada in 1960 and spent his first fourteen years at various technical jobs, while studying engineering at night. He moved to Kitchener in 1974, and four years later mortgaged his house to start a small business making special purpose machines. Today, Automated Tooling System (ATS) employs more than 4,000 people around the world, and is one of the world's foremost companies dealing with automatic manufacturing equipment.

Grenco Industries was founded in 1969 by Eduard and Arthur Grenke, two German immigrants who arrived in Canada in 1953. It manufactures and sells progressive cavity pumps, wellhead drives, variable frequency drives and other products for the oil industry. When the company was sold in 2010 it had some sixty employees, and sold its products not only in North America but also in other parts of the world.

Started by Hugo and Helmuth Eppich, two brothers who emigrated from Yugoslavia in 1953, Ebco Industries grew from a small tool and die making company into a major industrial enterprise in Western Canada. With headquarters near Vancouver, the company produces advanced Computer Numerical Control (CNC) machines, large steel and alloy fabrication and welding equipment and other products for pulp and paper production, the oil industry as well other industrial undertakings in North America and around the world.

Robert Schad arrived in Canada from Germany in 1951 with $25.00 in his pocket and a not yet finished degree in engineering. After an unsuccessful attempt to build a snowmobile, he founded Husky Injecting Molding, a company that designs and makes the machines that produce recyclable PET (polyethylene terepthalate) plastic bottles, food containers, car bumpers and other plastic products. Selling its products globally, the company grew rapidly. With the profits, Schad launched the Schad Foundation in 1987, to give money - $4.6 million in 2000 – to environmental concerns. In 2007, Schad sold Husky Injecting Molding Systems Ltd. for $960 million to devote himself to philanthropic activities.

John Volcken was another German immigrant who left a successful business career to devote himself to philanthropy. Born in East Germany in 1941, Volcken came to Canada in 1960. Having little money, he worked at a variety of jobs for the next two decades, until he bought a used furniture store, United Buy and Sell. Deciding to sell only new furniture, he changed the name of his store to United Furniture Warehouse. He built the chain up to 148 locations across North America, with an annual sale in excess of 200 million. In 2004, he sold his United Furniture Warehouse stores to the Brick and founded the John Volcken Foundation, with a capital base of 100 million. The foundation funds the Welcome Home Addiction Recovery Academy in Surrey, B.C., and Seattle, Washington, as well as Lift the Children, which supports needy orphanages in Africa.

Another successful enterprise was launched by Andrew Peller, a German Hungarian who arrived in Canada in 1927, just before the outbreak of the Depression. Deciding that Canada lacked premium quality wines, he established Andrés Wines Ltd. in Port Moody, B.C., in 1961. In 1964, the winery expanded its operations to Calgary, Alberta and Truro, Nova Scotia. It entered the Ontario market with the purchase of Beau Chatel Wines in Winona, and in 1974 moved into Quebec with the establishment of Les Vins Andrés in St. Hyacinthe. In 1994 Andrés acquired the Hillebrand Estates Winery, Canada's largest producer of VQA and premium wines, located in Niagara-on-the-Lake, Ontario. The winery's operations became centered in Niagara-on-the-Lake, under the name Andrew Peller Limited, in honor of the company's founder.

Land scarcity and expanding business opportunities also encouraged a number of established German wine makers to establish themselves in Canada. For example, Konzelmann Estate Winery was founded in the 19th century by Friedrich Konzelmann, who left the culinary trade to make wine. He released his first vintage in 1893 and would eventually produce over 200,000 gallons of excellent wine per year.

When in 1980 Friedrich's great grandson, Herbert Konzelmann, found the demand for his product increasing faster than the land could sustain, he decided to relocate in Canada. By 1984, the Konzelmann family had emigrated to Canada, purchased a lakefront peach orchard and started replacing the trees with vitis vinifera grape vines. At present, the Konzelmann Estate Winery produces over thirty wines, with a total output of 500,000 bottles per year, for which it has received hundreds of rewards and accolades.

The Reif family started making wines in the Rhein River Valley nearly five hundred years ago. Their tradition of wine making was transferred to Canada in 1977, when Ewald Reif purchased a plot of land on the banks of the Niagara River, on which he planted vinifera grape vines. In 1987, Ewald's nephew took over the Reif Estate Winery, after having completed his studies in Viticulture and Oenology at the Geisenheim Institute, a prestigious winemaking school in Germany. Currently, the winery produces some 50,000 cases of wine per year, including German Riesling, Cabernet Savingnon, as well as other wines.

Other Germans became distributors for German enterprises in Canada. Germany had taken the initiative to establish either branch plants or distributing centres for its industries prior to World War I. However, most German investments and businesses in Canada were lost during and after the Great War. The inter-war period provided few opportunities for German investments abroad. However, once German industry had again recovered after World War II, it sought to expand into different areas of the world. In Canada, local Germans often were recruited to help in this expansion. As a result, numerous German industries, banks and other businesses established themselves in Canada. This includes automobile manufacturers such as Volkswagen, Mercedes, or BMW. It includes banks such as Dresdner Bank, the Deutsche Bank, and the Westdeutsche Landesbank. The major German transportation enterprises, such as Lufthansa, Schenker, and Kuehne and Nagel, are represented in Canada. To encourage trade relations between Germany and Canada and facilitate the growth of German enterprises in Canada, the German-Canadian Chamber of Commerce, with offices in Toronto and Montreal, was established.

Summary

Looking at the different enterprises started by Germans shows a pattern. German enterprises tended to be started by immigrants who came over, not with an excessive amount of money, but with a skill on the basis of which they later established an industry. Also, they often found their first clients in the local or regional German Canadian community, and from there branched out to serving the larger society. Furthermore, they tended not to expand through the manipulation of the market, but on the basis of providing a product or service.

There are several reasons why so many enterprises by Germans were founded by immigrants. Emigrating to another country, in particular a country different in culture and language, involves risk taking. It requires a willingness to see things differently and adjust. The same is true of founding a business. Thus, it is likely that the same attributes that led a person to emigrate also led to his starting a business enterprise.

Looking at the different places in which businesses grew and flourished, it becomes evident that businesses prospered best in areas where Germans had formed group settlements. These offered businesses a clientele without the necessity of having to compete with better funded enterprises. Also, the block settlements offered businesses an industrious, reliable work force. At the same time, as may be seen in some of the joint ventures launched in Berlin, they offered entrepreneurs a network of likeminded people with whom they could co-operate in their undertakings.

Businesses in Canada were founded and prospered in particular during periods of economic expansion. For example, the relatively long period of peace in Canada between the establishment of Berlin, Ontario, and the outbreak of World War I offered industries established at that time a fairly long period of growth. The outbreak of civil war in the United States provided new market possibilities for Canadian industry, as American businesses during this period would have been hindered in their development by the war.

The Depression not only made it difficult for people to find work in Canada, but also had a negative effect on business life in this country. This altered after World War II when the general industrial expansion of the country offered a broad range of opportunities to establish a business enterprise.

Also, the attitudes of the larger society influenced business opportunities for Germans in this country. Canada's major industrial expansions occurred during and immediately after the two world wars, periods during which Germany was under attack and Germans encountered a great deal of suspicion and hostility. In particular, businesses owned by Germans were confiscated or attacked. Attitudes leading to these extremes led to products produced by German Canadian enterprises being boycotted. This was the case in particular during and after World War I.

The growth of tolerance after World War II, with its emphasis on multiculturalism, had a positive effect on business opportunities for Germans in this country. This may help explain the development and growth especially of companies producing and marketing German food products. It would also have had a positive effect on the development and expansion of German industrial enterprises in other areas, enabling them to market their products, not only in the German community, but in the larger society.

GERMAN CANADIANS IN CANADIAN POLITICAL LIFE

Germans participated in several ways in the Canadian political process. For the most part, they were passive observers that Canada's major political parties sought to involve in politics, essentially to obtain their support. Some Germans ran for office, with varying degrees of success. The following is an examination of German Canadian participation in the political process, in particular at the federal and provincial levels. I will look at where they ran for office and why, as well as explore the forces that influenced their ability to be elected.

The major Canadian political parties attempted to recruit the support of the German minority as soon as the democratic electoral process was organized in Canada. They did so in several ways. They had special leaflets printed in German, lauding their policies in regards to a specific issue and denigrating those of the opposition. They supported German language newspapers through placing ads in them in return for a newspaper's support at election time. In the cases of *Der Nordwesten* and the *Germania,* in Manitoba, or the *Saskatchewan Courier,* political parties took majority ownership in German language papers to control their political orientation, in particular at election time.

Also, political parties started political clubs in the German community, usually immediately before an election. For example, looking at *Der Nordwesten,* which was published in Winnipeg, one would see ads placed in the paper prior to an election, inviting people to attend the meeting of a Conservative or a Liberal club that had just been organized. In this case, leading members of the German community recruited by the different parties would use their influence to persuade community members to throw their support behind this or that political aspirant running for office.

For the most part, Germans were little more than passive participants awaiting recruitment by the dominant sponsor groups or more active ethnic groups. Even where Germans sought office, except in block settlements they seldom had enough support in their own community to succeed to office. That is because they were too divided by religious background and area of origin to be able to fully co-ordinate their effort to support a specific candidate. In some of the block settlements, as in the Mennonite block settlements, they failed to put up one of their own for election for some of the period under discussion because of their belief in the separation of Church and state.

Nevertheless, despite these drawbacks, Germans or people of German background were at different times elected to office. These tended, for the most part, to be second or third generation Canadians, who can be recognized as being of German background because of their family name. Included among them are Fathers of Confederation, who were of partial German origin, including Charles Fisher and William H. Steeves. Charles Fisher came from a Loyalist family. His grandfather, Lodewick (Ludwig) Fischer, was a Loyalist who came to St. John from New York. A member of the New Brunswick Legislature since 1854, Charles Fisher was elected Prime Minister of New Brunswick in 1857, a position he held until 1861 when he resigned but kept his seat in the Legislature. In 1864, he represented New Brunswick at the Quebec Conference. His advocacy of confederation cost him his seat following the election of 1865. William Steeves was the son of Heinrich Stief, who came to New Brunswick from Philadelphia in 1766. A successful businessman and able politician, Steeves was a strong advocate of confederation. He served as a representative for New Brunswick both at the Quebec City and the Charlottetown conferences. It is difficult to determine whether Sir Charles Tupper, another Father of Confederation, was of German origin. The name could have been derived from the German "Töpfer," an occupational name for potter. It could also have been derived from the occupational name for a herdsman who was in charge of rams, from a derivative of Middle English *to(u)pe* ("ram"). However, there is little doubt as to the origin of another Father of Confederation. The son of ethnically-German parents, Claus Helmcken and Catherine Mittler, John Sebastian Helmcken was a member of the team that negotiated British Columbia's entry into the Canadian federation, on July 20, 1871.

To gain insight into the German Canadian involvement in the Canadian political process, I made a survey of German names among members of parliament and of the different provincial legislative assemblies that had been elected since the time of confederation. The statistics show that only about half a dozen members of parliament were born in Germany during this period. Looking at both their first names and their family names, and those of their parents, suggests that most of the people of German origin elected to office at the provincial or federal level were second or third generation Canadians, or people whose family had arrived even earlier. Looking at cases where the name of the father and the maiden name of the mother are given, shows that many of the people who gained political office were only partially of German background. At other times, both the mother and father had German names, but the wife of the politician did not. This would suggest that most politicians of German background would have had a divided loyalty insofar as they represented the German community.

Their occupational background and their membership in different community organizations show that German candidates tended to be leaders in their particular community. Many of them worked as teachers, business people, doctors, lawyers, successful farmers. They also belonged to the major clubs in the community, to mutual benefit associations and had a leading role in their church and in other community organizations.

A study of the names of members of parliament shows that Germans have been consistently underrepresented in the House of Commons. At a high, they comprised about 6 per cent of the membership in the House of Commons, while Germans generally constituted about 10 per cent of Canada's population. There are a number of reasons for this. One is the German Canadian lack of experience with the democratic process. Another is that they were fractured by origin and religious affiliation. At the same time, while English Canadians repeatedly were elected to political office in predominantly German areas, for most of the period under study Germans were seldom chosen by the political parties to run for office in areas where they didn't constitute a significant portion of the voter base.

While generally low from the time of confederation to the present, German representation in both the national and provincial legislatures tended to be especially low between World War I and the mid-1960s. In these instances, the wars appear to have had a significant effect on German representation. During this period, while the number of elected officials from the German community declined, the political representation from the Scandinavian, Ukrainian or Italian communities increased. At this time, also, Germans tended to be represented essentially in areas where the German population base was of some significance. Even here, German candidates seldom gave "German" as their national background. Rather, to enhance their chances of success, they stated that they were of Alsatian, Austrian, or Russian origin.

The survey also suggests that Germans were most consistently elected in areas of German concentration. This was especially true of North Waterloo, where a person of German origin tended to be elected about 90 per cent of the time. People with German names also were frequently elected in areas surrounding North Waterloo, including South Waterloo and Bruce and Grey counties, in particular prior to World War I.

Germans tended to be elected in Nova Scotia's South Shore, which included Lunenburg County. In Western Canada, people with German names were frequently elected in areas of Mennonite settlement in southern Manitoba. Here, it seems, non-Mennonite Germans and non-Mennonites with English or Scottish names were frequently elected. Most of the people elected, in particular after 1917, tended to be members of the Conservative Party.[125] Germans were also frequently elected in areas where German Catholics had settled at the turn of the century, in particular in the Humboldt area of St. Peter's Colony.

Looking at German names, it also appears that, except for the city of Kitchener, few Germans were elected in major urban centers. This reflects German settlement patterns. Until World War II, most Germans who came to Canada tended to be attracted to the land. Furthermore, as a group, they tended to remain on the land longer than did other groups.

Another pattern evident in the election of German representatives concerns protest parties. Thus, one finds, in particular beginning in the 1920s, that Germans are frequently found representing protest movements. This might include farmer's parties, the CCF, the Social Credit Party or the Reform Party. This would suggest that, while Germans had difficulty being selected as candidates for political office by the major parties, they found easier access to the protest movements. Being less established, these movements would have had more difficulty finding delegates representing them. At the same time, being issue parties, they would likely have considered the views and attitudes of their political candidates more important than their ethnic background.

---

[125] V. Winkler, who had been elected to the provincial legislature as a Liberal in 1915, lost his seat to the Conservative John Kennedy in 1920. Following this, the Mennonites in this electoral district tended to give their support to Conservative candidates.

Germans were attracted to protest movements particularly in Western Canada, where these movements tended to have their genesis. In part, this was a result of the conviction that traditional parties were the agents of Eastern Canadian interests and therefore failed to represent the true interests of Western Canadians. Also, being newer settlements, these were more willing to experiment with new ways of dealing with the problems facing people. Protest movements found their expression primarily in the CCF and the Social Credit parties, with the CCF finding its main followers in Saskatchewan and, to some extent, in Manitoba, and the Social Credit movement finding its main advocates in Alberta and British Columbia.

In Saskatchewan, German delegates representing the CCF were elected to the Saskatchewan Legislative Assembly in considerable numbers in the 1957 election. The 1964, 1968, and the 1972 elections saw the German support for the CCF, and the later NDP, not only holding but increasing. These elections also witnessed an overall increase in the number of Germans elected to political office. In the 1984 election, in turn, German representatives elected to the Saskatchewan Legislative Assembly were largely Devine Conservatives. What we have here is politics centered on issues, with CCF supporters firmly opposed to Conservative solutions to the province's problems and vice versa.

In Alberta and British Columbia, the German protest vote went largely to the Social Credit Party rather than to the CCF and the later NDP. Thus, in particular in British Columbia, while the number of Germans elected to the provincial assembly wasn't high, the German delegates elected to the British Columbia Assembly in the 1955 election went largely to Social Credit. Almost all the German delegates elected to the Alberta Legislature in 1968 went to Social Credit. Almost all Germans elected to the Alberta Legislature in 1977 were members of the Progressive Conservative Party, while almost all the German representatives elected to the British Columbia Legislature at that time represented the Social Credit Party.

While Germans in Alberta continued to support the Progressive Conservatives provincially, they moved heavily toward the Reform Party in the 1997 federal election. Perhaps this was natural. The Reform Party was a party of the hinterland that found objectionable many of the things that the federal Conservatives and Liberals stood for. More so than other groups, Germans tended to remain on the farm rather than move to the city. One reason for this is their success as farmers. In some instances, also, as with Mennonites and Hutterites, their religion encouraged them to stay on the land. In other instances, especially Germans from Eastern Europe, from where many Germans in Western Canada originated, had a long tradition of seeking not only their livelihood but also their independence by establishing themselves as farmers. Their attachment to land made them similar to other groups who had remained on the land. The attraction to Reform, therefore, crossed ethnic boundaries, with the Reform Party representing people of a particular region rather than any ethnicity. The later union of the Reform and the Conservative parties, in turn, saw a significant shift of Germans into the Conservative party. It also witnessed an increasing number of German members in the House of Commons coming from Western rather than Eastern Canada.

Here I might comment on another pattern that becomes evident, in particular in the 1960s. Prior to this, Germans tended to be elected primarily in centres of German concentration. Since the 1960s, however, Germans were increasingly elected in areas where they were not concentrated. At the same time, non-German representatives were increasingly elected in places such as Kitchener. This, no doubt, was the result, to an extent, of the increasing importance of the non-German element among the new arrivals to the city. It also suggests that differences based on language and ethnicity were increasingly less important when people were selecting delegates to represent them in the House of Commons and in the different legislatures.

This change, seen in the light of the language transformation taking place in the German community, suggests that this alteration was encouraged by the loss of language among Germans themselves. As intermarriage was one of the forces encouraging language change, it also appears that people were becoming increasingly mingled. All this would have made language and ethnic differences less important when people chose delegates to represent them politically. This would have led to the increase of German representatives being elected in non-German areas and for a greater propensity of non-Germans being elected in German areas. In this situation, people were selected largely because of their ability to represent a certain region and specific issues rather than a particular nationality or linguistic group.

While linguistic assimilation had a role in this change, other factors also contributed to more Germans being elected to the provincial and national legislative bodies. Important in this regard is changing attitudes in Canadian society. Traditionally, the focus of the dominant sponsor group was the British connection. People were judged on that basis. This certainly was the case prior to World War I. During the inter-war years this changed somewhat, with people also being judged according to what side they were on during the war. This continued to an extent after World War II. However, in particular after the 1960s Canadian society increasingly tended to view itself as multicultural. This increased the possibility of having people not of British origin elected to political office. This contributed to German Canadians being increasingly elected not only to political office, but also appointed to take leading roles in parliament and the different provincial legislatures. Thus, since the 1960s there isn't a federal government, whose power base is in Western Canada, which doesn't have a minister who is of German origin. It is also at this time that we have people like Ed Schreyer and Gary Doer serving as premiers of Manitoba, Ralph Klein serving as premier of Alberta, and Brad Wall serving as premier of Saskatchewan.

Looking at the participation of Germans in the political process, one cannot help but ask: what benefits did the German Canadian community derive from its members participating in this process? This question is rather difficult to answer. The German Canadian presence in the political process was far too small to have a significant impact on decisions arrived at by the federal or provincial legislative bodies. Also, the ability of politicians of German origin or partial German origin would have been compromised by the fact that so many were intermarried or only partially of German origin. After the 1960s, elected politicians with German names increasingly were elected to represent ridings whose inhabitants were not predominantly German in origin. In these instances, the evidence suggests, politicians sought to represent, not any particular ethnic minority, but the community at large.

Prestige is one benefit derived from members of an ethnic group's rise to prominence in the political process either through election or appointment (for example, as governor-general). From this perspective, one could argue that Germans gained, for example, when Edward Schreyer was appointed Governor General of Canada, and when John Diefenbaker, who was partially of German origin, was elected prime minster of Canada. The same is true when Louis Orville Breithaupt, who was elected to parliament in 1940, served as Lieutenant Governor of Ontario from 1952 to 1956. The same was the case when Edward Schreyer was elected premier in Manitoba, William Aberhardt and Ralph Klein served as premier of Alberta, and Brad Wall served as premier in Saskatchewan.

The Right Honorable Edward Richard Schreyer, PC CC CMM OM CD, who served as Premier of Manitoba, 1969-1977, and as Governor General of Canada, Jan. 22, 1979-May 14, 1984. Author: Stevewashen. Created 10 Sept., 2015. CC BY-SA 4.0.

German Canadians who have been successful politically have also been successful in introducing programs that originated in large part in their own community. This is true in particular of Adam Beck, who was elected mayor of London in 1902 and a few months later was elected to the Ontario Legislature, representing London. Taking up an issue that was very much alive in Waterloo County at the time, he promoted the use of electrical power to light Ontario cities and run Ontario industries. He was largely instrumental in having the Conservative government of Sir James Whitney establish the Ontario Hydro-Electric Power Commission and using public funds to promote the use of electrical power in Ontario. This led to the introduction of electricity to replace in particular coal energy that prior to this ran the industries of both Berlin and other southern Ontario cities.

In a few instances, German Canadians were able to use the political process to forward their community goals. Prior to 1901, language instruction in the Canadian North-West Territories was limited to English and French. It was largely through the work of David Toews that the then Commissioner of Education of the Territories, F.W.G. Haultain, introduced legislation that permitted any School Board in the Territories to hire teachers to provide instruction in languages other than English for one hour a day, between the hours of three and four in the afternoon.

This permitted not only Germans but also other ethnic minorities in the Territories, and later in particular in Saskatchewan, to use the public school system to perpetuate their linguistic identity. The legislation was passed largely because of the favorable attitude English Canadians had towards the German minority at the time.

This provision was terminated during World War I, when the English Canadian majority decided to abolish it as well as the provisions in Manitoba and Ontario that provided to minority groups the opportunity to use the public school system to perpetuate their linguistic identity. German Canadians and other minorities could do little to prevent this. This suggests that German Canadians could attain goals they aspired to through the political process only insofar as these met with the concurrence of the English-Canadian majority.

The same appears to be the case in regards to the political influence German political representatives had on English Canadian attitudes during World War I. German Canadian representatives in the federal parliament helped them negotiate the difficulties faced by them during World War I. While co-operating with the Borden Conservatives, William George Weichel, who had been elected to represent Waterloo North in 1911, did his best to make the Borden Conservative government aware that German Canadians were British subjects and ought to be treated as such. After Weichel was defeated by William Daum Euler in 1917, over the conscription issue, Euler continued this policy. When the war was over, he served both his North Waterloo riding and Canadian society in general through his work as Minister of Finance and in other capacities.

William Daum Euler. Member of Parliament for Waterloo North, 1917-1940. Public Domain.

However, neither Weichel nor Euler had a significant influence on changing the negative stereotyping of Germans during the war, both in Europe and abroad, in which the Canadian government took a leading role. They could do little to stop innocent Germans from being arrested and sent off to internment camp during the war. The same is true of the negligible influence they had to prevent Germans from losing their jobs or from being beaten up in the street by the more rowdy elements in Canadian society.

From this it would appear that German political representatives, such as there were, did little to attain goals that were strictly in the interest of the German Canadian community. They were more successful when seeking to realize goals that served the interests, not of a particular community, but of Canadian society at large.

GERMAN CANADIANS IN SCIENCE AND SCHOLARSHIP

As in other areas of endeavour, Germans in Canada have been involved in scientific exploration and scholarship since the establishment of the country. Some of the scientists were recruited by Canada because of their expertise; others came because Canada, or the Canadian environment, offered them the opportunity to expand their field of study. In other instances, Canada offered them work opportunities. No matter what their field of expertise, the individuals involved all made a positive contribution to this country.

Some of the early medical personnel in Canada included Germans. Thus, Karl-Joseph Ferdinand von Felz is listed as serving as a surgeon for the Montreal garrison in 1738. Born in Quebec City, of a German father and French-Canadian mother, Anthony von Iffland in 1820 founded the first school of anatomy in Canada, in Quebec City. In 1847, Daniel Arnoldi, whose father had emigrated from Germany, was named the founding president of the Montreal College of Physicians and Surgeons of Lower Canada. He and Dr. Henry Loedel, also of German origin, were included among the group of doctors who worked out the memorandum that led to the founding of McGill University. A son of Dr. Arnoldi, D.F.T. Arnoldi, in 1843 became the first president of the École de Medicine et Chirurgie de Montréal, which evolved into the Université de Montréal. John Sebastian Helmcken, who came to Canada in 1850 to work as a surgeon for the Hudson's Bay Company, was a founding president of the British Columbia Medical Society in 1885, and in 1886 helped establish the Medical Council of British Columbia, which licenses B.C. doctors.

More recently, Dr. Raymond O. Heimbecker, born in Calgary, Alberta, in 1922, worked at the Department of Surgery of the University of Toronto and served as a cardiovascular consultant at Wellesley Hospital of that city when he performed the world's first complete heart valve transplant. In 1981, he performed Canada's first "modern" heart transplant.

Germans contributed to our understanding of native peoples and their environment in various capacities. The Moravian missionary, David Zeisberger, not only helped to establish different native settlements, but also created an English-German-Iroquois-Delaware dictionary to forward the communication between Europeans and native peoples. In addition, he translated hymns as well as sermons into Delaware as well as publicized the first "pronunciation" book in Delaware and English.

The Moravian missionaries worked among the Inuit in the Labrador since 1752. They Christianized the natives and, in the process, translated the Bible and German hymns into Inuktitut. They established schools to educate Inuit children. At the same time, their mapping of the Labrador coastline, as well as their work on plant species in the Labrador and their meteorological observations enriched our understanding of the plant life of the Labrador and of its environment.

The Moravian Brother, Johann Miertsching, who acquired a knowledge of Inuit languages through his work in Labrador, served as a translator for the Arctic expedition of Sir Richard Collinson, 1850-1854, while it explored Arctic waters in search of a sea route from the Pacific to the Atlantic. While accompanying the expedition, Miertsching made numerous observations regarding the land and its people. Similar observations were carried out by Franz Boas, who had emigrated from Germany to the United States before coming to Canada. In the 1880s, he made extensive studies of the Inuit population of Baffin Island and of the Indians of the north-west coast of North America. Another anthropologist, Bernard Adolf Hantzsch, who was born in Dresden, Germany, in 1875, conducted ethnological and geological investigations in Labrador in 1906. He undertook an expedition to Baffin Island, where he investigated Arctic ornithology, examined Eskimo life and carried out extensive mapping. More recently, the Vienna-born musicologist Ida Halper (born Ruhdoerfer), helped us to better understand the musical tradition of native peoples. Coming to Canada in 1939, she became a pioneer in the study of the music of Indian peoples in the Canadian West.

Otto Julius Klotz (1852-1923), along with W.F. King, was responsible for establishing the astronomical branch of the Department of Interior, and the building of the Cliff Street Observatory in 1899. With King, he planned the Dominion Observatory and succeeded him as director in 1917. In his work, he established positions along the CPR right of way through B.C. in 1885, and in 1903-04 extended the longitude from Vancouver across the Pacific along the new cable route.

Born in Cornwallis, Nova Scotia, Abraham Gesner (1797-1864) trained to be a doctor. Practicing medicine near Parrsboro, Nova Scotia, he collected fossils on his way from and to house calls. In 1838, he was appointed Provincial Geologist of New Brunswick and became the first government geologist in a British colony. In 1842, he opened the first museum in Canada, which later was acquired by the Natural History Society of New Brunswick. Later, Gesner emigrated to the United States, where he developed and patented a process for the manufacture of kerosene.

Born in Breslau, Germany, in 1841, Eugene Emil Felix Richard Haanel came to Canada in the 1870s to take the chair of chemistry and physics at Victoria College, Cobourg. He is generally regarded as the founder of the first institute of applied sciences in Canada. Born in New York of German parents, in 1890, Otto Maass became Macdonald Professor at McGill University in 1923. Maass was instrumental in the establishment of the Defence Research Board of Canada. He established the first graduate school in Science at McGill. He published more than 200 papers in such areas as calorimetry and the preparation of pure hydrogen peroxide, which was first prepared by him and is used today as a rocket fuel.

In the area of cultural studies, the political refugee from Nazi Germany, Hellmuth Kallmann worked for years in the Music section of the National Library. In 1960, he completed a detailed study of music in Canada, entitled *A History of Music in Canada*. Karl Klinck, who was born in Elmira, Ontario, worked long to have Canadian studies introduced into the curriculum of schools and universities. In 1965, he published his comprehensive study, *Literary History of Canada*. Through his work in publishing *The German-Canadian Yearbook* and other work, as well as in his leadership in the Historical Society of Mecklenburg Upper Canada, Professor Hartmut Froeschle made an invaluable contribution to our better understanding of German Canadian life. This has been further advanced by the establishment of the Chair of German-Canadian Studies, in 1989, through a grant from the Department of the Secretary of State and the financial support of families in Winnipeg's German community. The Canadian Association of University Teachers of German, which brings out the publication *Seminar*, has for years taken a leading role in structuring German language studies at Canadian high schools and universities.

In the area of botany, Frederick Pursh spent years studying Canadian flora. Unfortunately, he lost his extensive collection of plants in a fire and therefore could not complete the detailed study he was preparing on this subject. However, his *Flora Americae Septentrionalis* makes an important contribution to this field of study. The specialist in plant pathology and bacteriology, Hans Theodor Gussow, who in 1909 left Europe to take a position with the Experimental Farms Branch of the Dominion Department of Agriculture, helped forward our knowledge of diseases affecting plants. In a related field, Elizabeth Mann-Borgese, a daughter of Thomas Mann, devoted herself to the cause of protecting the environment, in particular the oceans. She was a founding member - and for a long time the only female member – of the Club of Rome. She also founded the International Ocean Institute (an international NGO with five centres around the world). A recognized expert on maritime law and policy, she held a position as a Senior Research Fellow, Adjunct Professor of Law, and Chair of the International Oceans Institute at Dalhousie University, Halifax, Nova Scotia.

Born in Prussia, Bernhardt E. Fernow was trained as a forester. Falling in love with Olivia Reynolds, a young American visitor, he followed her to the United States. There he was appointed to head the Forestry Division of the Department of Agriculture in 1886. As no foresters were being trained in the United States, Fernow established the first training school for foresters at Cornell University in 1898. Pressure from logging interests forced the school to close.

By the 1890s Canada was beginning to realize the value of forestry, although lands were not managed in a large-scale way. By 1905 the Dominion government had reserved nine and a half million acres of national parks, and Sir Wilfred Laurier called a convention to discuss the issue of forest management. It was here that the idea of a school of forestry came to the fore, with Fernow participating in the discussions. When in 1907 the faculty of forestry was established at the University of Toronto, Fernow became its first dean.

Born in Chester, Nova Scotia, Don Olding Hebb traces his roots back to the early settlers of Lunenburg County. Hebb has been considered one of the outstanding psychologists of this century and the father of neuropsychology and neural networks. In his work, he explored the role of neurons in psychological processes such as learning. Working at different universities, primarily at McGill, in Montreal, Hebb's central concern was to develop his neurophysiological theory of mental functions such as thought, imagery, volition, attention and memory - all problems which orthodox behaviourism tended to avoid or dismiss. In addition to his important monographs, *The Organization of Behaviour* (1949) and *A Textbook of Psychology* (1958), he wrote over 50 scholarly articles.

After graduating from the University of Berlin in medicine, Heinz E. Lehman (1911-1999) came to Canada in 1937. While working in psychiatry in private practice, he also taught at McGill University, where he became a full professor in 1965, and between 1971 and 1974 served as Chairman of the Department of Psychiatry. An avid researcher, teacher and clinician, he had some 300 publications in the area of psychiatry. In recognition of his work, he received numerous prizes, including the Albert Lasker Award of the American Association of Public Health. In addition, he has his name on the annual prize for excellence in psychiatry, awarded by the Quebec Psychiatric Association.

Henry Taube was born in 1915 in Neudorf, Saskatchewan. His parents were Germans from Ukraine, who had settled in Saskatchewan in 1911. He was the first Canadian-born chemist to win the Nobel Prize, which he won "for his work on the mechanisms of electron-transfer reactions, especially in complex metals." Teaching at Cornell, the University of Chicago and Stanford, he had over 600 publications, including one book.

Born in Hamburg, Germany, in 1904, Gerhard Herzberg taught at the Darmstadt Institute of Technology after obtaining his doctorate from the Institute in 1928. He was relieved of his position by the national Socialist regime because his wife was Jewish, and came to Canada in 1935 to join the Department of Physics of the University of Saskatchewan. He then spent three years at the University of Chicago, returning to Canada as head of the Physics Division of the National Research Council, a position he held until his retirement in 1969. In 1971, he was awarded the Nobel Prize in chemistry for his work on the electronic structure and geometry of molecules. Another Nobel Prize winner, John Charles Polanyi, born in Berlin, Germany, of Hungarian parents, won the Nobel Prize in Chemistry in 1986 for his research in chemical kinetics. Another chemist who made a notable contribution is Axel Becke. Born in Esslingen, Germany, Becke completed his Ph.D. in 1981 from

McMaster University. While working at Queen's University, Kingston, and Dalhousie University, Halifax, he developed a computational technique that allows us to calculate the molecular properties of large and complex molecular systems with greater accuracy, which has contributed to important advancements in both chemistry and physics. In recognition of his work, Becke was awarded the Gerhard Herzberg Canada Medal for Science and Engineering in 2015.

Gerhard Herzberg. Nobel Prize Chemistry, 1971. Photo courtesy of the National Research Council of Canada.

Arthur C. Heidebrecht was born in Alberta and served as a professor in the Department of Engineering of McMaster University, Hamilton, where he became renowned for his research in earthquake engineering. A graduate of Ludwig-Maximilians-Universität, in Munich, Claus Wagner-Bartak (b. 1937) contributed extensively to the application of robotics for industrial purposes. He pioneered and coordinated the research and development of the Shuttle Remote manipulator System (SRMS), or Canadarm 1, a mechanical arm used on the NASA Space Shuttle to manoeuvre a payload from the payload bay of the orbiter to its deployment position from where it is released. In the 1980s, he established a joint venture (Atlas Polar Systems, Inc.) with a reputable Canadian manufacturer with the objective of developing a fully robotized loading system mounted on specialized trucks. In addition to other projects involving the use of robotics in industry, he was instrumental in the development of robotic devices for quadriplegics. In recognition of his pioneer achievements, he received a number of international awards, including the Joseph Engelberger Award (1986).

Another person of German origin involved in creating the Canadarm was George Johann Klein, who has been mentioned as possibly the "most productive inventor in Canada in the 20th century," his career spanning the "stick and string" era of aviation to the space shuttle. Born in Hamilton, Ontario, in 1904, he was the offspring of Alsatian immigrants who had settled in Perth County in 1835. Klein designed the National Research Council's first wind tunnels and carried out research designed to fit skis to aircraft, which led to designing the Weasel army snowmobile. He designed aiming systems for artillery and naval submarines during World War II, and, from 1944-45 headed the team designing the Zero Energy Experimental Pile, the first atomic reactor outside the United States. In his seventies, he was chief consultant on gear design for the Canadarm. His other inventions include the STEM (Storable Tubular Extendible Member), a radio antenna that can be retracted into a flat screen and rolled out again, a wheelchair for quadriplegics and a microsurgical staple gun used to suture blood vessels.

Often cited as the most productive inventor in Canada in the 20th century George J. Klein worked at NRC for over forty years. George Johann Klein (standing) and his electric chair, 1953. Public Domain.

Roberta Lynn Bondar was involved in advancing the space program as an astronaut. Of German-Ukrainian origin, born in Sault St. Marie, she received her Ph.D. in neurobiology and a medical degree before she assumed her training as an astronaut in 1984. In 1992, she was designated a prime Payload Specialist for the first International Microgravity Laboratory Mission. On the NASA Space Discovery Mission from January 22-30, 1992, she performed experiments to help us better understand the mechanisms underlying the body's ability to recover from exposure to space.

Another person who might be mentioned is Joseph Gerald Hagey (1904-1988). A Canadian businessman, he founded and was the first president of Waterloo University, which in many ways laid the groundwork for Kitchener-Waterloo's prosperity during the high-tech era. Born and raised in Hamilton, Hagey took a job in sales for B.F. Goodrich, a Kitchener-based rubber company. While working as an advertising and public relations manager, he continued to be involved in his *alma mater*, Waterloo College. He left Goodrich to become president of Waterloo College in 1953. Anticipating expanding student enrolment because of the rapid post-war economic expansion and the baby boom, he sought to transform Waterloo College into a university, concentrating on science and technology, which would be closely linked to industry through co-operative education. Experiencing resistance from others at the college, he encouraged the science and engineering faculty, which he had established, to break away from Waterloo College, which eventually became Wilfrid Laurier University. The science and engineering faculty eventually evolved into the University of Waterloo, which by the time Hagey retired in 1969, had become a large campus with a student population of 9,000.

From the above survey, it becomes quite evident that the majority of Germans who contributed to Canada in the sciences were immigrants. One reason may be the rapid assimilation of German Canadians. Children from intermarriage with a German woman would be difficult to identify as German Canadian. In other instances, assimilation involved name changes, making it difficult to determine the national origin of a person.

Other influences may result from opportunity. When Canada was still largely at a developing stage, it did not yet have the schools to train top-notch scientists. To this would be added the orientation of immigrants themselves. Most of these, at least during the early period of settlement, were attracted to the land. As may be seen in the case of George Johann Klein, he left the land only because of illness. Unable to carry out the hard work demands of the farming life, he went on to pursue a higher education.

German scientists who contributed to the scientific evolution in Canada were generally trained in universities outside the country. They were often recruited by Canada. At times, they came to Canada as part of their fieldwork. At other times, they were forced to leave Germany and came to Canada because this country offered them work opportunities that were unavailable to them in their homeland.

GERMAN CANADIANS IN THE ARTS

People need the time and opportunity to pursue artistic endeavours. Art requires a fairly sophisticated public that can appreciate its value and support it. Institutions such as schools are needed to permit those with talent to develop and perfect their skills. Publishing houses, as well as art galleries, are necessary to help creators of art market their work. All these have for the most part been absent in the German Canadian community. Despite this, a number of people have emerged who have made a noteworthy contribution to the arts, be this in literature, fine art or music.

Literature

A number of influences shaped the literary heritage in the German Canadian community. German immigrants, in particular during the early period, were for the most part poor people from a rural background who often didn't know how to read or write. Preoccupied with making their daily living, they seldom had time for the arts. At the same time, they were faced with the problem of adapting to a new country in which they didn't speak the dominant languages. Although the immigrants established schools, these, for the most part, tended to pass on to the child a rudimentary German. Of course, some fairly good schools were established in some of the settled areas such as in Waterloo County or in the group settlements in Western Canada. Even here, however, the purpose of the school wasn't to train men of letters. Rather, it was to pass on a sufficient knowledge of German so that people attending these schools could communicate in German in their everyday life and understand the language well enough so as to be able to follow the Sunday sermon.

It was especially at this time that the literature which was being produced in the community was the work of priests, pastors, as well as of the few people who found work with the German language press.

Members of the clergy who wrote combined this with their daily duties in the ministry. Their work reflects their concerns and their spiritual quest.

One of the earliest poets to emerge was Eugen Funcken, a German Catholic priest serving the German Catholic community which emerged in Upper Canada during the 1830s. Born in Wankum, in Rhenish Prussia in 1831, Eugen Fucken was ordained to the priesthood on June 6, 1857. On August 14, 1857, he arrived in St. Agatha, Upper Canada, to serve the German Catholic parishioners in Waterloo County. Funcken's existent poetry is gathered in two collections. One of his miscellaneous pieces was published in 1868, largely to help defray the cost of the orphanage being built in St. Agatha. The second, *Immanuel,* was not published. While not of the highest literary quality, the works nevertheless provides an insight into 19th century Catholicism and into Funcke's view of Canada and his mission here.

Another poet with a religious background was Heinrich Rembe. Originating from Eisleben, Germany, Rembe (1858-1927) studied theology at the Kropp-Seminary in Germany as well as in Philadelphia prior to coming to Canada. Here he served German Lutheran parishioners in different centres, be this in Montreal, Arnprior, Hamilton, as well as in Bridgeport in Waterloo County. For a time, he served as president of the Canada Synod as well as editor of its synodical paper. He is known to have published four volumes of poetry: *Herz und Natur, Stimmungen in Liedern und Gedichten, Neue Gedichte* and *Aus der Einsamkeit einer canadischen Landpfarre.* The Doon Pioneer Village Archives holds one of his volumes, *Herz und Natur,* which displays not only profoundness and sensitivity, but also considerable artistic merit.

In addition to the religious poetry, a certain amount of popular writing was also produced, in particular in the Pennsylvania Dutch dialect. This includes poems, which appeared in the papers under assumed names or as anonymous. This dialect literature found expression in particular in the form of letters that appeared in the weeklies. Such letters took an art form especially in the work of John Adam Rittinger. Born in Berlin (Kitchener) in 1855, Rittinger attended St. Jerome's College as well as learned to be a typesetter at the firm of his father, Rittinger & Motz. He worked at papers in Toronto, Buffalo and elsewhere before he purchased the *Walkerton Glocke* together with Dr. A. Eby, in 1875. When the *Berliner Journal* took over the *Glocke* in 1904, Rittinger became editor of the paper. In order to appeal to the local readers, he brought out humorous stories in the Pennsylvania Dutch dialect, dealing with the life and problems of local farmers. Writing of John Adam Rittinger, who wrote under the pseudonym Joe Klotzkopp, Professor Herbert K. Kalbfleisch states: "Had John A. Rittinger written in English, he would be counted among the great humorists of this country. His work is in the tradition of Thomas Chandler Haliburton and Stephen Leacock. Even in translation, the subtle sallies are not lost."[126]

John Adam Rittinger. Courtesy of the Waterloo Region Hall of Fame.

Of the different groups among Germans, the Russian Mennonites who arrived in Canada during the 1920s created a literature of some note. For the most part relatively well educated, many had been unable to pursue their aspirations as a result of the socio-economic changes engendered by the outbreak of the Russian Revolution. Among these, Heinz Kloss, in his analysis of German Canadian literature, identifies Gerhard Friesen (1894-1983), who wrote under the name Fritz Senn, as being one of the most gifted among the Russian Mennonite poets who came to Canada following the Russian Revolution.[127] Born in Halbstadt, Ukraine, Friesen came to Canada in 1924. While making his living as a farmer, he frequently contributed to the Mennonite cultural publication

---

[126]   H. K. Kalbfleisch, *The History of the Pioneer German language Press of Ontario, 1835-1918* (Toronto: University of Toronto Press, 1968) 71.

[127]   Heinz Kloss, ed. *Ahornblaetter. Deutsche Dichtung aus Kanada* (Wuerzburg: Holzner Verlag, 1961) 26.

Mennonitische Warte. A selection of his poems was brought out in 1974 by Elisabeth Peters under the title of *Das Dorf im Abendgrauen.*

Another highly talented writer in the group was Arnold Dyck (1889-1970). Writing of Dyck, Al Reimer states: "By any critical standard, Arnold Dyck must be regarded as an important literary artist whose considerable body of fiction, plays, and other writings has not received the attention it deserves. One is tempted to say that had this master of comedy written in English rather than in his beloved *Plautdiesch* (the low German dialect spoken by the Mennonites since the sixteenth century), he would today be counted among Canada's finest humorists.[128] Born in the Mennonite village of Hochfeld in the Ukraine, Dyck aspired to be an artist and persuaded his father to send him to Germany to study art. He returned to Russia prior to the outbreak of war and served in the Red Cross office as a non-combatant. After the war he returned to his native colony, Yazykovo, to teach at the Nikolaipol *Zentralschule.* Permitted to leave Russia with other Mennonites, Dyck came to Canada in 1923 naively expecting to make a living as an artist. Unable to establish himself in Winnipeg, he settled in the Mennonite town of Steinbach, Manitoba, where for the down payment of one dollar he purchased the German weekly *Steinbach Post* and began his career as editor, writer, publisher and cultural entrepreneur.

Dyck's *Koop enn Bua opp Reise* began as a series in the Low German dialect, written for entertainment for his Mennonite readers. It was later turned into a novel, to which he also added *Koop enn Bua faore no Toronto* and *Koop enn Bua enn Dietschland,* his last published work. During the war, Dyck started his *Bildungsroman* entitled *Verloren in der Steppe,* which is considered by critics to be his finest work.

While there is no group of writers in the German Canadian community that is comparable to that of the Russlander Mennonites who came to Canada during the 1920s, individuals among the other groups created significant work. One of these is Else Seel (1894-1974). Writing of her work, Hermann Boeschenstein writes that in contrast to German lyricists, Else Seel is in the enviable position of having her work rooted in her experiences rather than in the alchemy of artificially inspired

---

[128] Al Reimer, *Annalen* VI (1987) 1.

language.[129] Born Else Lübcke in Schivelbein, Pomerania, Seel worked for a brief period in the Archives of the German Annuity Bank after graduating from high school. In 1927, she emigrated to Canada to marry George Seel of Ootsa Lake, B.C., with whom she had been corresponding for some time. Living in the backwoods as a trapper's wife, she was forced to adjust quickly to primitive backwoods conditions. She read voraciously, receiving her books from the Vancouver Public Library. She continued writing, communicating her experiences to the German-speaking world in the form of articles for various newspapers and periodicals. She also continued her creative work, which includes *Haus im Urwald*, a book of poems published in Vancouver in 1956, and *Kanadisches Tagebuch*, published in Tübingen in 1964.

As the number of educated people emigrating to Canada increased, the creative literature produced also expanded. This was true in particular for the post-World War II period. Among post-World War II poets, Walter Bauer (1904-1976) warrants special mention. When Walter Bauer emigrated from West Germany to North America in 1952 at the age of 48 he was already a well-established author in his homeland, with some 50 books published in German-speaking countries. He emigrated essentially for personal renewal, feeling he had reached the end of his creative output in Germany and needed new inspiration. Canada meant for him immense distances, freedom not only in the political sense but also from old forms. It meant sky, light, silence and snow. Bauer worked at first as a dish washer and labourer. In 1954, he started to take courses at the University of Toronto, specializing in German studies. After completing his Masters, he started to teach at the University of Toronto, at first as an instructor and eventually as an assistant professor.

Writing of Bauer, Professor Froeschle states that while Bauer cannot be counted among the giants of German literature, in the context of German Canadian literature, Bauer holds a significant position if not the most significant position.[130] Of Bauer's Canadian works, several might

---

[129]   Translated from the German by the author. Quoted in Rodney T. K. Symington, "Else Seel: Eine Biographie im Nachlass," *German – Canadian Yearbook* III (1976) 197.

[130]   Hartmut Froeschle, Walter Bauer. "Sein dichterisches Werk mit besonderer Berücksichtigung seines Kanada-Erlebnisses." *German-Canadian Yearbook V* (1979), 99.

be mentioned: *Nachtwachen des Tellerwaschers* (poetry, 1957); *Die tränen eines Mannes* (narratives, 1961); *Fremd in Toronto* (narratives, 1963); *Ein Jahr* (diary notes, 1967). These works are significant not only because of their literary merit. Through different literary forms, they provide a sensitive account of the immigrant experience: the fears, hopes and difficulties faced by someone seeking to make a start in the New World.

Among emigrants of the post-World War II period Ullirch Schaffer might also be mentioned. Born in 1942 in Pomerania, his family fled west during the war. He and his family emigrated to Canada in 1953, settling at first in Lethbridge, Alberta, and then in Kitimat, British Columbia. Studying German and English literature in Canada as well as in Germany, Schaffer took a job teaching German at Douglas College, in Vancouver. A poet of considerable talent, his work is largely of a religious nature and includes works such as *im gegenwind* (Karlsruhe 1964), *gurluana* (Karlsruhe 1965), and *umkehrungen* (Wuppertal 1975).

Rather than writing in German, a number of German Canadian writers have chosen to write in English. One of the earliest of these is Felix Paul Berthold Friedrich Greve. Born in Germany, he came to Canada in 1909. Here he worked as a school teacher in Mennonite settlements in southern Manitoba. Between 1922 and 1947 he wrote seven popular novels, short stories, as well as *In Search of Myself,* a fictionalized autobiography for which he received the Governor General's Award for Fiction.

Born in 1927 in Heisler, Alberta, Robert Kroetsch, of German Catholic background, wrote some nine popular novels, over twelve books of poetry, as well as autobiographical works. In his novels, he adopted in particular the tall tale rhetoric of the prairie tavern literary form. His poetry is largely experimental and his exploration of poetry often includes the structure of fiction, which is evident in particular in *The Hornbooks of Rita K* (2001), which was a Governor General's Literary Award Nominee. His *The Studhorse Man* (1969) won the Governor General's Literary Award. Kroetsch has often been referred to as "Mr. Canadian Postmodern," with his work often exploring myths and the magical/fabulous.

Paul Hiebert, who worked as a professor of chemistry, was one of the early Mennonite writers who wrote in English. He is best known for his book, *Sarah Binks* (1947), for which he was awarded the Stephen Leacock Medal for Humour in 1948. Mennonite writing in English has flourished in particular since the publication of Rudy Wiebe's *Peace Shall Destroy Many* (1962). Wiebe's novel became a landmark because it highlighted contradictions in Mennonite faith and behaviour that Mennonite leaders did not want to have aired in the outside world. Since the publication of this seminal work, Wiebe has published other novels, including *The Temptations of Big Bear* (1973) and *A Discovery of Strangers* (1994), for both of which he won the Governor General's Award for Fiction. Other publications include collections of short stories, essays, children's books, as well as a volume of memoirs about his childhood. His work is characterized by its ambitious scope and his focus on moral issues.

Wiebe was among the first Mennonite writers after World War II who turned to writing in English. Others include Patrick Friesen, Armin Wiebe, Sandra Birdsell, John Weier, David Bergen, Di Brandt, Vern Thiessen and Miriam Toews. A central focus for many of these writers is reconciling the restrictive religious outlook in which they grew up with the more free, cosmopolitan and, at times, irreligious outlook they encountered in the outer world.

Art and Sculpture

Unlike German Canadian literature, which depended to a large extent upon a German-speaking audience, the work of German Canadians in the visual arts tended to have an appeal not so much in the German Canadian community as in the larger Canadian society. This was due essentially to the nature of the media, with the artist not being restricted by language to communicate with his or her audience. Also, the artists, who for the most part were immigrants, tended to be of a cosmopolitan nature. They often came to America, not to settle, but to search for adventure or to paint the American landscape. They tended to have little contact with the German Canadian community but sought their contacts in the larger Canadian society, and their inspiration in the Canadian landscape.

A number of influences caused German painters to come to Canada. One was the thirst for adventure or travel. Another was the romance of America, be this the attraction of the North American landscape or the uniqueness of its people. One of the earliest was Cornelius Krieghoff (1815-1872). Born in Ufhoven, Thurungia, Krieghoff's father moved to

Amsterdam where he married I.L. Mauters, a woman of Flemish origin. Cornelius Krieghoff was born in 1815 in Amsterdam. In about 1822 the family returned to Germany, with Cornelius growing up in Mainberg, Bavaria, where his father was in charge of a carpet factory. It is uncertain whether he went to study art in Rotterdam or in Germany. In any case, some of Krieghoff's work, painted in Quebec City, shows the influence of the Düsseldorf school of painting, with its love of genre, its attention to detail, and its figures silhouetted against gloomy interiors.

In 1837, Krieghoff emigrated to the United States, primarily in search of adventure. While serving in a military campaign against the Seminole Indians, he prepared numerous sketches of campaign incidents, but these were burned. His life altered when he met a French Canadian girl, Louise Gauthier *dite* Saint-Germain, from Longueuil, near Montreal. He fell in love with her and soon after they were married. He was discharged (or deserted) from the American army in 1840. He moved to Toronto with his bride, where his brother Ernst worked, possibly as a pioneer daguerreotypist. Following this, he and his wife stayed briefly with her parents, in Longueuil, before settling in Montreal.

Meanwhile, Krieghoff concentrated on his art, with his wife and daughter becoming favourite subjects. Other works, such as views of Indian encampments in the Thousand Islands, still retain a brown cast which the artist abandoned for livelier hues in later years. Occupying a two-bedroom apartment near Beaver Hill, Krieghoff peddled his paintings from door to door, selling them for $5 to $10 each. Briefly, he also supported himself teaching at an art school.

He supported himself and his family as best he could through his art, painting teams of horses, sketching pieces of furniture, or decorating tilt-top tables with miniature landscapes. In 1851, he met with John Budden of Quebec, who had heard of his work. Several years later, Krieghoff and his family moved in with Budden. Krieghoff threw himself into painting the Quebec City scene, including scenes of revellers at Jean-Baptiste Jolifou's hostelry. He painted numerous landscapes as well as other works. Popular subjects he painted repeatedly, with minor variations. Insofar as possible, he supplemented his income from his art with prints of his work. While some may question Krieghoff's artistry, few will deny that his ability to capture the spirit and vitality of Quebec habitant life remains unmatched even today.

The Toll Gate, oil on canvas by Cornelius Krieghoff, 1859.
National Gallery of Canada. Public Domain.

Another painter of German origin who gained a degree of
prominence in Canada was William von Moll Berczy. Raised in Vienna,
where his uncle served as the German ambassador, he rebelled against
entering the diplomatic service, attended Leipzig University, and
then wandered through Central Europe. After he married Charlotte
Allemande, a painter from Berne, the two spent five years in Italy, where
he painted watercolours of family groups and then became drawing
master of the Marquis of Bath's daughters in England. Their London
friends were expatriate Germans, one of their circle being Johann
Zoffany, favourite court painter to Queen Charlotte and George III.

Serving as land agent for the Marquis of Bath, Berczy came to North
America in 1792 to bring a party of German colonists to the United
States. Getting into a quarrel with the New York State authorities, he
moved his settlers to Markham Township outside of Toronto. Thereafter
he considered himself Canadian, and soon after his arrival was painting
portraits, with Joseph Brant's portrait being one of his early Canadian
works.

Litigation over title to the Markham lands took Berczy to England
about 1800. The dispute was never settled and, on returning to Canada,
Berczy became a full-time professional painter. As Montreal offered a
more appreciative and larger clientele than Toronto, he moved there. He
continued concentrating on portraiture, with his *Woolsey Family*, painted
during a visit to Quebec in 1808-9, probably his strongest work. Berczy's

best-known works are portrait heads drawn with the precision and clarity of a classical medallion. In addition, he also did life-sized oil busts. Other members of the Berczy family also painted. His wife taught art, and William Jr. was almost as talented as his father at miniatures, small watercolour portraits and landscapes.

Other German artists also came to live and work in Canada just prior, or soon after, the formation of the new Dominion. Adolph Vogt (1843-71) came to Montreal in 1865 and worked for some time at the Notman photographic studios. Born in Liebenstein (Sachsen-Meiningen), Vogt had come to Philadelphia when twelve, where he had taken painting lessons from German immigrants. Later, he studied in Munich, Zurich and Paris. In 1869, he made an impressive painting of Niagara Falls, which may have led to his employment as "special artist" by *l'Opinion Publique* and the *Canadian Illustrated News*. His *Approaching Storm* was widely praised at the second exhibition of the Society of Canadian Artists in 1870.

Vogt was one of three well-known German painters who settled in Montreal at the time of Confederation. The others were Otto Reinhold Jacobi and Wilhelm Raphael. Jakobi left Europe for New York to paint portraits, and after a short stay came to Quebec, in 1860, to paint a presentation canvas of Shawinigan Falls for the Prince of Wales. He remained in Canada, painting waterfalls, autumn foliage and blue hazes in both oil and watercolour. Raphael, who had studied at the Berlin Academy first went to the United States and in 1860 came to Canada. Concentrating on sleighing scenes and scenes of winter storms, he introduced genre to add interest to his landscapes. His paintings, combining realism with romantic and classical traditions, often depict Montreal harbour and market scenes.

Germans have always been fascinated with North American wilderness. One of the most noteworthy painters depicting the Canadian scene was Carl Rungius. He emigrated to the U.S. at the age of twenty-five. After exploring the wilderness in Wyoming and New Brunswick, he left to hunt and paint in the Yukon. In 1910, he explored the Alberta Rockies, where he remained, painting Rocky Mountain scenes until his death in 1959.

Born of a noble family in Germany, Count Berthold von Imhoff began to paint at the age of seven. In his training as an artist, he focussed on religious subjects. In 1900, he and his family left Germany for Pennsylvania to escape the effects industrialization was having on his homeland. Although he did well as a painter, he found that industrialization was also transforming Pennsylvania. He decided to move to Saskatchewan, which he had found attractive while on a hunting trip to the province, in 1913. From 1914, until his death in 1939, he painted hundreds of religious works free of charge, essentially for his artistic and spiritual satisfaction. He got most of his income by decorating Roman Catholic churches in Saskatchewan and the United States. Many of his commissioned works can be seen in churches in St. Walburg, Muenster, St. Benedict, Bruno, Denzil, Humboldt and North Battleford.

Born in Dresden, Germany, Hans Erich Bergmann (1893-1958) was an apprentice to a commercial engraver before coming to Canada in 1913. Settling in Winnipeg, he worked as an illustrator with Bridgen's Limited. He pursued his personal artistic interest in his free time during which he worked on wood engraving as well as with watercolours and oils. He gained prominence as both a painter and engraver and has representative works in local and provincial galleries as well as in the National Gallery of Canada. Commenting in particular on Bergman's wood engravings, Dr. Ferdinand Eckhardt, when introducing two Bergman exhibitions, in 1960 and 1969, states that they have a near-abstract organization: a cedar branch becomes a filigree of perfect patterns, a moth on oak leaves a wonder of texture and lines.[131]

Born in Danzig, Fritz Brandtner (1896-1969) studied art at the University of Danzig. After travels in France, Germany, Poland and Russia, he returned to his home city and for a year taught at the University of Danzig, in life classes for the Department of Architecture. In 1928 he came to Canada. Starting work as a house painter, he later was employed by a photo-engraving firm as commercial artist, designer and letterer, while also doing murals and stage sets for local firms and societies. He left Winnipeg for Montreal in 1934, where he became active in children's art and in the use of art as therapy. His work was strongly influenced by the German expressionists and, later, by the semi-abstract and abstract movements. He worked in both oils and watercolours.

---

[131]   Gunda Lambton, "Contributions of German Graphic Artists in the History of Canadian Printmaking, *German Canadian Yearbook*, vol. IV (1978) 196.

Potato Pickers. Oil Silkscreen on Paperboard, c. 1943. By Fritz Brandtner. Courtesy of Mayberry Fine Art.

Christiane Pflug (née Schütt) was born in Berlin Germany, in 1936. When her family emigrated to Canada, she went to Paris to study fashion design. On the train to Paris, she met her future husband, Michael Pflug. With his encouragement and that of the artists Viera de Silva and Arpad Scenes, she began to paint. She painted while her husband practiced medicine in Tunis. She continued her work after her family settled in Toronto in 1959. Here, among other works, she painted a series of landscapes from a window on Yonge Street, from 1960-1962, and a series of interiors, doors and windows with dolls, in her home on Woodlawn Avenue, from 1962-1967. Her work expresses a surreal dreamlike quality.

Born in Bohemia, Karl May (1901-1975) studied art in Prague and Vienna and in 1928 became a professor of art at the Academy in Prague. During the 1930s, his art was condemned as subversive by the Nazis. He came to Canada in 1952, when the Iranian Academy, to which he served as advisor, mounted an exhibition of Persian art at the Canadian International Trade Fair. Deciding to stay here, he quickly made a name for himself. He had one-man exhibits of his art both in Europe and in private galleries in Canada, as well as major exhibits of his work at the Arts Centre in Ottawa and at the Montreal Museum of Fine Arts. His work includes oils and acrylics, pastels, charcoal and tar drawings, handprints, lithographs, as well as "Hinterglas" (behind glass) paintings, a traditional European medium which Karl May adapted as his own. It has been said that his realistic paintings suggest the abstract qualities that a nonobjective man might seek, while his semi-abstract paintings include as much objective reality as a die-hard representative painter might want to offer.

While most artists among German Canadians were born in Germany, some were born in Canada. One of these is Carl Fellman Schaefer. Born in Hanover, Ontario, in 1903, Schaefer worked with such artists as J.E.H. MacDonald and Emmanuel Hahn after he finished his studies at the Ontario College of Art in 1924. He taught art at the Central Technical School, Toronto, as well as at Trinity College School, Port Hope. Between 1943 and 1946, he served as official war artist. In 1948, he was appointed instructor at the Ontario College of Art, where he taught until 1970. With works in different galleries across Canada as well as in the National Gallery, Schaefer is especially well known for his landscapes of Waterloo County. Rather than flamboyant colours, he preferred austere yellows, grey-blues and dull greens. Often he painted and repainted his grain fields, with each retry enhancing the inner glow which transformed the grain into a living organism.

Born in Reutlingen, Germany, Emmanuel Otto Hahn came to Canada with his parents at a young age. He studied at the Ontario School of Art and Industrial Design (now the Ontario College of Art and Design University). On the completion of his studies, he travelled in Europe, taking post-graduate work in Stuttgart. On his return, he was appointed to the staff of the old Toronto Technical School, later the Ontario College of Art, becoming in time head of the Department of Sculpture. His best-known work is the statue of Sir Adam Beck on University Avenue, Toronto. His other noted work is the statue of Dr. Doughty, in Ottawa, in front of the Library and Archives Canada building. He also created sculptures that stand in the Canadian Bank of Commerce and Bank of Montreal buildings in Toronto, as well as designed the Canadian Jubilee dollar in 1935 and the Bluenose and caribou head coins of 1937.

Hahn was a member of a large family, some of whom also had distinguished careers. His brother Gustav studied in Stuttgart before coming to Canada. As both muralist and interior decorator, he pioneered the *Jugendstil* or Art Nouveau style in Canada. As teacher at the Ontario College of Art and the Royal Ontario Museum, he contributed to the development of many young Canadian artists. Examples of his work are

"1913 Great Meteor Procession" and "Hail Dominion" (1906), held by the National Gallery. Gustav's daughter, Sylvia Hahn, became especially well known for her wood engravings and her murals at the Royal Ontario Museum and also gained considerable importance as a talented graphic artist.

Other sculptors include Harry Wohlfarth, who has taught art at the University of Alberta since 1953, whose sculptures can be found in different cities in Canada and in other parts of the world; and Almuth Luetkenhaus who specialized in bronze sculptures. Both her realistic works as well as her whimsical sculptures, in particular of dancers, can be seen in plazas in Ottawa, Toronto, and in Europe.

Crafts

Woodcuts for the purposes of printmaking made their first appearance in Canada in the 1770s. Woodcuts, at that time, were the only prints possible in Canada, as they could be printed on simple wooden presses imported into Halifax from Boston, and into Quebec from England. Woodcuts used to illustrate newspapers, government documents or almanacs were precious and often travelled from printer to printer. The first woodcut in Canada, a "View of Halifax," appeared in 1777 in the English-language Nova Scotia Calendar, which was then published by Anthon Heinrich. Born in Alsace, he had come to Canada as a bandsman with a Louisburg regiment and appeared in Halifax in 1758. He took over the print shop of John Bushnell, a Boston immigrant, in 1761. As woodcuts remained anonymous, it is impossible to determine who prepared the cuts.

Although woodcuts remained anonymous, we find the signature of what appears to be a German copper engraver, J.C. Hochstetter, on works dating to the 1890s. J.C. Hochstetter worked in Quebec City between 1792 and 1799. Little is known about him other than his name. Included in work signed by him is an engraving of Montmorency Falls, found in the 1793 *Quebec Almanac*. It appears that the artist both engraved and drew the scene. Another of his engravings shows not only the city of Quebec (as seen from Point Lévy) but also sailing vessels and small boats manned by neatly engraved rowers.

Toronto, which by the 1840s had developed from a muddy village into a town, attracted a number of German craftsmen. Included among them was Hoppner Meyer, nephew of the famous English painter of German extraction, John Hoppner. Meyer came to Toronto in 1842, the year he also made an engraving of the governor general, Lord Sydenham. Both a talented artist and engraver, Meyer's engraving of Sydenham as well as of the Reformer Robert Baldwin, illustrate both skill and sensitivity.

A number of German-born lithographers worked in Toronto in the mid-1800s, including Jacob Hauer, Louis Enneker, Valentin Schreiber and Hermann Bencke. In the first exhibition of the Toronto Art Association, in 1847, Hauer exhibited maps and a lithographed portrait of Queen Victoria. Born in Berlin, Germany, in 1827, Hermann Bencke went into partnership with the younger Charles Fuller in 1856, and together they produced a number of lithographs. These included a colour (or chromo) lithograph (probably the first of its kind in Canada) of Paul Kane's painting, "Death of Big Snake."

Germans were also involved in the design and manufacture of furniture. This was especially the case in the former Berlin and the present Kitchener-Waterloo, which during its early days became a centre of furniture manufacturing in Canada. The furniture produced tended to combine beauty, simplicity and functionality.

German names also appear frequently in association with glass art. Thus, Robert Hold, who in 1968 founded the glass blowing section at Sheridan College in Mississauga, made an important contribution. Other important glass artists include Karl Schantz and Max Leser. Glass artists of a younger generation include Russel Kehler, Candace Reimer, John Reichert and others.

Architecture

Among the vestiges of folk culture brought to southern Ontario from Pennsylvania is the so-called Pennsylvania German bank barn, a large structure distinguished by its size, earth ramp to the upper floor, mow overhang, and hex signs. German farmers from Pennsylvania also transplanted their typical log cabin, characterized by a centrally located chimney with fireplace openings to the living and sleeping quarters. The farm layout common in south-western Ontario, with the detached residence, barn, and grain elevator, can also be traced to the Pennsylvania German pioneers.

While different German architects worked in Canada or taught at Canadian schools of architecture, few have made a name for themselves. An exception is Eberhard Heinrich Zeidler. Born in Braunsdorf, Germany, in 1926, Zeidler studied at the Bauhaus, Weimar, and the Technische Hochschule, Karlsruhe, before coming to Canada in 1951. He joined Blackwell and Craig in Peterborough, in 1975, which led to the Zeidler Partnership in 1975 and to the Zeidler Roberts Partnership/ Architects, with offices in different parts of Canada, in the United States and Europe.

McMaster University Medical Centre, 2007, designed by Eberhard H. Zeidler. Public Domain

In his work, Zeidler displays the factory look of the Bauhaus style, which includes exposed conveyor systems and air ducts. In all instances, the appearance of mechanical efficiency is softened by colourful interiors, greenery, and spacious courtyards. His most notable works include Ontario Place, Toronto (1968-1971), the Eaton Centre, Toronto (1974-81), Queen's Quay Terminal, Toronto (1979-83), Canada Place for Expo 86. Works completed since 1990 include the Hospital for Sick Children, the Princess Margaret Hospital, as well as the Joseph L. Rotman School of Management, at the University of Toronto. All his designs make use of dramatic interior central spaces. In recognition of his work, Zeidler received numerous awards, including the Gold Medal of the Royal Architectural Institute of Canada and the Toronto Arts Lifetime Achievement Award.

Another architect of German origin was Philip Ruh (OMI). Born in Alsace-Lorraine in 1883, Ruh entered the Oblate Order in 1910. He came to Canada in 1913 to serve Ukrainian Catholic settlements in Saskatchewan. Although he had limited training as an architect, Ruh designed many churches, which show a blend of Byzantine, Latin and modern Canadian influences. Churches he designed during the 1920s include the Mountain Road Church of St. Mary's, the Church of the Blessed Virgin Mary, Portage la Prairie; the Holy Ascension Church, Winnipegosis, and the St. Basil the Great Church, Regina.

In 1930, he began to design and oversee the construction of the Church of the Immaculate Conception, a monument completed in 1952. St. Josaphat's Church was built in Edmonton in the 1940s. At least 40 of the buildings he designed across Western Canada and Ontario remain as his legacy. The *Canadian Encyclopedia* names him as one of the "greatest church builders of Canada. Adopting the plans he brought with him to his adopted land, he achieved an often stimulating fusion of the grand style and the vernacular."[132]

While Ruh and Zeidler gained national and international stature through their work, most German architects made a significant contribution at the local level. One of these was Werner Ernst Noffke. Born in 1878 in Germany, Noffke came to Canada as a child. Here he studied architecture at the Ottawa School of Art. During his 60-year career, he became one of Ottawa's most prolific and influential architects. When he died in 1964, he left a legacy of some 200 buildings in Canada's capital. These include gracious houses in Ottawa's upscale neighbourhoods, as well post offices, hospitals and churches. It has been said that in Ottawa one "could be born in a Noffke hospital, grow up in a Noffke house, attend a Noffke school, worship in a Noffke church or synagogue, work in a Noffke office, and be laid to rest in a Noffke funeral home."[133]

---

[132] William P. Thompson, "Philip Ruh" *The Canadian Encyclopedia* (2008)

[133] Maria Cook, "Book fetes work of W.E. Noffke," *Ottawa Citizen* (April 12, 2013) C.1.

Music

Music, in particular choral music, has had a long tradition in German culture. It is therefore not surprising that choirs were among the first organizations Germans established in the new country. These have been discussed previously.

German Canadians established not only their community choral societies but also participated in the musical life of British North America since early times. For example, the 4,000 Brunswick soldiers who fought for the British during the American War of Independence included as many as 102 'tambours and oboists.' Many of these musicians later settled in Quebec, where they sought to continue their musical careers. Thus, the military band leader Friedrich Heinrich Glackemeyer (1759-1836) imported musical instruments during the six years that he was in Quebec City, and in 1819 he founded the Quebec Harmonic Society, Canada's first symphony orchestra. Glackemeyer's son-in-law, Theodore Frederick Molt, who originated from Württemberg, worked as a music teacher in Quebec City and Montreal, and wrote the well-known Canadian patriotic song "Sol canadien, terre chérie," as well as the first bilingual book for musical instruction, *Elementary Treatise on Music* (1828).

German band leaders were active in the Maritimes, where, for example, bandmaster Kästner led a musical society in Antigonish, NS, in the 1840s. Professor Weisbecker served as director of the Sacred Music Society in the same city, in 1842. He presented not only simple vignettes but also works by Mozart, Haydn and Handel.

Early piano builders who settled in Canada included Isaac Reinhardt (1808-1846) who worked in Montreal, and the piano manufacturers H. and J. Philips, who established themselves in Halifax in 1845, as well as Frederick Hund, who was active in Quebec City in 1816 and later in partnership with Gottlieb Seebold. None of these were as successful as later manufacturers and dealers in musical products. The A. & S. Nordheimer Company, established by Samuel and Abraham Nordheimer, imported not only musical instruments and sheet music into Canada but also printed Canadian compositions and organized tours of European artists in Canada. In addition, Samuel served as president of the Toronto Philharmonic Society.

In the second half of the 19th century, there were few major cities in English Canada that didn't have a German conductor. Among these was Gustav Schilling, who for several years served as conductor of the Oratorio Society in Montreal. When his attempt to establish a Conservatory of music failed, he left for the United States. In 1880, Joseph Hecker founded the first symphony orchestra in Western Canada, the Winnipeg Philharmonic Society. In the 1850s, Theodoric Wichtendahl served as conductor of the Harmonic Society of St. John, New Brunswick. Ferdinand Oscar Telgmann (1855-1946) founded the Kingston Symphony Orchestra and also wrote the popular operetta "Leo, the Royal cadet." In the area of semi-classical and popular music, Dr. Augustus Vogt launched the renowned Mendelsohn Choir in Toronto in 1894.

The ascent to power of Adolf Hitler in Europe brought a number of musically gifted emigrants to Canada. Dr. Arnold Walter, who was born in Moravia and came to Canada in 1937, founded the International Society for Music Education in Toronto. Teaching music at the University of Toronto for some sixteen years, he had a considerable influence on the training of future performers, in particular of classical music. Among this group also belong Hans Blume, who for many years taught at the McGill University Faculty of Music, the director Heinz Unger, and the pianist John Newmark (Hans Neumark).

Post World War II immigrants who made a contribution to Canadian music include the pianist Anto Kuerty, the composer Wolfgang Bottenberg, and Franz Paul Decker, who in 1967 became director of the Montreal Symphony Orchestra. Robert Dietz, who came to Halifax in 1951, was a driving force behind the founding of the Atlantic Symphony. Nicholas Goldschmidt, who was born in Moravia, served as first music director of the Royal Conservatory Opera School, in Toronto. Together with Walter and Herman Geiger-Torel, who were born in Frankfurt and left Europe after Hitler came to power, he helped found the Royal Conservatory Opera Company, which later became the Canadian Opera Company. From 1949 to 1957, he served as first music director of the CBC opera. In 1978, in recognition of his services, Goldschmidt was made an Officer of the Order of Canada, and was promoted to Companion in 1989.

Composer, violinist, and teacher Otto Joachim was born in Germany in 1910 and became a Canadian citizen in 1957. Together with his brother Walter (cellist and teacher) and others, he founded the Montréal String Quartet, in which he played the viola, 1955-62. He also founded the Montreal Consort of Ancient Instruments, which he directed until

1968 when he decided to devote himself more fully to composing. His compositions include *Katimavik*, which he composed for the Canadian Pavilion at Expo 67, as well as *Illumination II*, which was awarded the Grand prix Paul-Gilson of the Communauté radio-phonique des programmes de langue français in 1969. In 1990, he received the Prix Musique Calixa-Lavallée in recognition of his work.

Born in Hamburg, Germany, Lothar Klein taught at the universities of Minnesota, 1962-1964, and of Texas, 1964-1968, before taking a position with the faculty of Music of the University of Toronto, in 1968. His musical compositions, which reflect influences as disparate as Varèse's "organized sound" and jazz, have won the Rockefeller New Music Prize (1965 and 1967), the Greenwood Choral Prize (for *Three Chinese Laments*, 1968) and the Floyd S. Chalmers Performing Arts Creative Award (for *Tale of a Father and a Son*, 1982). His work has been performed in North America, Europe and elsewhere. Commenting on Klein's works, Hans-Berthold Dietz states that all of Klein's works, "whether light or serious, attempt to find parallel points of reference between old and new music. Klein's collage compositions, based on pre-existent older music, are profound pieces. They successfully bridge differences of time and culture, and offer a rich source of stylistic analysis" (PRO Canada Pamphlet).

R. Murray Schafer, of German and Scottish origin, was born in Sarnia Ontario. After his expulsion from the University of Toronto Faculty of Music, in the mid-1950s, he undertook a tour of Europe. Here, he familiarized himself, among other things, with German Bauhaus artists as well as with German Romantic poets and German Romantic music, influences that later found expression in his own work, following his return to Canada, in 1961. His compositions include his *World Soundscape Project*, designed to study the individual's relations with his acoustic environment. A prolific composer, others of his works that might be mentioned include *Canzoni for Prisoners, Dream Rainbow Dream Thunder, Scorpius, The Crown of Ariadne, Patria II, Magic Songs, Ra*, as well as concertos for guitar, harp and flute.

Composer R. Murray Schafer. Public Domain.

Hildegard Westerkamp was influenced in her work by Schafer. Born in Osnabrück, Germany, in 1946, she came to Canada to further her studies. After completing her studies in music in the early seventies, she joined the *World Soundscape Project* under the direction of Murray Schafer, which developed in her a deep concern about noise and the acoustic environment. In particular after 1991, Westerkamp sought to combine her interest in acoustics and music. While some of her early music features traditional instruments, most of her work draws material from the acoustic environment, be this the noise and silence of urban, rural or wilderness soundscapes, the human voice, or the sound of media and foreign cultures.

Much of Wsterkamp's music is personal in nature, incorporating her own texts or the poetry of her husband. At the same time, her work demonstrates her commitment to social causes such as the environment and feminism. Her other music is more whimsical, such as her Harbour Symphony, written to celebrate the opening of Canada Place at Expo 86, which was performed by more than 100 boat horns in Vancouver harbour.

Notable performers of classical music among German Canadians include the tenors Thomas Bernard (Ben) Heppner, Victor Martens, and Michael Schade, as well as the baritones Victor and Russell Braun (father and son), and the soprano Barbara Fris. Andreas Thiel, who was just one when his family emigrated to Canada, had his first award-winning performance at the age of seventeen when he won first place in the Edward Johnson Piano Competition in Guelph. This was followed by other awards and appearances throughout Ontario, culminating in his first appearance as soloist with an orchestra in Kitchener, Ontario, playing a Mozart Concerto. Since then, he has appeared as a soloist with symphonies in both Canada and the United States. Learning to play the piano at the age of nine, Frederic Grinke won a Dominion of Canada scholarship at the age of 16, to the Royal Academy of Music in London. In a long and distinguished career, Grinke performed in Europe, the USA, Australia and New Zealand, at the London Promenade Concerts, and at festivals in Edinburg and Salzburg. He began teaching at the Royal Academy in 1939, with many of his students becoming distinguished performers. Between 1937 and 1939, he served as concertmaster for the Boyd Neel Orchestra, quitting to pursuer a solo career. He became especially well known for his performance of 20th-cetury English music, much of which was recorded for English Dacca. In 1979, he was named a commander of the Order of the British Empire in recognition of his work.[134]

Canadians of German origin contributed not only to classical music but also to the creation and performance of more popular music in this country. An example of this is Alfred Kunz. Composer, conductor, administrator, Kunz was born in Neudorf, near Regina, Sask., in 1929. He studied composition and conducting, 1949-55, at the Royal Conservatory of Music and also spent several summers in the 1960s with Stockhausen and others in Europe. In 1965, he completed the state examinations in choral conducting at the *Musikhochschule* in Mainz. He commenced teaching in Kitchener, Ont., in 1955, where he organized the Kitchener-Waterloo Chamber Music Orchestra and Choir in 1959. He has extensive experience as a choral conductor and has worked with the Concordia Male and Mixed Choirs (1962-), the Germania Male Choir (1963-5), the German-Canadian Choir (1965-79 and 1981-), the Waterloo Regional Police Chorus (1968-86), and the 200-voice regional Music Alive mixed choir (1989-). With the German-Canadian Choir, which is made up of Ontario choristers, he has toured Germany four times and organized all-Ontario song festivals with orchestra. He served as principal (1965-7) of the Canadian Music Teachers' College, Burlington, Ont., and as director of musical activities at the University of Waterloo. He also had a leading role in the revival (1969, 1970) of the International *Sängerfest* in Kitchener.

---

[134] See Giles Bryant, "Frederic Grinke", *"Encyclopedia of Music in Canada"*

A prolific composer, Kunz emphasizes choral works of medium difficulty. His compositions *Fanfares for the Centre, A Time to Celebrate, Canada Song, Abner's Fiddle*, and *Runner's Boogie* were included in the 'Kitchener Sings' program of the September 1980 opening ceremonies of Centre in the Square. His orchestral pieces such as the *Saskatchewan Suite* and *Oktoberfest Overture* have been well received.

Another conductor who might be mentioned is Elmer Iseler. Born in Colborne, Ontario, in 1927, Elmer Iseler taught music in Toronto high schools from 1952 to 1964. In 1964, he became conductor of the Toronto Mendelssohn Choir. He founded the Festival Singers of Canada, and, in 1979, the Elmer Iseler Singers. He was made an Officer of the Order of Canada in recognition of his many services in the field of music in Canada.

Michael Kaeshammer, who had been classically trained in Germany, came to Canada at the age of 17. He has released a series of award-winning, critically acclaimed records, as well as developed a large, international following through his performances. In addition, he uses his encyclopedic knowledge of piano styles, to compose hip, well-crafted originals. In his music, stride, ragtime and Jelly Roll Morton's stylings fuse easily into romantic ballads, funk-inspired behop and modern jazz.

John Kay, born in 1944 as Joachim Fritz Krauledat, came to Canada from Germany in 1958. Here, he joined a blues rock and folk music group called "The Sparrows," in 1965. The group had moderate success in Canada before leaving for California, where it changed its name to Steppenwolf. With music that pioneered heavy metal and hard rock, Kay's Steppenwolf won an international following for songs such as *Born to be Wild, Magic Carpet Ride,* and *The Pusher.* In recognition of his early work in Canada, Kay was inducted into Canada's Walk of Fame, in 2004.

Born in 1961, in Edmonton, to parents of Icelandic and German origin, Kathryn Dawn Lang (k.d. lang) is probably one of Canada's best-known pop and country singer-songwriters. In 1983, she formed her first band, the Reclines, which that same year released its debut album *Friday Dance Promenade. A Truly Western Experience* was released in 1984 and led to national attention in Canada. Lang made other records while singing County and Western venues in Canada, which earned her a 1985 Juno Award for Most Promising Female Vocalist. Since then, she has won at least eight other Juno awards. She also won other awards, including the American Grammy Award for Best Female Country Vocal Performance, for her 1989 album *Absolute Torch and Twang.* Her song *Constant Craving* brought her million-dollar sales, critical acclaim, and the Grammy Award for Best Female Pop Vocal Performance. She also wrote sound tracks for films such as *Even Cowgirls Get the Blues*, as well as for James Bond films. She ranked # 33 on V H 1's 100 Greatest Women in Rock and Roll in 1999 and # 21 on C M T 40 Greatest Women in Country Music in 2002. In addition, she played the lead in the 1991 drama film *Salmonberries*, as well as starred in other films.

John F. Mann is the lead vocalist and one of the principal songwriters for the folk rock band Spirit of the West. In addition, he has released solo albums such as *Acoustic Kitty* and *December Looms*. He has also appeared as guest actor for television shows such as *Dark Angel*, *Whistles*, and *Da Vinci's Inquest*.

The Oster family left Vanguard, Saskatchewan, soon after Albert Adam Oster was born and moved to Langley, B.C. to escape the severe prairie drought. Al moved through central B.C. and western Alberta ranches as a singing ranch hand and cowboy. He wrote numerous country and western songs. In 1957, he relocated to Whitehorse, where he began work as a TV anchor/operator. He began the half hour music Al Oster TV show featuring Yukon artists and legends. At the same time, he wrote and recorded compositions about Yukon folklore. Between 1961 and 1962, he toured Western Canada with Jake Doell and "The Chuck Wagon Drivers" on the Yukon Gold Show. During that time, he also started a 3-year CBC radio show called *Northland Echoes*. He continued writing and recording historical songs and ballads. In total, since 1959, Oster wrote and recorded some 14 albums worth of original music, many of the songs celebrating Yukon pioneers. As such, Oster was one of the first since Robert Service to write and publish poetry about Klondike Gold Rush folklore; one of the first Canadians to compose and sing folk music about historical Canadian folklore legends and to preserve the compositions on LP Records. In recognition of his work, Oster received the Yukon Heritage Award, and in 1999, he was appointed a Member of the Order of Canada for his contribution to Canadian heritage.

Matt Thiessen, born in St. Catharines, Ontario, is one of the founders, and lead singer, guitarist, pianist, and main songwriter of the Christian rock band Relient K. Jason Heinrichs, who was born in Kingston, Ontario, in 1970, produced and remixed songs for albums such as *Lucy Ford* for the hip-hop group Atmosphere. He also plays piano, guitar, and drums in many of his productions.

Of German-American descent on her father's side, Lynn Feist is a singer-songwriter who performed as a member of the indie rock group Broken Social Scene and also worked as a solo artist under her own name. At the Juno Awards in Calgary, in 2008, she won five awards: Songwriter of the Year, Artist of the Year, Pop Album of the Year, Album of the Year, and Single of the Year. Other awards include Grammy Award nominations for Best Pop Vocal Album, for the *Reminder*, and the 2008 nomination for the Artist of the Year award.

Randolph Charles Bachman, whose father was of German and mother of Ukrainian background, was lead guitarist, songwriter and founding member of the 1960s to 1970s rock band The Guess Who, and the 1970s rock band Bachman-Turner Overdrive. In addition, Bachman has also recorded numerous solo albums. In recognition of his achievements, Bachman was awarded the Order of Manitoba in 2005, the highest award in Manitoba. Along with other members of The Guess Who, Bachman also received the Governor General's Performing Arts Award in 2002, Canada's foremost distinction for excellence in the performing arts. In 2008, he was made an Officer of the Order of Canada.

I include Bieber, as I did Lang, because both, in their own way, in the not so distant future will describe the majority of people identified as German Canadian. For example, Justin Bieber's grandfather was German and his grandmother was Anglo-Irish. His mother is French Canadian. He can readily be identified as being, in part, of German origin because neither his grandfather nor his father changed their family name. At the same time, there is little evidence that his German background influenced his music.

Justin Bieber, pop musician, dancer, actor, singer-songwriter, was discovered in 2008 by American talent scout Scooter Braun, who came across Bieber's videos posted on YouTube. Braun signed Bieber with the Raymond Braun Media Group, and then to an Island Records recording contract. Bieber's extended play, *My World*, released in 2009, was certified platinum in the U.S. Bieber's first full-length studio album, *My World 2.0*, was released in March 2010. Not only did it debut near number-one in several countries, but also was certified platinum in the U.S. This was followed by his first headlining tour, the My World Tour, the remix albums *My World Acoustic* and *Never Say Never*. Other albums followed, all of them at or near number-one on the Billboard 200.

Bieber's numerous awards include Artist of the Year Award, at the 2010 American Music Awards. He was nominated for Best New Artist and Best Pop Vocal Album at the 33rd Grammy Awards. With a global fan base and over 40 million followers on Twitter, Forbes Magazine, in 2011, named him the third-most powerful celebrity in the world.

When one looks at German Canadian contributions to the arts in Canada, it becomes quite evident that this is often a contribution of immigrants. In these cases, it often involves applying skills people had learned in the homeland in a new environment. This is most clearly evident in the literary arts, where German language literature is essentially the product of people who were educated in Europe. Most artists, sculptors or architects mentioned were trained in Europe but spent a good portion of their working years in Canada. In the case of music, several trends are evident. On the one hand, in particular German immigrants were very much involved in transmitting the European classical tradition to Canada. At the same time, in particular the children or grandchildren of immigrants were turning to Canadian and North American popular music, both as performers and creators. In other instances, more recent immigrants, as well as the children or grandchildren of immigrants, are active in blending old traditions with North American styles and themes.

CONCLUSION

When one looks at Germans in Canada, several generalizations can be made. First, the German community in Canada, wherever it established itself, was not monolithic, but rather was comprised of people who differed in origin and religious belief. In particular during the settlement of the Canadian West, Germans came from different areas of the Austro-Hungarian and Russian empires where they constituted sizable minorities. At the same time, they had a sense of a common origin and shared a common language.

Secondly, rather than speak of a single German community made up of many parts, it would be more logical to speak of different German communities that emerged in Canada at different times and in different places. The first German Canadian community arose in Nova Scotia with the coming of the Foreign Protestants. It was well on the way to being absorbed into the larger Anglo-Canadian milieu when a new wave of German-speaking immigrants established themselves in Upper Canada. Next, German Canadian communities emerged in Western Canada. Being spatially separated from Germans in Upper Canada, these communities essentially developed separately.[135] When World War I ended, the German Canadian communities in Ontario were on the way to giving up the German language. The German communities in Western Canada, still dominated by the immigrant generation German speakers, were positively affected by the inflow of post-World War I immigrants.

---

[135] That does not mean that they developed in total isolation from each other. Thus, during the settlement period, there was a flow of farmers from Waterloo County to Western Canada in search of land. Institutional contacts existed between Germans in Eastern and Western Canada. For example, General Council Lutherans in both Western and Eastern Canada received and published in the mission paper *Siloah*. Missouri Synod Lutherans in Eastern and Western Canada both received *Der Lutheraner* out of St. Louis. However, these contacts were not important or frequent enough for Germans in Eastern and Western Canada to significantly influence each other's community developments.

However, these communities were undergoing rapid assimilation when the next wave of German immigrants arrived, after World War II. German churches in Western Canada were in the process of changing to English. German clubs were essentially defunct by the end of the war. German communities which emerged after the war were again essentially immigrant in nature.

All German communities were initially organized to meet the needs of the immigrant generation. Their basic institutions were established by immigrants. These included churches, schools, secular social organizations, newspapers, all of which helped communities function and perpetuate themselves. German was the language of their churches, clubs, schools, and of their media. Insofar as possible, Germans sought to perpetuate the use of their mother tongue in the institutions established. Their newspapers urged its preservation. Religious leaders, in particular those originating from Europe, encouraged its use. Insofar as possible, Germans established schools to teach the language to future generations. At the same time, they sought to take advantage of the larger educational system in the country to help them preserve the language and pass it on to future generations.

Despite such endeavors, as community organizations came under the control of the Canada-born generation, the language was in most instances gradually lost. This transition can most readily be traced in German language churches, essentially because, more than any other German community organizations, churches tended to retain their membership even after a congregation gave up the German in favor of the language spoken by members of the larger society. Church records, therefore, provide fairly reliable information, not only on when a congregation gave up the German, but also give insight into the reasons for the change. As the church is the most important organization in the German Canadian community, one can well conclude that the language transition in the churches reflects the language transition in the community in general.

The rate of German language loss differed for the different groups and for the different institutions involved. Rural communities gave up the language more slowly than urban ones. Religious affiliation influenced language retention, with language change being much slower among the Mennonites, who had integrated language and other aspects of their old-country tradition into their religious practices, using these to establish boundaries to separate them from the larger society, which they identified as the "world." Hutterites, who not only used language as a means of separating themselves from the "world," but also developed a well-functioning educational structure to pass the German language on to their children, have been most successful among German Canadians in preserving their linguistic heritage.

Of course, the closed Hutterite community helped in this. The German language disappeared fastest in areas where Germans were sparsely settled. This made it difficult for them to use the German in their everyday life. Also, they generally didn't possess the financial resources or the educational structure to establish educational institutions that would help them pass on the language. This means that in most instances the German language ceased functioning as the main language of communication by the second generation in the more scattered settlements and by the 3rd or 4th generation in areas such as Lunenburg, even though Germans there had established a fairly cohesive settlement.

Similar factors were operative in Ontario, where German settlements were often not cohesive enough to permit them to establish and support schools offering German language instruction. It was only in areas such as Kitchener-Waterloo, where Germans had formed larger block settlements, that they were able to use the educational system with some success to pass on their linguistic identity. Their endeavors foundered, however, when these conflicted with the attempt by the larger society to use the educational system to assimilate the minorities. This was the case in particular during the war years.

Similar trends are evident in Western Canada. Here, the larger German religious groupings, in particular the Mennonites and the German Catholics in Saskatchewan, were able to set up a fairly elaborate institutional framework that helped them to transmit their linguistic identity to their offspring. With nearly a hundred parochial schools and a Normal School in Melville and one about to open in Alberta when war broke out in 1914, German Lutherans were gradually laying a base for perpetuating their linguistic and religious heritage. Most other groups tended to be too scattered for them to raise the financial resources to establish effectively functioning educational institutions or to use the public school system to help them transmit their linguistic identity. No matter whether they used the public school system or the parochial schools, German endeavors to use the educational system came to naught in the face of the determination of the host society to use the schools to assimilate the minorities.

The end result is that most churches that had at one time used German today use English in their services. In almost all churches this change occurred when the Canadian-born members of congregations lost their knowledge of the German so that they could no longer follow the church service in that language. The transition usually included an examination by the different congregations of the purpose served by the church: did it exist to perpetuate the Gospel of Jesus Christ, or was its purpose the transmission of a particular cultural identity? The answer in all instances where the change occurred was the same. That is, the different congregations decided that the purpose of the church was to transmit the Gospel rather than any specific cultural identity, which resulted in their giving up the language. The end result is that, except in cases where language serves a religious function (usually helping separate the community of God from the "world"), the use of German in the churches is essentially confined today to serving the older members of the immigrant generation.

The language transition didn't affect secular German community organizations in quite the same way as it did the churches. That is because secular organizations were not as important to community life as the churches. In fact, the vast majority of Germans, in particular those settled in rural areas, didn't even belong to clubs. This was true in particular of the pre-World War II immigrants. The result is that German secular social organizations had a much shorter life span than the churches, which was the case especially of national organizations. The *Nationalverein*, founded by German immigrants just prior to the outbreak of World War I, faltered soon after it was organized. Attempts to revitalize the organization during the 1920s didn't get off the ground. The Trans-Canada Alliance, the first organization to unite Germans from coast to coast, lasted longer than any other German national secular organizations. It foundered after some thirty years, destroyed largely through disagreements among immigrants who had arrived shortly before the war and those who had arrived shortly after.

German local clubs lasted much longer than their national secular organizations. They did so despite their inability to retain their membership much beyond the immigrant generation. They did so, essentially, by serving as a gateway through which new arrivals were introduced into the country. Many left once they had adjusted to the majority Canadian culture. This was true in particular for the inter-war and post-war World War II periods. The clubs were also more severely affected by the wars. Unlike the churches, the conflicts forced most clubs to close their doors and essentially brought German secular community life to a halt. By the time the wars were over, the clubs had lost most of their members. They were revitalized again through a new influx of immigrants, which gave them renewed vitality and purpose.

German language schools declined as the Canada-born generations adopted other priorities than passing the German language on to future generations. The German language media declined as it lost the clientele that made use of its services. In the latter half of the 20th century, the Canadian German language media was also negatively affected by increasing competition from European competitors.

Language loss did not occur independently, but was part of a larger pattern of change. Other than language use, Germans differed little from members of the larger society. For example, except for groups such as the Mennonites and Hutterites, German religious organizations had their counterparts in the larger society. Thus, German Catholics and Baptists were but one segment of the Baptist and Catholic communities in Canada. German Lutherans had counterparts in the different Scandinavian and Baltic communities. Once the language was lost, there was little that differentiated Germans from non-Germans among these groups. Even Mennonites, once they lost the language and their strong rural orientation, and exchanged their identity for the sixteenth century Anabaptist vision, in many respects became little more than another fundamentalist group competing with other fundamentalist groups for adherents. Thus, language and beliefs associated with it, was the basic feature that identified Germans. Once it was lost, a key element of the German identity was lost.

This encouraged intermarriage. Although not common prior to the twentieth century, except in areas of scattered settlement, it accelerated during the twentieth century. Today, most German Canadians are partially of German background. One effect of intermarriage is an increase in the number of people who identify themselves as being of German origin. In time, however, as intermarriage continues, and people link one-quarter or one-eighth of their blood line to their German ancestor, the number of Canadians claiming German ancestry will decrease and another more prevalent identity will predominate.

The decline in German language use will result in an increasing number of Canadians of German origin growing up with English or French as their mother tongue, in particular the former. German, insofar as it will survive, will continue among small segments of the German community, such as the Hutterites. For the most part, however, it will continue insofar as it is taught at the university or high school level, learned for personal reasons or because people find it useful when dealing with German-speaking parts of Europe.

One might well ask, what will remain of what is German in Canada once the German language no longer serves as the community's media of communication. Manfred von Vulte seeks to answer this in *Where have all of Toronto's Germans Gone?* Looking at the city's post-World War II immigrants and their children, many of whom no longer speak German, he maintains that the community can continue to sustain an identity, even without the language, because of its common experience in both Europe and Canada.[136] Although von Vulpe's focus is too narrow to be applicable to Germans in Canada, there is evidence of the German identity being maintained after language loss. In the case of Lunenburg, for example, the German language had been given up over a hundred years ago. In this case, the village itself has become a focus of the German identity. Ancestors of present-day Lunenburgers, coming from German-speaking lands, turned woodland into farms. It is in this territory that the community turned from the land to the sea. Pride in the community's achievements very much forms the basis of the present-day Lunenburg identity. Lunenburgers are proud of their German origin, but this is only one dimension of their pride in being Lunenburgers.[137] Similar developments are evident in the case of Kitchener-Waterloo.

More important than this, however, for most Germans, will be family influences, with children, grandchildren and great-grandchildren tracing their identity back to the first of their family to establish himself or herself in this land. The best example of this is probably Jean-Pierre Wilhelmy who traces his ancestry back to a German mercenary who had

---

[136]   Manfred J. Vulte, *Where Have All of Toronto's Germans Gone?* (Ottawa, 2003) 1-96.

[137]   Laurie Lacey, *Ethnicity and the German Descendants of Lunenburg County, Nova Scotia* (Halifax, N.S., 1982) 1-21.

settled in New France over a hundred years ago.[138] In this case, the family name served to sustain a connection with the German roots. Here, the link is a genealogical chart that identifies a grandfather or grandmother or great grandfather or great grandmother in someone's genealogical background. In this case, the link will become increasingly more tenuous through intermarriage, leading to a situation where a person is of so many backgrounds that any particular background becomes insignificant.

Looking at this transformation, which involves the gradual disintegration of the German Canadian community and its integration into the larger society, one may ask whether this transformation is of benefit to Canada. One may obtain an idea of this by looking at the German Canadians this study identifies as having made a significant contribution to Canada's economic, scientific or cultural life.

Thus, one area in which German Canadians have made an important contribution to Canada is in opening its frontier and turning the wilderness into farmland. Among Germans, this contribution was made largely by the immigrant generation. It was this generation, for the most part, who settled the land, cleared it, and established their farms.

It was also primarily the immigrants among Germans who made major contributions to Canada's business life. This may be observed when looking at the contribution of German entrepreneurs. No matter whether they established their enterprises in the larger society or in a German enclave, it was largely the immigrant generation or the first or second generation offspring of immigrants, or those people who had not yet totally lost the language, who expanded their businesses into larger concerns. In fact, the most successful entrepreneurs, such as those in Kitchener-Waterloo, had established their enterprises in German enclaves. This suggests that the German workers as well as the German community environment in which these enterprises were established contributed to their success. The community environment would, of course, include the network these entrepreneurs were able to establish among themselves.

When one looks at German contributions in the sciences, it becomes evident that the training that German immigrants had received in the old country and then brought to Canada contributed to their success in this country. Almost all German-Canadian scientists of note had been trained

---

[138] Jean-Pierre Wilhelmy, *German Mercenaries in Canada*. Trans. Honey Thompson (Boloeil, Quebec, 1986) 1-332.

in Europe. Canada provided them with the opportunity to apply their skills for the benefit of this country.

The majority of German Canadian artists had received their training in Europe. Some came to Canada in search of adventure. Others were attracted by the Canadian landscape. Still others came to escape persecution in their homeland. Once here, they found the country to their liking and remained.

The vast majority of writers and poets creating in the German language were trained in Europe. They came in search of adventure, to escape persecution, or because they had difficulty making their livelihood in Europe. This tended also to be true of conductors and other classical musicians. At the same time, German immigrants and second, third or fourth generation German Canadians have gained considerable recognition in music. Also, Canada-born writers of German origin have produced notable works in the English language. This is true in particular of Mennonite writers.

Nevertheless, when looking at the overall contribution of German Canadians to Canadian life, it becomes quite evident that such contributions were made primarily by immigrants and, if not by immigrants, then the children or grandchildren of immigrants. That is, by people who still had some contact with their German background and the immigrant experience, including the German language.

This suggests several things. It suggests that the majority of German Canadians had already assimilated by the third, fourth, or fifth generation and were hard to identify by their ethnic origin. It can also suggest that the process of assimilation in which Germans gradually lost their language and their cultural identity not only destroyed their language, but was also detrimental to their creative and innovative spirit? That is, the energy that especially the immigrant generation had expended in various creative or entrepreneurial endeavors was consumed by the attempt by later generations to integrate into the Canadian environment, which, in particular during the last hundred years, has often been a hostile environment. Acculturation and assimilation, in this situation, came at a cost, not only for German Canadians, but also for Canadian society.

BIBLIOGRAPHY

Government Records

Department of Agriculture. Records. Library and Archives Canada.

Immigration Branch. Records. Library and Archives Canada.

C.N.R. Records. Devlin Files. Library and Archives Canada.

Department of National Defence. Records. Library and Archives Canada.

R.C.M.P. Records. Library and Archives Canada.

Department of Secretary of State. Chief Press Censor. Records. Library and Archives Canada.

Published Canadian Government Documents

Canada. *Census of Canada*, 1885-Present.

_____. *Report of the Royal Commission on Bilingualism and Biculturalism: The Cultural Contributions of the Other Ethnic Groups*, Book IV. Ottawa, 1970.

Secondary Sources: Machine Readable Articles and comments on the Internet

Secondary Sources: Print

Immigration and Settlement

Amstatter, Andrew. *Tomslake: History of the Sudeten Germans in Canada.* Saanichton, B.C., 1978.

Anderson, Alan B. *German Settlements in Saskatchewan: The Origin and Development of German Catholic, Lutheran, Baptist, Mennonite and Hutterite Communities.* Saskatoon, Sask., 1990.

Atwood, Rodney. *The Hessians: Mercenaries from Hessen-Kassel in the American Revolution.* Cambridge, 1980.

Bassler, Gerhard P. "The 'Inundation' of British North America with the 'Refuse of Foreign Pauperism': Assisted Emigration from Southern Germany in the mid-19th Century," *German Canadian Yearbook,* IV (1978) 93-113.

_____. *The German Canadian Mosaic Today and Yesterday: Identities, Roots, and Heritage.* Ottawa, 1991.

_____. *Vikings to U-boats: The German Experience in Newfoundland and Labrador.* Montreal, 2006.

Bausenhart, Werner. *German Immigration and Assimilation in Ontario 1783-1918.* Ottawa 1989.

Bell, Winthrop Pickard. *The 'Foreign Protestants' and the Settlement of Nova Scotia: The History of Arrested British Colonial Policy in the Eighteenth Century.* Toronto, 1961.

Bickelmann, Hartmut. *Deutsche Überseeauswanderung in der Weimar Zeit.* Wiesbaden, 1980.

Burkholder, Lewis J. *A Brief History of the Mennonites in Ontario.* Toronto, 1935.

Cook, Maria. "Book fetes work of W.E. Noffke," *Ottawa Citizen* (April 12, 2013) C.1&2.

Cutting, James William. "The Canadian National Railway and the German Baptist Settlement of the Canadian Prairie Provinces." Research Essay, Carleton University, 1975.

Debor, Herbert Wilhelm. *1664-1964: Die Deutschen in der Provinz Québec.* Montréal, 1963.

_____. "Early German Immigration to Nova Scotia," *German Canadian Yearbook,* I (1973) 67-70.

_____. "German Soldiers of the American war of Independence as Settlers in Canada," *German Canadian Yearbook,* III (1976) 71-93.

DeBrisay, Mather Byles. *History of the County of Lunenburg.* Toronto, 1895.

DeMarce, Virginia Easley. *The Settlement of Former German Auxiliary Troops in Canada After the American Revolution.* Arlington, Va., 1984.

England, Robert. *The Colonization of Western Canada; A Study of Contemporary Land Settlement, 1896-1934.* London, 1936.

English, John and Kenneth McLaughlin. *Kitchener: An Illustrated History.* Waterloo, 1983.

Epp, Frank. *Mennonites in Canada, 1920-1940: A People's Struggle for Survival.* Toronto, 1982.

Froeschle, Hartmut. "Walter Bauer. Sein dichterisches Werk mit besonderer Berücksichtigung seines Kanada-Erlebnisses," *German-Canadian Yearbook* V (1979) 77-100.

Gerwin, Elizabeth B. "A Survey of the German-speaking Population of Alberta," M.A. thesis, University of Alberta, 1938.

Gow, B.A. "A Home for Free Germans in the Wilderness of Canada: The Sudeten German Settlers of Tupper Creek, B.C.," *Canadian Ethnic Studies,* X:1 (1978) 62-74.

Gradish, Stephen Francis. "The German Mercenaries in Canada, 1776-1783," M.A. thesis, University of Western Ontario, 1964.

Grams, Grant. "Der Volksverein deutsch-canadischer Katholiken: The Rise and Fall of a German-Catholic Cultural and Immigration Society, 1909-52," *The Catholic Historical Review,* vol. 99, no. 3 (July, 2013) 480-498.

Grenke, Arthur. "The Formation and Early Development of an Urban Community: A Case Study of the Germans in Winnipeg, 1872-1919," Ph. Thesis, University of Manitoba, 1975.

_____. "Settlement Patterns of German-Speaking Immigrants on the Canadian Prairies, 1817-1914," *German Canadian Yearbook,* XIV (1995) 1-16.

_____. "German Land Settlement in Eastern Canada and Its Influence on Community Development and Assimilation," *German Canadian Yearbook,* XV (1998) 31-56.

_____. "From Dreams of the Worker State to Fighting Hitler: The German-Canadian Left from the Depression to the End of World War II," *Labour/Le Travail, 35 (Spring 1995)* 65-105.

Grossman, John. "Streiflichter vom Rande der Zivilisation: Die Erlebnisse eines deutschen Heimstätters im Peace River-Gebiet – Parts 1 and 2," *German Canadian Yearbook,* I (1973) 191-244, and II (1975) 193-246.

Hedges, James B. *Building the Canadian West: The Land and Colonization Policy of the Canadian Pacific Railway.* New York, 1939.

Helling, Rudolf A. *A Socio-Economic History of German-Canadians: They, Too, Founded Canada.* Wiesbaden, 1984.

Hempel, Rainer L. *New Voices on the shores: early Pennsylvania German settlements in New Brunswick.* Toronto, 2000.

Hessel, Peter. *Destination Ottawa Valley.* Ottawa, 1984.

Jakobsh, Frank K. "German and German-Canadian Literature as Contained in the 'Berliner Journal'," *German Canadian Yearbook* vol. 5 (1979) 108-120.

Kalbfleisch, H. K. *The History of the German language Press of Ontario, 1835-1918.* Toronto, 1968.

Kiesewalter, Dieter. *Kanada – gelobtes Land? Aus dem Leben einer deutschen Auslandsgemeinde: Erzählungen, Dokumente, Fotos, Erlebnisse, Geschichte.* Ottawa, 1994.

Küster. Mathias. "Die Baltendeutschen in Kanada," *German Canadian Yearbook,* V (1979) 55-65.

Lambton, Gunda, "Contributions of German Graphic Artists in the History of Canadian Printmaking," *German Canadian Yearbook,* vol. IV (1978) 180-204.

Lavallee, Omer S. A. *Beloeil.* Montreal, 1965.

Lee-Whiting, Brenda. *Harvest of Stones: The German Settlement in Renfrew County.* Toronto, 1985.

_____. "The Opeongo Road – An Early Settlement Scheme," *Canadian Geographical Journal,* 74 (1967) 76-83.

Lehmann, Heinz. *The German Canadians, 1750-1937: Immigration, Settlement and Culture.* Trans. Gerhard P. Bassler. St. John's, 1986.

Lewis, Gertrud J. "Germans in Northern Ontario," *Laurentian University Review/Revue de l'Université Laurentienne* XV:1 (Nov. 1982) 21-40.

Leibbrandt, G. *Little Paradise: The Saga of the German Canadians of Waterloo County, Ontario, 1800-1975.* Kitchener, 1980.

Liddell, Peter. "The First Germans in British Columbia?" *German Canadian Yearbook,* VI (1981) 74-77.

Lutz, Otto. *A Mother Braving a Wilderness: Told by her Son, Otto Lutz.* Muenster, 1977.

MacKinnon, Neil. *The Unfriendly Soil: The Loyalist Experience in Nova Scotia, 1783-1791.* Kingston and Montreal, 1986.

Martin, John D.P. "The Regiment de Watteville: Its Settlement and Service in Upper Canada," *Ontario History*, 52:1 (March, 1960) 17-30.

Meune Manuel. *Les Allemands du Québec: Culture et identité, entre nationalismes et multiculturalisme.* Thèse de doctorat, Université de Strasbourg.

Mika, Nick and Helma. *United Empire Loyalists: Pioneers of Upper Canada.* Belleville, Ont., 1976.

Möllmann, Albert. *Das Deutschtum in Montreal.* Jena, 1937.

Ramsay, Bruce. *A History of the German-Canadians in British Columbia.* Vancouver, 1958.

Renneberg, Werner, ed. *Homesteading to Homecoming, 1903-1971: A History of St. Gregor and District.* Muenster, Sask., 1971.

Schmalz, Ronald E. "Former enemies come to Canada: Ottawa and the postwar immigration boom, 1951-1957." Ph.D. thesis, University of Ottawa, 2000.

[Schulte, W., ed.] *Pictures and Pages on the Silver Jubilee of St. Joseph's Colony, compiled by the Oblate Priests in the Colony.* Translated by Lambert and Tilly Schneider. Saskatoon, [1986].

Sturhahn, William J. H. "Bemerkungen über die Einwanderung deutscher Baptisten nach dem Zweiten Weltkrieg," *German Canadian Yearbook*, IV (1978) 122-126.

_____. *They Came from East and West: A history of immigration to Canada.* Winnipeg, 1976.

Tischler, Kurt. "The German Canadians in Saskatchewan, with Particular Reference to the Language Problem, 1900-1930," M.A. thesis, University of Saskatchewan, 1978.

Toews, John B. *Lost Fatherland: The Story of the Mennonite Emigration from Soviet Russia, 1921-1927.* Scottdale, Pa., 1967.

von Vulte, Manfred J. *Where Have All of Toronto's Germans Gone? The state of the German-Canadian identity.* Ottawa, 2003.

Wanka, Willi. "Tomslake 1939: The Sudeten Story," in Lillian York, ed., *Lure of the South Peace: Tales of Early Pioneers to 1945.* South Peace, 1981.

Warkentin, A. *Reflections on Our Heritage: A History of Steinbach and the R.M. of Hanover from 1874.* Steinbach, Man., 1974.

Waseem, Gertrud. "Die Fahrt nach Nova Scotia: Zur Vorgeschichte der Gründung Lunenburgs, N.S." *German Canadian Yearbook,* III (1976) 140-159.

_____. "Neue Heimat im fremden Land: Zur Geschichte der Gründung Lunenburgs, N.S." *German Canadian Yearbook,* IV (1978) 74-92.

Wilhelmy, Jean-Pierre. *German Mercenaries in Canada.* Boloeil, 1985.

Zurich Centennial Committee. *A Century of Progress, Zurich, 1856-1956: Centennial History.* [Zurich, Ont., 1956].

The Wars

Bassler, Gerhard P. "The Enemy Alien Experience in Newfoundland, 1914-1918," *Canadian Ethnic Studies/etudes ethniques au Canada* XX:3 (1988) 42-62.

Bausenhart, Werner A. "The Ontario German language Press and its Suppression by Order-in-Council in 1918," *Canadian Ethnic Studies/etudes ethniques au Canada* IV:1/2 (1972) 35-48.

Boudreau, J.A. "Western Canada's Enemy Aliens in World War I," *Alberta History* XII:1 (1964) 1-9.

Carter, David J. *Behind Canadian Barbed Wire: Alien and German Prisoner of War Camps in Canada, 1914-1946.* Calgary, 1980.

Chadwick, William Rowley. *The Battle for Berlin, Ontario. An Historical Drama.* Waterloo, Ontario, 1992.

Entz, W. "The Suppression of the German language Press in September 1918 (with special reference to the secular German language press in Western Canada) *Canadian Ethnic Studies/etudes ethniques au Canada,* VIII:2 (1976) 56-70.

Friesen, Gerhard. "The Presentation of German-Canadian Concerns in the *Berliner Journal,* 1914-1917," *German Canadian Studies Annals,* 6 (1988) 138-153.

Grenke, Art. "The German Community of Winnipeg and the English-Canadian Response to World War I," *Canadian Ethnic Studies/etudes ethniques au Canada,* XX:1 (1988) 21-44.

Hilmer, John. *Ein deutsches Schicksal in Kanada. Einwanderung, Internierung, Ringen um Rehabilitierung.* Ed. and compiler Lothar Zimmermann. Toronto, 1996.

Kelly, John Joseph. "The Prisoner of War Camps in Canada, 1939-1947," M.A. thesis, University of Windsor, 1976.

Keyserlingk, Robert H. "Which fatherland in War? The Canadian Government's View of German Canadian Loyalties in World War Two," in T. Yedlin, ed. *Central and East European Ethnicity in Canada: Adaption and Preservation.* Edmonton, 1985.

_____. "Agents Within the Gates: The Search for Nazi Subversives in Canada During World War II," *Canadian Historical Review,* 66 (1985) 211-239.

McKegney, Patricia P. *The Kaiser's Bust: A Study of Wartime Propaganda in Berlin, Ontario, 1914-1918.* Bamberg, Ontario, 1991.

Morton, Desmond. "Sir William Otter and Internment Operations in Canada during the First World War," *Canadian Historical Review*, LV:1 (1974) 32-58.

Nagler, Joerg A. "Enemy Aliens and Internment in World War I: Alvo von Alvensleben in Fort Douglas, Utah, a Case Study," *Utah Historical Quarterly*, 58 (1990) 387-405.

Thompson, John Herd. *The Harvest of War: The Prairie West, 1914-1918.* Toronto, 1978.

_____. *Ethnic Minorities during two World Wars.* Canadian Historical Association, 1991.

Churches

Baumann, Paul S. "The Unchanging Old Order Mennonites," *German Canadian Yearbook*, III (1976) 97-105.

Beringer, Walter. "Deutsche Pastoren aus Breklum und Kropp in Nordamerica," *German Canadian Yearbook*, VII (1983) 22-27.

50th Anniversary, 1901-1951, Bethany Ev. Lutheran Church, Inglis, Manitoba. [Inglis, Man., 1951].

Canada District, American Lutheran Church. Jubilee Yearbook. 1958.

50th Anniversary Christ Lutheran Church Neudorf, Saskatchewan. [Neudorf, Sask., 1964].

60th Anniversary Christ Lutheran Church, 1914-1974. Neudorf, Saskatchewan. [Neudorf, Sask., 1974].

The Year of Jubilee, Lutheran Church of the Cross, 1905-1965.

Cobb, John. "German Speaking Lutherans in the Prairie Provinces Before the First World War." Ph.D. thesis, University of Manitoba, 1991.

Cronmiller, Carl R. *A History of the Lutheran Church in Canada.* Vol. I. Toronto, 1961.

Denkschrift zum Silber-Jubiläum der Evangelisch-Lutherischen Synode von Manitoba u.a. Provinzen, 1897-1922. Winnipeg, Man., 1922.

Edinger, Gerhard C. *Crossing the Divide: Language Transition Among Canadian Mennonite Brethren.* Winnipeg, Man., 2001.

Ens, Adolf. *Becoming a National Church: A History of the Conference of Mennonites in Canada.* Winnipeg, Man., 2004.

Ertis, Waldemar. *50 Jahre, 1916-1966, Bethel Baptisten Gemeinde, Prince George, B.C.* [Prince George, B.C., 1966].

Kept by his Power, 1874-1974: The Evangelical Lutheran Church of St. Paul Wisconsin Synod – Ottawa, Ont. [Ottawa, Ont., 1974].

Festschrift der deutschsprachigen Kirchen Hamiltons zur Jahrhundertfeier Kanadas, 1877-1967. [Hamilton, 1967].

Gerbrandt, H.J. *Adventure in Faith: the background in Europe and the Development in Canada of the Bergthaler Mennonite Church of Manitoba.* Altona, Man., 1970.

Gerein, Frank. *Outline History of the Archdiocese of Regina, 1911-1961.* Regina, 1961.

_____. *History of Odessa to Commemorate the 50th Anniversary of the Advent of Odessa's First Settlers and the 40th Anniversary of the Founding of Holy Family Parish, Odessa, Saskatchewan, 1904-1954.* Regina, Sask., Western Printers Association, 1954.

Gerhard, Karl. *100 Jahre Johannesgemeinde Montreal.* Montreal, 1953.

Getz, Henry J., ed. *1864-1964, A Century in Canada: The Canadian Conference of the Evangelical United Brethren Church.* Kitchener, Ont., 1964.

Gingerich, Orlando. *The Amish of Canada.* Waterloo, 1972.

Goegginger, Wolf. "Religiöse Arbeit in deutscher Sprache in Kanada: evangelische Gemeinden (Lutheraner)," *German Canadian Yearbook,* III (1976) 273-278.

Goos, Ernst George. *Pioneering for Christ in Western Canada. The Story of the Evangelical Lutheran Synod of Manitoba and other Provinces: Synod's Golden Jubilee, 1897-1947.* [Winnipeg, 1947].

Herzer, John E. *Homesteading for God: A Narrative History of Lutheran Mission Work in Alberta and British Columbia, 1894-1946.* Edmonton, 1946.

Holst, Wayne A. "Ethnic Identity and Mission in a Canadian Lutheran Context," *German Canadian Yearbook,* V (1979) 20-24.

1904-1954. 50th Anniversary Holy Cross Lutheran Congregation, Winnipeg, Manitoba. [Winnipeg, Man., 1954].

Horsch, John. *The Hutterite Brethren, 1528-1931: A Story of Martyrdom and Loyalty.* Cayley, Alta., 1977.

Hostetler, John A. *Amish Society.* Baltimore, 1963.

———. *Hutterite Society.* Baltimore, 1974.

Johnson, Gilbert. *"In His Service" 75 Years St. Paul's Evangelical Lutheran Church at Langenburg.* [Langenburg, 1965].

Jubiläums-Büchlein. Festschrift zur Feier des 50-jährigen Jubiläums der evang.-luther. Synode von Canada, 1911.

Klaassen, H. T. *Birth and Growth of the Eigenheim Mennonite Church, 1892-1974.* Rosthern, [1974].

Kleiner, C. *Jubiläums-Büchlein der Evangelisch-Lutherischen Synode von Manitoba und andern Provinzen, 1897-1947.* N.p., 1947.

Kluttig, R. L. *Geschichte der Gnaden Baptisten Gemeinde in Kelowna, B.C.* [Kelowna, 1964].

Koehler, L. W. *The 75th Anniversary (1892-1967) Immanuel Lutheran Church, Winnipeg, Manitoba.* Winnipeg, 1967.

Krause, Emil, "Origin, Life, and Accomplishments of the Lemberg Lutherans." Unpublished paper, November, 1970.

Golden Jubilee and History of Our Lady of Grace Parish, Sedley, Saskatchewan, 1906-1956. [Sedley, Sask., 1956].

Link, Edward B. "North American (German) Baptists," in *Baptists in Canada*, ed. Jarold K. Zeman. Burlington, Ont. (1980) 90-92.

Lizee, Simon, ed. *A Cross in the Clearing: A History of Annaheim and District, 1902-1980.* Melfort, Sask, 1980.

Liefeld, Waldemar C. "Lutheranism in Western Canada," B.D. Diss. Capital University, Columbus, Ohio, 1942.

McCartney, James R. "Sectarian Strife in Dundas County: A Lutheran-Episcopalian Land Endowment Controversy," *Ontario History* LIV:2 (June 1962) 69-86.

1889-1964. 75th Anniversary, McDermot Avenue Baptist Church. Winnipeg. 1964.

The Edmonton Moravian Church, 1905-1955. [Edmonton, Alta., 1955].

Metzger, H. "Historical Sketch of St. Peter's Parish and the Founding of the Colonies of Rastatt, Katharinenthal and Speyer," *Saskatchewan Genealogical Society Bulletin.* V:4 (1974) 7-29.

Meyer, Elisabeth. "Lutherische deutschsprachige Gottesdienste in Victoria, B.C., 1891-1982," *German Canadian Yearbook*, VII (1983) 28-39.

Muenster Catholic Women's League. *Memories of Muenster's 70 Progressive Years, 1903-1973*. Muenster, Sask., [1973].

Peter, Karl. *The Dynamics of Hutterite Society: An Analytical Approach*. Edmonton, 1986.

Pleasant Prairie Baptist Church Wetaskiwin Alberta Golden Jubilee, July 12th and 14th 1946, 1896-1946. [Wetaskiwin, 1946].

Plemel, Sister Benedict. *Sail On: Ursuline Convent 1913-1973 Diamond Jubilee*. Bruno, Sask., 1973.

1968-2008. 40 Jahre Pfarrgemeinde St. Albertus, Ottawa, Ont.: Festschrift. Ottawa, 2008.

20 Jahre St. Bonifatius-Gemeinde, 1956-1976. Hamilton, Ontario, Canada. Hamilton, 1976.

1866-1966. Centennial of St. James Evangelical Lutheran Church, St. Jacobs, Ontario. St. Jacobs, Ont., 1966.

Die ersten hundert Jahre der Deutschen Evangelisch-Lutherischen St. Johannes Gemeinde in Montreal. Montreal, 1953.

St. John's Lutheran Church, Bonnechere, Ontario. 1863-1988: 125th Anniversary. [Bonnechere, 1988].

Centennial History, 1867-1967, St. John Lutheran Church, Patawawa, Ontario. [Patawawa, Ont., 1967].

60th Anniversary St. John's Lutheran Church, Winnipeg, Manitoba. [Winnipeg, Man., 1967].

1946-1971. 25 Years St. John's Evangelical Lutheran Church Aylmer Ontario. Aylmer, 1971.

60th Anniversary, 1906-1966. This is a Story of a People of God; St. Joseph's Parish, St. Joseph's School. [Winnipeg, 1967].

Fiftieth Anniversary, 1915-1965, St. Luke Ev. Lutheran Church, Ottawa, Ontario, October 24, 1965. [Ottawa, Ont., 1965].

St. Mary's Province, 1926-1976. Battleford, Sask., [1976].

1900-1950. St. Mary's Church Kitchener Ontario. Kitchener, Ont., 1950.

St. Paul's Evangelical Lutheran Church of Steinbach, Steinbach, Man., 1966.

Kept by his power, 1874-1974. The Evangelical Lutheran Church of St. Paul Wisconsin Synod – Ottawa. [Ottawa, Ont., 1974].

1903-1953. St. Paul's Evangelical Lutheran Church Golden Jubilee, Langenburg, Saskatchewan. [Langenburg, Sask., 1953].

The Dedication of St. Paul's Lutheran Church, Saskatoon, May 27, 1962. [Saskatoon, Sask., 1962].

"One Hundred Years with Christ." St. Peter's Lutheran Church, Zurich, Ontario, 1861-1961. Zurich, 1961.

Souvenir of the Silver Jubilee of St. Peter's Colony. 1903-1928. Zum Andenken an das Silberne Jubiläum der St. Peters-Kolonie. [Muenster, Sask., 1928].

In Commemoration of the Seventieth Anniversary of the Erection of the Present Church Building, St. Peter's Evangelical Lutheran Church. Services June 27th and 28th, 1948, Zurich, Ontario. Zurich, Ont., 1948.

Sixty Years of Grace: St. Peter's Evangelical Lutheran Church, Edmonton, Alberta. Diamond Jubilee, 1904-1964. [Edmonton, Alta., 1964].

St. Peter's Evangelical Lutheran Church, Winnipeg, Manitoba, 25th Anniversary, Sunday, September 18th, 1955. [Winnipeg, Man., 1955].

Sautter, Udo. "Ein deutscher Geistlicher in Neuschottland: Johann Adam Moschell (1795-1849), *German Canadian Yearbook,* I (1973) 71-75.

Scharf, Gilbert A. *Anniversary Sixty Years, 1915-1975: Lutheran Church of the Resurrection.* Halifax, 1975.

Scheidt, David L. "Some Effects of World War I on the General Synod and General Council," *Concordia Historical Institute Quarterly,* XLIII:2 (May 1970) 83-92.

Schindler, K.J. "Die deutschsprachigen katholischen Kirchengemeinden in Kanada – Teil 2," *German Canadian Yearbook,* II (1975) 276-284.

Slack, J.M. et. al. *On to Zion: A Souvenir of the Bicentennial Anniversary of Zion's Lutheran Church, Lunenburg, Nova Scotia, 1772-1972.* Lunenburg, 1972.

Schmieder, John. *St. Matthews Lutheran Church Twenty Fifth Anniversary Report, 1924-1929.* Kitchener, Ont., 1929.

_____. *Souvenir of the Golden Jubilee St. Matthews Lutheran Church.* Kitchener, ON, 1954.

Schulte, W. *St. Joseph's Colony, 1905-1930.* Trans. Lambert and Tilley Schneider. [Regina, Sask., 1930].

Spetz, Theobald. *The Catholic Church in Waterloo County.* Hamilton, Ont., 1916.

1934-1959. Springside Baptist Church Silver Jubilee Anniversary. [Springside, Sask., 1959].

Threinen, Norman J. *Immanuel Evangelical Lutheran Church, Landestreu, Saskatchewan, 1895-1970.* Ms. N.p., [1970].

_____. "The Stuermer Union Movement in Canada," *Concordia Historical Institute Quarterly,* 46:4 (Winter 1973) 148-157.

_____. "Lutherans in Canada," *German Canadian Yearbook*, V (1979) 13-19.

Service of Dedication. Trinity Lutheran Church, Winnipeg, Manitoba, Sunday, June 9, 1968. [Winnipeg, Man.], 1968.

65th Anniversary of Founding of Trinity Lutheran Church, 1906-1971, Lemberg, Saskatchewan. [Lemberg, Sask., 1971].

Vitt, Kurt H. *Bruderfeld Moravian Church 75th Anniversary, 1895-1970.* Edmonton, Alta.: Bruderfeld, 1970.

_____. *Heimthal Moravian Church.* Edmonton, Alta., 1971.

_____. *Clement Hoyler, God's Peacemaker for Moravians in Canada. Impressions.* Edmonton, Alta. 1972.

_____. *New Serepta, Alberta, Founded in 1904. History and Development in Pictures.* Edmonton, Alta., 1974.

Wadel, Viola R. "The German Lutheran Settlement of Rainham Township, County of Haldimand, Ontario," *German Canadian Yearbook*, VIII (1984) 129-132.

Wahl, James A. "Father Louis Funcken's Contribution to German Catholicism in Waterloo County, Ontario," *Canadian Catholic Historical Association*, 50 (1983) 513-531.

Ward, Kenn. "A Brief Historical Account of the Lutheran People in the Upper Ottawa Valley of Ontario," unpublished article, 1976.

Windschiegl. Peter. *Fifty Golden Years, 1903-1953: A Brief History of the Order of St. Benedict in the Abbacy Nullius of St. Peter, Muenster, Saskatchewan.* Muenster, Sask, 1953.

Woyke, Frank H. *Heritage and Ministry of the North American Baptist Conference.* Oakbrook Terrace, Il., 1979.

Zion Evangelical Lutheran Congregation. Pembroke, Ont., 1933, 1954, 1958.

Zion Augsburg: 110 Anniversary, 1874-1984. Augsburg (Ont.), 1984.

Zurbrigg, Howard G. *Songs of Zion: The Story of Zion Church, Crediton, Ontario.* [Crediton, 1969].

Schools and Language maintenance

Anderson, Alan B. "Linguistic trends among Saskatchewan Ethnic Groups," in M.L. Kovacs, *Ethnic Canadians: Culture and Education* (Regina, 1978) 3-86.

Auburger, L. and H. Kloss. *Deutsch als Muttersprache in Kanada.* Wiesbaden, 1977.

_____. "Factors Contributing to the Assimilation of the German United Empire Loyalists of the Upper St. Lawrence and the Bay of Quinté," *German Canadian Studies Annals,* 5 (1985) 20-31.

Driedger, Leo and Peter Hengstenberg. "Non-Official Multilingualism: Factors Affecting German language Competence, Use and Maintenance in Canada, *Canadian Ethnic Studies,* XVIII:3 (1986) 90-109.

Ediger, Gerald C. "Language Transition in the Vineland Mennonite Brethren Church." *Historical Papers, Canadian Society of Church History* (1988) 97-116.

_____. *Crossing the Divide: Language Transition Among Canadian Mennonite Brethren, 1940-1970.* Winnipeg, Man., 2001.

Epp, Georg K. "Ein Verein zur Pflege der deutschen Sprache in Kanada: Mennonitischer Sprachverein (Mennonite German Society)," *German Canadian Yearbook,* III (1976) 271-272.

Gumpp, Ruth. "Language Loss and Language Retention among German Post-War Immigrants in Vancouver, 1945-1971," *German Canadian Yearbook,* XIV (1995) 75-88.

Guenther, Bruce L. "The Origin of the Bible School Movement in Western Canada: Towards an Ethnic Interpretation," *Canadian Society of Church History*. Historical Papers (1993) 135-173.

Kalbfleisch, Herbert K. "German or Canadian?" *Waterloo Historical Society*. Fortieth Annual Report (1952) 18–29.

Lacey, Laurie. *Ethnicity and German descendants of Lunenburg County, Nova Scotia. Halifax, 1982.*

Lorenzkowski, Barbara. *Sounds of Ethnicity: Listening to German North America, 1850-1914.* Winnipeg, Man., 2010.

McKegney, Patricia Pearl. "The German Schools of Waterloo County, 1851-1930," *Waterloo Historical Society, Annual Report,* 58 (1970) 54-67.

Prokop, Manfred. *The German language in Alberta. Maintenance and Teaching.* Edmonton, 1990.

Prokop, Manfred and Gerhard Bassler. *German language maintenance across Canada: a handbook.* [Sherwood Park, Alta. c. 2004].

Roger, Dieter. "Deutsch in Manitoba. Vom ersten Deutsch Westkanadas bis zum heutigen Deutschunterricht," *German Canadian Yearbook,* VII (1983) 136-147.

Toepper, Robert M. "Rationale for Preservation of the German language in the Missouri Synod of the Nineteenth Century," *Concordia Historical Institute Quarterly* XLI:4 (November 1968) 156-167.

Von Oesen, Anne. "Sprache und Heimat," *German Canadian Yearbook,* III (1976) 66-70.

Von Vulte, Manfred J. *Where have all of Toronto's Germans gone?: the state of the German-Canadian identity.* Ottawa, 2004.

White, Clinton O. "Education Among German Catholic Settlers in Saskatchewan, 1903-1918: A Reinterpretation," in Nancy Sheehan, ed.

Schools in the West: Essays in Canadian Educational History (Calgary, 1986) 175-192.

Secular Organizations

Bassler, Gerhard P. "Franz Straubinger and the Deutsche Arbeitsgemeinschaft Ontario," *German Canadian Yearbook*, VIII (1984) 225-235.

130 Jahre Deutsche Gesellschaft zu Montreal, 1835-1965. [Montreal, 1965].

Fahnenweihe 1988. 30 Jahre Deutsch-Kanadischer Sängerbund. Toronto, Ont., 1988.

Froeschle, Hartmut. "Der 'Verband für deutschkanadische Geschichtsforschung," (German-Canadian Historical Association) *German Canadian Yearbook*, II (1975) 271-275.

1864-1989 = 125 Jahre Germania Club: Jubiläumsausgabe. Hamilton, Ont, 1989.

Grenke, A. "From Dreams of the Worker State to Fighting Hitler: The German-Canadian Left from the Depression to the end of World War II," *Labour/Le Travail*, 35 (Spring 1995) 65-105.

Gürttler, Karin. *Geschichte der Deutschen Gesellschaft zu Montreal, 1835-1985*. Montreal, 1985.

_____. "Das Manitoba Siedlungsproject der Deutschen Gesellschaft zu Montreal," *German-Canadian Yearbook*, X (1988) 33-71.

25 Harmonie. 100 Jahre Deutsches Vereinsleben in Toronto, 1853-1953. [Toronto, Ont., 1953].

Junker, Wolfgang. "Kulturarbeit ohne Maske und Make-Up. Der 'Deutsch-Kanadische Kulturkreis' unter der Leitung von Eva Kastens," *German Canadian Yearbook*, II (1975) 265-270.

Kliem, Ottmar. "Deutsche in Kanada: Eine Empirische Orientierstudie über den Integrationsprozess der Mitglieder des deutschen Klubs in Calgary, Alta. Im Vergleich zu den Führern der deutschen Klubs in ganz Kanada." Ph.D. thesis, University of Erlangen-Nürnberg, 1969.

Kluckert, Richard W. "14 Jahre 'Verein deutscher Ingenieure' in Toronto," *German Canadian Yearbook,* II (1975) 285-286.

Kuester, Mathias F. "Die Deutschen Tage – ein historischer Rückblick," in *German-Canadian Association of Alberta, ed. Deutsche Tage 1987,* Edmonton (1987) 12-14.

Leibbrandt, Gottlieb. *Canadian German Society (Canadian Society for German Relief), 1947-1972.* Kitchener, [1972].

_____. "100 Jahre Concordia," *German Canadian Yearbook,* I (1973) 263-274.

Wagner, Jonathan F. *Brothers Beyond the Sea: National Socialism in Canada.* Waterloo, Ont., 1981.

Wekherlien, Robert P. "The German-Canadian Association of Alberta, Past and Present," *German Canadian Yearbook,* IV (1978) 295-311.

Wieden, Fritz. *The Trans-Canada Alliance of German Canadians: A Study in Culture.* Windsor, Ont., 1985.

The German language Media

"Berliner Journal," *Waterloo Historical Society,* vol. 47 (1959) 62-69.

Entz, Werner. "Der Einfluss der deutschsprachigen Presse Westkanadas auf die Organisationsbestrebungen des dortigen Deutschtums, 1889-1939," *German-Canadian Yearbook,* II (1975) 92-138.

Kalbfleisch, Herbert Karl. *The History of the Pioneer German language Press of Ontario, 1835-1918. Toronto, 1968.*

St. Matthew's Lutheran Brotherhood, *Kirche Daheim: Church at Home – A Souvenir Booklet.* Kitchener, [1930].

Leibbrandt, Gottlieb. "Deutschsprachiges Fernsehen in Kitchener-Waterloo," *German-Canadian Yearbook*, II (1975) 287-289.

Lochhead, Douglas G. "Henry, Anthony (also Anton Heinrich or Henrich)," *Dictionary of Canadian Biography*, vol. IV (1979).

The Lutheran Church: A Series of Broadcasts. [St. Peter's Evangelical Lutheran Church, Kitchener, 1942].

Politics

Entz. Werner. "William Hespeler, Manitoba's First German Consul," *German-Canadian Yearbook*, I (1973) 149-152.

Meilicke, E. J. *Leaves from the Life of a Pioneer: Being the Autobiography of Sometime Senator Emil Julius Meilicke.* Vancouver, 1949.

Riedel, Walter E. "John Sebastian Helmcken: Pioneer Surgeon and Legislator (1824-1920)," *German Canadian Yearbook*, IV (1978) 250-256.

Smith, Dorothy Blakey, ed. *The Reminiscences of Dr. John Sebastian Helmcken.* Vancouver, 1975.

Weissenborn, Georg. "Adam Beck – The Human Dynamo (1857-1925)," *German Canadian Yearbook,* III (1976) 234-236.

Business

Cardinal, Clive H. "A Note on Martin Nordegg (1868-1948)," *German Canadian Yearbook*, IV (1978) 246-249.

Cobb, David. "A Rare Wine Success," *Report on Business Magazine* (April 1986) 60-67.

Cyr, Céline. "Wurtele, Josias," *Dictionary of Canadian Biography*, vol. VI (1987).

Frisse, Ulrich. *A history of success: Paul Tuerr: a German-Canadian life.* Kitchener, ON, c. 2007.

Fryer, Mary Beacock. "Captain John Walden Meyers: Loyalist Spy," *German Canadian Yearbook*, II (1975) 70-82.

Heffner, John. *From Hungary to Canada: the building of my dream.* Kitchener, ON, c. 2009.

Johnson, J.K. "Zimmerman, Samuel." *Dictionary of Canadian Biography*, VIII (1985).

Laue, Ingrid E. "Gustav Konstantin Alvo von Alvensleben (1879-1965): Ein Lebensbild," *German Canadian Yearbook*, V (1979) 154-173

Matas, Robert. "Furniture Baron to make room for poor," *The Globe and Mail* (Monday April 30, 2001). Also, "John Volken built a furniture empire from nothing," *Immigrant Stories* (June 17, 2001).

Momryk, M. "Ermatinger, Lawrence," *Dictionary of Canadian Biography*, vol. IV (1979).

Nordegg, Martin. *The Possibilities of Canada are Truly Great: Memoirs 1906-1924.* Toronto, 1971.

Stackhouse, John and Sandy Nicholson. "Robert's Show," *Report on Business Magazine* (December 2001) 46-52.

Vincent, Dorothea. "Deutschkanadisches Geschäftsleben in Toronto zu Beginn der 70er Jahre," *German Canadian Yearbook*, II (1975) 168-179.

Weissenborn, Georg K. "Samuel Zimmerman (1815-1857)," *German Canadian Yearbook*, V (1979) 177-180.

Zimmermann, Lothar. "Franz von Ellershausen: Entrepreneur and Dreamer of Legendary Proportion (1820-1914), *German Canadian Yearbook*, XVIII (2004) 175-186.

Science

Hempel, Rainer. "Abraham Gesner: Father of the Petroleum Industry," *German Canadian Yearbook*, XVII (2002) 129-137.

Landon, Fred. "Otto Julius Klotz," *Waterloo Historical Society*, 40th Annual Report (1952) 30-37.

Stuart, E.R. "Bernhardt Fernow, First Forestry Dean," *German Canadian Yearbook*, V (1979) 174-176.

Macpherson, Alan G. "Early Moravian Interest in Northern Labrador Weather and Climate: The Beginning of Instrumental Recording in Newfoundland," in Donald H. Steele, ed. *Early Science in Newfoundland and Labrador*. St. John's (1987) 30-41.

Ratz, Alfred E. "Frühe Kulturarbeit deutscher Herrnhuter in Labrador," *German Canadian Yearbook*, II (1975) 50-69.

Weissenborn, Georg K. "David Zeisberger. The Apostle of the Indians," *German Canadian Yearbook*, II (1975) 185-188.

Weissenborn, Georg K. "Johann Daniel Arnoldi: The Pioneer Doctor of Lower Canada (1774-1849)," *German-Canadian Yearbook*, IV (1978) 254-256.

Art

Arend, Angelika. "Verführte, Hexe, Hure, Weib: Frauenbilder aus der Hand der Dichterin Else Lübke Seel," *German Canadian Yearbook*, XVII (2002) 47-58.

Bird, Michael and Terry Kobayashy. *A Splendid Harvest: German Folk and Decorative Arts in Canada*. Toronto, 1981.

Bird, Michael. "Beauty and Simplicity: Germanic folk art in Canada," *German Canadian Yearbook*, VIII (1983) 63-81.

Boeschenstein, H. "Else Seel, Eine deutsch-kanadische Dichterin," The *German Canadian Review*, 10:1 (Spring, 1957) 17- 19.

Boeschenstein, Hermann, (Hrsg). *Heiteres und Satirisches aus der deutsch-kanadischen Literatur. John Adam Rittinger, Walter Roome, Ernst Loeb, Rolf Max Kully.* Toronto, 1980.

Brock, Daniel J. "Zeisberger, David," *Dictionary of Canadian Biography*, V (1983).

Christy, Jim and Pete Skov. "Prairie Cathedrals: Philip Ruh was a tireless missionary who adorned the western landscape with ornate Ukrainian churches," *Canadian Geographic* (November/December '96) 68-76.

Cook, Maria. "Book fetes work of W. E. Noffke," *Ottawa Citizen* (April 12, 2013) C. 1&2.

Erb, Peter C. "The Canadian Poems of Eugen Funcken, C.R." *German Canadian Yearbook*, IV (1978) 225-233.

Friesen, Gerhard K. (ed.). "Fritz Senn (1894-1983), Kurze Selbstbiographie (1975)," *German Canadian Yearbook*, VIII (1983) 89-92.

_____. "Overlooked Canadian Poetry by Johann Gottfried Seume," *German Canadian Yearbook*, XIV (1995) 267-278.

Froeschle, Hartmut. "Gibt es eine deutschkanadische Literatur?" *German Canadian Yearbook*, III (1976) 174-187.

_____ Hrg.). *Drei frühe deutschkanadische Dichter. Eugen Funcken – Heinrich Rembe – Emil Querner.* Toronto, 1978.

_____. "Walter Bauer. Sein dichterisches Werk mit besonderer Berücksichtigung seines Kanada-Erlebnisses," *German Canadian Yearbook*, V (1979) 77-100.

German Society, Montreal, ed. *German Canadian Artists in Québec.* Montreal, 1985.

Hadley, Michael L. "Education and Alienation in Dyck's "Verloren in der Steppe": a Novel of Cultural Crisis," *German Canadian Yearbook,* III (1976) 199-210.

Jakobsh, Frank K. "German and German-Canadian Literature as Contained in the "Berliner Journal," *German Canadian Yearbook,* V (1979) 108-120.

Kalbfleisch, H. K. "A Word About Joe Klotzkopp," *German-Canadian Review,* 10:1 (Spring, 1957) 2-5.

Kallmann, Helmut. "The German Contribution to Music in Canada," *German Canadian Yearbook,* II (1975) 152-166.

_____. "Nordheimer, Abraham," *Dictionary of Canadian Biography,* vol. IX (1976).

Klippenstein, Lawrence. "Canadian Mennonite Writings: A Survey of Selected Publications, 1980-1995," *German Canadian Yearbook,* XIV (1995) 279-293.

Kloss, Heinz, ed. with Arnold B. Dyck. *Ahornblätter. Deutsche Dichtung aus Kanada.* Würzburg, 1961.

Kloss, Heinz. "Bemerkungen zur deutschkanadischen Literatur," *German Canadian Yearbook,* III (1976) 188-192.

Lach, Friedhelm. "Deutschkanadische Kunst in Québec," *Annalen Deutschkanadische Studien,* 5 (1986) 125-132.

Lambton, Gunda. Contributions of German Graphic Artists in the History of Canadian Printmaking," *German Canadian Yearbook,* IV (1978) 180-204.

Mackay, Donald C. "Nordbeck, Peter," *Dictionary of Canadian Biography*, vol. IV (1976).

Pache, Walter. "Der Fall Grove – Vorleben und Nachleben des Schriftstellers Felix Paul Grove," *German Canadian Yearbook*, V (1979) 121-136.

Peters, Victor. "Russlanddeutsches Schrifttum in Nordamerika," *German Canadian Yearbook*, III (1976) 281-283.

Riedel, Walter. "Der Deutschkanadische Expressionist Herbert Siebner," *German-Canadian Yearbook*, VI (1981) 172-177.

Riedel, Walter and Rodney Symington, eds. *Der Wanderer. Aufsätze zu Leben und Werk von Walter Bauer*. Berlin, 1994.

Roger, Dieter. "From German Pioneer Building to 'Bauhaus' and Beyond," *German Canadian Yearbook*, IV (1978) 135-167.

Roger, Dieter. *Vom Pionierbau zur Moderne*. Winnipeg, Man., 1994.

Stabler, Hedy. "German Contributions to Our Heritage," *Saskatchewan Multicultural Magazine*, VI:4 (Fall 1985) 12-13.

Sturm, Ellen. "Toronto und das deutsche Theaterleben in den Nachkriegsjahren," *German Canadian Yearbook*, III (1976) 225-233.

Symington, Rodney T.K. "Else Seel: Eine Biographie im Nachlass," *German Canadian Yearbook*, III (1976) 193-198.

Weiselberger, Carl. *Eine Auswahl seiner Schriften*. Hg. Peter Liddell and Walter Riedel. Toronto, 1981.

Zeidler, Erhard A. "Architecture in our Time - Necessities and Possibilities," *German Canadian Yearbook*, IV (1978) 168-179.

Printed in the United States
By Bookmasters